# ethics, *governance* & *accountability*

## a professional
## perspective

# ethics, *governance* & *accountability*

## a professional perspective

**Steven Dellaportas**
La Trobe University

**Kathy Gibson**
University of Tasmania

**Ratnam Alagiah**
Griffith University

**Marion Hutchinson**
University of Queensland

**Philomena Leung**
Deakin University

**David Van Homrigh**
KPMG Australia

**WILEY**

John Wiley & Sons Australia, Ltd

First published 2005 by
John Wiley & Sons Australia, Ltd
33 Park Road, Milton, Qld 4064

Offices also in Sydney and Melbourne

© Steven Dellaportas, Kathy Gibson,
Ratnam Alagiah, Marion Hutchinson,
Philomena Leung, David Van Homrigh 2005

Typeset in 11/13.5pt Minion Light

National Library of Australia
Cataloguing-in-Publication data

Ethics, governance and accountability: a professional
perspective.

　　Includes index.
　　For undergraduates.
　　ISBN 0 470 80499 8.

　　1. Business ethics — Textbooks. 2. Professional ethics —
　　Textbooks. 3. Corporate governance — Textbooks.
　　I. Dellaportas, Steve.

174.4

Cover and internal design images: © PhotoDisc, Inc

Edited by Amanda Morgan

Printed in Singapore by
Kyodo Printing Co (S'pore) Pte Ltd

10 9 8 7 6 5 4 3 2 1

# About the authors //

**Steven Dellaportas** CPA BBus (Acc) VU, Dip Ed La Trobe, Grad Dip (Tax) RMIT, MAcc RMIT, PhD RMIT is a senior lecturer in the School of Business, La Trobe University. Steven worked in public accounting prior to entering academia in 1991. Since then, he has taught both undergraduate and postgraduate students in the principles and practice of financial and managerial accounting, and auditing. In recent years, Steven has developed an increasing interest in 'accounting ethics'. He has authored a number of ethics-related publications and is actively involved in continuing education with the accounting profession.

**Kathy Gibson** is Associate Dean, Teaching and Learning, and coordinator of off-shore programs in the Faculty of Commerce, University of Tasmania. Beginning her career in stockbroking and merchant banking in London and later Australia, she then moved into the hospitality industry as Company Secretary and Finance Director of an Australian restaurant group. She began her academic career in 1987, and moved to the University of Tasmania in 1994. Prior to taking up her Faculty role, she was a senior lecturer in the School of Accounting & Finance, and was Acting Head of School in 2002–2003. Kathy is a Fellow of CPA Australia, Past President of the Tasmanian Division, and a former Chair of the CPA's national Ethics and Corporate Governance Centre of Excellence. She is also an author of materials in triple bottom line reporting and financial accounting for the CPA Program, and has authored government discussion papers on triple bottom line issues.

**Ratnam Alagiah** BCom MCom Auck PhD Woll CMA is a lecturer at Griffith Business School, Griffith University at the Gold Coast Campus. Ratnam has taught accounting in four countries and in seven universities, both at the undergraduate and postgraduate levels, and specialises in Accounting Theory, Company Accounting and International Accounting. Ratnam has presented papers at numerous conferences and published papers in several accounting journals, including *Abacus*. As part of a research team at Griffith University, Ratnam is undertaking research to determine the role of ethical education in accounting, with a view of introducing *Virtues* into accounting education. He is also the Australian representative of A Single Global Currency Association, Newcastle, Maine, USA.

**Marion Hutchinson** Phd Deakin University; MCom Deakin University; GradDipEd(Sec) Monash University; BBus WIAE; CPA. Marion is a senior lecturer in accounting at the UQ Business School and has a PhD in the area of corporate governance from Deakin University. Marion's main research interests are in the areas of corporate governance, management controls and incentives, and agency and contracting theory. She has published in several leading international journals including the *Journal of Corporate Finance*, the *Asia-Pacific Journal of Accounting and Economics*, *Managerial Finance* and the *Review of Accounting and Finance*, among others. Prior to joining the UQ Business School in 2004, Marion worked as a Senior Lecturer in the School of Accounting, Economics and Finance at Deakin University. In addition to her academic career, she has the experience of assisting in the management of a manufacturing firm.

**Philomena Leung** is Associate Professor of Auditing and Ethics in the School of Accounting and Law at RMIT University. Her PhD in accounting ethics provides an insight into the issues relevant to the accounting profession. Philomena has received her auditing training with one of the Big Four in Hong Kong and has taught auditing for more than 20 years. She has written for a number of academic and professional journals in the areas of auditing, ethics, internal auditing and accounting education. Her research interests, apart from ethics and auditing, include corporate governance and accounting education. Philomena is extremely active in promoting professionalism. She is a regular contributor to professional development programs, presenting papers at numerous international and national conferences. She is sought after for public debates on professional issues. Philomena is a pioneer of ethics education in Hong Kong and Australia.

**David Van Homrigh** is the managing partner of KPMG Forensic in Australia and for the Asia–Pacific region. He is a member of the KPMG International Steering Group with general responsibility for the development of forensic services in the Asia–Pacific region. David has given evidence in many judicial proceedings, including litigation in the Supreme Court, the Federal Court, and in various arbitrations and mediations. He has provided advice in cross-border disputes, international arbitrations and multi-jurisdictional investigations.

# Contents //

**chapter 3**    **Professional ethics and self-regulation   57**
Steven Dellaportas

**chapter 4**    **Ethical decision making   87**
Steven Dellaportas

## part 2    Ethics in a regulatory environment    115

### chapter 5    Corporate governance    117
Marion Hutchinson

## chapter 12    Ethics in a corporate environment    310
Steven Dellaportas

# Preface //

During the nineteenth century, universities included courses on ethics and values as part of the curriculum. The academic curriculum and the entire campus environment clearly viewed the formation of student character as a central mission. Throughout most of the nineteenth century, moral philosophy was regarded as the most important course in the university curriculum. Ethics education gave meaning and purpose to the student's university experience that would benefit them and society. However, the rise of research universities in the twentieth century, and the fragmentation of knowledge that accompanied the evolution of academic disciplines, contributed to the decline of the direct curricula approach to the development of students' character and moral sensitivity. Ethics education in the twentieth century appears to have been overlooked in favour of vocationally based education that centres on providing students with credentials rather than educating them.

In recent years, there has been an upsurge in the support for ethics education in business programs, caused largely by instances of questionable conduct in practice. Accounting led scandals, and recurring failures in business such as WorldCom Enron, Parmalat and HIH, invite questions about the appropriateness of accounting and business education. In response to such questions, the International Federation of Accountants (IFAC) issued International Education Standard (IES) 4 *Professional Values, Ethics and Attitudes*. IES 4 prescribes the professional values and responsibilities that should be acquired by accountants during their education so that professional accountants are equipped with the appropriate professional values, ethics and attitudes when they enter the profession. IES 4, effective from 1 January 2005, imposes an obligation on member bodies including CPA Australia and the Institute of Chartered Accountants in Australia to ensure that their prospective members receive adequate ethics education during their university education and throughout their professional life. With ethics education now a core component of accounting education, the twenty-first century is witnessing a return to the direct curricula approach to ethics education in business programs. Calls for the expansion of ethics education in the business curricula are not new. Derek Bok (former President of Harvard University) has criticised business education for its lack of ethics education since the 1970s. It has simply taken three decades to respond to such calls.

There are many reasons why educators and program managers have been slow to respond to the call for ethics education in business programs. These include:
- a lack of expertise and training among business educators to properly teach ethics;

- the ambiguous nature of ethics and the inability to provide satisfactory moral conclusions confuse students as well as educators, because questions of morality become unanswerable, thus promoting a cynical attitude about ethics;
- the lack of rewards for accounting ethics research (compared with other disciplines) provides little incentive for educators, who themselves are under pressure to perform in an increasingly competitive academic environment, to research and teach ethics;
- the inability to introduce new topics or courses such as ethics into overcrowded degree programs;
- the perception that ethics education is created largely for the sake of appearances, to silence the critics, without any real intent to impact the ethical awareness or reasoning skills of students;
- conflicting views on whether ethics should be taught, and conflicting expectations on how it might affect ethical decision making and behaviour; and
- the lack of resources available for educators to teach ethics.

In regard to teaching materials, there are a number of existing limitations. First, research that examines prescribed references suggests only a limited number of case studies in accounting and finance textbooks. Second, business ethics textbooks have been criticised for being too philosophical and emphasising cases and examples directed at upper-level managers and CEOs. The bias toward top executive dilemmas presents an irrelevant dimension to the learning of business ethics, when the majority of students will end up in lower and middle-level posts. Third, in accounting, textbook coverage of ethics is generally limited to one chapter, which is devoid of ethical principles or reduced to a mechanistic following of rules espoused in the code of professional conduct. Fourth, ethics education is limited because of the high degree of correlation between textbook coverage of ethics and the extent of ethics instruction. Fifth, superficial textbook treatment creates the impression in the students' minds that ethics is relatively unimportant. Finally, the extensive time and commitment required by educators to prepare course materials in an era of increasing responsibilities where universities demand more for less is a barrier to the development of adequate materials.

This textbook is a direct response to the limitations identified above. It is designed to provide educators with a local textbook that is up-to-date, relevant, and has a practical emphasis. This book is dedicated to ethics education, which means it can be used to teach ethics as a separate course or can be used as a reference book for courses that integrate ethics material throughout a number of accounting or businesses courses. The book has a dual focus: first, it examines ethics from an individual perspective (chapters 1 to 4), and second, it examines ethics in organisational and regulatory environment (chapters 5 to 12). Even though the book emphasises ethics in accounting, much of the material (for example chapter 4, Ethical decision making) is equally valuable to other business disciplines, and it should not be viewed as a reference strictly for accounting students. Overall, the book aims to provide students with an easy to understand and practical perceptive on ethics, with insights on how to deal and resolve ethical issues in business and accounting.

Accounting and business professionals have often been criticised for lacking the ethical sensitivity to recognise ethical dilemmas when they arise. They focus too much on the technical issues and fail to see the moral dimension of a problem. Hence, the ethical issues associated with a problem are inadvertently overlooked in the resolution process. It is crucial for students — soon to be professionals — to be sensitive to the moral components of seemingly technical questions. Chapter 1, An ethics framework; chapter 2, Understanding ethics and moral judgment; and chapter 3, Professional ethics and self-regulation, introduce students to theories of ethics and professional responsibilities, which provide the framework for recognising and understanding ethical problems. However, the answers to many ethical dilemmas are not always clear and the principles established in chapters 2 and 3 are not easily applied. Therefore, chapter 4, Ethical decision making, provides students with a structured approach to ethical decision-making incorporating the basic elements of chapters 2 and 3.

The roles of accountants range from scorekeeping to decision making. Chapters 7 to 12 examine ethical issues in accounting practice and organisational ethics. Issues in financial reporting are dealt with in chapter 6, Fraud and forensic accounting; chapter 7, Creative accounting; and chapter 8, Social responsibility accounting. Issues particular to the accountant, or the firm of accountants, rather than practice of accounting are dealt with in chapter 10, Professional independence, and chapter 11, Client-centred conflicts of interest. Ethics from an organisational and managerial perspective are dealt with in chapter 5, Corporate governance; chapter 9, Environmental responsibility; and chapter 12, Ethics in a corporate environment. The practical nature of this book allows it to be used as a reference book for students in all year levels of a degree program. However, the book is primarily aimed at latter-year undergraduate students and is ideally suited to a capstone subject that brings together knowledge that has been acquired in the earlier stages of their education. The book is also suitable for postgraduate programs, particularly programs where students are dealing with concepts in accounting and business at an introductory or broad-based level.

Ethics, as a practical discipline, demands the acquisition of moral knowledge and the skills to properly apply such knowledge to the problems of daily life. Ethical dilemmas in accounting and business are common, and it is a mistake to assume that a professional may never face an ethical dilemma. Empirical evidence suggests that all professionals will face many ethical dilemmas throughout their professional life. Therefore, competence in ethics is not an optional extra; it is an important component of being a professional. With the advent of courses in ethics and development of ethics subject material such as this textbook, students will finally being taught how to recognise and resolve ethical issues.

Steven Dellaportas
Kathy Gibson
Ratnam Alagiah
Marion Hutchinson
Philomena Leung
David Van Homrigh
October 2004

# Acknowledgments //

There are many people deserving of gratitude in the actualisation of this book. First, I would like to express my appreciation to the employees at John Wiley & Sons Australia for their assistance, professionalism, and tireless efforts in publishing this book. In Australia, few textbooks have been published on ethics and professionalism, therefore, I applaud John Wiley for their imagination and foresight in publishing such a book. I express my sincere appreciation to the reviewers for their invaluable comments during the draft stages of this book: Frances Chua, Dawn Cable and Vivienne Brand, and to my co-authors: Kathy Gibson, Ratnam Alagiah, Marion Hutchinson, David Van Homrigh and Philomena Leung for their contributions to this book without which the book would not exist. I offer a special thank you to my wife for her endless support and for giving the space which allows me the freedom to undertake and complete such projects. Finally, I would like to thank my children, Kathryn and Dion, who remind me of the important things in life, my family.

Every effort has been made to trace the ownership of copyright material. Information that will rectify any error or omission in subsequent editions will be welcome and the publisher will be happy to pay the usual permission fee. Please contact the Permissions Department of John Wiley & Sons Australia, Ltd.

**Images:**
p. 98: Copyright © 2002 by the American Institute of Certified Public Accountants, Inc. Adapted and reprinted with permission from the AICPA.

**Text:**
• p. 10: © Mallen Baker • pp. 66, 75–7: Copyright © International Federation of Accountants. All standards, guidelines, discussion papers and other IFAC documents are the copyright of the International Federation of Accountants (IFAC), 545 Fifth Avenue, 14th Floor, New York, 10017, USA; tel: 1-212/286-9344, fax: 1-212/286.9570, Internet: http://www.ifac.org. All rights reserved. No part of this publication may be reproduced, stored in a retrieval system, or transmitted, in any form or by any means, electronic, mechanical, photocopying, recording or otherwise, without the prior written permission of IFAC. The IFAC pronouncements in this volume have been reproduced by John Wiley & Sons, Australia with the permission of IFAC. The approved text of all IFAC documents is that published by IFAC in the English language • pp. 84–5, 102, 120, 263–4, 265–6, 274, 274–8, 295: Copyright. Reproduced with the permission of CPA Australia. CPA Australia

has used reasonable care and skill in compiling the content of this material at the time of publication. No part of these materials are intended to be advice, whether legal or professional. You should not act solely on the basis of the information contained in these materials as parts may be generalised and may apply differently to different people and circumstances. Further, as laws change frequently, all practitioners, readers, viewers and users are advised to undertake their own research or to seek professional advice to keep abreast of any reforms and developments in the law • p. 99: © Harold Q. Langenderger and Joanne W. Rockness, *Issues in Accounting Education*, vol. 4, no.1. Spring 1989 • p. 101: *Ethical decision making in everyday work situations*, by M. Guy, Quorum Books. Copyright 1990. Greenwood Publishing Group, Inc., Westport, CT • pp. 104–7: © Institute of Chartered Accountants in Australia and CPA Australia • p. 113: © William W. May/ American Accounting Association • pp. 123, 128, 129, 131, 135, 147: © Australian Stock Exchange Limited ABN 98 008 624 691(ASX) 2002. All rights reserved. This material is reproduced with the permission of ASX. This material should not be reproduced, stored in a retrieval system or transmitted in any form whether in whole or in part without the prior written permission of ASX • p. 138: © Gerald Vinten, *Corporate Governance*, 2002, Reproduced with permission of Emerald Group Publishing Limited • pp. 205–6: © DuPont Company, *Business Conduct Guide*, 2004 • p. 228: © Orica *Annual Report 2003* • p. 228: © AGL • pp. 232, 238, 242: © R. Kendall, *Ethical Investor*, December/January, 2004. Reproduced with permission of Lifecraft Pty Ltd • pp. 234–6: Kathy Gibson FCPA has been a practising accountant in the finance and hospitality industries for over 20 years, in the UK and Australia. A lecturer in accounting at the University of Tasmania, Kathy has research interests in accounting theory and environmental accounting. This article was printed in *Australian Accountant*, February 1996 • p. 244: © IASB • pp. 251, 252: © MCU • p. 292: Commonwealth Copyright Administration/© ATO, copyright Commonwealth of Australia, reproduced by permission • p. 324–6: © Transparency International www.transparency.org.

# part 1

# Ethics & the individual

Instances of professional misconduct have led to increasing calls for ethics education that will improve students' ethical awareness and their ability to deal effectively with ethical challenges. Part 1 of this book introduces students to the significance of ethics in a business environment (chapter 1), theories of ethics (chapter 2), professional responsibilities and obligations (chapter 3), and structured approaches to ethical decision making (chapter 4).

# 1

# An ethics framework

**Learning objectives**

After studying this chapter, you should be able to:

- Discuss the concepts of ethics, governance and accountability in the business environment.
- Describe the ethics framework within which accountants work.
- Relate the ethics expectations of the market.
- Examine the ethics environment faced by accountants.
- Identify different ethics risks.
- Appreciate the significance of regulatory reforms which impact upon the accountant.
- Understand the approach adopted by the rest of the book in addressing the concepts of ethics, corporate governance and accountability as introduced in the ethics framework.

'The day Arthur Andersen loses the public trust
is the day we go out of business.'
**Steve Samek, Country Managing Partner, Arthur Andersen US, 1999,
in Toffler, BL 2003, *Final accounting, ambition, greed,
and the fall of Arthur Andersen*, p. 1.**

# Introduction to an ethics framework //

Recalling the statement made on the firm's *Independence and Ethical Standards* CD-ROM in 1999, Barbara Ley Toffler, former partner-in-charge of the Ethics and Responsible Business Practices Division of Arthur Andersen United States (1995–99), wrote:

> It is Arthur Andersen's lack of accountability that has inspired me to write this book. As an observer of corporate cultures, I believe strongly that the suicide of Arthur Andersen — and the assault on the investing public's trust — could have been avoided had people paid attention to the danger signs flashing everywhere in the late 1990s... [This] is a book about what it was like to work at a respected company as its culture began to decay. It is also about what happens when the values of an organization begin to distort your own.[1]

This book, *Ethics, governance and accountability: a professional perspective*, is a timely reminder for accountants and auditors of their roles in the competitive, highly regulative and complex business environment. This book has one theme: the long-term viability of a fair market is dependent on the effective and ethical interactions of individuals, the governance body, organisations and regulators. The **ethical dispositions** of individuals underpin behaviours, which, collectively, provide the framework for ethical cultures, sound values and good leadership, resulting in a fair and transparent system of accountability and responsible practices. This is the **ethics framework** that affects us all. Hence, this book aims to build the basic foundation for ethics, applicable for accountants and finance professionals in business. The book offers a rich base of knowledge, theories and principles, which are relevant for the ethics framework.

This chapter aims to provide the background to contextual matters concerning accountants. It sets the scene for readers to appreciate the significance and value of ethics in the corporate environment. An ethics framework is introduced, showing how ethics, corporate governance and accountability are interrelated and support the functioning of a fair market. We shall explore the risks and supports of the ethics framework for business. Within the framework, we will identify the typical issues that accountants and the accounting profession need to address. The typical issues are dynamic in nature, and a discussion of the current demands for accountability will provide an insight. Following a historic surge of corporate collapses in the early years of the 21st century, the accounting profession has embarked on regulatory and other reforms in response to the increasing amount of public scrutiny.

The remaining chapters of this book focus on the ethics framework for entities, in two main parts. Part 1 examines individual ethics and part 2 looks at ethics in a regulatory environment, integrating the debates in corporate governance with workplace issues.

# What is ethics, governance and accountability? //

**Ethics** is about choices. It is a concept that signifies how we act in order to make the 'right' choice, and produce 'good' behaviour. It encompasses a thorough (and objective) examination of principles, values, duties and norms, the consideration of available choices or alternatives in order to make the right decision and the strength of character to act in accordance with the decision. Ethics concerns individuals, groups, institutions and society.

**Governance** and **accountability** are about relationships. The word governance refers to authority and control. Governance means the strategy, method and manner in which a group of people (the governance body) directs, controls and manages an organisation. The governance body of a corporation normally rests with the board of directors and senior management, who possess the authority to govern or control. With authority comes responsibility. Accountability is the responsibility of those charged with governance to account for their choices, decisions and actions.

**Corporate governance** has been around for many years, and has traditionally been defined as 'the way a corporation is directed and controlled to maximise shareholders' value'. However, recent corporate events and the apparent failures of the governance system highlight the need to review not only systems and structures, but also relationships, cultures, ethics and leadership within organisations. The latest debates on corporate governance focus on the following issues:

- the structures of boards and committees, including independence of directors, committees, required expertise, appointment, compensation, performance assessment, and their accountability to shareholders, regulators and the public
- the relationships between the board, management, the shareholders, the auditors and the employees
- transparency and fairness in disclosure of financial reporting matters, the audit function, the independence of auditors, their engagement and reporting matters
- treatment and the rights of shareholders and stakeholders
- ethics, compliance and cultural issues within organisations
- shareholders' and stakeholders' interests.

What is right for individuals is highly subjective. How to define and perhaps develop an equitable balance in dealing with governance matters (such as between **conformance** and **performance**) is a delicate issue. These aspects will be further dealt with in other parts of this book. After reading this book, you will realise that ethics, corporate governance and accountability are all interrelated within an ethics framework.

## The ethics framework for businesses //

Figure 1.1 shows a schematic of the ethics framework for businesses. Three forces operate in the framework. They are the market (which includes the environment), the business entity and the regulatory regime. The ethics framework shows the interactive relationships among parties within each of these forces and among the forces. The market provides the resources and opportunities (and threats) for the entity to operate in a competitive world. The entity operates as an ongoing concern for the interests of its owners and forms a part of the marketplace. The government, industry regulators and professional organisations, on the other hand, provide support and oversight functions to the market and its entities. Interested parties such as the Australian Shareholder Associations, the unions and the Australian Institute of Company Directors are subgroups that pursue the interests and voice the concerns of their members to exert influence on all three forces.

The actions and performance of an entity can be seen by market participants such as shareholders, fund providers, and other stakeholders, including customers and the general public. The performance of the entity is also under the oversight of the **regulatory regime**. The market responds to the actions of entities and regulatory authorities and increases demand for relevant information, responsible behaviour, safety, protection of the environment, with the long-term expectations of returns and security. The regulatory regime corrects and minimises opportunities for malpractice by enacting legal restrictions and legislative reforms, and through persuading the industry and related professional organisations to introduce stronger self-regulatory standards and rules.

Within the entity, the governing body defines the overall strategy and implements control systems to exercise proper governance. Three levels of ethics are found within an entity: the ethics of the **governing body** (and its management), workplace ethics and individual (employee) ethics.

### Ethics of the governing body

The ethics of the governing body and its management concern the priorities given to the formulation of goals, mission and overall direction in the interests of the shareholders and stakeholders, thus implementing them into policies, procedures and control systems. The governing body of an entity is typically represented by the board of directors, the senior management and relevant board committees. The primary responsibility of the directors and management is to provide and facilitate good corporate governance practices, and to satisfy key corporate drivers for both performance and conformance. Corporate governance is not only about structures and processes, but also strategies for addressing stakeholder needs, in the form of products, services and information. Governance is characterised by an entity's priorities in values and leadership. Chapter 5 examines corporate governance in greater detail.

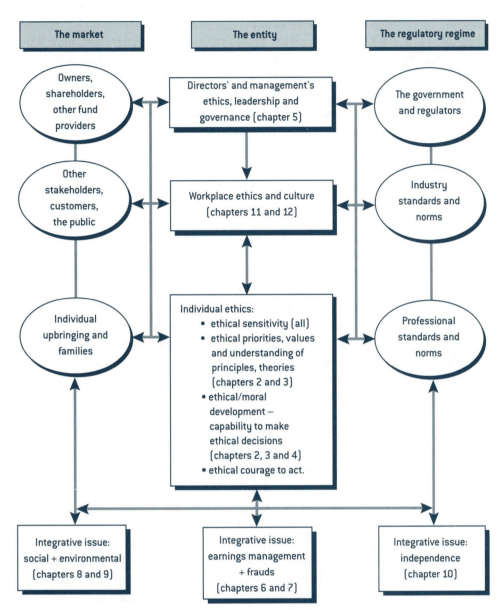

**FIGURE 1.1**  A schematic for an ethics framework

## Ethics of the workplace

The ethics of the workplace are influenced by the visibility of the values and leadership practised by the governing body. Workplace ethics can be characterised by the transparency of information and operation, open communication between levels, equitable treatment among and within subgroups and a generally supportive workplace environment. Workplace ethics concerns the implementation of governance polices and procedures, while monitoring the soft issues of 'unwritten norms' or cultures. The existence of a code of conduct, for example, is an incomplete feature when there is a lack of constant review regarding its adequacy, or when there is no monitoring procedure (i.e. supporting mechanism when an individual within an entity enforces the code or disciplinary measures when an individual breaches the code). Whistle-blowing programs, workplace conflicts, bribes or other conflicts of interests are issues which must be addressed in order to provide the contexts for ethical behaviour in a healthy workplace. Chapters 4 and 12 of this book examine both conflicts of interest and workplace ethics.

The ethics of the governing body and workplace ethics shape the entity's culture through their interactions and support. Culture in turn influences individuals.

### Individual ethics

Individual ethics, as a foundation, is dealt with in part 1 of this book. Individual ethical behaviour is influenced by four interrelated components, according to James Rest.[2] Individuals must be capable of identifying ethical problems (**ethical sensitivity**); appreciating the values and priorities through their understanding of principles, rules, norms and theories (**ethical priorities**); developing their individual sets of reasoning and judgment (**ethical judgment**); and developing the strength of character to act upon such decisions (**ethical courage**). So when an individual employee encounters a situation, he or she (1) acknowledges the ethical dimensions of the problem; (2) assesses available principles, rules and norms; (3) evaluates the adequacy of existing policies, practices and workplace standards; and (4) acts. All four components have to be present, according to James Rest, to result in ethical behaviour. Ethical approaches, priorities and theories, which underpin individual moral development and ethical decision making are dealt with in chapters 2, Understanding ethics and moral judgment, 3, Professional ethics and self-regulation, and 4, Ethical decision making. While this entire book aims to sensitise readers to ethical issues, ethical courage is a character trait developed by individuals, and which is enhanced by education and experience.

Although the integral part of the ethics framework concentrates on the entity, three accounting issues are examined to demonstrate the inter-dependencies between the market expectations, the system within entities and the regulatory regime — such relationships giving rise to more complex ethical issues. The issue of earnings management and its relationship to corporate collapse is discussed in two chapters: chapter 6, Fraud and forensic accounting, critically examines the role of accountants in fraudulent activities and chapter 7, Creative accounting, describes the problems (and incentives) of earnings management and creative accounting. Social and environmental issues (a topic increasingly prominent in annual reports), management strategies and corporate social responsibilities are dealt with in chapter 8, Social responsibility accounting, and chapter 9, Environmental responsibility. The cornerstone of the profession's credibility, professional independence, is the focus of chapter 10, Professional independence.

# Ethical expectations of the markets //

The growth of Australia's markets and financial services industry has been rapid and sustained. Statistics have shown that nearly one in two Australian adults now directly own shares, which is the highest proportion in the world, ahead of the United States, United Kingdom, Canada, Germany and New Zealand, in both direct and indirect share ownership. Different from Europe, Australia's market profile is also increasingly skewed towards retail investors. Millions of Australian investors are eager to help fund their retirement through some kind of equity ownership. Three out of four working Australians invest in superannuation, and over five million Australians use financial advisers. This growth in market size and coverage inevitably means that many investors are participating for the first time in financial markets, which they may not entirely or adequately understand. During the late 1990s, many inexperienced financial services consumers bought a complicated range of products and services and were caught out, losing their life savings.

The market, including owners and investors, public stakeholders and the general public, has certain **ethical expectations**. The market's support for an entity depends upon the credibility of the entity's corporate commitments and reputation, and the strength of its competitive advantage. Credibility depends on the trust that stakeholders place in the entity's activities, and trust, in turn, depends upon the values underlying such corporate activities. As Brooks (2004) points out, stakeholders increasingly expect an entity's activities to show respect for their values and interests. This respect for stakeholder values and interests determines the ethical standing and success of a corporation. The example on page 10 shows the importance of respect for stakeholder values and interests.

With an increasing amount of interest in corporate activities and accountability, the public expectations of businesses and the professions have become far more concerned with stakeholder interests and ethical matters than has been the case in the past. Directors, executives and business managers, who serve the often conflicting interests of shareholders directly, and the public indirectly, must be aware of the public's ethical expectations, and manage the related ethics risks accordingly. More than just to provide financial outcomes, their awareness must be combined with traditional values and incorporated into a framework for ethical decision making and action. Otherwise, just as with Enron and Arthur Andersen, the credibility, reputation and, eventually, competitive advantage of capital markets — as well as the organisation, management and the profession — will suffer.

In the aftermath of the corporate failures in the early 2000s, the general community has been caught up with extensive financial and other injuries. The collapse of HIH, one of Australia's largest home-building market insurers, left the building

## Johnson & Johnson and others

Crisis may strike a company unexpectedly. A huge amount of blame can be placed on a company if it fails to respond properly to a crisis. In 1982, Tylenol commanded 35 per cent of America's over-the-counter analgesic market, contributing about 15 per cent of Johnson & Johnson's profits. Unfortunately, an individual succeeded in lacing the drug with cyanide and seven people died as a result. After that incident, there was panic about Tylenol and the market value fell by $1 billion. When the same situation occurred in 1986, the company acted quickly. It recalled all Tylenol products from every outlet, not just the outlets where the products had been tampered with. The company also decided the product should not be re-established until something had been done to provide better product protection. As a result, tamper-proof packaging was developed. The cost was high and the lost production and destroyed goods of the recall were considerable. However, the company won praise for its quick and appropriate action, and achieved the status of consumer champion. Within five months of the disaster, the company regained 70 per cent of its market share for the drug. The company had succeeded in preserving the long-term value of the brand and its loyalty.

Contrast that with the case of Bridgestone/Firestone in 2001. In Washington, it paid US$41.5 million in a settlement to fend off lawsuits by states over defective tyres the company recalled in late 2000. The United States investigators had documented 271 deaths from thousands of accidents involving the tyres and the Attorneys-general raised doubts as to whether Bridgestone/Firestone and Ford were aware of the problems with the tyres long before the recall was announced.

Can you think of any other real-life cases similar to these?[3]

industry in turmoil. Home owners were left without compulsory home warranty insurance, owners of residential dwellings found that cover for defective building work had vanished, and builders were unable to operate because they could not obtain builders' warranty insurance. Thousands of other individual cases of hardship also emerged. For example, about 200 permanently disabled people no longer received their regular payments from HIH. A 50-year-old school principal who had developed a brain tumour, and who had relied on an income protection insurance policy, found his monthly cheque from HIH was dishonoured and his policy worthless.[4] Corporate collapses and the extensive damages to the community were a wake-up call for ethics in business.

In summary, market participants have ethical expectations from both the entity and its accounting and finance personnel.

Table 1.1 illustrates some of the ethical expectations of the market.

**TABLE 1.1**

### EXAMPLES OF ETHICAL EXPECTATIONS BY THE MARKET

| MARKET PARTICIPANTS | ETHICAL EXPECTATIONS OF THE ENTITY | ACCOUNTANTS' OR EXECUTIVES' ROLES |
|---|---|---|
| Owners, shareholders and fund providers | • Ongoing viability<br>• Reputation and credibility<br>• Integrity of information and returns<br>• Accountability. | • Effective governance and objective risk management process<br>• Integrity in financial management<br>• Transparency, objectivity and disclosure. |
| Other public stakeholders, employees, and individuals etc. | • Product safety and product quality<br>• Socially responsible activities<br>• Fairness and equity<br>• Honesty and respect for the public interest<br>• Professional and other developments<br>• Open communications<br>• Fair compensation. | • Understand corporate social responsibility and triple bottom line reporting<br>• Integrity in judgments for operations, financial and other business dealings<br>• Ensure compliance with standards, legal and regulatory matters<br>• Maintain integrity and the duty of care<br>• Undertake corrective actions in cases of wrongdoings<br>• Implement and monitor codes and whistle-blowing programs. |

# The accountant in the ethics framework //

Accountants provide skilful services. These services have developed from a traditional financial focus to a broad range of services including auditing, advisory, assurance and consultative roles, on matters which have economic outcomes, in the short or long term. Accountants therefore may assume responsibilities in any part of the ethics framework, providing services either as an employee, a financial expert or an independent service provider.

## Accountants as the moral agent //

Accountants are also said to be the moral agents of organisations, and provide an objective account of matters in a **fiduciary relationship**.[5] They are relied upon because of their professional status and ethical standards. Hence, within an entity, accountants have a duty towards their employer, loyalty to the governing body and management, and the responsibility to ensure such duties are performed with the objectivity, integrity and ethics of a professional person. Accountants providing independent services, such as in auditing, have a duty to their own employers, while maintaining an independent but cordial relationship with their clients.

One complication of the accountant's role in public accounting firms is the relationship between the accountant and the client. The cosy relationship, which often develops as a result of an accountant's increasing assistance to management in the form of consultancy and other services, may in turn jeopardise the perceived independence of the accountant as an auditor. It has been reported that, over the period 1992–2002, the total audit fees paid by the Australian Stock Exchange (ASX) top 100 companies grew by 99 per cent, while the total non-audit fees paid by these companies to their audit firms grew by 501 per cent.[6] The Australian Securities and Investments Commission (ASIC) also reported in 2002 that audit firms were earning substantial fees for non-audit services and that most companies lacked robust processes for ensuring that the independence of audit was not prejudiced by the provision of non-audit services.[7] The spate of audit and financial disclosure reforms in the *Corporate Law Economic Reform Program (Audit Reform and Audit Disclosure) Act 2004* is partly the result of the extensive nature of auditor involvements in their audit clients, which has led to the alleged failure of objectivity and integrity in major corporate collapses. Although there are historical and economic reasons in support of the broadening of services provided by accountants and auditors, the evidence presented after recent corporate collapses has rendered stringent rules for audit independence inevitable.

On the other hand, accountants employed within an organisation can be challenged with matters that are not necessarily financial in nature, but which have ethical implications. For example, an operational disaster which leads to human injuries involves financial compensation and the accountant may either be aware of the situation or part of the investigation. Or, an accountant may be involved in alerting a management to internal fraudulent activities, which could expose the organisation to potential financial losses. Outside the entity, accountants may be involved in providing professional forecasts and analyses, or undertaking investigative projects to evaluate investment proposals. Accountants representing the regulatory regime contribute to the understanding, development and interpretation of the law, industry and professional standards, with possible involvements in forensic issues. In sum, the roles of accountants in the ethics framework are diverse and complex.

All accountants are expected to observe the standards of care, **professionalism** and ethical behaviour as part of their primary professional duty to safeguard the public interest. This, of course, is an extremely simplistic description of the principles regarding accountants' roles in the ethics framework. The complex ethical positions of the accountant are briefly discussed here and explored further in the later parts of this book.

## The impact of competitive pressures and environmental concerns //

The development of the global market has given rise to the free flow of capital, goods and services throughout the world. Corporations try to combat competitive pressure through greater productivity and lower costs. Questionable behaviour, undertaken to increase short-term profitability, such as in the case of Bridgestone/Firestone, does not outweigh the risk of long-term reputation damage. There are also increasing concerns regarding environmental matters, excessive management compensation and bad business judgments. These issues, together with the corporate collapses and financial scandals, have led to the general public becoming less trusting of business executives and professionals, such as accountants and auditors. Some of these cases are illustrated in the following section.

## Ethical problems faced by accountants //

Accountants are educated to possess the competence and skills to deliver their services in the public interest. They are regarded as professionals who have a fiduciary relationship with those whom they service. Accounting bodies traditionally exercise a self-regulatory system in order to ensure that members safeguard the public interest by performing their tasks professionally, competently, ethically, responsibly and with due care.

As shown in figure 1.1, accountants, like other individuals employed within an entity, be it commercial or professional in nature, are subject to the same complex framework of relationships and influences. Furthermore, the requirement of allegiance towards professional standards and behaviour means that accountants must regard the public interest as their top priority. Any conflicts between **the public interest** and **self-interest**, loyalty to the entity and its governing body, may result in ethical dilemmas and possibly lapses. A choice has to be made. The choice made may even have very far-reaching consequences.

In a professional environment, such as within an accounting firm, an accountant's role requires performance under tight budget and timelines, maintaining relationships with clients and firm management, and applying strict accounting rules and professional standards. Hence, the ethics framework for an accountant working in a professional entity can be both demanding and complex, resulting in ethical issues to be faced by individual accountants.

The technology market bubble of the late 1990s and its puncturing in 2000 occurred alongside major collapses in corporate governance. Those who had contributed to the accounting scandals also contributed to the loss of public confidence in the accounting profession. High profile collapses such as Enron, WorldCom, Global Crossing, Adelphia Communications and Tyco in the United States, HIH, One.Tel and Harris Scarfe, in Australia, were largely the result of a period of disguise, restatement of the financial statements and a general disregard of ethics and integrity by business management, the board and the accountants involved. Parallel to this was great concern regarding the fairness of the operation of a market system where shareholders, employees in general, and pensioners lost large sums, while those running companies, exercising bad business and ethical judgments, had enriched themselves with massive compensation pay-outs.

Some argued that the catalyst for these events was the fierce battle by many managers and directors to meet investors' expectations that the company in which they purchased shares would report a steady stream of high and ever-increasing quarterly profits and revenues. In the struggle to deliver results, management, as well as investment bankers and analysts, with lawyers working alongside, lost sight of their responsibility and accountability. Some auditors also lost their autonomy and good judgment, and blurred the line between right and wrong. On too many occasions professionals in our largest and most respected accounting firms yielded to management pressure, permitting misleading financial information to be published.

To some extent, there have been some lapses in the way accounting firms have structured compensation policies and other incentives, rewarding those partners who generated the greatest amount of new auditing or consulting assignments rather than those who delivered the best quality audit work.

The following examples show how accountants have been involved in ethical lapses.

- A forensic audit by PricewaterhouseCoopers at HealthSouth, an Alabama-based rehabilitative clinic, reported a revised fraud of US$4.6 billion on 22 January 2004, representing fraudulent accounting entries from 1996 to 2002, incorrect accounting for goodwill and other aggressive accounting in that period to March 2003. Fifteen former executives, including five former chief financial officers, have pleaded guilty to charges related to the fraud. Former auditors at Ernst & Young, and former investment bankers at UBS Warburg, were said to have known about the fraud even as they signed off on financial statements and sold HealthSouth securities to the public.[8]
- Parmalat Finanziaria, the parent company of the Italian dairy group, has removed Deloitte & Touche SpA and Grant Thornton SpA as auditors following the discovery of a phoney asset certificate in the Cayman Islands. Two accountants at GT SpA were arrested on suspicion of falsely certifying Pamalat's balance sheets. Both firms were cited in a class action suit brought on behalf of United States investors.

- Former HIH Insurance financial executive Bill Howard was the first person convicted for his role in the HIH collapse when he was sentenced in the New South Wales Supreme Court to a three-year suspended jail term in December 2003. He admitted he received AUD$124 000 in bribes to organise payments to companies linked with Brad Cooper, including a $737 500 payment from HIH, which HIH was not obliged to make. It was alleged that when Cooper made an offer to 'look after' Howard, in return for retrieving funds from HIH, the HIH executives had their hands full trying to keep the company afloat. They asked Howard to 'deal' with Cooper. When Howard was asked at the HIH Royal Commission as to the reason for his action, he said, 'I don't know. I think I just gave in to the incessant battering ... I have been punting all my life'. [9]
- Alan Hodgson, the CFO at Harris Scarfe, admitted that for about five years he had in effect been keeping two sets of books. He had artificially increased the company's profits in the monthly financial reports, as well as the half-yearly and annual financial statements for the board and the Australian Stock Exchange (ASX). Hodgson stood to gain nothing from his actions other than the 'approval' of those around him. When the executive chairman said he wanted to achieve a particular profit margin, Alan interpreted it as an order to do whatever it took to get that margin. Hodgson was sentenced in 2001 to a six-year jail sentence, with a non-parole period of three years. [10]

These examples are just some of those appearing in the media about the corporate collapses in recent years, other than Enron and WorldCom. Many of the cases had similar features: a strong and dominating leader, a dysfunctional board, an aggressively results-driven corporate culture, manipulation of accounts, and accounting personnel caught in the middle, trying to balance the pressure to perform and to maintain their own position, possibly within an ethics lapse situation.

# Threats to ethics, corporate governance and accountability //

In light of the current environment of competition and drive for performance, accountants, auditors and other finance executives face issues which pose threats to their ability to maintain their ethical position and implement good governance practices. The sources of **threats** can include:

- stakeholders — where one group of stakeholders has an unfair advantage over other groups
- products or services — where the poor quality of products or performance of service compromises the standards (e.g. of safety and health)
- organisational culture, norm and objectives — where there is a lack of responsible leadership, combined with a self-interested culture and objectives

being defined by the 'bottom-line' and short-term financial benefits for individuals

- social status and reputation — professional and organisational misconduct where the organisation or the industry acts in a way perceived to be detrimental to society, leading to loss of credibility.

Threats to ethics, or ethics risks, have not been well researched. Carris and Duska (2003, p. 28) argue that unethical behaviour can expose a company to potential loss, liability torts and other risks.[11] They identify internal and external ethical hazards and suggest that the risk manager could mitigate both internal and external ethical hazards by using traditional risk management processes of identifying, evaluating, treating and monitoring the risk of, or exposure to, poor ethical behaviour within organisations. Earlier, Dr Enrico Nicolo (1996, pp. 153–162) designed a Total Ethical Risk Analysis method as an auxiliary approach for decision making in project management leadership.[12] He divided ethical risks into direct ethical risks and negative-feedback ethical risks and devised analytical methods to manage these risks. Although Enrico Nicolo focused on problems in managing distributed multimedia and other communicative systems, his paper introduced a few fundamentals of the total ethical-risk analysis method as a possible way of implementing ethical risk analysis that can contribute to developing policy frameworks and protocols. The latest edition of Brooks (2004) also discusses ethics risks and strategies (p. 358) and uses similar classifications to Nicolo and Carris and Duska.[13]

In describing the 'bill our brains out' culture of Arthur Andersen, Barbara Toffler referred to the fact that, by the late 1990s, all of the firm's employees were expected to be 'masters of creativity' when it came to figuring out ways to sell more services — auditing or consulting — to clients. There were regular meetings of SOAR teams ('Sales Opportunities and Resources'), 'Crown Jewel' teams and 'Elephant Target' teams. They were there to exploit every possible void. Everyone from auditors, internal auditors, tax specialists and consultants attended these meetings. Over the course of an hour or two, the status of a client's account would be reviewed, and then everyone would pitch in with ideas about how to increase revenue. 'It was all about cross-selling — offering the soup, the nuts, and everything in between ... the meetings also had the effect of increasing the pressure.'[14] Such a culture of pressure on individual employees led to the only way to get ahead, or to keep up, was to compromise quality. 'So that's what we did,' wrote Toffler.[15]

**Ethics threats** or risks can be defined as the risk of failure to achieve a certain expected standard of behaviour. An ethics risk for the professional accountant is the risk of failing to achieve the standards of behaviour expected of him or her. Such standards of behaviour are assumed within a fiduciary relationship, a professional arrangement, an accredited affiliation with a profession, or criteria established in a code of ethics or a set of mission statements.

## Threats to accountability at Barings and NAB

In August 1994, Barings' internal auditors had issued a report highlighting 'significant general risk' that Nick Leeson could circumvent controls, as he had responsibility over both trading and settlement activities. Although the warning has created tremendous pressures, the management wrote, 'Leeson should continue to take an active role in the detailed operation of both the front desk and the back office'. Leeson's ability to generate large profits was emphasised. In February 1995, the 233-year-old British investment bank collapsed. [16]

A decade later, a similar case occurred in the National Australia Bank (NAB), although it reacted swiftly to correct the situation. NAB lost AUD$360 million on currency options trading, as a result of poor operational and monitoring controls. PricewaterhouseCoopers (PwC), which conducted the investigation into the activities, reported that there were inadequate or non-existent controls which allowed trading losses to be concealed. Moreover, warnings signs were ignored. PwC reported that the concealment of the true trading position began as early as 1998. The traders 'smoothed' profits and losses by shifting them from one day to the next. It was a practice not dissimilar to Nick Leeson's at Barings — a lack of internal checking, concealing true transactions through the timing difference of recording, a lack of reconciliations, and a disregard for breaches of trading limits by management — practices that appeared to have been acceptable to NAB and Barings. Responsibility was 'passed on, rather than assumed'.

KPMG, which also reviewed the case, said that the NAB's culture or 'tone at the top' was a key to understanding how the losses developed. The focus was on procedure manuals (rather than the substance of the issues) and said that the board must accept that it is ultimately responsible for the culture that kept it in the dark.

NAB announced the departure of its executive general manager of risk management, alongside the earlier departure of its former chairman and chief executive — a casualty list of 10 so far. [17]

Some examples of ethics risks from different sources are described in table 1.2.

Table 1.2 shows that ethics risks can be embedded in a variety of relationships, hence the sources of ethics risks classifications include individuals, organisations, groups, products and objectives. Some ethics risks originate from a self-interest motive, in which individuals and organisations attempt to maximise their own benefits or avoid losses.

**TABLE 1.2**

## EXAMPLES OF ETHICS RISKS UNDER EACH SOURCE

| NATURE | STAKEHOLDERS | PRODUCTS/ SERVICES | CULTURE, NORMS AND OBJECTIVES | SOCIAL STATUS AND REPUTATION |
|---|---|---|---|---|
| Self-interest | Institutional investors' pressure for earnings / forecast targets leading to earnings management | Concealing prohibitive nature of products (e.g. ill effects of drugs to protect profit) | Maximising bonus and commission by manipulating accounts and budgets by senior staff | Building monopolised services (e.g. anti-trust practices, low-balling by accounting firms) |
| Incompetence (technical or ethical) | Failure to manage staff disputes leading to employee fraud | Failure to acknowledge product safety standards resulting in customer injuries | Wrong tone set at the top, non-compliance culture leading to staff tendency to cut corners | Failure of accountants or auditor to apply standards of integrity and objectivity in financial reporting |
| Conflict of interests | Conflicts between shareholders and management leading to misleading information released to the public | Extensive non-audit services rendered by auditors leading to compromised audits being performed | Inappropriate handling of complaints or staff concerns leading to whistle-blowing situations | Failure to discharge fiduciary duties in an independent and objective manner by accounting firms |

Ethics risks can also derive from incompetence. Here, competence includes both technical competence and ethical competence. A failure to understand the nature of a transaction which results in a wrong judgment of accounting policies (e.g. capitalising expenses) is an error caused by technical incompetence, leading to inappropriate financial statements being furnished. An inability to withstand the influence and pressure of management to manipulate the earnings figures is an example of ethical incompetence. Both cases would result in an unethical conduct (i.e. misleading users of the financial statements). Although it is difficult to distinguish between the two, and indeed they overlap sometimes, an ethical problem often arises from an error of judgment. Worse still is when, in some cases, an intentional error is committed to conceal an unintentional error. In terms of ethics, it is called a 'slippery slope', as seen in many corporate collapse cases — in HIH, One.Tel and Harris Scarfe, or in the collapse of the Barings Bank in the early 1970s.

# Corporate collapses and the need to restore credibility and trust //

Recent corporate collapses did not happen in a vacuum. Gittens (2002)[18] argues that the prevalence of materialism in many developed countries is the key motivation of fraudsters. Motivations for material advantages and pursuits of self-interests are shown by economic and political agendas, the growth in compensation for executives and the apparent declining ethical standards among company directors and auditors. The chairman of the Australian Securities and Investments Commission (ASIC) also lamented the extent of management greed, the failure of boards to exercise good corporate governance practices such as remuneration payouts, and the record level fees and commissions earned by analysts and accountants on advisory services (Knott 2002).[19]

In July 2003, the International Federation of Accountants (IFAC) released a research report entitled, *Rebuilding public confidence in financial reporting — an international perspective*. The report concluded that the financial scandals experienced in recent times were symptoms of deeper problems and not the prime cause of the loss of **credibility**. The research reported the following key findings:

- Methods of ensuring the effectiveness of corporate ethics codes and active monitoring are needed.
- Financial management and controls are a prime concern for corporate management.
- Incentives and awareness of financial misstatements are required in order to reduce such opportunities.
- Board oversight of management must be improved.
- Attention to potential threats to auditor independence and corporate governance issues is needed.
- The effectiveness of audit quality processes should be monitored.
- Compliance with codes of conduct should be monitored.
- The regulatory, standard setting and financial reporting processes and practices should be strengthened.[20]

In sum, the findings concern ethics, adequacy of financial management, reporting mechanisms, audit quality and strengthening of governance regimes. As the IFAC research report quite rightly put it, there are 'deeper problems' faced by accountants and auditors. Such deeper problems are the impediments and threats which jeopardise the objectivity and integrity of all parties in the supply chain of financial management and corporate governance.

> As the bubble economy encouraged corporate management to adopt increasingly creative accounting practices to deliver the kind of predictable and robust earnings and revenue growth demanded by investors, governance fell by the wayside. All too often, those whose mandate was to act as a gatekeeper were tempted by misguided compensation policies to forfeit their autonomy and independence.[21]

Never in its history has the accounting profession been subject to such criticism and challenges, which eroded public confidence and led to the sweeping changes in legislation and government intervention. From the enactment of the Sarbanes–Oxley Act in 2002, as well as the Public Company Accounting Oversight Board in the United States, we witnessed the publication of numerous papers of reforms and research reports. In Australia, the more recent developments are:

- CLERP Discussion Paper No. 9: *CLERP (Audit Reform and Corporate Disclosure) Act 2004*
- the ASX Corporate Governance Principles and Best Practice Guidelines 2003
- Standard Australia's Australian Standards for Corporate Governance, which includes Good Governance Principles, Fraud and Corruption Control, Organisational Codes of Conduct, Corporate Social Responsibility, and Whistleblower Protection Programs for Entities. These standards were issued in 2003 as AS8000 Standards.
- the HIH Royal Commission reports (three volumes), which detail the problems and recommendations for parties such as the accounting profession, governments, auditors, corporate managers and board of directors.

In an address in March 2004 to the Institute of Chartered Accountants in Australia, the Acting Chairman of ASIC emphasised the priorities of ASIC in 2004. The address reiterated the increased responsibilities of ASIC, which are to maintain, facilitate and improve the performance of the financial system and the entities within it, which includes reducing business costs and improving the efficiency and development of the economy. The collapse of entities such as HIH, Enron and WorldCom have moved regulatory reforms higher up the public agenda, particularly as they relate to disclosure and audit.[22]

An example of these is the regulation S1013D(1) of the *Financial Services Reform Act 2001* (FSRA), which requires the issuer of financial services products, including superannuation funds, to disclose 'the extent to which labour standards, or environmental, social or ethical considerations are taken into account in the selection, retention or realisation of the investment'. Another example is the CLERP (Audit Reform and Corporate Disclosure) Act 2004, which strengthens the obligations of auditors to report breaches of the law to ASIC. ASIC regards the administration of the Financial Services Reform Act, CLERP (Audit Reform and Corporate Disclosure) Act 2004 and surveillance programs as its priorities. All three have major implications for the role of accountants and finance professionals.

The introduction of the financial services reform (FSR) regime set new standards, which meant that the entire financial sector was brought under a consistent set of regulations. There is a harmonised licensing system, disclosure and conduct framework and a single regime for financial product disclosure. The CLERP (Audit Reform and Corporate Disclosure) Act 2004, on the other hand, is the government's response to the series of corporate governance and accounting failures.

Examples of the CLERP (Audit Reform and Corporate Disclosure) Act 2004 provisions include:

- expanding the role of the Financial Reporting Council, which is to be responsible also for the oversight of the accounting and auditing standards-setting regime
- providing legal underpinning for auditing standards
- strengthening auditor independence, including requiring rotation of audit partners of listed company clients after five years
- providing greater protection for those who report breaches of the law to ASIC
- enhancing disclosure and accountability to shareholders, including on executive and director remuneration
- introducing a new duty for financial services licensees to manage conflicts of interest.

As stressed by the acting chairman in his address, one of the foundations of good governance is the provision of adequate, timely and reliable information about corporate performance. This is the responsibility of those who direct and control the corporation, its finance personnel and the experts brought in under the law as independent judges — that is, the auditors. Auditors, in particular, have always faced the dilemma of trying to reconcile a commercial service provider-client relationship with the responsibility of a watchdog or a 'contracted regulator' of corporate financial reporting. The two roles conflict and are not equally supported. All the commercial incentives support the service provider role, and very little, if anything, has supported the watchdog role. The CLERP (Audit Reform and Corporate Disclosure) Act 2004 tries to redress the balance, and supports the public responsibility or 'watchdog' aspect of auditing. Not only that, in the opinion of the acting chairman, a clear market expectation now is that auditors should be bloodhounds, not just watchdogs. It expects auditors to take the initiative where they discern something amiss — to find and reveal what is hidden.

To remain a profession, therefore, accounting must address issues ranging from the underlying potential problems or conflicts created by the consolidation of the financial industry to the need to restore its credibility by critically re-examining its fundamental values and roles. This book offers not only an understanding of the role of accountants and finance professionals but also provides the theoretical framework for the future development of the profession.

## Summary //

This chapter has set the scene and provided the structure of the rest of the book. The aim of the book is based on the theme that the ongoing viability of a fair market is founded on ethical inter-relationships among the market players. The market and the regulatory regime influence the functioning of an entity, and demand and support an effective framework of ethics in business entities. The ethics framework was introduced to illustrate the impact of individual ethics, workplace ethics and corporate governance. The chapter discussed the elements of the ethics framework, the ethical expectations of the market, the role of the accountant and the latest developments and expectations of the regulatory regime in the framework. Various types of ethics threats or risks were discussed. The remaining chapters deal with the bases of individual ethics and how individual ethics interacts with corporate ethics and governance.

## Key terms //

Accountability . . . p. 5
Corporate governance . . . p. 5
Conformance . . . p. 5
Credibility . . . p. 19
Ethical courage . . . p. 8
Ethical dispositions . . . p. 4
Ethical expectations . . . p. 9
Ethical judgment . . . p. 8
Ethical priorities . . . p. 8
Ethical sensitivity . . . p. 8
Ethical threats . . . p. 16
Ethics . . . p. 5
Ethics framework . . . p. 4
Fiduciary relationship . . . p. 12
Governance . . . p. 5
Governing body . . . p. 6
Performance . . . p. 5
Professionalism . . . p. 13
Public interest . . . p. 13
Regulatory regime . . . p. 6
Self-interest . . . p. 13
Threats . . . p. 15

# Questions //

**1.1** What is meant by ethics and how do ethics relate to an accountant's role?

**1.2** Explain the relationship between 'governance' and 'accountability'.

**1.3** What are the ethical expectations of the market for the accountant? Explain how the ethical expectations have not been met.

**1.4** Discuss the role of regulation in corporate governance.

**1.5** Ethics is an individual matter, and it should not be influenced by an individual's employment status. Discuss this contention with examples.

**1.6** After some years of complacency and even cynicism, corporate governance again became a topic of some international interest. Do you think the debate on corporate governance is purely a knee-jerk reaction to the recent corporate collapses? Explain your answer.

**1.7** What is the current state of the accounting profession's credibility? Why is credibility so important to the profession?

**1.8** Provide three examples of ethical threats for each of the following categories:
- **a** stakeholders
- **b** products or services
- **c** culture of an organisation
- **d** reputation

**1.9** How does incompetence give rise to ethical problems? Provide an example to illustrate an accounting ethical problem resulting from the incompetence of an auditor.

**1.10** Discuss the implications of CLERP (Audit Reform and Corporate Disclosure) Act 2004 as it affects the accountant.

## CASE STUDY 1

After graduating with an accounting degree, Ai Ming joined Wholesalers Ltd, a textile wholesale company, as an assistant accountant 6 months ago. He encountered the following situations:

1. For the past five months, the chief accountant, Bing Ho, authorised a number of expense invoices, which Ai Ming was instructed to include as company expenses. Ai Ming discovered last Friday that these expenses were household expenses incurred by Bing Ho's family. Ai Ming felt uneasy about the situation, especially when Bing Ho came in with another invoice of $12 000 for an entertainment system installed at Bing Ho's address. Bing Ho told Ai Ming to put it through to the Repairs and Maintenance account.

2. Bing Ho's daughter Alice, who is studying accountancy at a university in Melbourne, has obtained a part-time job in Wholesalers Ltd, working as

an accounting clerk in Ai Ming's office. Alice has become very friendly with Ai Ming and they have gone out a few times. Alice asked Ai Ming to help her with her studies, as she wishes to be as successful as her father, referring to her father Bing Ho's motto that 'being a professional accountant holds the key to all'.

**Required**

*1*

For case scenario 1, what are the duties owed by Ai Ming? Is there any conflict of interest faced by Ai Ming as an assistant accountant in Wholesalers Ltd?

*2*

For case scenario 2, explain any ethics risks and possible consequences faced by Ai Ming when dealing with Alice. Comment on Bing Ho's motto and advise of Ai Ming's possible actions.

*3*

Taking both scenarios 1 and 2 together, what are the ethical and professional issues faced by Ai Ming?

## CASE STUDY 2

The following appears in an article entitled 'NAB struggling to regain customer trust' by Stewart Oldfield, *Australian Financial Review*, 8 April 2004, p. 11.

> One fact is certain. The impact on NAB of its currency option scandal goes well beyond the $360 million it has owned up to, when issues such as reputation and staff morale are included. It goes well beyond the mispricing of a book of options written against a US dollar that was meant to rally over Christmas. Bank staff have complained of 'gridlock' in internal processes after a spate of executive departures and expectations of many more . . .

**Required**

As an independent ethics consultant, write a report to a competitive organisation regarding the significance of internal control failures, taking into consideration the lessons learned from the NAB case. You may make assumptions about the organisation's internal processes.

## FURTHER RESOURCES AND WEBSITES //

### Journal articles

Australian Council of Superannuation Investors Inc. 2002, *Non-audit services performed by auditors in the top 100 companies*, ACSI, Melbourne.

Barrier, M 2003, 'One right path — Cynthia Cooper', *Internal Auditor*, December, pp. 52–7.

CLERP (Audit Reform and Corporate Disclosure) Act 2004.

Corporate Governance Australian Standards 2003, *Standards Australia*, Standards Australia, Melbourne.

Eakin, J 2003, 'H Norman "fails" governance', *Sydney Morning Herald*, 10 November, p. 33.

Gettler, L 2002, 'Audit fees soar after scandals', *The Age*, 26 November, viewed 23 January 2004, www.theage.com.au.

Flanagan, J 2004, 'Role of personal values in ethical decisions', *Australian Financial Review*, 5 January, p. 43.

*Illawarra Mercury* 2003, 'Ex HIH finance boss walks free from court', *Australian Financial Review*, 24 December, p. 35.

Jennings, MM 2003, 'The critical role of ethics', *Internal Auditor*, December, pp. 47–51.

Peaple, A 2004, 'Survey reveals poor reporting practices', *Australian Financial Review*, 8 January, viewed 23 January 2004, www.afr.com.au.

Ryan, M 2002, 'The inside job', *The CFO Magazine*, 1 October, p. 20.

Sarbanes–Oxley Act 2002, United States Congress.

Sexton, E 2003, 'Secret meetings, cash bribes and dirty deals', *Sydney Morning Herald*, 17 December, p. 6.

### Websites

Australian Stock Exchange 2003, *Corporate governance principles and guidelines*, viewed 12 April 2004, www.asx.com.au.

Commonwealth of Australia 2003, *HIH Royal Commission Report*, vols 1–3, Canberra, viewed 10 June 2004, www.hihroyalcom.gov.au.

Horwath and the University of Newcastle 2003, *Key Findings from the Horwath 2003 Corporate Governance Report*, Horwath, Melbourne, viewed 28 February 2004, www.horwath.com.au.

### ENDNOTES //

1. Toffler, BL 2003, *Final accounting — ambition, greed, and the fall of Arthur Andersen*, Broadway Books, New York, p. 1.
2. Rest, J 1983, 'Morality', in P Mussen (ed.), *Handbook of child psychology: vol. 4*. Wiley, New York, pp. 556–619 and Rest, JR 1986, *Moral development: Advances in research and theory*, Praeger, New York. James Rest provides a framework for understanding moral behaviour. His Four Component Model includes moral sensitivity, moral judgment, moral decision making and moral action. Moral sensitivity is the recognition that a situation exists in which moral action may be needed and that these actions may have consequences for others. Moral judgment is a judgment about what one ought to do, while moral decision making involves considering alternatives and weighing pros and cons in light of their probable consequences for the self and others. Finally, moral action includes the will and skill to implement the decision (Rest 1983). Rest concludes that his framework should be used as a basis for formulating objectives for moral education programs.
3. The case of Johnson & Johnson and Tylenol has been reported on many ethics websites. This one is an extract of an article that appeared on www.mallenbaker.net, viewed 8 June 2004. The case of Bridgestone/Firestone was reported in a series of articles from www.motoring.co.za, viewed 17 March 2004.

4. Commonwealth of Australia 2003, *HIH Royal Commission Report*, vols 1–3, Canberra, viewed 10 June 2004, www.hihroyalcom.gov.au.

5. Schweiker, W 1992, 'Accounting for ourselves: accounting practice and the discourse of ethics', *Accounting, Organizations and Society*, April, pp. 231–62. The author argues that giving an account is basic to understanding the moral dimension of accounting practice: a discursive act in which the identity of the agent is displayed as inter-subjective and constituted by fiduciary relations through time.

6. Survey results by Institutional Analysis Pty Ltd (www.institutionalanalysis.com) reported in its submission to the review of independent auditing by registered company auditors, August 2002. Viewed 18 March 2004.

7. Australian Securities and Investments Commission 2002, *ASIC announces findings of auditor independence survey*, media release, Australian Securities and Investments Commission, 16 January.

8. 'Auditors find fraud at HealthSouth could total $4.6 billion', reported on AccountingWEB.com, viewed 22 January 2004.

9. From Commonwealth of Australia 2003, *HIH Royal Commission Report*, vols 1–3, Canberra, viewed 10 June 2004, www.hihroyalcom.gov.au

10. Reported by Ryan, M 2002, 'The inside job', *The CFO Magazine*, 1 October, p. 20.

11. Carris, R & Duska, R 2003, 'Ethics and the risk manager', *Risk Management*, vol. 50, no. 4, April, pp. 28–32.

12. Enrico N 1996, 'Fundamentals of the total ethical-risk analysis method (TERAmethod) with a study of crucial problems in managing distributed multimedia', *International Journal of Project Management* vol. 14, no. 3, pp. 153–62.

13. Brooks, L 2003, *Business and professional ethics for directors, executives, and accountants*, 3rd edn, Thomson & South-Western, USA.

14. Toffler, BL (op cit), pp. 101–26.

15. Toffler, BL (op cit), pp. 101–26.

16. Allen, RD 1996, *Internal auditor*, Aug, Institute of Internal Auditor Inc, USA.

17. 'NAB faces task of rebuilding corporate culture', 13 March 2004, *The Age*.

18. Gittens, L 2002, 'Invasion of the money snatchers', *The Age*, 28 August.

19. Knott, D 2002, 'Corporate governance — principles, promotion and practice', Monash University Governance Research Unit, Inaugural Lecture, Melbourne, 16 July.

20. International Federation of Accountants 2003, *Rebuilding public confidence in financial reporting — an international perspective*, July, International Federation of Accountants, New York.

21. The American Assembly, 2003, 'The current state of the accounting profession: what went wrong', *The future of the accounting profession report*, the 103rd American Assembly, Columbia University, New York.

22. Lucy, J 2004, 'FSR, CLERP 9 and surveillance programs: ASIC priorities over the next 12 months', an address by the Acting Chairman, ASIC, Jeffrey Lucy AM, FCA, to the Institute of Chartered Accountants in Australia, Queensland CA Business Forum, 13 March.

# 2

# Understanding ethics and moral judgment

## Learning objectives

After studying this chapter you should be able to:

- Explain why ethics is important in accounting education.
- Describe the normative ethical theories of utilitarianism, rights and justice.
- Evaluate the strengths and weaknesses for each of the normative ethical theories.
- Recommend a course of action using the normative ethical theories.
- Describe the challenges to ethical behaviour.
- Distinguish the normative theories of ethics from Kohlberg's theory of cognitive moral reasoning and development.
- Describe the six stages of cognitive moral reasoning and development.
- Discuss the implications of moral reasoning judgment in accounting.
- Discuss the effect of accounting education on students' moral development.
- Explain the concept of select-socialisation in the accounting profession.

---

'. . . CPA respondents appear to have reached the moral maturation level of adults in general, instead of maturing even to the level of college students, much less to the level of college graduates.'

**Mary Beth Armstrong (1987, p. 33)**

# Introduction //

To facilitate an ethical decision, we must first decide what is ethical. Decision making that relies on intuition and personal feelings does not always lead to the right course of action. For example, an act fixed on revenge, often rationalised on the notion of justice, is unlikely to produce the best course of action. Ethical decision making requires a criterion to ensure good judgment. In the same way managers compare actual activity with expected outcomes to judge performance, people require a criterion for judging the ethics of an act or decision. In ethics, we rely on philosophy to provide that criterion. In the first half of this chapter we introduce three philosophical theories of ethics: *utilitarianism*, *rights* and *justice*. Each of these theories provides different and distinct criteria for good, right or ethical judgment.

In the latter part of this chapter, we introduce the concept of cognitive moral reasoning and development. Moral reasoning is the process that people use to evaluate the facts, principles, and consequences of a dilemma when arriving at a decision. While ethics provides us with principles of right and wrong, moral reasoning explains how decisions are actually made. Understanding the theory of moral reasoning is important if we are to comprehend the decisions accountants make in resolving ethical dilemmas.

# Why learn ethics? //

The accounting profession has suffered a series of setbacks with the financial collapse of business firms involved in financial fraud without detection from their auditors (Clark 2002). Critics usually cite a breakdown in the ethical standards and behaviour of accountants as a contributing factor in such scandals (Gaa 1994). Consequently, a number of organisations recommend the inclusion of ethics into business curriculums. For example, The National Commission on Fraudulent Financial Reporting 1987 (Treadway Commission) recommends the inclusion of ethics education in business curriculums to help prevent, detect, and deter fraudulent reporting. The two major Australian accounting bodies (CPA Australia and the Institute of Chartered Accountants Australia) and universities now include ethics in their educational programs.

The phrase 'ethics education' has a variety of connotations. For some, it means instruction to obey the law, while for others it is improving moral character. Critics of ethics education argue that a student's moral standards have been fully developed and firmly entrenched by traditional institutions such as church and family by the time they reach university. The university curriculum, therefore, is unlikely to influence students' attitudes. However, supporters of ethics education claim that changing students' habits, beliefs and values is not, and should not be, a primary function of a course in ethics. The primary function should be to teach ethical systems of analysis, not moral standards of behaviour.

The goal of ethics education is not related to value-shaping, but to helping the fundamentally decent, well-intentioned student by introducing skills to deal effectively with ethical challenges (McDonald & Donleavy 1995). Ethics education will not convert a 'deviant' to a 'virtuous human being', but students with good instincts and a genuine concern for others will be able to detect issues more perceptively, think about them more carefully and to understand more clearly the reasons for acting morally. Therefore, one goal of this chapter is to provide you with a framework to identify, analyse and resolve ethical problems. Whether or not you choose to utilise these skills in your professional life is a separate issue.

# Normative theories of ethics //

In this section we identify and classify three approaches to ethical judgment, which will not only help you to understand the language of normative ethics but also provide a framework for moral discourse in later chapters. As you read through the following material you should bear in mind that theories of ethics are not based on utopian notions of idealistic living — they reflect the way people make decisions in their everyday lives.

A **normative theory** is represented by a value judgment on what 'should' or 'ought' to happen, it is not concerned with what does happen. For example, fidelity as a normative principle suggests that people *should* always be truthful even if deception is common or usual practice. In ethics, a normative theory provides a principle, standard or value on how we ought to behave toward others by considering the right and wrong of our actions. Ethics is about doing good instead of harm and it does this by setting a standard of virtuous conduct. Therefore, a **normative ethical theory** provides a principle on how we ought to behave irrespective of current social norms and practices. Understanding principles of good behaviour is important if we are to make ethical decisions and behave appropriately.

It is customary to divide normative ethical theories into two broad classifications, consequential and non-consequential. **Consequential theories** define good in terms of its consequences, thus giving rise to the term consequential. The best-known example of a consequential theory is utilitarianism. In contrast to consequential theories we have **non-consequential theories**, which define good not by its consequences, but by its intrinsic value, regardless of whether its obedience produces undesirable outcomes. For a non-consequentialist, an act or decision is right because it is the right thing to do. The best-known examples of non-consequential theories are the rights and justice theories. Each of these theories is discussed on the following pages.

## Consequential theories of ethics //

In ethical decision making, even the best intentions are of little value unless an ethical outcome is achieved. Proponents of this view support the notion that consequences are important for assessing the moral worth of an act or decision. In general terms, consequential theories determine right from wrong based on the results or consequences of the action or decision, and if the good consequences outweigh the bad consequences, the decision or action is morally correct. There are a variety of consequential theories; in this chapter we examine the theory of utilitarianism.

## The theory of utilitarianism //

The theory of **utilitarianism** is concerned with making decisions that promote human welfare. According to this theory, the ethical alternative is the one that maximises good consequences over bad consequences. Expressed as a guiding principle, something is morally good to the extent that it produces the greatest balance of good consequences over bad consequences for the greatest number of people. The principle is commonly expressed as 'the greatest benefit for the greatest number'. This should not be confused with producing the greatest total benefit, but the action that produces the greatest benefit after allowing for total costs.

Jeremy Bentham (1784–1832), the father of utilitarian ethics, defined utilitarianism as the *greatest happiness principle*. The greatest happiness principle measures good and bad consequences in terms of happiness and pain. To this end, acts are right to the extent that they promote happiness (which makes life more content) and avoid pain (which makes life worse). The terms happiness and pain have broad meaning and encompass all aspects of human welfare, including pleasure and sadness, health and sickness, satisfaction and disappointment, positive and negative emotions, achievement and failure, and knowledge and ignorance.

Applying the utilitarian principle is a procedural process involving five simple steps. They are:
1. Define the problem.
2. Identify the stakeholders affected by the problem.
3. List the alternative courses of action for resolving the problem.
4. Identify and calculate the short- and long-term costs and benefits (pain and happiness) for each alternative course of action.
5. Select the course of action that yields greatest sum of benefits over costs for the greatest number of people.

The theory of utilitarianism is attractive because it fits neatly into people's intuitive criteria for deciding moral problems. People make crude comparisons between their likes and dislikes every day and are quick to point out the benefits and harms of proposed actions. For example, a proposal to introduce fees for education will immediately conjure up notions of affordability and accessibility. Utilitarianism is appealing to many people because it takes a pragmatic, common-sense, and even unphilosophical, approach to ethics. Actions are right to the extent that they benefit people. Alternatively, actions that produce more benefits than harms are right, and those that do not, are wrong. Therefore, the advantage of utilitarianism lies in its simplicity and defensibility. This comparative cost–benefit approach to ethical decision making provides a straightforward method of ana-lysing and resolving ethical problems. Once resolved, decisions can be explained and justified with utilitarian reasoning.

## Limitations of utilitarianism

The cognitive process required for utilitarian decision making appears similar to the cost–benefit analysis that is normally applied in business decisions. However, there are three important distinctions between the application of the utility prin-ciple and the traditional cost–benefit analysis: the nature of the consequences, the measurability of the consequences and stakeholder analysis.

### The nature of the consequences

In analysing the consequences of the various alternative courses of action, we must be careful not to consider consequences in strict economic terms. As stated above, costs and benefits are defined as pain and happiness, which encompass all aspects of human welfare and emotions. Consequences in utilitarian analysis are not restricted to financial matters. This does not mean that economic outcomes should be ignored, but should receive the same consideration as non-economic outcomes. The problem for most accountants, and business people generally, is that they are inclined to focus on the economic outcomes and ignore other non-quantifiable variables. This typically occurs in business where cost–benefit analyses are meas-ured predominantly in economic terms and for their impact on the profit motive. The comfort and objectivity associated with measurable outcomes tempts people to favour quantifiable criteria and, in doing so, ignore non-quantifiable variables, even though they may be sometimes more important. This kind of faulty analysis displays a quantitative bias that may exclude other more attractive courses of action that rely more heavily on non-quantifiable outcomes.

### The measurability of consequences

The utilitarian principle assumes that we can somehow measure and add the quan-tities of happiness produced by an action and subtract them from the quantities of measured pain, thereby enabling the selection of a course of action that produces the greatest net happiness. However, not all benefits and harms have an easily determined unitary or monetary value. How can sadness, pleasure or contentment be measured? Even when unitary measurement is possible, the relative weighting given to outcomes will vary with different people. What is good for one person may be harmful to another. It is likely that two people applying a utilitarian analysis to the same problem will arrive at different conclusions simply because of the way in which outcomes are measured and weighted. Fortunately for accountants, they, more than many other professions, possess the skills for measuring and assigning values to uncertain outcomes.

### Stakeholder analysis

Proper application of the utility principle requires a deliberation of the consequences on *all* people affected (stakeholders) including, but not restricted to, the decision maker. Whereas the typical cost–benefit analysis in business considers the impact of the consequences primarily in terms of the entity or person that is making the decision. Other stakeholders are considered only in so far as it affects the business entity. A utilitarian analysis goes beyond that of the decision maker and seeks to maximise net happiness to as many stakeholders as possible. An act that promotes self-interest at the expense of others is unethical on utilitarian grounds.

## Non-consequential theories of ethics //

The alternative to consequential theories such as utilitarianism are non-consequential theories. A non-consequentialist affirms that duties must be obeyed regardless of the outcomes, hence the term non-consequentialism. A non-consequentialist would argue that the end does not justify the means and the intention to do the right thing is more important than the result. The question here is what is the right thing? We examine two examples of non-consequential theories: the theory of rights and the theory of justice.

## The theory of rights //

The rights principle stems from the belief that people have an inherent worth as human beings that must be respected. Therefore, according to the theory of **rights**, a good decision is one that respects the rights of others. Conversely, a decision is wrong to the extent that it violates another person's rights. When confronted with a moral dilemma, consideration must be given to the rights of the individuals involved and ensure that decisions respect the rights of others.

Having rights or entitlements, such as freedom of speech, is worthless unless individuals are free to pursue their entitlements unhampered. For example, in Australia people have a right to speak freely on all matters of their choosing. This right imposes an ethical obligation on others to ensure that the right to speak freely is respected. Similarly, in education, lecturers have a right to be heard; in turn, this right imposes an obligation on students to ensure that those who want to listen, can. Therefore, not only does the rights principle give due recognition to individual rights, but it also imposes an obligation on individuals not to interfere with others' privilege to pursue and enjoy their rights.

## Natural rights

In general, rights can be divided in two categories: rights that exist independently of any legal structure and rights that are created by social agreement. The former are known as natural rights, and these rights are commonly referred to as human rights or constitutional rights. A detailed discussion of the various natural rights is beyond the scope of this book; however, a list of the rights that are commonly advocated in western societies includes:

- *freedom of choice* — the right to be able to make decisions without fear of reprisal
- *right to the truth* — the right to be accurately informed of all matters that affect decisions
- *right to privacy* — the right to live life as one chooses
- *freedom of speech* — the right to speak freely and be heard
- *right to life* — the right to be protected from injury, including safety in the workplace
- *right to due process* — the right to a fair hearing
- *right to what is agreed* — the right to have promises and contracts honoured.

Drawing from this list, the right to the truth is central to the function of accounting. The public, particularly users of financial statements, has a right to truthful and accurate financial information when making choices on alternative investment strategies. This right imposes a moral obligation on the accountant and the reporting entity to prepare and issue, true and fair financial reports. Upholding the integrity of the financial reports is critical if members of the accounting profession are to respect the users' right to make fully informed choices.

## Legal rights and contractual rights

The second category of rights consists of rights created by agreement, which include legal rights and contractual rights. It is this type of right that is important in the accountant–employer and the accountant–client relationship. Accountants are employed by companies or commissioned by clients for their expert knowledge and skills. In return for their professional services, accountants are financially rewarded with fees or a salary. The contractual relationship between the parties means that clients and employers have a legal right to expect professional and competent service. In turn, accountants have a corresponding legal duty to perform their tasks to the best of their ability within the constraints of their expertise. If an accountant does not possess the requisite skill to perform the task properly, he or she has a professional and moral obligation to seek specialist advice or, if necessary, decline the task. A list of the rights and corresponding duties peculiar to the accounting profession are presented in table 2.1.

TABLE 2.1

## STAKEHOLDER RIGHTS AND THE ACCOUNTANT'S CORRESPONDING DUTIES

| VALUE | STAKEHOLDER | STAKEHOLDER RIGHTS | ACCOUNTANT'S DUTIES |
|---|---|---|---|
| Privacy | Clients and employers | The right to expect that information regarding their activities will not be disclosed to a third party. | To ensure that all information discovered in the course of their work is not disclosed to a third party without the stakeholder's express permission. |
| Competence | Clients and employers | The right to receive a service that is expertly applied. | The duty to maintain expertise and apply their skills diligently. |
| Wellbeing | Clients, employers and the public | The right to expect that the service provided by the accountant will advance the stakeholder's best interests. | The duty to ensure that accountants subordinate their self-interest in favour of their client or employer and to avoid any relationship or event that may compromise objective judgment. |
| Respect for peers | Members of the accounting profession | The right to expect that their reputation as competent and trustworthy professionals is not discredited by the behaviour of their peers. | The duty to ensure that their behaviour does not adversely affect the good reputation of the accounting profession. |
| Truth | Users of accounting information | The right to receive complete, accurate and truthful financial information. | The duty to comply with accounting standards in the preparation of accounting reports and to be prepared to depart from accounting standards if compliance will produce misleading statements. |

You will observe from your perusal of table 2.1 that a corresponding duty imposed by a right can fall on all members of a group as well as individuals. For example, the duty of a professional accountant to 'respect peers' imposes an obligation on all members of the accounting profession. Accountants should be mindful that their responsibilities extend not only to individual clients, employers and other accountants, but also to the public and the community of accountants. The values discussed in table 2.1 are embedded in the Joint Code of Professional Conduct, which is discussed in detail in chapter 3.

### Limitation of the rights principle

One problem associated with the rights principle is that it does not always provide satisfactory solutions to many problems. Difficulties arise when the dilemma involves a conflict among two or more equally compelling rights. Take, for example, a situation involving a client behaving illegally. Which right has priority: the client's right to privacy or the public's right to the truth? Unfortunately, the theory does not prioritise or give weight to the various rights — it merely states that individuals have rights that must be respected. Therefore, there is no clear way to address problems of conflicting rights. This lack of hierarchy is a major problem of the rights principle.

## The theory of justice //

Understanding the theory of **justice** is complicated by the various notions of justice. In everyday language, justice is often described as **fairness**, which refers to the correlation between contributions and rewards. However, fairness alone does not adequately define the concept of justice as there is as much subjectivity in fairness as there is in justice. For instance, what one person may think is fair or just, another may not. Other forms of justice include **equality**, which assumes that all people have equal worth, **procedural justice**, which is concerned with due process and **compensatory justice**, which aims to redress the loss from a wrongful act (Velasquez 2002). A comprehensive theory incorporating the various domains of justice has yet to be developed. Until such time, the justice principle and its application will have different meanings in different contexts. In this chapter, we focus our discussion on the principle of distributive justice.

### Distributive justice

Disputes between people often arise because one person accuses another of unfair treatment or failing to accept a fair share of responsibilities. Resolving these types of disputes means that we must compare, weigh up and strike a balance between the conflicting claims. This comparative approach to problem solving is based on the principle of distributive justice, which is primarily concerned with the fair and equal distribution of benefits and burdens. The theory of **justice**, based on the principle of distributive justice, focuses on how fairly our decisions and actions distribute benefits and burdens among members of the group. An unfair distribution of benefits and burdens is an unjust act and an unjust act is a morally wrong act.

Applying the justice principle to the resolution of an ethical problem is a three-step process. First, the decision maker identifies the benefits and burdens that are likely to result from a proposed action and decision; second, the benefits and burdens are assigned to the stakeholders affected by the action or decision; and third, a judgment is made to determine whether the distribution of benefits and burdens is fair and equal to the people affected. What constitutes a fair allocation will depend on the circumstances. A fair distribution of benefits and burdens does mean an equal distribution. The third step implies a reasonable allocation or sharing of both benefits and burdens among the stakeholders. Benefits and burdens that are singularly allocated to different stakeholders is unacceptable. For example, a decision that results in the allocation of benefits to one stakeholder and burdens to a different stakeholder is unjust.

You may have noticed the similarities between utilitarianism and justice. Both systems of analysis require a comparative approach to ethical decision making. While the two theories have parallel processes, it is a mistake to assume that utilitarianism and justice are similar. The difference lies in the respect afforded to people as individual beings. Justice is concerned with individual fairness and liberties, whereas utilitarianism is concerned with total net happiness. Utilitarianism supports the maximisation of utility but is indifferent to the distribution of benefits to individuals, particularly the minority. By definition, a utilitarian act is one that maximises total net happiness to the majority. Therefore, harm to the minority can be justified on utilitarian grounds so long as there is a net benefit to the majority. In some cases, the rights and wellbeing of some individuals may be disadvantaged for the benefit of the majority. There are many examples of racism and exploitation, such as depriving Aboriginal people of their land rights, which have occurred because of the greater happiness rule.

## Limitations of justice principle

Applying the justice principle is as problematic as defining it, particularly when the decision affects the wellbeing of others. The difficulty in applying the justice principle becomes apparent when the rights of some may have to be sacrificed in order to ensure a more equitable distribution of benefits. For example, in business many employers have instituted **affirmative action** policies designed to reduce the effects of past discrimination on women and minorities in employment. The 'glass ceiling' is a term that is commonly used to describe the barriers that women face in reaching senior positions within organisations. The preferential treatment afforded to men means that women are under-represented in senior ranks. Under affirmative action, companies must establish policies to correct this deficiency. However, awarding jobs or promotions to women or minorities, based solely in the interests of affirmative action is arguably another form of discrimination — reverse discrimination. More qualified people may be passed over for less qualified people. If discrimination is wrong in the first instance, it couldn't possibly be right in the second instance.

In conclusion, we must be careful to distinguish just results from just procedures. Procedural justice deals with rules or procedures that result in fair and just outcomes. Procedures should be well defined and communicated and corresponding rules should be administered fairly and impartially enforced. Doling out rewards in accordance with procedures that have been unjustly determined is as morally wrong as an unfair distribution of benefits.

## Why three normative theories of ethics? //

The theories described in this chapter represent well-accepted theories that can be applied in the day-to-day decision making in every day life and the world of business and accounting. Being aware of a broad range of ethical theories provides alternative approaches to analysing a situation with moral implications. A range of theories provides insights from a number of perspectives — this is generally not achievable from a single theory. However, a range of theories provides different perspectives to the same problem and, in doing so, is likely to improve the decision maker's awareness and understanding of the ethical issues involved in the dilemma. An overview of the theories described in this chapter is presented in table 2.2.

**TABLE 2.2**

### SUMMARY OF THE NORMATIVE THEORIES OF ETHICS

|  | UTILITARIANISM | RIGHTS | JUSTICE |
|---|---|---|---|
| TYPE | Consequential | Non-consequential | Non-consequential |
| PRINCIPLE | Maximising the wellbeing of the majority | Respecting individual rights | Fair and equal distribution of benefits and burdens |
| DECISION RULE | An ethical decision is one that produces the greatest benefit to the greatest number of people. | An ethical decision is one that does not impinge on the rights of another. | An ethical decision is one that produces the fairest overall distribution of benefits and burdens. |

## Applying the normative theories of ethics //

Understanding ethical theories such as the ones presented in this chapter is beneficial for two reasons. First, the principles derived from normative ethical theories serve as the criteria for judging the moral rightness of an act or decision (after the event); and second, ethical principles provide a structured approach for making ethical decisions (before the event). The process and issues associated with decision making are discussed more fully in chapter 4. At this point we provide you with an example demonstrating the application of the normative ethical theories in an accounting related problem. See 'In practice: Cooking up a venture'.

### IN PRACTICE

### Cooking up a venture

Vincent is desperate to secure an additional loan to fend off insistent creditors. Vincent believes he can secure a loan from the bank so long as he can support his claims with a positive financial report. Vincent asked his public accountant, Jane, to 'cook the books' so that the financial statements appear more favourable than they really are. Vincent asked Jane to do whatever she could to make the reports appear as favourable as possible. Vincent emphasised, 'whatever it takes'. When Jane questioned his motives, Vincent became apprehensive and threatened to withdraw Jane's services unless she complied with his request.

Jane was left contemplating her choices; she may either accept or reject Vincent's request. What should Jane do?

**Utilitarianism**

According to the utilitarian principle, the ethical solution is the course of action that produces the greatest net benefit to the greatest number of stakeholders. We begin our utilitarian analysis by listing the possible consequences and stakeholders affected for each alternative course of action:

#### IF JANE COMPLIES WITH VINCENT'S DEMAND

| POSITIVE CONSEQUENCES | NEGATIVE CONSEQUENCES |
|---|---|
| • The probability of Vincent receiving a loan will be enhanced. | • Jane's integrity as a professional accountant will suffer. |
| • Vincent and the bank will benefit financially if the loan is used to improve the profitability of the business. | • Based on the revised financial reports, the loan carries an unknown risk. Vincent and the bank will be financially poorer if Vincent defaults on the loan. |
| • Jane will retain Vincent as a client and her billings will not diminish. | |

## IF JANE REJECTS VINCENT'S DEMAND

| POSITIVE CONSEQUENCES | NEGATIVE CONSEQUENCES |
| --- | --- |
| • Jane's integrity and her reputation remain intact. | • Jane may lose Vincent as a client (this could also be a positive outcome) and reduce her billings. |
| • The bank is protected from an investment that carries an unknown risk. | • Based on the existing financial reports, Vincent is unlikely to raise the loan. He must find alternative methods to fend off the creditors. |
| • Vincent will avoid further financial stress from servicing an additional loan. | |
| • Vincent may avoid additional financial losses if the loan does not improve the profitability of the business. | |

Choosing an ethical alternative based on the consequences will often depend on the probability of the outcomes occurring. Unfortunately, the uncertainty or the lack of predicability of outcomes is a major problem with utilitarian analysis. In this dilemma, we must consider the likelihood of the loan improving the profitably of the business. If the subsequent outlay from obtaining the loan is successful, the majority of stakeholders (Vincent, the bank, creditors, employees and Jane) will be better off. If the subsequent outlay is unsuccessful, the majority of stakeholders will be financially poorer. The success of the investment is difficult to determine from the facts stated above; however, the probability of a successful return on investment must be questioned when the acquisition of the loan relies on questionable financial reports. On the basis that an adequate return on investment is unlikely, the majority of stakeholders will be worse off if Jane complies with Vincent's demand to 'cook the books'. Therefore, Jane should reject Vincent's request.

### Rights
Individuals have a right to the truth. In accounting, this means users of financial statements have a right to receive true and accurate financial reports and accountants have a corresponding duty to prepare the financial reports accordingly. To do otherwise is unethical. Therefore, Jane should refuse Vincent's request to cook the books as she has an ethical obligation to prepare the financial statements in accordance with the applicable accounting regulation to ensure as far as practicable the truthfulness of the reports.

**Justice**

Jane must identify the benefits and burdens that are likely to result from her decision and assess the fairness of the distribution of such benefits and burdens to the various stakeholders. In this case, Vincent will benefit from the acquisition of the loan that he may not have otherwise acquired. On the other hand, the bank must shoulder the burden of an investment that is riskier than the financial reports indicate. This is clearly unfair, as one party, Vincent, receives the benefits, and a different party, the bank, is shouldering the burden. Jane must, once again, refuse Vincent's request.

## Challenges to ethical behaviour //

There are many reasons why good people make bad decisions. In this section, we briefly examine three factors that challenge ethical behaviour. The first reason returns us to the issue raised in the opening section of this chapter: why learn ethics? The traditional notions of accounting education and practice possess a mechanistic perspective that focuses on techniques rather than the broader questions of human values and morality. The lack of attention given to ethical values means that accountants lack the skill or sensitivity to recognise and deal with ethical issues when they arise. The implication for accountants is that ethical issues are inadvertently overlooked because they focus too much on technical issues. Gandz and Hayes (1988) claim that it is not that people in business are devoid of moral values, but that they are deficient in tools of ethical analysis, which allow them to reconcile their responsibilities as professionals and individuals. According to Jones (1988–89, p. 4), 'These are people who basically want to do the right thing, but who lack the intellectual background and the attendant moral courage to actively and forcefully defend their views'. With ethics education, accountants will be able to identify predicaments when they arise, determine how to resolve problems and, more importantly, provide them with the rationale and vocabulary to take and defend their ethical positions.

Contextual factors in the workplace are the second reason why people make bad decisions. Professionals must often balance competing demands from superiors, peers and subordinates while simultaneously pursuing organisational goals which can often temper the quality of ethical decision making at work. The organisational context can influence the direction of either higher or lower levels of ethical decision making. Workplace pressures, often driven by the profit motive, can sometimes compromise personal and ethical values. Accountants will make morally defendable decisions only if the business environment, particularly superiors, supports that view. As employees, accountants will give the 'official position', rather than their individual judgment. This sometimes explains why people make decisions at work that are quite different from their personal decisions, which are unaffected by job concerns. Decision making in a work environment is examined more closely in chapters 4 and 12.

The third reason why people make questionable decisions is selfishness. Selfishness, also known as psychological **egoism**, is a theory that describes human nature. In this context, psychological egoism explains how people *do* behave rather than how they *should* behave. According to this view, people in their natural state are selfish and motivated by self-preservation and self-gain. Egoists (selfish people) are driven by self-interest and their actions are motivated by the desire to achieve their own interests without concern for others. The problem with the pursuit of self-interest is that it is sometimes at odds with the interests of other parties. Questionable acts such as discrimination and dishonesty may be justified if they promote self-interest. Moral reasoning based on selfishness is discussed further in the next section.

When analysed further, acts of self-interest are not always self-serving acts. In many instances, the egoist will consider others because ultimately their relationship will become mutually advantageous. An egoist will seek to further the interests of others if it is believed that reciprocity will advance the egoist's self-interest. Advocates of egoism claim that if everyone adopts a policy of pursuing self-interest, then eventually everyone is better off. If societal interest is equal to the sum of individual interests, the promotion of self-interest adds to the total value of societal interest.

# Kohlberg's theory of cognitive moral reasoning and development //

The most noted author in the area of moral development psychology is Lawrence Kohlberg. He is best known for his theory of **cognitive moral reasoning and development**. The theory describes the stages of moral development through which individuals pass as they mature in their moral judgments. Kohlberg (1969) argues that moral reasoning abilities develop according to a stage sequence framework. According to Kohlberg, a **stage of moral development** represents a structure of thought that is concerned with how judgments are made and why the judgment was made. Each stage is characterised by the reasons a person gives for making what they consider the right or moral decision when confronted with an ethical dilemma.

You should be careful not to confuse the theory of moral reasoning from the philosophy of ethics that was discussed earlier in this chapter. Ethics is concerned with the principles of right and wrong, whereas the theory of moral reasoning is concerned with the rationale that people use in making moral decisions. The former establishes the principles of ethical behaviour and the latter establishes the rationale for why the decision was arrived at. In practical terms, philosophy is concerned with making the right decision, whereas moral reasoning is concerned with how the decision is formulated. Therefore, developing an appreciation of moral reasoning will help us to better understand how decisions are actually made, even if they are not always the best decisions.

# Stages of moral development //

Kohlberg distinguishes three levels of moral development: 'pre-conventional', 'conventional', and 'post-conventional', and within each level are two distinct stages. An individual's moral judgment develops through a series of six progressive stages and, according to Kohlberg, each individual can be identified as being at a specific stage in the development process. The three levels and six stages of moral development are described in the following sections.

## Level 1 — pre-conventional

Level 1, the **pre-conventional level**, reflects a level of moral reasoning that is exclusively self-centred. Individuals at this level are concerned about consequences that result from their behaviour. The motivation for making moral decisions is interpreted in terms of good and bad consequences to the decision maker. Unlike utilitarianism, individuals at this level are not concerned about the impact of their behaviour on others, only the impact on themselves. The pre-conventional level of moral reasoning is consistent with the notion of selfishness discussed in the previous section.

The driving force behind personal decisions at the pre-conventional level is the minimisation of personal harm (stage 1) or the maximisation of personal gain (stage 2). At this level, individuals are likely to commit an unethical act when they perceive a personal advantage with minimal risks and penalties. These stages are regarded as pre-conventional because they are judged to solve moral dilemmas less satisfactorily than higher levels of moral reasoning.

### Stage 1

At stage 1, a moral course of action is defined as obedience to fixed rules. The individual does not see any purpose for the rules; it is merely assumed that punishment is inevitable following disobedience. To this end, the motivation for behaviour is governed by the desire to avoid penalty. In general terms, individuals are likely to act ethically simply to avoid the consequences of wrongful behaviour. Conversely, individuals are likely to pursue the wrong course of action if the perceived risk of detection is low, and punishment from wrongful behaviour is unlikely or insignificant. In colloquial terms, people will do the wrong thing if they believe they can get away with it.

### Stage 2

At stage 2, people are viewed as independent agents motivated to pursue their own **self-interest**. In general, a course of action is considered ethical if the benefits to the decision maker exceed the costs. While generally concerned with serving their own needs and desires, stage 2 people will occasionally consider the interests of others, but only in so far as there is a mutual advantage in exchange and deals. The distinguishing feature of stage 2 over stage 1 is the recognition of others in addition the self, exemplified by 'you scratch my back, I'll scratch yours' reasoning.

## Level two — conventional

At the **conventional level**, the notions of living within a community, conformity and maintaining relationships assume increasing significance. Individuals at this level exhibit loyalty to the immediate group and its norms by living up to the expectations of their families, peer groups and society. Individuals take a 'member of society' perspective and, unlike the pre-conventional level, are now able to see situations from others' points of view.

### Stage 3

At stage 3, individuals conform to the norms of the group and subordinate their individual needs to that of the group. Ethical decisions are motivated by the need to be seen as 'good people' by those for whom they feel loyalty and affection, such as family, friends and colleagues. Good behaviour is defined as that which pleases or helps the members of the group. Shame or disapproval from members of the group is likely to be a deterrent to dishonesty or unethical behaviour. In the absence of identifiable group norms, a person reasoning at stage 3 is likely to conform to stereotypical images of majority behaviour. In this sense, individuals act according to what is expected of them in their roles, whether that be a 'good son', a 'good parent' or a 'good accountant'. In this way, a stage 3 person pleases others by conforming to stereotypical images of good behaviour (Kohlberg 1971).

### Stage 4

Like stage 3 people, stage 4 people are also concerned with loyalty; however, they are concerned with loyalty to their larger nation rather than their immediate group. In this stage, the moral course of action is defined by compliance to authority and laws. Laws are upheld because they are seen as the means for maintaining social order, and deviations from the law are seen as bad because they threaten the social order (Kohlberg 1971). This stage is commonly referred to as the 'law and order' stage because of this strict adherence to the law. However, the notion of a 'law-follower' may be too narrow for a person in accounting or business. In business, you should view a person with stage 4 reasoning as a 'rule-follower' rather than a 'law-follower'. An accountant with stage 4 reasoning will be guided by codes of conduct, company policies and regulations, such as auditing and accounting standards, as well as the laws of the nation.

## Level 3 — post-conventional

Moral reasoning in the **post-conventional level** shifts from strict compliance with established rules to reliance on personally held principles as a means for making moral choices. The third level, also known as the principled level, reflects a growing moral autonomy defined by self-determined but not selfish moral reasoning. In this level, individuals think beyond society's laws to make decisions based on universal moral principles.

**Stage 5**

Moral conduct in this stage is the result of written consensus achieved by due process, such as that achieved by the writers of the Constitution. In stage 5, an individual recognises differences in society and emphasises fair ways of reaching consensus by agreement. Individuals at this stage will respect laws but will evaluate, question and seek to change laws if they are inconsistent with the principles of justice and welfare. This differs from stage 4 people, who blindly accept laws without question or evaluation. Accountants at this stage are primarily concerned with protecting and serving the public interest. That is, to produce and attest to financial reports that present fairly the economic activities of the entity so that users may make rational economic decisions. In this stage, accountants may not comply with accounting standards if strict compliance does not result in fair presentation. This is unlike accountants with stage 4 reasoning, who are likely to comply with accounting standards because of their obedience to the rules.

**Stage 6**

The stage 6 scheme of reasoning goes beyond due process and social consensus and rests on a commitment to universal ethical principles in which there is clearly an awareness of the moral point view. Decision-making behaviour is governed by self-chosen ethical principles founded on the non-consequential ethical theories of justice, duties and equal human rights. At this stage, moral decisions are independent of any external influence to the self. Moral decisions are made entirely based on ethical principles without influence from authority, rules, consequences or the group. Therefore, stage 6 represents a universalistic, principled notion of moral reasoning in which individuals would be prepared to challenge 'bad' laws which frustrate natural justice. While stage 6 is hypothesised and theoretically supported by Kohlberg, few people ever attain stage 6 moral reasoning. We can assume, however, that accountants capable of reasoning at stage 6 would base their actions on universal ethical principles, which would supersede formal rules and regulations. A summary of Kohlberg's stage framework is presented in table 2.3.

**TABLE 2.3**

### SUMMARY OF THE SIX STAGES OF MORAL REASONING

| LEVEL | FOCUS | STAGE | ORIENTATION |
|---|---|---|---|
| Post-conventional | Universal principles | 6 | Self-chosen ethical principles |
| | | 5 | Just rules determined by consensus |
| Conventional | Community | 4 | Rule-follower |
| | | 3 | Pleasing others |
| Pre-conventional | Self-centred | 2 | Self-interest |
| | | 1 | Avoiding punishment |

## Decision making through the stages //

Consider the ethical motivations of accountants at different stages of moral development. At stage 1, accountants will avoid an unethical act and comply with professional duties if they believe that detection and punishment from the boss or regulators is likely. At stage 2, accountants choose to comply with regulations such as accounting standards, ethical codes or the law only if they deem that ethical behaviour is less harmful or costly than unethical behaviour. At stage 3, accountants may feel pressured to abide by peer group norms (colleagues and superiors), even though such behaviour may result in violation of company policy or accounting regulation. At stage 4, accountants feel obligated and committed to the policies of the firm or the standards of the profession and are better able to withstand peer pressure. At stage 5, accountants see society's rights and values as outweighing the corporation's rules, policies and practices. The right thing to do is to protect the public interest even though it may conflict with corporate policy. Similarly, at stage 6, ethical principles with universal character transcend corporate culture and policies. These principles, such as honesty, not corporate policies, determine ethical behaviour.

A comprehensive example demonstrating the application of Kohlberg's theory in an accounting-related problem is presented in 'In practice: Who's controlling Helen?'

## IN PRACTICE

### Who's controlling Helen?

Suppose Helen, a young audit assistant, is given the task of evaluating the internal control structure of a client's accounting information system. She discovers several significant weaknesses in the system. Jon, Helen's supervisor, is fearful of the client's reactions to an adverse report, so he instructs Helen to modify the report. Jon feels that management may appoint a new auditor if the client receives the report in its current form. Jon is eager to impress his seniors and wants to maintain this client as a continuing engagement.

What is Helen's likely response at each stage of Kohlberg's theory of moral development?

**Stage 1**

Helen's decision to modify the report will be determined by her aversion to harm. If Helen feels threatened by her supervisor and believes that he will act on his threats, she will probably abide by his wishes and modify the report. However, if Helen believes that a higher authority such as a partner will discipline her for modifying the report, then she is unlikely to modify the report.

### Stage 2

Helen will modify the report if she believes it is in her best interests to do so. The perceived benefits may come from exhibiting a sense of loyalty to her supervisor and the firm that might one day reward her.

### Stage 3

Helen may modify the report in order to win the approval of her colleagues, particularly her supervisor. Alternatively, she may comply with her professional responsibilities simply because this is what is expected of her as a professional accountant.

### Stage 4

The need to abide by the rules of the profession will oblige her to report truthfully and fairly. Despite personal risk, the interests of the client and the firm take precedence.

### Stage 5

Helen will resist pressure from her superior to modify the report and uphold the principles of professional conduct. In this way she is acting in a manner consistent with the authority bestowed her as a professional accountant — to act in the public interest.

### Stage 6

Helen will resolve the dilemma by exercising fundamental principles such as honesty, which do not rest on particular needs. She will not modify the report.

A stage of moral development implies that Helen will respond similarly in different circumstances. However, you should be cautious when predicting behaviour based solely on a person's stage of moral development. Consistency of action should not be defined by the behaviour itself but in terms of the person's rationale. At stage 1, Helen may act appropriately on one occasion, but not on another. In both situations, however, the reasoning will be consistent — to avoid penalty. Behavioural predictions become clearer in the latter stages of moral development. In Helen's case, she may or may not modify the report in the first three stages of moral development. But in stages 4 to 6, her decision becomes more predictable. Since unethical behaviour is difficult to reconcile with properly developed rules and regulations and post-conventional considerations, Helen is more likely to adopt the ethical course of action at the higher stages of moral reasoning.

## Moving through the stages //

Empirical research consistently shows that moral reasoning development is highly correlated with age. Therefore, as people mature, the more morally developed they become. In general, children develop moral reasoning abilities commencing from stage 1 and attain stage 3 reasoning when they reach their mid teens. They then develop from stage 4 from ages 16 to 24. Even though people progress through the stages, there is no guarantee of continued moral development. It is possible for people to remain stuck at one of the earlier stages.

Kohlberg further argues that the post-conventional level of moral reasoning is likely to require a high degree of maturation on the part of the individual, and expectations of such levels of moral reasoning should not be anticipated until people are in their late 20s and possibly beyond. In fact, few are ever likely to achieve post-conventional stages of moral reasoning, and most will never develop beyond the conventional stages. In general, people move forward through the stages at a rate determined by their own life experiences and, as stated above, there is no guarantee of continuous growth. Movement through the stages occurs one stage at a time and only in one direction. This means people never skip a stage and only move forward through the framework, never backward.

## Why is the study of moral reasoning in accounting important? //

The study of moral reasoning in accounting is important because the level of moral development will directly influence how accountants will consider and resolve dilemmas. At the pre-conventional level, accountants will seek to satisfy their own interests. At the conventional level, accountants are influenced by the group or community, and it is not until they reach the post-conventional level that they develop autonomous reasoning. With each successive stage, the moral judgment grows less and less dependent on outside influences and moves from a self-centred conception of what is right to a broader understanding of the importance and principles of justice and rights. However, as noted above, the majority of the adult population, including accountants, is reported to possess conventional levels of moral reasoning and never acquires post-conventional levels of moral reasoning. This is unfortunate because principled reasoning is necessary to satisfy professional responsibilities such as objectivity and autonomous judgment.

Autonomy or independent judgment is often cited as a key attribute of a professional accountant. This is evident in public accounting where the auditor's independence is important to withstanding pressure from client management when providing audit and assurance services. The problem for the accounting profession is that they, like the majority of the adult population, possess conventional levels of reasoning and do not have the moral maturity (post-conventional) to make independent judgments. Therefore, independent judgment, from a moral reasoning perspective, is doubtful. For example, Windsor and Ashkanasy (1995) discovered that auditors with lower levels of moral reasoning were less resistant to client pressure and favoured clients who were financially sound and offered large fees. Conversely, auditors with high levels of moral reasoning were more resistant to client pressure. An understanding of the factors that are associated with elevated levels of moral development is of practical value in ensuring that accountants always adhere to high moral standards in their exercise of moral judgment (Thorne 1999).

## Moral reasoning development in accounting //

Research on moral reasoning in the accounting profession has shown that the majority of accountants do not mature beyond the conventional level (Armstrong 1987; LaGrone, Welton & Davis 1996). This means that the moral reasoning levels of accountants are no higher than the general population of adults, who also never develop beyond the conventional stages. This is a significant finding because tertiary qualified professional groups, on average, demonstrate higher levels of moral reasoning than the general population. Therefore, accountants, as university graduates, should also score higher than the general population. Yet, the moral reasoning levels of the accounting profession are consistent with the adult population. There appears to be something peculiar about accountants, accounting education or the environment in which they study and work, that prohibits moral development beyond the levels displayed by the general population.

### Accounting education and rule-based learning

The deficiency displayed by the accounting profession in moral reasoning development may be caused, in part, by the accounting curriculum, which emphasises training in 'hard and fast rules'. As students, accountants are taught to obey the rules of accounting, which is reinforced throughout their professional careers with increasing regulation. This rule-based approach to accounting education and practice has inadvertently instilled a preference for stage 4 reasoning, reflecting the internalisation of Generally Accepted Accounting Principles. Lampe and Finn (1992) conclude that rule-based reasoning is the most significant influence on auditors' ethical decision making. Arguably, rule-based reasoning has become so ingrained in accountants' mindsets that they appear to be stuck at stage 4, and unable to develop to higher stages of moral reasoning. As stated earlier in this chapter, this is unfortunate because principled reasoning is a key attribute of autonomous judgment. For example, Ponemon and Gabhart (1993) and Sweeney and Roberts (1997) found that auditors whose moral development was primarily conventional in nature were more likely to comply absolutely with professional standards, and were more influenced by penalties for non-compliance than post-conventional auditors. They further discovered that auditors with higher levels of moral development rely more on judgment and less on technical standards for problem resolution.

## Select-socialisation and career advancement

Kohlberg's stage framework has been used to investigate the average levels of moral development in public accounting firms. Researchers have found an association between the average level of moral reasoning and position levels. However, rather than detecting an increasing level of moral development within the firm hierarchy, the accountants' moral reasoning decreases steadily as they progress to higher levels within the firm (Ponemon 1990, 1992). We might conclude from these findings that the moral reasoning abilities of accountants regress to lower stages of moral development with increasing seniority. However, a basic tenet of Kohlberg's stage framework is that moral development is sequential and invariant, which means individuals develop one stage at a time and do not regress. Therefore, moral reasoning regression cannot be accepted without contradicting the validity of Kohlberg's theory. Ponemon (1990) suggests that the net decrease in measured moral cognition is not the result of moral reasoning regression but the self-selection or the selection-socialisation process within public accounting firms.

The notion of **selection-socialisation** suggests that career advancement and opportunities are offered to employees who are perceived by management as having personal characteristics commensurate with the culture and philosophy of the firm. Therefore, promotions are awarded to employees who have similar values and share common views with senior management. This process of advancement is known as self-selection or selection-socialisation. It can be inferred from this concept that senior managers promote only those members who have similar levels of moral development to their own. Individual accountants who are unable to fit or adapt to the culture of the firm (too high or low levels of moral reasoning) have little hope of senior career advancement. They become frustrated and eventually leave the firm in search of an alternative future. In the end, if senior managers possess low levels of moral development, only those individual accountants with similar levels of moral development remain in the firm, conscious of career opportunities that may not be available to other accountants with higher levels of moral development. By giving preference to accountants with low levels of moral development, the measured moral cognition at senior levels within the firm hierarchy will be lower than the measured moral cognition at less senior ranks.

## Is gender a factor?

We conclude this section by examining gender as a potential factor influencing moral judgment development and, in particular, whether female accountants reason differently from male accountants. In the case of the adult population, research shows that gender differences are trivial and women do not reason any differently from men (Rest 1986). However, research has regularly shown that female accountants and female accounting students score higher than their male counterparts (Shaub 1994; Sweeney 1995; Etherington & Schulting 1995; Abdol-mohammadi, Gabhart & Reeves 1997). It appears that the moral reasoning abilities of female accountants are fundamentally different from those of male accountants. The cause of this difference is unknown, but Gilligan (1982) argues that male social development is highlighted by a sense of individuality, while female social development stresses connectedness between people driven by relationships and obligations to others known as the 'ethic of care'. According to Gilligan, the recognition of relationships and responsibilities by females is more prominent in their ethical decision making than for men.

If female accountants demonstrate higher levels of moral reasoning, the accounting profession may benefit by recruiting, mentoring, advancing and retaining female accountants (Shaub 1994). However, this would require an increasing understanding of barriers inhibiting women advancing in public accounting firms. Maupin and Lehman (1994) found that women cannot advance to partnership level without exhibiting stereotypical masculine characteristics. Therefore, being successful may mean suppressing typical feminine attitudes and behaviour.

## Summary //

Judging right from wrong is best achieved by applying an ethical principle derived from normative theories. Utilitarianism, a consequential theory, defines a moral action as one that maximises net benefit for the majority. Non-consequential theories (namely rights and justice) are concerned with maintaining a duty to respect their fellow human beings by applying rules of moral behaviour irrespective of the outcomes. The theory of rights defines a good decision as one that respects the rights of others and the theory of justice centres on the distributive effects of actions or policies.

Kohlberg's stage framework provides a hierarchical continuum, which consists of six stages of cognitive moral reasoning and development. In general, the stages proceed from self-oriented thinking to the community point of view, and ultimately to an abstract principle orientation. Movement from the pre-conventional level to the conventional level is common, and generally reflects a growing awareness of the self in relation to others. However, movement to the post-conventional level is less common and movement to this level may require intervention. The problem for the accounting profession is that reasoning centred on conventional reasoning has serious implications for autonomous judgement.

In this chapter, we have shown you what it means to be ethical. In chapter 3, we show you what it means to be a professional accountant.

## Key terms //

Affirmative action . . . p. 36
Cognitive moral reasoning and development . . . p. 41
Compensatory justice . . . p. 35

# Questions //

**2.1** Explain the difference between a consequential and a non-consequential theory of ethics.

**2.2** Briefly describe the normative ethical theories of utilitarianism, rights and justice, and give an example of an action or decision that is consistent with each of these theories.

**2.3** Describe the benefits and limitations of each of the normative ethical theories of utilitarianism, rights, and justice. Is any one normative ethical theory superior to another? Explain.

**2.4** Discuss the differences between a utilitarian analysis and the cost–benefit analysis that is normally applied in business.

**2.5** What is the relationship between individual rights and correlating duties?

**2.6** Two audit assistants, Fred and Ginger, have applied for the same 'audit senior' position. Both candidates work hard, taking on extra work when needed but Fred's performance reports are slightly superior. Ginger was offered the job because of the firm's affirmative action policy. Was this decision just? Discuss.

**2.7** Most social and economic institutions are founded (underlying reason for their existence) on a normative ethical theory; for example, unions exist to protect the rights of workers. Give an example of a social and economic institution that is founded on each of the following ethical theories: utilitarianism, rights and justice. In your opinion, which theory underpins the philosophy of your university or employer?

**2.8** Why do good people make bad decisions?

**2.9** Explain the difference between normative theories of ethics and the theory of cognitive moral reasoning and development.

**2.10** Briefly describe the six stages of cognitive moral reasoning and development and give an example for each stage.

**2.11** Select a stage of moral reasoning that best describes each of the following statements. Justify your choice.

   (i) 'This is a win-win deal for everyone and no-one will ever know about it.'

   (ii) 'I have no choice but to tell the truth, the fact that someone may be hurt is irrelevant. Respect for my fellow human beings is more important.'

   (iii) 'Why shouldn't I cheat on my tax return? Everyone else is doing it.'

   (iv) 'I'm afraid I might get caught if I cheat on my tax.'

   (v) 'Company policy prohibits me from making personal long-distance telephone calls.'

   (vi) 'The law is not fair; it was rushed through parliament without due consideration by interested parties.'

**2.12** In your opinion, which stage of moral reasoning best describes the community of accountants as a profession? Justify your answer.

**2.13** Describe the selection-socialisation process and its effect on the moral reasoning levels in public accounting firms.

**2.14** What is autonomous judgment? Are accountants capable of making autonomous judgments? Discuss this question in relation to Kohlberg's theory of cognitive moral reasoning and development.

## CASE STUDY

### Alan Bond — the salesman

At one point, Alan Bond was Australia's most famed businessman. His victory in the Americas Cup in 1983 tugged at the heartstrings of all Australians. He started his career as an apprentice sign-writer in Perth, made a fortune in property deals and eventually built a global empire. In the late 1980s the Bond Corporation became the ninth largest enterprise in Australia, with a reported asset value of $9 billion. The Bond empire, which included interests in media, energy and property, grew to be a global conglomerate with hundreds of subsidiaries, including the world's largest privately owned gold mining company and the fifth largest brewing group. Bond amassed his empire by acquiring assets, revaluing them and then borrowing on the revaluation to purchase more assets. However, this form of growth was not sustainable. Struggling to service the debt acquired by the Bond group of companies, bankers called up huge loans and in 1991 liquidators were called in to cease further additions to the mountains of unpaid debt.

In order to understand what led to the rise and fall of the Bond empire it is necessary to understand Bond himself. Bond was an entrepreneur with no formal education, but what he lacked in knowledge, he made up for in his ability to 'make a deal'. He made his fortune on property dealings and exchanging billions of dollars in buying and selling assets. Bond was a wheeler and dealer, who borrowed as much as he could, bought, and then sold. Deal making is in Bond's blood.

Bond had been a salesman all his life and was a better salesman than he was a businessman. In 1985, Bond purchased Castlemaine Tooheys, a brewery that dominated sales in Western Australia, Queensland and New South Wales. Bond attempted to cash in on his investment by reducing the terms of credit for beer sales to publicans from 30 to 7 days. This was a major blow to the publicans in Queensland. In New South Wales, Bond allowed the leases on Tooheys pubs to expire without renewal or payment for goodwill so that he could sell the hotels for a quick profit. The hoteliers won their battle in court, but Tooheys' market share fell markedly.

In 1987, the auditor of the Bond Corporation, Price Waterhouse, agreed to recognise only one half of the $200 million profit-making deal that was sought by management. Soon after this disagreement, the Bond group went shopping for a new auditor. The Bond group invited audit firms to tender for the audit engagement. Prospective auditors were interviewed, briefed and quizzed with hypothetical scenarios. Arthur Andersen was the eventual winner. When Arthur Andersen was offered the engagement in 1988, they agreed not to restate or qualify the 1987 balances.

Bond treated the company assets like his own, seemingly with little regard for the rights of the minority interests. Large sums were moved from one part of the group to another to circumvent the loan covenants that were implemented by banks to avoid this very practice. In 1997, Bond admitted to moving money out of Bell Resources Ltd — considered one the jewels of the Bond empire group of companies — into his own private companies. According to some reports, tens of millions of dollars were diverted to private companies, trusts and offshore bank accounts in tax haven countries. Australian authorities tried unsuccessfully to recover some of these moneys but without Bond's cooperation they found it difficult and eventually gave up.

In 1997, Bond pleaded guilty to the nation's biggest fraud and was convicted and sentenced to four years in jail for his role in stripping Bell Resources Ltd of $1.2 billion. In prison, Bond ran business classes for the inmates; it is not known whether the in-house lessons included a component on business ethics. Bond was freed in 2000 to spend the millions of dollars of his family's wealth acquired from the Bond empire. Since his release from prison he has been spotted dining at some of London's more exclusive restaurants and appears to enjoy a comfortable lifestyle in London, one of the world's most expensive cities.

In spite of his admission to fraud, Bond believes he has done nothing wrong. Some people applaud Bond for facing the Australian judiciary and the consequences of his actions, unlike other corporate rogues, such as Christopher Skase, who fled the Australian legal system never to return.

### Required

1 As a businessman, which stage of Kohlberg's theory best describes Alan Bond? Justify your answer.
2 Is there a relationship between Bond's stage of moral development, identified in question 1 above, and the downfall of the Bond empire? Explain.
3 As an auditor, would you accept Alan Bond as a client? Why or why not?
4 'Bond treated the company assets like his own, with little regard for the rights of the minority interests.' Describe the ethics of this statement from a *rights* perspective.
5 Alan Bond remained in Australia to face the consequences of his behaviour. Christopher Skase did not. Does this mean Alan Bond is more ethical than Christopher Skase? Explain.

## FURTHER RESOURCES AND WEBSITES//

### Further resources

Beauchamp, TL & Bowie, NE 1997, *Ethical theory and business*, 5th edn, Prentice Hall, New Jersey.

Boatright, JR 1997, *Ethics and the conduct of business*, 2nd edn, Prentice Hall, Upper Saddle River.

Chartered Practising Accountants Australia 2003, *CPA108 reporting and professional practice*, CPA Program, Melbourne.

Donaldson, T & Werhane, PH 1996, *Ethical issues in business: a philosophical approach*, Prentice Hall, New Jersey.

Icerman, RD, Karcher, JN & Kennelley, M 1991, 'A baseline assessment of moral development: accounting, other business and nonbusiness students', *Accounting Educators' Journal*, Winter, pp. 46–62.

Lovell, A 1995, 'Moral reasoning and moral atmosphere in the domain of accounting', *Accounting, Auditing and Accountability Journal*, vol. 8, no. 3, pp. 60–80.

Purtill, RL 1976, *Thinking about ethics*, Prentice Hall, Englewood Cliffs.

Shaw, WH & Barry, V 1998, *Moral issues in business*, 7th edn, Wadsworth Publishing Company, Belmont.

Shenkir, WG 1990 'A perspective from education: business ethics', *Management Accounting*, June pp. 30–3.

St Pierre, KE, Nelson ES & Gabbin AL 1990, 'A study of the ethical development of accounting majors in relation to other business and nonbusiness disciplines', *The Accounting Educators' Journal*, Summer, pp. 23–35.

### Websites

Institute for Business and Professional Ethics 2001, De Paul University, College of Commerce, Chicago, viewed 9 February 2004, www.depaul.edu/ethics.

Center for Accounting Ethics, University of Waterloo, 2004, viewed 9 February 2004, http://arts.uwaterloo.ca/ACCT/ethics/index2.html.

Markkulla Centre for Applied Ethics, 2003, Santa Clara University, viewed 9 February 2004, www.scu.edu/Ethics.

The Carol and Lawrence Zicklin Center, for Business Ethics Research, 2003, Wharton University of Pennsylvania, viewed 9 February 2004, www.zicklincenter. org/Home.htm.

## REFERENCES //

Abdolmohammadi, MJ, Gabhart, DRL & Reeves, MF 1997, 'Ethical cognition of business students individually and in groups', *Journal of Business Ethics*, vol. 16, no. 16, November, pp. 1717–25.

Armstrong, MB 1987, 'Moral development and accounting education', *Journal of Accounting Education*, vol. 5, pp. 27–43.

Clark, C 2002, 'Perspectives on corporate governance, corporate failure and business ethics in Australia and USA', *CPA Australia*, viewed 1 July 2003, www.cpaaustralia.com.au/01_information_centre/16_media_releases.

Etherington, LD & Schulting, L 1995, 'Ethical development of accountants: the case of Canadian certified management accountants', *Research on Accounting Ethics*, vol. 1, pp. 235–51.

Gaa, JC 1994, *The ethical foundations of public accounting*, CGA-Canada Research Foundation, Vancouver.

Gandz, J & Hayes, N 1988, 'Teaching business ethics', *Journal of Business Ethics*, vol. 7, pp. 657–69.

Gilligan, C 1982, *In a different voice*, Harvard University Press, Cambridge.

Guy, M 1990, *Ethical decision making in everyday work situations*, Quorum Books, New York.

Jones, TM 1988–1989, 'Ethics education in business: theoretical considerations', *The Organizational Behaviour Teaching Review*, vol. 13, no. 4, pp. 1–18.

Kohlberg, L 1969, 'Stage and sequence: the cognitive developmental approach to socialization', in DA Goslin (ed.), *Handbook of socialization theory and research*, Rand McNally, New York, pp. 347–480.

Kohlberg, L 1971, 'From is to ought: how to commit naturalistic fallacy and get away with it in the study of moral development', in T Mischel (ed.), *Cognitive development and epistemology*, Academic Press, New York, pp. 151–235.

LaGrone, RM, Welton RE & Davis JR 1996, 'Are the effects of accounting ethics interventions transitory or persistent?', *Journal of Accounting Education*, vol. 14, no. 3, pp. 259–76.

Lampe, JC & Finn, DW 1992, 'A model of auditors' ethical decision processes', *Auditing: A Journal of Practice & Theory*, vol. 11, (supplement) pp. 33–59.

Maupin, RJ & Lehman, CR 1994, 'Talking heads: stereotypes, status, sex-roles and satisfaction of female and male auditors', *Accounting Organizations and Society*, vol. 19, no. 4/5, pp. 427–37.

McDonald, GM & Donleavy, GD 1995, 'Objections to the teaching of business ethics', *Journal of Business Ethics*, vol. 14, no. 10, pp. 839–53.

Committee of Sponsoring Organizations of the Treadway Commission 1987, *Report of the National Commission on Fraudulent Financial Reporting (Treadway Commission)*. Committee of Sponsoring Organizations of the Treadway Commission, USA.

Ponemon, LA & Gabhart DRL 1993, *Ethical reasoning in accounting and auditing*, CGA-Canada Research Foundation, Vancouver.

Ponemon, LA 1990, 'Ethical judgments in accounting: a cognitive-developmental perspective', *Critical Perspectives on Accounting*, vol. 1, pp. 191–215.

Ponemon, LA 1992, 'Ethical reasoning and selection-socialisation in accounting', *Accounting Organizations and Society*, vol. 17, no. 3/4, pp. 239–58.

Rest, JR 1986, *Moral development: advances in research and theory*, Praeger, New York.

Shaub, M K 1994, 'An analysis of the association of traditional demographic variables with the moral reasoning of auditing students and auditors', *Journal of Accounting Education*, vol. 12, no. 1, pp. 1–26.

Sweeney, JT 1995, 'The moral expertise of auditors: an exploratory analysis', *Research on Accounting Ethics*, vol. 1, pp. 213–14.

Sweeney, JT & Roberts, RW 1997, 'Cognitive moral development and auditor independence', *Accounting Organizations and Society*, vol. 22, no. 3/4, pp. 337–52.

Thorne, L, 1999 'An analysis of the association of demographic variables with the cognitive moral development of Canadian accounting students: an examination of the applicability of American based findings to the Canadian context', *Journal of Accounting Education*, vol. 17, pp. 157–74.

Velasquez, M 2002, *Business ethics concepts and cases*, 5th edn, Prentice Hall, Englewood Cliffs.

Windsor, CA & Ashkanasy, NM 1995, 'The effect of client management bargaining power, moral reasoning development, and belief in a just world on auditor independence', *Accounting Organizations and Society*, vol. 20, no. 7/8, pp. 701–20.

# 3

# Professional ethics and self-regulation

## Learning objectives

After studying this chapter you should be able to:

- Outline the pathway to professionalisation.
- Describe the attributes that distinguish a profession from a non-profession.
- Discuss the importance of ethics and public trust in accounting.
- Describe the objectives of the code of professional conduct.
- List and describe the fundamental principles of professional conduct.
- Explain the conceptual framework approach to the code of professional conduct.
- Describe the factors that limit the effectiveness of the code of professional conduct.
- Outline the profession's disciplinary procedures.

'Society's demands for moral authority and character increase as the importance of the position increases.'
John Adams, 18th-century American Founding Father,
Second US President

# Introduction //

The nature of accountants' work puts them in a special position of trust in relation to their clients, employers and the general public. This trust is evident when you consider the willingness of people to share confidential information about their personal financial affairs and to entrust the administration of their assets to their accountant. In turn, recipients rely on accountants for their professional judgment, guidance, adherence to ethical values and a commitment to advance recipients' interests. This special relationship is founded on a notion of trust that is automatically bestowed on advisers because of the integrity that is associated with the title 'professional accountant'. The key to maintaining the confidence of individual clients as well as the public is professional and ethical conduct. In this chapter we examine what it means to be a 'professional' and the significance of public confidence to the survival of the profession.

# Professionalisation //

A **profession** is defined as a community of people bounded by the activities they perform, founded on a common theoretical background acquired through formal education. Professions occupy an important position in society. Their roles, whether they be in medicine, law, engineering or business, affect the lives of many people, and as societies develop and become more complex, existing professions mature and new professions are created. Professions are neither made nor are they born; they evolve out of efforts from large numbers of people with a common interest and a commitment to a set of ideals. The initial criterion for the establishment of a professional association is primarily a self-identified interest or practice in a discipline. In the beginning, formal training and qualifications are not a prerequisite for membership but as associations mature, technical qualifications become increasingly important, particularly when the group achieves some standing as representing an occupational speciality or intellectual discipline. Eventually, technical criterion becomes the permit for membership.

Initially, accounting in Australia was seen as a trade or vocation, rather than a profession. Accountants were trained on the job rather than formally educated. Consequently, heavy emphasis was placed on the recording function rather than evaluation or judgment (Bloom & Kantor 1991). It was not until the 1960s that a university degree was established as the licence for membership and educational qualifications became prominent.

## Professionalisation in Australia //

Within a profession, there are often a number of professional associations, and each individual association has its own entry and membership requirements. Australia has two major professional accounting bodies: CPA Australia and the Institute of

Chartered Accountants in Australia (ICAA or the 'Institute'). Generally, the requirements for becoming a professional accountant in Australia are three-fold (see figure 3.1). First, candidates must complete an accredited academic qualification to qualify for membership with one of the professional bodies. In Australia, this consists of a three-year university degree or its equivalent. Second, candidates must acquire three years of mentored practical work experience, which is viewed by some as a form of apprenticeship or on-the-job training. Third, in order to be granted full membership status, candidates must complete the professional development program with the respective professional accounting association. **Professionalisation** is therefore a process that includes the acquisition of formal education combined with professional development and practical work experience.

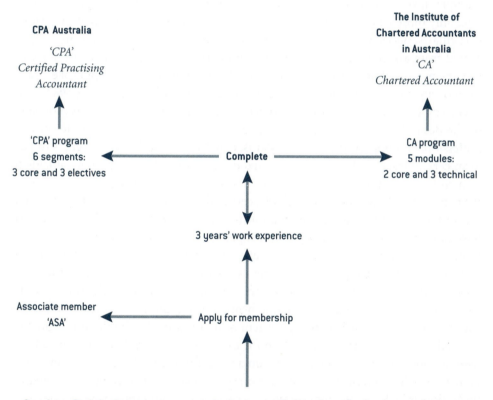

Complete a Bachelor degree in commerce or business accredited by the professional accounting bodies

FIGURE 3.1    Professionalisation in Australia

Professionalisation is a form of licensing that achieves two objectives. First, it ensures that members have acquired the requisite skill and knowledge to call themselves professional accountants; and second, it develops a sense of occupational identity that is committed to professionalism. A graduate enlisting with CPA

Australia automatically qualifies for 'associate membership' status upon entry and is conferred the designation 'ASA'. Members of CPA Australia who undertake and complete the 'CPA program' qualify for advancement in status to certified practising accountant and are conferred the designation 'CPA'. Members of the ICAA who undertake and complete the 'CA program' attain chartered accountant status and are conferred the designation 'CA'.

### The profession as an exclusive franchise //

A recognised profession acquires an exclusive franchise in the field of work with which it is identified. In some fields, such as medicine, where public health would be endangered if unqualified persons were permitted to practise, the law guarantees this profession a monopoly. Similarly, in accounting, the public and clients would suffer if unqualified or undisciplined persons were permitted to practise accounting. Therefore, only those who are licensed to practise are given the exclusive right to perform particular services, such as auditing and taxation, and unlicensed persons are prevented from assuming professional titles and performing certain tasks. In this context, the process of professionalisation controls and often limits the supply of entrants to an occupation in order to safeguard or enhance its market value (Saks 1983, p. 6).

Guarding entry and establishing criteria for continuing membership is motivated by the desire to be recognised by the larger society as a profession and to create a professional monopoly. Professional status, combined with the exclusiveness to perform certain tasks, makes the professional designations of CPA and CA valuable to its members. The professional achieves a new identity on entering the profession — the person is no longer bookkeeper but a certified practising accountant or chartered accountant. The professional designation is highly desired because it sets the professional apart from wider society. People aspire to be professionals because professional status brings higher social status, respect and greater wealth. For example, the ordinary person normally ranks the doctor above many other professions, undoubtedly because doctors are commonly seen as people who serve the community. Not only does this ranking bring prestige and respect from the general community, but also it brings higher economic rewards. In simple terms, doctors generally receive greater remuneration for their services than do accountants. Likewise, accountants receive greater remuneration for their services than do bookkeepers, which is a quasi-profession. In a survey of salaries for accounting and finance professionals by Hays Personnel Services, a qualified accountant, on average, receives double the salary of an experienced bookkeeper (Hays Personnel Services 2003).

# Characteristics of a profession //

In this section we attempt to distinguish the characteristics that help influence us to speak of one occupational group as professional, such as doctors, and deny the label to other occupational groups, such as plumbers. In general, professions are defined according to a checklist of attributes that can be applied to distinguish the professional from the non-professional. This approach rests on the belief that professions possess unique characteristics, which set them apart from the wider community. Greenwood's (1957) pioneering work, repeatedly referred to by other researchers, formulated a list of attributes, outlined in table 3.1, that represent core features common to professional occupations. In this chapter we focus our discussion on two attributes, 'professional authority' or 'the power of knowledge' and the code of professional conduct.

## TABLE 3.1

### DEFINING CHARACTERISTICS OF A PROFESSION

| 1. A systematic body of theory | involves the mastery of theory rather than manual skills, underpinned by extensive tertiary education, professional updates, practical experience and research |
| --- | --- |
| 2. Professional authority | is based on knowledge that creates a dependent relationship with those who are reliant on the professional's services |
| 3. Community sanction | confers powers on the profession to self-regulate |
| 4. Codes of ethics | regulate members' conduct by compelling a minimum standard of ethical behaviour |
| 5. Professional culture | consists of values that are oriented toward the public rather than self-interest |

## The power of knowledge //

The primary quality that distinguishes a professional from a non-professional is the reliance that clients place on their professional advisers due to their superior knowledge and expertise. In simple terms, professionals know things that others do not. If this knowledge is considered important to those who do not have it, then the professional has a relative advantage that is useful to others. Clients and employers generally do not share the expertise held by accountants, which is why accountants are hired. Consequently, accountants are placed in a position of power because of their special expertise and skill. This power is not based on any kind of legal sanction, but on knowledge underpinned by formal education and practical experience. This is not to say that the technical training of the plumber is trivial, but it is not outside the grasp of people who want to do it themselves. The same cannot be said of professionals such as accountants and lawyers.

Superior knowledge places the professional in a dominant position in their role-relationships with clients and employers, so much so that the client has no choice but to trust or rely on the judgment and expertise of the professional. Trust in the professional is important because the client cannot appraise the quality of service due to the knowledge differentiation. Clients must therefore take it on faith that the professional is competent and committed to helping them. However, unbending loyalty to their professional advisers renders clients vulnerable to the questionable practices of unscrupulous practitioners. This risk occurs in part because the ordinary person is unable to judge the competence of the accountant or to assess the quality of the accountant's work. Consequently, people have no choice but to rely on their accountant for expert advice and professional judgment.

Historically, professional accountants were viewed as public servants, motivated not by profit but by a desire to serve the public. In this context, accountants are accepted as highly skilled persons who have the desire to serve the public, and who place that service ahead of personal gain. If they were not regarded in this light, they would not have clients or employers. Only ethical conduct on the part of the professional accountant will ensure that this power is not abused.

## The implications of losing the public's trust //

The status of any profession rests on social consent, and in return the profession accepts a responsibility to subordinate self-interest to the public interest. The credibility of the accounting profession is maintained only when accountants are perceived to be honest, independent and to provide quality service. If a professional loses credibility in the eyes of the public, the consequences can be quite severe, not only for the offending professional, who may face disciplinary action, but also for the entire accounting profession. The very existence of the accounting profession depends on public confidence in the accountant's determination to safeguard the public interest. When accountants continually put their own interests before those of the client or the public, a lack of confidence can develop, which can trigger public inquiries into the affairs of the profession.

Subscribers to this view argue that accounting is too important to leave to accountants. If there were genuine concern that the accounting profession was unable to discharge its duties properly, the government would intervene to ensure the public's protection. To this end, the government would regulate accounting practice to ensure a fully informed market and to guarantee, to the best of its ability, economic and market efficiency. Increasing regulation would mean that accountants would subscribe more to formal rules and rely less on professional judgment in the performance of their duties. In the extreme, accounting practice would be dictated by regulations that tell accountants what to do and how to do it. In these circumstances the practice of accounting would be reduced to a bookkeeping function. Accounting would no longer be a profession, but a vocation.

# The ethics of self-regulation //

The phrase **self-regulation** denotes control by a governing body over its membership and the activities of its members. The self-regulatory processes of the accounting profession include entry qualifications, quality assurance processes, conformity with accounting regulations and rule enforcement. One prominent way in which professional associations operate as agencies of self-regulation is in the development and enforcement of rules to direct members' behaviour. The rules that direct and influence ethical behaviour are embodied in the code of professional conduct. It is this aspect of the self-regulatory process that will be explored in this chapter.

The ethics of protecting the profession's economic monopoly is a vexed issue. Professional accountants are expected to be altruistic by advancing the interests of clients, employers and users before their own; however, by being seen to serve the interests of others, accountants effectively benefit themselves by enhancing their reputation and ultimately their financial wellbeing. As Parker (1994) states, the 'public interest is readily declared but the private interest remains submerged yet powerful'. Is protecting the public interest altruism or egoism? It is up to you to ponder this question. The fact remains, however, that protecting the public interest necessitates ethical behaviour, which in turn is vital to enhancing the good reputation of the profession and maintaining its high status in the eyes of the community. If high status brings high economic rewards, then acting ethically for the benefit of others is good for business. Therefore, the motivation for self-regulation is twofold. On the one hand, self-regulation preserves and even enhances members' ethical and professional standards for the benefit and protection of the public; on the other hand, it is used to enhance occupational prestige and self-interest.

# Professional ethics and the code of professional conduct //

**Professional ethics** is often described as ethics in a professional situation. While this definition is technically correct, it does not help guide the professional to resolve ethical dilemmas. In chapter 2 we defined ethics as principles derived from normative theories such as utilitarianism, rights and justice. A key element in this definition of ethics is a rule or standard by which right and wrong behaviour can be sought and judged. The principle underlying professional ethics is exactly the same as that of ethics: a rule or standard by which right and wrong can be sought and judged. However, rather than rely on the philosophy of ethics to define the rule or standard, in professional ethics, the rules or standards that define right from wrong are the 'principles of professional conduct'. These principles are crystallised in the code of professional conduct and form the basis of professional ethics. Therefore, the test of professional ethics is not how professionals serve their own interests but whether they act in ways that are consistent with the duties entrusted to them. In this regard, accounting professionals are guided by the code of professional conduct that has been established by the professional accounting bodies.

## Why have codes of professional conduct? //

Some commentators distinguish terms such as codes of ethics, codes of conduct and codes of practice, on the basis of their content. For example, codes of ethics are statements of values and principles that define the purpose of the organisation, codes of conduct are statements of rules that define acceptable and unacceptable behaviours, and codes of practice interpret and illustrate the principles of professional conduct with examples that guide decision making (Clarkson & Deck 1992). In practice, codes tend to include all three elements and, for the purpose of this chapter, the terms are used interchangeably.

The trust afforded to professional accountants because of their particular knowledge renders clients and employers vulnerable to the actions of accountants. Unfortunately, the power derived from differential levels of knowledge, like any other form of power, is subject to abuse. For example, accountants who receive privileged communications from clients may violate that confidence in ways ranging from inadvertent gossip to using the information for personal gain. To ensure this power is not abused, high standards of ethical conduct are required. The profession inculcates such standards in its members by issuing and enforcing a code of professional conduct. Thus, a **code of professional conduct** is a set of rules designed to induce a professional attitude and behaviour consistent with the high ethical standards expected by the public.

The major benefits of a code of professional conduct are twofold. First, the code serves as a public relations tool because it fosters a positive image of the profession which serves to build and retain public confidence. Codes provide assurance to the public that the profession is monitoring itself by establishing high standards of conduct with disciplinary procedures in place to deal with violations. Second, the code is designed to protect the potentially gullible client from incompetent and unscrupulous practitioners, and also protect the qualified practitioner from unfair competition. Codes provide the moral foundation by conveying principles of professional conduct, which establish the minimum standards of professional behaviour. Establishing minimum standards of behaviour has two aims: to provide a reference tool for members making ethical decisions, and to provide the benchmark for assessing the ethics of a member's conduct. The first aim, ethical decision making, is discussed in chapter 4. The second aim, assessing whether behaviours are inconsistent with the principles of professional conduct, forms the basis for a system of self-policing, which is the focus of this chapter.

### The Joint Code of Professional Conduct

In Australia, ethical rules first emerged with the incorporation of a number of professional bodies in the late nineteenth century (Parker 1987). Throughout the twentieth century ethical rules were developed on an ad hoc basis, usually in response to the issues of the day. This process existed until 1978, when the Joint Standing Committee of the Australian Society of Accountants (now CPA Australia) and the ICAA issued ethical pronouncements that were respectively entitled, 'Ethical Pronouncements' and 'Ethical Rulings'. Parker (1987) suggests that this is the first evidence of a code of ethics to be developed by the two professional bodies. However, it was not until 1998 that the two professional associations, CPA Australia and the ICAA, reached agreement and issued the Joint Code of Professional Conduct (the joint code). For the first time, members of both professional bodies had common ethical requirements as well as a set of common accounting and auditing standards.

The code is divided into six sections (see table 3.2). Each section contains mandatory requirements along with supportive narrative. In this chapter we focus discussion on Section B of the joint code, which sets out the fundamental principles of professional conduct, which in turn form the basis of accountants' professional and ethical responsibilities. Various other sections of the joint code will be referred to where appropriate to provide a better understanding of the principles' meaning and their application.

### TABLE 3.2

### STRUCTURE OF THE JOINT CODE OF PROFESSIONAL CONDUCT

| | |
|---|---|
| A. Introduction | Provides an introduction to the code, gives definitions for terms used within the code, and outlines the format of the code |
| B. Fundamental principles of professional conduct | Sets out the fundamental principles of professional conduct that are applicable to all members of the profession |
| C. Matters applicable to all members | Sets out various guidelines and responsibilities for particular circumstances such as members practising overseas and the preparation of legal documents |
| D. Matters applicable mainly to members in public practice | Covers matters applicable to public practitioners such as trust accounts, practice names, advertising, and referrals |

# STRUCTURE OF THE JOINT CODE OF PROFESSIONAL CONDUCT

| E. Statements, regulations and by- laws contained in other parts of the members' handbook and relevant to specific aspects of professional conduct | Cross-references rules contained in other parts of the *Members' handbook* that relate to specific aspects of professional conduct |
|---|---|
| F. Professional statements | Contains professional statements that detail matters of particular importance such as professional independence and professional fees |

## The proposed revised code of ethics for professional accountants

In July 2003, the Ethics Committee of the International Federation of Accountants (IFAC) issued an exposure draft to a new code of ethics entitled the Proposed Revised Code of Ethics for Professional Accountants. The original IFAC code of ethics was a model on which member bodies could base their national code, but the code itself was not regarded as a standard. The proposed revised code issued by IFAC has significant implications for the accounting profession because the code now represents an international standard for all member bodies (including CPA Australia and the ICAA) to follow. As an international standard, no IFAC member body or firm is allowed to apply less stringent standards than those stated in that section unless imposed by national law or regulation (IFAC, 2003, Part A, Paragraph 1.5). Therefore, CPA Australia and the ICAA are likely to adopt the proposed revised code as their own when it becomes effective on 1 January 2006.

Part A of the proposed revised code sets out the fundamental principles of professional conduct and explains the conceptual framework approach to assessing and dealing with threats to the fundamental principles. The conceptual framework is discussed in the latter part of this chapter. The fundamental principles of professional conduct discussed in Part A of the proposed revised code of ethics and Section B of the Joint Code of Professional Conduct contain considerable overlaps. Therefore, the fundamental principles and explanatory commentary from both codes are discussed as a single concept in the next section. The particular references to the Joint Code of Professional Conduct and the IFAC equivalent are presented in table 3.3 (opposite).

**TABLE 3.3**

## REFERENCES TO FUNDAMENTAL PRINCIPLES OF PROFESSIONAL CONDUCT

| Principle of professional conduct | CPA Australia and the ICAA The Joint Code of Professional Conduct | IFACs Proposed Revised Code of Ethics for Professional Accountants |
|---|---|---|
| Public interest | Section B.1 | Part A: Paragraph 1.6– 1.8 |
| Integrity | Section B.2 | Part A: Paragraph 1.14 (a) and Section 2 |
| Objectivity | Section B.3 | Part A: Paragraph 1.14 (b) and Section 3 |
| Independence | Section B.4 | Part B: Section 8 |
| Confidentiality | Section B.5 | Part A: Paragraph 1.14 (d) and Section 5 |
| Technical and professional standards | Section B.6 | Subsumed within Part A: Paragraph 1.14 (c) and 1.14 (e) |
| Competence and due care | Section B.7 | Part A: Paragraph 1.14 (c) and Section 4 |
| Ethical behaviour | Section B.8 | Part A: Paragraph 1.14 (e) and Section 6 |

## Fundamental principles of professional conduct //

The fundamental principles of professional conduct provide the framework for the profession's technical standards and ethical rules. In effect, the principles provide the benchmark by which accountants' behaviour is compared and judged. In a professional context, the ethics of an accountant's actions are judged by comparing that behaviour with the responsibilities espoused by the codes of conduct. In simple terms, behaviour consistent with the principles of professional conduct is ethical, and behaviour inconsistent with the principles of professional conduct is unethical, or at the very least, unprofessional. Professional codes are often criticised because the fundamental principles are subject to broad interpretations due to vague and general wording. Without interpretation, members must rely on their own values when making decisions, which may or may not be consistent with the code's objectives. The principles of professional conduct define the accountant's professional responsibilities, which in turn form the basis of professional ethics; therefore, it is important to understand the meaning of the fundamental principles and the limits of their tolerance. In the next section, we examine in some detail the fundamental principles of professional conduct.

## Public interest

The **public interest** principle states that 'members must at all times safeguard the interests of their clients and employers provided that they do not conflict with the duties and loyalties owed to the community and its laws' (Section B.1). According to this principle, accountants have a fundamental duty to safeguard and advance the interests of their clients and employers subject only to the public interest. The profession recognises that members have obligations beyond the immediate client or employer relationship that extend to shareholders, creditors, employees, suppliers, government, the accounting profession, and ultimately, the public at large. Therefore, accountants have an obligation to a number of stakeholders and, in discharging their responsibilities, they may encounter conflicting pressures from among each of these groups. In the case of these conflicts, accountants' principal responsibility is not to themselves, the client or the employer, but to the public. Expressed as a guiding rule, accountants are obliged to advance the interests of their client or employer as long as they do not conflict with the public's interest. If the interests of the client are at odds with the interests of society, accountants' first obligation is to the public.

An orientation toward the community rather than self-interest is fundamental to the role of the professional — so fundamental that professionals have traditionally been expected to make personal sacrifices if the welfare of the client or the public is at stake. Careful examination of the wording of the public interest principle affirms an obligation to a number of stakeholders (clients, employers, community and the law), but not to the self. The accountant is omitted from the wording of the public interest principle, which implies that accountants have final priority in conflicts of interest situations. In general, the accountant's interest must never supersede the interests of others.

This public interest perspective is a distinguishing feature of any profession; however, in accounting, protecting the public interest presents a unique dilemma. On the one hand, accountants have a contractual obligation to their clients or employers, but on the other hand, they are expected to give their primary loyalty to the public. This set of circumstances is unlike other professions. Take, for example, the legal profession: in serving a client in a court of law the lawyer's first priority is to protect the client's interest. Guilt and harm to the public from the client's behaviour is irrelevant to this dimension of the lawyer's responsibility. While lawyers have a paramount obligation to their clients, accountants owe their primary obligation not to their clients, but to the public.

Accountants' duties are better understood if they are viewed as a triad consisting of the accountant (the first party), the client or employer (the second party) and the public (the third party). Unfortunately, this triad of responsibilities presents an in-built conflict of interest for accountants. Accountants are sometimes placed in positions where their loyal and faithful service to the client or employer may result in less than perfectly trustworthy information being reported to the public. In turn, full disclosure to the public may be perceived as a disservice to the client or employer (Lindblom 1997). In these circumstances, accountants may bend to the demands of their clients or employers at the expense of the public. In difficult situations, accountants must remember their third party obligations. Users of financial reports are their prime concern, not preparers or clients who may have ulterior motives.

## Integrity

The principle of **integrity** is vital to maintaining public trust because without integrity users would have no faith in accountants' work or their opinions. Section B.2 states that 'members must be straightforward, honest and sincere in their approach to professional work'. The significance of this principle in maintaining the trust and confidence of the public is undeniable, yet the code provides the least amount of supporting narrative to interpreting its meaning. We can infer from this principle that integrity implies honesty as well as fair dealing. However, integrity is more than being truthful. It can accommodate the inadvertent error and the honest mistaken opinion but it cannot accommodate deceit. In addition to honesty, integrity has a second dimension — courage. Accountants are often placed in difficult situations where they must choose between the interests of the client or the public. Such decisions involve difficult trade-offs and can often be influenced by personal consequences. Accountants must summon the courage to stand up for what is right and not surrender to the pressures and demands of significant others.

In regard to financial reporting, integrity is violated when the accountant knowingly misrepresents the facts, such as permitting or failing to correct a false or misleading accounting entry or attesting to the financial reports when they are untrue. Overall, the accountant has an obligation to ensure that users are not misled. In general, a violation of integrity occurs when an act or decision:

- is dishonest
- is evasive
- omits pertinent facts
- subordinates the public interest for personal gain and advantage
- takes personal advantage or profit from the knowledge of the client's affairs
- accepts exorbitant fees even when the client is innocently willing to pay them
- succumbs to pressure from clients and employers to overlook professional obligations.

## Objectivity

The principle of **objectivity** states that 'members must be fair and must not allow prejudice, conflict of interest or bias to override their objectivity' (Section B.3). In the main, the principle imposes an obligation to be impartial and free from conflicts of interest. When reporting and attesting to the financial statements, accountants have an overriding obligation to maintain an impartial attitude. Objectivity, therefore, may be described as a state of mind that has regard for considerations relevant only to the situation or the facts at hand. It is primarily a condition of mind that is focused on making judgments with an unbiased view. Objectivity is especially important to the audit profession, where the professional opinion is likely to affect the rights between parties and the decisions they make. For auditors, the maintenance of objectivity and independence requires a continuing assessment of client relationships and public responsibilities. In this regard, objectivity is better understood when it is read in conjunction with the principle of independence.

## Independence

The issues surrounding professional independence are dealt with in detail in chapter 10. In this chapter, we define independence and highlight its major features. The principle of **independence** states that 'members must be and should be seen to be free of any interest which might be regarded, whatever its actual effect, as being incompatible with integrity and objectivity' (Section B.4). Two essential attributes comprise the principle of independence: 'independence of mind' and 'independence of appearance'. Independence of mind and thus the ability to provide unbiased viewpoints requires integrity (candour) and objectivity (impartiality). Independence of mind is achieved when the accountant avoids situations or relationships that impair objectivity or create personal bias which could influence delicate judgments, even subconsciously. For example, an auditor, concerned for its investment, may compromise professional judgment when dealing with clients in which it has a financial interest.

Accountants must not only be independent of mind but also they must appear to be independent. Paragraph 10 of Professional Statement F.1, 'Professional Independence', applies the 'reasonable person test' as the criterion for evaluating the appearance of independence. That is, whether a reasonable person, having knowledge of the relevant facts and taking into account the conduct of the member and the member's behaviour under the circumstances, could conclude that the member is in a position where objectivity could be impaired. This is not about the professional or the professional's independence of mind, but how others view the professional and his or her behaviour. In conclusion, accountants should avoid relationships that might suggest to a reasonable observer that conflicts of interest exist, whether it is in fact or appearance.

## Confidentiality

Confidentiality is one principle that appears in almost all professional codes. The principle of **confidentiality** states that: 'members must respect the confidentiality of information acquired in the course of their work and must not disclose any such information to a third party without specific authority or unless there is a legal or professional duty to disclose it' (Section B.5). The accountant is under a strict obligation, which continues after the termination of the client or employer relationship, not to disclose any confidential information without the specific consent of the client or employer. Clients and employers have a right to expect that accountants will not reveal their affairs to third parties as it could lead to significant personal and financial loss. Confidentiality is particularly important to the provision of auditing and attestation services where open and honest discourse with the client is necessary if the auditor is to provide a fully informed opinion on the status of the financial reports. However, willingness on the part of the client to discuss confidential matters is likely only if confidentiality is maintained. In addition to maintaining confidentiality, Section C.5 of the Joint Code of Professional Conduct imposes an additional obligation on accountants to ensure that confidential information obtained in the course of professional work is not used for personal advantage or for the advantage of a third party. This obligation prevents members from using privileged information for personal gain.

The duty of confidentiality is not without limits. Section C.5 of the joint code and Paragraph 5.6 of Part A of the proposed revised code suggest that accountants may sometimes find themselves in circumstances that require disclosure and absolution from confidentiality. These situations include:

- disclosure authorised by the employer or client
- disclosure required by law — for example, to produce documents or to give evidence in legal proceedings
- a professional duty or right to disclose, such as **compliance** with mandatory technical or ethical requirements, compliance with a quality review conducted by CPA Australia or ICAA, or to respond to a formal investigation by CPA Australia or the ICAA.

The major limitation of the principle of confidentiality is the apparent conflict with the public interest principle. Consider a situation where the client or employer is participating in tax evasion by deliberately misrepresenting taxable income. The accountant faces a quandary because the duty of confidentiality prohibits the accountant from informing the tax authorities, even though it is in the public's best interest. At present, the accountant must maintain confidentiality and may only counsel the client or employer against such behaviour but not report the matter to the authorities. At times, the principle of confidentiality may unwittingly cover up malpractice. Knowing when it is ethical to disclose confidential information is always difficult. Section C.5 of the joint code and Paragraph 5.7 of the proposed revised code provide some guidance by listing a number of issues that the accountant should consider before determining whether confidential information can be disclosed:

- whether or not all the relevant facts are known and substantiated, to the extent that it is practicable to do so
- the member should be satisfied that the parties to whom the communication is addressed are appropriate recipients and have the responsibility to act on it
- whether or not the member would incur any legal liability having made a communication and the consequences thereof.

In all such situations, the accountant should consider the need to consult legal counsel and/or CPA Australia or the ICAA.

## Technical and professional standards

In the performance of their professional duties, accountants are expected to conform to accounting and auditing standards, and rules promulgated by private and government standard setting authorities, such as the ASIC and the Australian Taxation Office. The principle states that 'members must carry out their professional work in accordance with the technical and professional standards relevant to that work' (Section B.6). In simple terms, this principle mandates compliance with applicable accounting and auditing standards and other relevant rules or regulations. A true and fair view of the reporting entity's financial performance and state of affairs is likely when the financial reports are prepared in accordance with accounting standards. Any deviation from applicable accounting standards must be properly disclosed and supported with the reasons for the deviation and its financial effects (*APS 1.12: Conformity with Accounting Standards and UIG Consensus Views*).

## Competence and due care

The two components of this principle, *competence* and *due care* are conceptually different and therefore discussed separately. **Competence** represents the attainment and maintenance of a level of knowledge that enables an accountant to render services with expertise. When accountants are approached to perform professional services, they must have the requisite technical qualifications and knowledge to perform the job properly. Serving the client's interest is unlikely when accountants do not possess the necessary skills for the tasks they undertake. Therefore, accountants must not provide services that they are not competent to render. They must ensure that they comply with the highest level of technical expertise because only by maintaining the highest standards will the client be protected. To accept a task without the requisite skill is unethical. Providing services competently will not only avoid harm to the client but it will also protect accountants from potential litigation from negligent practices.

Competence is achieved initially through formal education and the attainment of an accredited university degree. However, Section C.4 of the joint code imposes an obligation to achieve not only a minimum level of education but also to maintain a commitment to learning and professional improvement throughout professional life. In this regard, continuing professional development is a key component of maintaining competence. Currently, full status members of CPA Australia and the ICAA must commit to approximately 40 hours annually of continuing professional development, which may include formal education (postgraduate degrees), training, seminars, and events or programs offered by employing organisations or professional associations.

Competence also establishes the limitations of accountants' capabilities by dictating referrals when an engagement exceeds their personal competence. If accountants are approached to perform tasks for which they do not possess the requisite skill, they should not refuse the job in the first instance as this will result in a loss of professional fees, but refer the job to other accountants or specialists. Referrals are consistent with protecting the client interest and should be encouraged. In order to protect the interests of the referring accountant, a member who receives an engagement by referral must not extend their services beyond the specific engagement without first consulting with the referring accountant (Professional Statement F.4, 'Referrals'). The system of referrals is discussed further in chapter 11.

**Due care** is the quest for excellence. It requires accountants to discharge their professional responsibilities with diligence. Due care imposes an obligation to perform professional services to the best of one's ability with concern for the best interests of those for whom the services are performed. Not only does due care impose a responsibility to render services promptly and carefully but also to be dutiful of the profession's responsibility to the public and to observe applicable accounting and ethical standards. Due care also imposes an obligation on accountants in senior and supervisory positions to plan and supervise professional activities adequately. Larger firms will no doubt have strategies in place to monitor the work of colleagues; however, there should always remain a tradition of expecting each person to be able to assess the quality of their work.

### Ethical behaviour

The principle of **ethical behaviour** is a general catch-all principle sometimes referred to as 'the conduct unbecoming' rule (Henderson & Henderson 2001). The principle states that 'members must conduct themselves in a manner consistent with the good reputation of their profession and refrain from any conduct which might bring discredit to their profession' (Section B.8). The principle is not clear about what constitutes behaviour that is discreditable to the profession. However, it presumably includes behaviour that violates state or Commonwealth laws, whether it is in the course of duty or their private lives. Through appropriate and professional behaviour, accountants have a responsibility to their professional peers to protect the good reputation developed by their predecessors, but this does not precede their duty to protect the public interest. Therefore, while the principle imposes a duty to protect the image of the profession, this is second to protecting the public interest. Assigning priority to the profession's image over the public interest may tempt cover-ups purely to avoid damaging the profession's reputation, without regard for those who have been wronged. Acts that protect the profession's image ahead of the public interest can only protect crooked accountants at the expense of their victims. Such behaviour is unethical and therefore unacceptable.

## The conceptual framework approach //

Following the success of the conceptual framework approach to the revised standard on independence (discussed in chapter 10) in 2002, IFAC extended this approach to the entire code of ethics. The proposed revised code begins by establishing the fundamental principles of professional conduct, then provides a conceptual framework for applying those principles. The conceptual framework imposes an obligation on accountants to identify, evaluate and address threats to compliance with the fundamental principles, rather than merely comply with a set of specific rules (IFAC, 2003, Part A, Paragraph 1.10). Evaluating the threats to the fundamental principles calls for accountants to determine the significance of the risks associated with the threat. Where the risk of compliance is insignificant, no action is required. However, where the risk is significant, accountants must respond by eliminating the threat or reducing it to an acceptable level by implementing appropriate safeguards such that compliance with the fundamental principles is not compromised. If the threats cannot be reduced to an acceptable level, accountants should decline or discontinue the specific service or engagement (IFAC 2003, Part A, Paragraph 1.11). See figure 3.2 for a diagrammatic view of the conceptual approach to the application of the fundamental principles.

### Threats to fundamental principles

Part A of the proposed revised code sets out the categories in which the threats to compliance with the fundamental principles may fall. Parts B and C of the proposed revised code provide examples of circumstances that may give rise to such threats for accountants in public practice (Part B) and accountants in business (Part C). The box entitled, 'In practice: Threats to compliance with fundamental principles' lists the different threats and circumstances that may give rise to such threats.

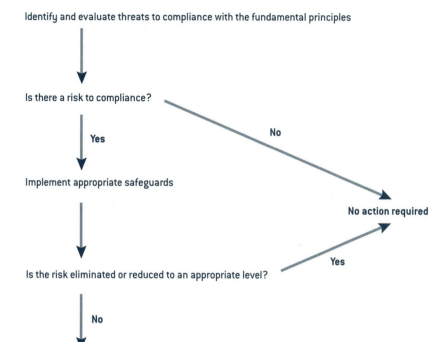

Identify and evaluate threats to compliance with the fundamental principles

Is there a risk to compliance?

Yes      No

Implement appropriate safeguards

No action required

Is the risk eliminated or reduced to an appropriate level?

Yes

No

Decline or discontinue the specific service or engagement

FIGURE 3.2   The conceptual framework approach to professional ethics

## IN PRACTICE

### Threats to compliance with fundamental principles

| THREAT | SELF-INTEREST | SELF-REVIEW |
|---|---|---|
| Definition | may occur as a result of the financial or other interests of professional accountants or of immediate or close family members | may occur when a previous judgment needs to be re-evaluated by the professional accountant responsible for that judgment |
| Examples of threats in public practice | • A financial interest in a client where the performance of professional services may affect the value of that interest<br>• A loan to or from an assurance client or any of its directors or officers where the performance of professional services may affect the value of that loan | • The discovery of a significant error during a re-evaluation<br>• Reporting on the operation of financial systems after being involved in their design or implementation<br>• A member of the engagement team for an assurance client being, or having recently been, a director or officer of that client |

75   chapter 3   Professional ethics and self-regulation

| | | |
|---|---|---|
| **Examples of threats in public practice** *(cont'd)* | • Concern about the possibility of losing a recurring client<br>• Potential employment with a client | • A member of the engagement team being, or having recently been, employed by the client in a position to exert direct and significant influence over the subject matter of the engagement<br>• Having prepared the original data used to generate records that are the subject matter of the engagement |
| **Examples of threats in business** | • Financial interests, loans or guarantees<br>• Incentive arrangements<br>• Concern over employment security<br>• Commercial pressure from outside the employing organisation | • Business decisions or data being subject to review and justification by the same person responsible for making those decisions or preparing that data |

| THREAT | ADVOCACY | FAMILIARITY |
|---|---|---|
| **Definition** | may occur when a professional accountant promotes a position or opinion to the point that subsequent objectivity may be compromised | may occur when, because of a close relationship, a professional accountant becomes too sympathetic to the interests of others |
| **Examples of threats in public practice** | • Promoting shares in a listed entity when that entity is an audit client<br>• Acting as an advocate on behalf of an assurance client in resolving disputes with third parties | • A member of the engagement team having a close or immediate family relationship with a director or officer of the client<br>• A member of the engagement team having a close or immediate family relationship with an employee of the client who is in a position to exert direct and significant influence over the subject matter of the engagement<br>• A former partner of the firm being a director or officer of the client or an employee in a position to exert direct and significant influence over the subject matter of the engagement<br>• Accepting gifts or preferential treatment, unless the value is clearly insignificant |

| Examples of threats in business | • Commenting publicly on future events, in particular, circumstances where outcomes may be doubtful or where information is incomplete<br>• Acting publicly as an advocate for a particular position where bias may arise or where the validity of that position may later be called into question | • A person in a position to influence financial or non-financial reporting or business decisions having an immediate or close family member who is in a position to benefit from that influence<br>• Long association with business contacts influencing business decisions<br>• Acceptance of gifts or preferential treatment, unless the value is clearly insignificant |
|---|---|---|

| THREAT | INTIMIDATION | |
|---|---|---|
| Definition | which may occur when a professional accountant may be deterred from acting objectively by actual or perceived threats | |
| Examples of threats in public practice | • Being threatened with dismissal or replacement in relation to a client engagement<br>• Being threatened with litigation<br>• Being pressured to reduce inappropriately the extent of work performed in order to reduce fees | |
| Examples of threats in business | • Threat of dismissal or replacement of the professional accountant in business or a close or immediate family member over a disagreement about the application of an accounting principle or the way in which financial information is to be reported<br>• A dominant personality attempting to influence the decision making process — for example, with regard to the awarding of contracts | |

*Source:* International Federation of Accountants, 2003, *Proposed revised code of ethics for professional accountants*, IFAC, New York.

## Safeguards

The safeguards that may eliminate or reduce such threats to an acceptable level fall into two broad categories: (1) safeguards created by the profession, legislation, or regulation (see 'In practice: Safeguards created by the profession'); and (2) safeguards in the work environment (IFAC 2003, Part A, Paragraph 1.16). The safeguards in the work environment are too numerous to mention in this chapter. In brief, however, safeguards in the public practice work environment consist of three types: firm-wide safeguards such as leadership and policies, which provide guidance on appropriate behaviour; engagement-specific safeguards such as consulting with third parties; and safeguards within the client's systems processes such as corporate governance structures (IFAC 2003,

Part B, Paragraphs 1.15–1.20). Safeguards in the work environment of business organisations (non-accounting firms) generally refer to the employing entity's governance and management procedures — for example, the company's ethics program, internal controls and disciplinary processes (IFAC 2003, Part C, Paragraph 1.18). The nature of the safeguards to be applied will vary depending on the circumstances. In exercising their judgment, accountants should consider what a reasonable and informed third party — having knowledge of all relevant information, including the significance of the threat and the safeguards applied — would conclude to be unacceptable.

**IN PRACTICE**

### Safeguards created by the profession

The safeguards created by the profession, legislation or regulation include, but are not restricted to:

- educational, training and experience requirements for entry into the profession
- continuing professional development requirements
- corporate governance regulations
- professional standards
- professional or regulatory monitoring and disciplinary procedures
- external review by a legally empowered third party of the reports, returns, communications or information produced by a professional accountant.

Safeguards that may increase the likelihood of identifying or deterring unethical behaviour include, but are not restricted to:

- effective, well-publicised complaints systems operated by the employing organisation, the profession or a regulator, which enable colleagues, employers and members of the public to draw attention to unprofessional or unethical behaviour
- an explicitly stated duty to report breaches of ethical requirements.

*Source:* International Federation of Accountants 2003, *Proposed revised code of ethics for professional accountants*, IFAC, New York (Part A: Paragraphs 1.17 & 1.19).

# Enforcing the code //

In exchange for the profession's autonomous and privileged existence, members are expected to obtain specialised training and demonstrate a high degree of ethical conduct in the performance of their duties to ensure the protection of the public interest. However, some accountants might be tempted to use the power of their position to maximise personal gain rather than satisfy their obligations to clients or employers. To assure the proper performance of duties, the profession is obliged to regulate the conduct of members by ensuring adherence to the ethical standards that are contained in the joint code. If a member behaves unethically, his or her conduct will be brought under review by the profession's disciplinary procedures, and the collective reputation of the profession may require the imposition of sanctions, ranging from reprimand to dismissal. To this end, codes and their enforcement play a strong role in maintaining public confidence.

## The disciplinary process //

The specific disciplinary procedures for CPA Australia and ICAA vary; however, the general processes have overlapping similarities. The procedure normally begins with the association receiving a complaint. The complaint, which may originate from a member of the public, a government agency or a fellow practitioner, is received by the professional association and duly investigated. The investigation involves gathering evidence and interviewing the complainant and member. If there is a case to answer, the matter is referred to the disciplinary committee for a hearing and determination. The committee hears the case, giving the member the opportunity to present his or her version of the facts. The committee then retires to make a determination. If the committee finds the member is guilty of misconduct, a penalty is imposed. At this point the member has the right to appeal the decision or the sanction imposed. The major phases of investigation and disciplinary procedures are outlined in figure 3.3.

The threat of punishment is an essential part of the disciplinary structure that deters unscrupulous behaviour. Sanctions are designed to reflect the impact of members' actions rather than to punish them. For the most serious of offences, the ultimate sanction is exclusion and withdrawal of the right to use their professional designation, CPA or CA. Under the Australian professional and regulatory framework anyone can provide accounting services. Only in specific specialisations, such as auditing, do they need to be a member of a professional accounting body. Therefore, exclusion or suspension may not preclude the accountant from continuing to provide basic accounting services. However, if members are excluded from the profession, they may no longer rely on their professional designation CPA or CA, which will undoubtedly diminish their ability to win clients or obtain gainful employment. Lesser sanctions include suspension from membership, a quality review of the member's practice, a fine, censure, admonishment, reprimand or a remedial action such as continuing professional development. Details of hearings are normally published in the associations' professional journals. Disclosing details of hearings promotes an effective and transparent disciplinary process but also presents a dilemma for the profession. Improved disclosure of disciplinary procedures strengthens the effectiveness of the code and improves behaviour but may diminish public confidence.

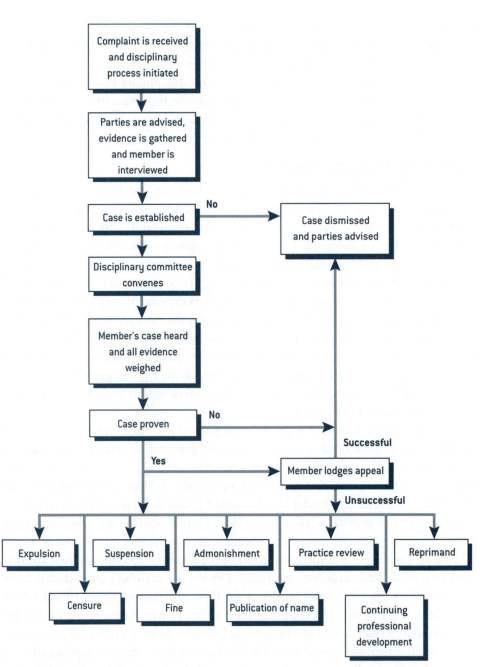

FIGURE 3.3   The major phases of investigation and disciplinary procedures

## Code effectiveness //

The extent to which the code will influence accountants' decision making and behaviour depends on their awareness of the code and its content and how effectively the code is enforced. According to Leung and Cooper (1995), accountants will be responsive to a professional code of conduct only if they know about it and it is relevant to their needs. In a survey of the members of CPA Australia, Leung and Cooper (1995) discovered that accountants had little or no knowledge of the code or its principles such as public interest, integrity and compliance. Even when accountants knew about the code, few believed it met their requirements, leaving respondents uncertain about its usefulness in helping them to resolve ethical problems. Similar results were discovered by Tan and Chua (2000), who discovered that members of the Australian and New Zealand professional associations did not have sufficient knowledge of the code, with some members admitting that that they had not even read the code. Leung and Cooper (1995) found that most accountants did not make frequent use of the code and, when faced with an ethical dilemma, members preferred to consult their superiors, colleagues or friends, and not the code. Leung and Cooper (1995) suggested that the lack of awareness of the code and its apparent lack of usefulness should be addressed to promote positive attitudes to its enforcement and its continuing benefits to accounting practice.

A commitment to the code from its members requires effective enforcement. One reason why members may lack commitment to the code is because they perceive the code to be ineffectively enforced (Leung & Cooper 1995). Without the threat of penalty, the motivation to comply is absent. This perception is based in part on the inherent limitations associated with the disciplinary process. The disciplinary process begins with a complaint raised against a member of the accounting profession. If there is no complaint, then there is no disciplinary action. The probability of a complaint depends on a number of factors, which include the victim being aware of the losses, their causes and the perceptions of whether the complaint will result in action (Henderson & Henderson 2001).

The perception that codes are ineffectively enforced is supported by evidence from the United States and Australia that only a small number of cases, relative to membership size, are ever investigated (Parker 1994). This finding may be evidence of a highly ethical profession but it could also be evidence of reluctance by the aggrieved parties to file complaints. Additionally, sanctions imposed are relatively minor, with forfeiture and suspension of membership rarely enforced. Inspiring a commitment to the code is difficult when detection is unlikely and sanctions are not significant enough to deter repeat behaviour.

A code that is not actively enforced suggests that it is a self-serving document employed to protect its own interests. Parker (1994) analysed the types of offences and penalties doled out in the Australian accounting profession during the years 1974 to 1987. His analysis supports the notion that codes and their enforcement are more concerned with protecting the profession's self-interest rather than protecting the public interest. A sceptic might conclude that codes are simply window dressing, designed to gain the confidence of the public without any real effect on members' behaviour. The motivation for a self-serving code is to protect the economic interests of the profession from the unethical conduct of its members (Jamal & Bowie 1995). However, more recent evidence suggests that we may be seeing a change in the way codes are enforced. The accounting profession in the United States appears to be improving the code's effective implementation, with an increasing number of sanctions, with increasing severity, for substandard professional service (Moriarity 2000). Until further evidence is gathered, effective implementation of the code remains an issue for the accounting profession.

## Summary //

The completion of formal training, passing qualifying examinations and being licensed to practise constitute a ticket of admission to a career in accounting. However, these characteristics alone do not guarantee success. Success requires a good reputation with clients and the public generally. This is achieved by growth in proficiency, wisdom and professionalism. Although most people strive to work skilfully, professionalism is more than doing your job well — it denotes a genuine regard for excellence that is focused on serving others.

Arguably, of all the professions that are closely allied to business, accounting is under the greatest ethical obligation to the public interest. To guide accountants the profession has imposed certain rules of conduct on their members. These rules, referred to as principles of professional conduct, come under the broad heading of professional ethics and are embodied in the Joint Code of Professional Conduct. To this end, the joint code is essential to ensuring good conduct and retaining the confidence of the public. If members fail to conduct themselves properly, they run the risk of forfeiting their privilege of membership.

In the next chapter, we examine how to apply the ethical principles learned in chapter 2, and the rules of professional conduct learned in chapter 3, to resolving ethical dilemmas. The principles of ethical and professional conduct are essential knowledge for graduate accountants entering the profession. However, having knowledge of these principles and being able to apply them are separate and distinct issues. One purpose of chapter 4 is to provide you with a decision-making structure that incorporates both ethical principles and professional obligations.

## Key terms //

Advocacy threats . . . p. 76
Code of professional conduct . . . p. 64
Competence . . . p. 72
Compliance . . . p. 71
Confidentiality . . . p. 71
Due care . . . p. 73

# Questions //

**3.1** Describe the characteristics that distinguish a profession from a non-profession.

**3.2** What is meant by the phrase: 'a profession is an exclusive franchise' and why is this important?

**3.3** Discuss the significance of public confidence to the accounting profession.

**3.4** Protecting the public interest: is this altruism or egoism? Explain.

**3.5** What are the major objectives of the code of professional conduct?

**3.6** Define the fundamental principles of professional conduct. Is any one principle contained in this section superior to the others? Why?

**3.7** For each of the following threats:
   (i) classify the threat as either self-interest, self-review, advocacy, familiarity or intimidation
   (ii) identify the principle(s) of professional conduct that may be violated
   (iii) explain why you think the principle(s) may be breached
   (iv) nominate one safeguard that might reduce the threat to an acceptable level
      **a** Accepting a gift from a client or employer
      **b** An auditor who maintains the accounting records and prepares the financial statements
      **c** An unreasonable boss with a dominant personality
      **d** An accountant who owns shares in their employing organisation.

**3.8** Are there any limits to an accountant's obligation not to disclose confidential information obtained in the course of a professional engagement? Explain.

**3.9** Discuss the role of mandating continuing education for accounting professionals.

**3.10** Describe the conceptual approach to the application of the fundamentals of professional conduct.

**3.11** A public practitioner recently published the following advertising slogan: 'Guaranteed to Surpass your Existing Accountant'. Which fundamental principle of professional conduct has been breached and why?

**3.12** Outline the profession's disciplinary procedures. How effective is the Joint Code of Professional Conduct in influencing members' behaviour?

## CASE STUDY

### Professional misconduct

Below are particulars of a case that was referred to the disciplinary committee of CPA Australia in 2002. This case represents the finding of the disciplinary committee on 1 October 2002, recorded by divisional council on 27 November 2002 and published in *Australian CPA* February 2003, pp. 78–9. The case involves a member who borrowed money from clients to finance personal expenses and property investments and then failed to repay the moneys. The member had two cases (referred to as 'particulars') to answer, they are:

**Particular A**

- On 6 August 1997 the member visited the home of his client, Mr X, and requested a loan of $30 000, to be repaid in one month, to purchase a property on the Central Coast. Mr X agreed and gave the member a cheque drawn on his bank account.
- On 2 November 1997 the member telephoned Mr X and asked for a further loan of $2000, which the member urgently needed to pay for his children's school fees.
- On 25 February 1998 in his own hand-written letter to Mr X's solicitor and by loan agreement the member acknowledged that he owed Mr X $32 000.
- On 29 November 2000 the member appeared in the Federal Magistrates Court of Australia in response to a bankruptcy notice issued on behalf of Mr X. Prior to appearing, a settlement was negotiated between the member's solicitor and Mr X's solicitor, on the basis that the member was to pay Mr X the sum of $29 000, the petition was to be dismissed and each party to release the other from any further claims.

**Particular B**

- The member's clients, Mr and Mrs Y, engaged a registered building contractor to carry out renovations.
- The builder commenced work at the beginning of November 1997 but by late February 1998 there were problems with a number of subcontractors and some suppliers of white goods and PC items.

//

- The builder realised that Mrs Y was worried about the problems and offered to return $53 000 to Mrs Y to put into her bank account until the matters in dispute were resolved. The money was then to be returned to the builder. Mrs Y refused to take the money and the builder suggested that Mrs Y speak to 'the member', her accountant.
- On or about 27 or 28 February 1998 the member accepted a cheque for $28 000 from his clients, Mr and Mrs Y, being a return of progress payments made by the bank to the builder and on or about 6 March 1998 the member accepted a further $25 000 from their builder also being a return of progress payments made by the bank. At the member's request, the builder agreed to lend the member the money as bridging finance for the purchase of a house. He was to repay the builder in six weeks.
- On 10 July 1998 the builder commenced legal action against the member following his failure to return his money.
- On 21 July 1998 in the member's own handwritten letter to the builder's solicitor, he admitted that he owed the builder $53 000.
- On 14 July 1999 in the district court an agreement, as to judgment, was lodged in which the member agreed that he owed the builder $58 603.03 and $2500 in costs.
- On 13 July 2001, he appeared in the district court for failing to pay the balance of the judgment debt and was examined as to his property and means of satisfying the judgment debt. The debt was repaid in October 2001.

**Required**

1 Identify the fundamental principles of professional conduct that the member has breached and explain why you think they have been breached.
2 The member was found guilty of professional misconduct. What penalties do you think are fitting for this member's behaviour?
3 Would your answer in questions 1 and 2 differ if the member repaid the loans when they were due?
4 Do you believe that a member's name should be published when they are found guilty of misconduct?

## FURTHER RESOURCES AND WEBSITES //

### Further resources

Bayles, MD 1981, *Professional ethics*, Wadsworth, Belmont CA.

Calhoun, CH, Oliverio, ME & Wolitzer, P 1999, *Ethics and the CPA: building trust and value-added services*, John Wiley & Sons, New York.

Carey, JL 1980, *Profession ethics of public accounting*, Arno Press, New York.

Coady, M & Bloch, S 1996, *Codes of ethics and the professions*, Melbourne University Press, Melbourne.

Lee, T 1995, 'The professionalization of accountancy: a history of protecting the public interest in a self-interested way', *Accounting, Auditing and Accountability*, vol. 8 no. 4, pp. 48–69.

Magill, HT, Previts, GJ & Robinson TR 1998, *The CPA profession: opportunities, responsibilities and services*, Prentice Hall, Upper Saddle River NJ.

Velayutham, S 2000, 'The professional accounting body of the 21st century: the global franchise', *Pacific Accounting Review*, vol. 11 no. 2, pp. 163–71.

### Websites

CPA Online 2003, CPA Australia, viewed 2 August 2003, www.cpaaustralia.com.au.

The Institute of Chartered Accountants 2003, viewed 2 August 2003, www.icaa.org.au.

The International Federation of Accountants 2003, New York, viewed 2 August 2003, www.ifac.org.

American Institute of Certified Public Accountants 2003, New York, viewed 2 August 2003, www.aicpa.org.

....................................................................................................................................................

## REFERENCES //

Bloom, R & Kantor, J 1991, 'Professional accounting education in England, the United States, Australia, and Canada: a status report', *Advances in International Accounting*, vol. 4, pp. 311–34.

CPA Australia and the Institute of Chartered Accountants in Australia 2002, 'Joint code of professional conduct', *Members' Handbook*, CPA Australia and ICAA, Melbourne.

Clarkson, MBE & Deck, M 1992, *Applying the stakeholder management model to the analysis and evaluation of corporate codes*, Clarkson Centre for Ethics, University of Toronto, Canada.

Greenwood, E 1957, 'Attributes of a profession', *Social Work*, July, pp. 45–55.

Hays Personnel Services 2003, *Salary Survey 2003*, viewed 2 August 2003, www.hays.com.au/salary/index.asp.

Henderson, S & Henderson, E 2001, 'A note on the public interest and ethical behaviour', *Australian Accounting Review*, vol. 11 no. 3, pp. 68–72.

International Federation of Accountants, 2003, *Proposed revised code of ethics for professional accountants*, IFAC, New York.

Jamal, K & Bowie, NE 1995, 'Theoretical considerations for a more meaningful code of professional ethics', *Journal of Business Ethics*, vol. 14, no. 9, pp. 703–14.

Leung, P & Cooper, B 1995, 'Ethical dilemmas in accountancy practice', *Australian Accountant*, May, vol. 65, no. 4, pp. 28–33.

Lindblom, K 1997, 'Functionalist and conflict views of AICPA code of conduct: Public interest vs. self interest', *Journal of Business Ethics*, vol. 16, no. 5, pp. 573–84.

Moriarity, S 2000, 'Trends in ethical sanctions within the accounting profession', *Accounting Horizons*, vol. 14, no. 4, pp. 427–39.

Parker, L 1987, 'A historical analysis of ethical pronouncement and debate in the Australian accounting profession', *Abacus*, vol. 23, no. 2, pp. 122–40.

—— 1994, 'Professional accounting body ethics: in search of the private interest', *Accounting, Organizations and Society*, vol. 19, no. 6, pp. 507–25.

Saks, M 1983, 'Removing the blinkers? A critique of recent contributions to the sociology of professions', *Sociological Review*, vol. 31, pp. 1–21.

Tan, LM & Chua, F 2000, 'Tax ethics education in New Zealand tertiary institutions: a preliminary study', *Accounting Education*, vol. 3, pp. 259–79.

# 4

# Ethical decision making

**Learning objectives**

After studying this chapter you should be able to:

- Describe the process of conventional decision making.
- Explain the importance of decision making in accounting.
- Describe the internal processes of problem resolution.
- Outline the seven steps of the AAA ethical decision-making model.
- Resolve an ethical dilemma using the AAA ethical decision-making model.
- Describe the strengths and weaknesses of the AAA ethical decision-making model.
- Understand that using an ethical decision-making model does not guarantee an ethical decision and explain the factors that influence decision making.

'It is our choices . . . that show what we truly are, far more than our abilities.'
**Professor Dumbledore in *Harry Potter and The Chamber of Secrets*,
J K Rowling, (1999, p. 245)**

# Introduction //

In this chapter, we highlight the significance of professional judgment in accounting and contrast the process of conventional decision making with a structured decision-making model known as the **AAA model**. The AAA model is an ethical decision-making model used by individuals to help them arrive at ethical and defendable decisions. The AAA model and its various components are described in detail and its application is illustrated with an extensive example. However, being aware of decision models and knowing how to use them does not mean that ethical decisions will always be made. Decision making is influenced by a number of situational and environmental factors, such as personal preferences and the pressures of time and stress. Although the process of following a decision-making model cannot guarantee an ethical decision, it is likely to minimise the likelihood of making an inappropriate decision.

# Routine versus non-routine decision making //

Straightforward problems are resolved by making routine decisions based on predetermined policy or procedure. For example, rules of professional conduct dictate how accountants should respond when clients understate their taxable income. These types of decisions are known as **routine** or **mechanical decisions** and form the bulk of workplace decisions. However, many problems are not straightforward and require decisions that are unique and non-recurring without clear-cut solutions. These types of decisions are known as **non-routine decisions** and although they form only a small percentage of the overall number of decisions made in the workplace, they usually carry the greatest significance. Non-routine decisions can arise in a number of ways; these include the resolution of new and unfamiliar problems and a genuine moral dilemma involving competing interests or claims. Although routine decisions are determined by reference to predetermined policy or procedure, the non-recurring nature of non-routine decisions means that predetermined polices or procedures are unlikely to exist. Therefore, determining non-routine decisions is best done by following a structured procedure known as a decision-making model.

# The process of conventional decision making //

**Decision-making models**, such as the one presented in figure 4.1, provide a systematic framework to arrive at the best course of action. The decision-making model presented in figure 4.1, generally known as the conventional decision-making model, is based on assumptions of rationality, which means, as rational human beings people will seek the best course of action after taking into account all known variables. The process of conventional decision making comprises three levels. The first level is concerned with identifying and clarifying the problem. The second level outlines the steps to making an informed decision. The third level deals with implementing and evaluating the decision to assess its effectiveness and to see what can be learned from the exercise. The eight identifiable steps in conventional decision making are briefly described in this section, and illustrated with an example involving the purchase of an asset (see 'In practice: The conventional decision making process — an illustration'). Familiarising yourself with the process of conventional decision making is important because it forms the basis of the 'AAA' ethical decision-making model, which is discussed in detail later in this chapter.

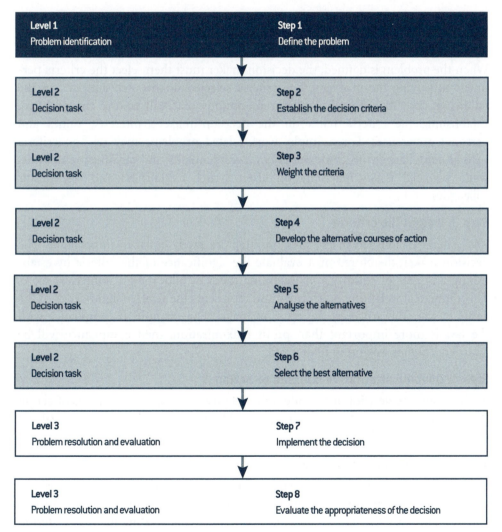

| Level 1 Problem identification | Step 1 Define the problem |
| Level 2 Decision task | Step 2 Establish the decision criteria |
| Level 2 Decision task | Step 3 Weight the criteria |
| Level 2 Decision task | Step 4 Develop the alternative courses of action |
| Level 2 Decision task | Step 5 Analyse the alternatives |
| Level 2 Decision task | Step 6 Select the best alternative |
| Level 3 Problem resolution and evaluation | Step 7 Implement the decision |
| Level 3 Problem resolution and evaluation | Step 8 Evaluate the appropriateness of the decision |

FIGURE 4.1    The conventional decision-making model

# Level 1: Problem identification //

### Step 1: Define the problem

The obscurity of problem identification is a major obstacle to effective decision making. Problems rarely come with warning signs that identify themselves as problems and, in many cases, what may often be a problem to one person may not be a problem to another. Accurately defining the problem is arguably the most important step of the decision-making process because it establishes the reason(s) for making a decision and it ensures the right answer to the right problem. Although problem identification is subjective, people must acknowledge that problems exist and be alerted to their existence. The remaining steps depend on the decision maker identifying the right problem.

# Level 2: The decision task //

### Step 2: Establish the decision criteria

When the problem is defined, the decision maker must then select the criteria pertinent to solving the problem. The criteria selected in this step are used in the following steps to evaluate the different options that will resolve the problem. Establishing the criteria relies on the decision maker's interests, values and personal preferences. For example, work-related problems may rely on criteria such as compliance with company policy, confidentiality and maximising revenue, while personal issues may rely on criteria such as fairness and respect for colleagues.

### Step 3: Weight the criteria

The criteria established in the previous step are rarely equal in importance. The decision maker, therefore, must evaluate the significance of the criteria by establishing an order of priority and weighting them by allocating a numerical score. This numerical weighting is arbitrary and represents the relative significance of the various criteria awarded by the decision maker. For example, if compliance with the law is more important than profit maximisation, then compliance will be awarded a higher weighting than profit.

### Step 4: Develop alternative courses of action

At this point the decision maker identifies all possible alternative courses of action that are likely to succeed in resolving the problem. No attempt is made to evaluate the alternatives at this stage.

### Step 5: Analyse the alternatives

Having identified a number of alternatives, the decision maker is now in a position to assess the different courses of action. The decision maker must critically analyse and evaluate each alternative course of action by giving a rating for each criterion developed and prioritised in the second and third steps. In straightforward decisions such as asset purchases, some ratings will be objective, such as performance and reliability, because these evaluations can be based on information provided by the manufacturer and independent test results. However some ratings will be based on personal judgment and are therefore subjective, such as style and appearance. Despite the lack of objectivity, assessment is necessary to compare the alternatives. Due to the complex nature of non-routine decisions, some criteria may be difficult to quantify by simple rating. Nonetheless, each alternative must be evaluated against the criteria in terms of its strengths, weaknesses, advantages, disadvantages, benefits and harms.

### Step 6: Select the best alternative

The final step in the decision task is to select a course of action by choosing the alternative that produces the greatest overall value. In this step, the alternative courses of action are assessed by assigning a total score for each criterion. The total score for each criterion is determined by multiplying the weighting determined in step 3 and the rating determined in step 5. The scores for each criterion are then summed to determine the overall value for each alternative course of action. The alternative with the greatest overall value is the best choice. In some cases the best alternative is not always clear because the overall scores for different alternatives are similar. In these circumstances, a compromise is sometimes necessary, particularly when the ratings are difficult to quantify. At this point, you should refer to 'In practice: The conventional decision-making process — an illustration' for a demonstration of the steps discussed thus far.

## IN PRACTICE

### The conventional decision-making process — an illustration

Assume David, after careful consideration of his annual work plan, has decided to purchase a new computer. The problem confronting David (*step 1*) is that he is unsure which brand he should buy. Contemplating his needs, David has identified four criteria (compatibility, quality, price and portability) that he believes are important to this decision (*step 2*). These criteria, presented in order of importance, are weighted accordingly. The weighting begins with a score of 4 for compatibility through to 1 for portability (*step 3*). David has investigated a number of recommended brands and identified two options that serve his needs, Brand A and Brand B (*step 4*). David examines the features of both brands of computer and assigns a rating between 1 and 10 (lowest to highest) for each criterion (*step 5*). The weights, ratings and total values are provided in table 4.1 on the following page.

TABLE 4.1 The conventional decision-making process — an illustration

| CRITERIA | WEIGHT (a) | BRAND A | | BRAND B | |
|---|---|---|---|---|---|
| | | RATING (b) | VALUE (a × b) | RATING (c) | VALUE (a × c) |
| Compatability | 4 | 5 | 20 | 8 | 32 |
| Quality | 3 | 9 | 27 | 8 | 24 |
| Price | 2 | 5 | 10 | 9 | 18 |
| Portability | 1 | 6 | 6 | 3 | 3 |
| **Total Value** | | | **63** | | **77** |

The total value for each criterion is determined by multiplying the weighted criteria with the assigned rating. A variation in the assigned scores (weights or ratings) will alter the total value and possibly the decision. The best alternative is determined by summing the total values for each criterion. In this example, Brand B produces the greatest overall value and is therefore the preferred choice of the two alternative computers (*step 6*). Even though computer Brand A rates more highly in quality and portability, Brand B is superior in compatibility and price, resulting in the greatest overall gain. The mechanistic process of decision making associated with this model makes it appealing for resolving simple problems. However, this model is equally applicable in solving more complex problems involving difficult choices. Although defining and weighting the criteria may be difficult at times, it remains an important part of the decision-making process and should not be ignored in favour of less sophisticated methods of decision making.

## Level 3: Problem resolution and evaluation //

### Steps 7 and 8: Implement and evaluate the decision

An effective decision must be conveyed and implemented, otherwise the decision will fail. Sound implementation is just as important as the decision itself. The decision must be appraised to determine whether the problem has been resolved and to provide feedback on its progress. Since many decisions are made based on imperfect information, some decisions will inevitably be wrong. Evaluation enables people to learn from the experience and improve their decision-making skills. In an ideal world, if the problem is not resolved, the decision-making process should be repeated until a satisfactory remedy is attained.

# Professional judgment and decision making in accounting //

One theme that emerges throughout this book is the need for accountants to exercise judgment and make decisions. For example, financial accountants continually deal with measurement, recognition and disclosure issues. Although one purpose of accounting standards is to reduce the number of decisions required in the preparation of financial reports, even the most comprehensive accounting standards require some judgment. It is impracticable for accounting standards to cover every possible circumstance; therefore, judgment is needed in relating the relevant standard to the particular circumstances of the problem. Decision making is evident in all fields of accounting, not just financial accounting. For example, in auditing, accountants are continually making decisions on sample size, materiality and the reliability of audit evidence. Management accountants make decisions concerning the allocation of costs, overhead recovery rates and capital budgeting. Irrespective of their level of responsibility, or their field of employment, accountants spend a great deal of time making decisions, which are then used to evaluate their performance.

Brooks (2004) claims that few financial scandals involving accountants are the result of methodological errors. Instead, most scandals are the result of errors in judgment. Some accountants' errors in judgment result from the sheer complexity of the problem at hand, but most are caused by the lack of attention given to ethical and professional values such as honesty, integrity, objectivity, due care, confidentiality, and the commitment to the interests of others before their own. In many cases such errors are accidental, but irrespective of the cause of such errors, the results are always the same. A lack of attention to ethical values, in most cases, brings the greatest harm to those most reliant on the accountant's judgment, typically clients, employers and, ultimately, the public. As explained in chapter 3, continual revelations of ethical transgressions by accountants will eventually lead to a weakening of society's belief that accountants act in the public interest, which will adversely impact the credibility of the accounting profession. Questions concerning public confidence are rarely directed at the accountant's ability to do his or her job properly but the ability to exercise proper judgment in difficult or complex situations.

In chapter 3, we defined an accountant as a professional who is an authority on the subject and application of accounting to remedy the problems presented by clients or employers. It goes without saying that expert knowledge in accounting is a requisite for professional judgment but the acquisition of knowledge is only the first step to becoming a professional. A professional must be able to identify and solve complex, unstructured problems. Accountants, as professionals, must have the ability to solve problems where routine or mechanical solutions are not apparent. It is not enough to offer clients or employers a menu of alternatives from which to choose; accountants are expected to make recommendations and act on them. Therefore, **professional judgment** is the process of making a decision that is carried out with objectivity, integrity and in recognition of the responsibilities to those affected by the judgment. Professional judgment, like **decision making**, involves making a choice from a number of alternative courses of action to resolve a problem or achieve a desired result. For the purpose of this chapter, the terms professional judgment and decision making are used interchangeably.

As the profession evolves, accountants will move further from their traditional role of gathering, measuring, recording and then auditing information, and closer to shouldering the burden of risks that come with leadership and making key decisions. However, the problem with an accounting industry that is obsessed with growth, and an ever-increasing range of services that appear to compromise independence, is that it brings new and unfamiliar challenges; these threaten to exceed the capabilities and resources of accountants, who are expected to meet those demands. It is under these conditions that poor judgment often results; consequently, accountants will face many new challenges that will test their judgment skills. Accountants, as principals, must develop strong leadership skills and the ability to make decisions that deal with difficult trade-offs.

## Ethical decision making //

In general, a course of action is justified when there are better reasons in favour of it than there are against it. In ethical decision making, this means showing that there are more or better ethical reasons in favour of a course of action than against it. Therefore, the chief differences between decision making and ethical decision making are the attention given to ethical values in the decision task and the aim of finishing with a decision that will be judged as ethical because it is supported by principles of good conduct. **Ethical decision making** is therefore the 'process of identifying a problem, generating alternatives, and choosing among them so that alternatives selected maximise the most important ethical values while achieving the intended goal' (Guy 1990, p. 39).

In the workplace, people often resolve difficult problems using easily understood **decision rules**. Decision rules, or rules of thumb, are appealing in difficult circumstances because they reduce the complexity of decision making by reducing the number of alternatives that must be considered. For example, the test of materiality states that a misstatement of 5 per cent or less is deemed immaterial. Based on this decision rule, auditors are no longer required to consider and make judgments on every misstatement, only misstatements greater than 5 per cent. Although decision rules may not always give the best results, they are often justified on the basis that they give adequate or satisfactory results. The problem with decision rules is that they can ignore the moral component of decision making and are therefore inadequate for dealing with ethical problems.

Ethical decision making is more than just making a choice; it involves critical thinking that acknowledges a range of views and values that occasionally conflict. In these circumstances, ethical decision making is difficult because it involves making a choice from a number of equally acceptable courses of action. In other words, the ethical dilemma does not present one clear course of action, but a choice between two or more 'right' courses of action or, alternatively, a choice between two or more 'wrong' courses of action. Choosing the lesser of two evils or the greater of two advantages is unlikely to satisfy everyone and could invite expressions of dissent. However, by adopting a structured approach to ethical making, the decision maker is better placed to defend their decision with reasoned and sound ethical judgment.

## The hierarchy of ethical decision making //

In accounting as well as business, **ethical decisions** can be viewed as a hierarchy consisting of three distinct levels. The first and simplest form of ethical decision making is lawful decisions that are governed by legally binding rules. In most cases, lawful decisions will lead to ethical decisions; however, this may not always be the case. Some laws are outdated and may not reflect current societal values. On some issues, laws may be silent or even permit questionable behaviour such as gambling and prostitution. Therefore, to suggest that lawful decisions are always ethical decisions is incorrect; it is more accurate to claim that the law sets the minimum acceptable standard for decision making and occasionally the decision maker must look beyond the law to arrive at an ethical decision.

Professional obligations and duties espoused in the codes of conduct form the basis for the next level of ethical decision making. These types of decisions are not legally binding but are based on a commitment to professionalism that is built on serving the public interest. This form of decision making goes beyond mere compliance with the law and is based on a professional and ethically binding commitment to the principles of professional conduct at the expense of self-interest. Accounting is clearly placed in this level of the hierarchy and the principles of professional conduct should be the first checkpoint in any situation involving professional conflict. Therefore, when faced with moral confusion, the accountant should turn to the Joint Code of Professional Conduct (the joint code) for guidance. The joint code and professional responsibilities were discussed in detail in chapter 3.

The joint code is particularly useful in resolving straightforward problems of a professional nature. However, there are many instances where a convenient rule is not always available and, even if a rule is available, it may appear to be inadequate to deal with complex issues. In this situation, the accountant may need to turn to the next and highest level of decision making — the level where decisions are made within a defined sense of right and wrong, which is based on moral values and philosophical reasoning, such as the normative theories of ethics discussed in chapter 2. In practical terms, making such decisions is best achieved by a following structured procedure known as an ethical decision-making model, which incorporates moral principles. An **ethical decision-making model**, like the AAA model, discussed in the next section, is a procedural model that directs the decision maker to take account of the norms and rules pertaining to the situation and to give a moral perspective to the problem and the alternative courses of action and their implications. In brief, it is a systematic method of obtaining a responsible and ethical decision.

## Ethical decision-making models //

According to the American Accounting Association (AAA) (1990), accounting educators play an important role in alerting students to ethical dilemmas that they may confront as professionals. However, until recently, the extent to which ethics was taught to accounting students was constrained by the dearth of ethics cases and teaching materials available. This prompted the AAA to develop a book of cases relating to professional conduct and ethical issues in each of the functional disciplines of accounting (AAA 1990). The book, *Ethics in the accounting curriculum — cases and readings*, contains real-world cases supported by analysis and discussion using an ethical decision-making model, which has since been known as the **AAA model**.

The AAA model, based on the ethical decision-making model developed by Langenderfer and Rockness (1989), is a seven-step ethical decision-making model that students can adopt in their professional lives for the resolution of ethical dilemmas. The purpose of the seven-step model is to develop a systematic approach to making decisions that can be used in any situation that has ethical implications. In 2002, the Australian accounting profession officially adopted the AAA model. CPA Australia and the Institute of Chattered Accountants in Australia published the model in a joint guidance note entitled, GN 1 Members in Business Guidance Statement. The purpose of the guidance note is to provide members with a framework (AAA model) to resolve ethical problems. Paragraph 3.1 refers members to section A.6 Resolution of Ethical Conflict of the joint code, which states that, when faced with a significant ethical conflict, members should first follow the established policies of their employer. If this does not resolve the problem or the employer's policies do not extend to the particular problem, members should consider applying an ethical decision-making model such as the AAA model. The guidance note is non-mandatary and advisory only, but using the model ensures that members can adequately defend and justify their decisions by showing that it was made in a systematic manner which clearly reflected a consideration of their duties and the consequences of different actions in particular circumstances (section 3.2). Before considering the AAA model, we will first explore what it means to follow the established policies of the employer.

## The ethics decision tree //

The procedures for dealing with ethical conflict within an organisation are outlined in section A.6 Resolution of Ethical Conflicts of the joint code. When employees are challenged with an ethical issue, they should first follow the established policies of their employer to try and resolve the conflict. If established policies fail to resolve the dilemma, employees should discuss the problem with their immediate superior. If the immediate superior is believed to be involved in the conflict or satisfactory resolution cannot be achieved, the problem should be presented to the next higher managerial level. If the next higher superior is the chief executive officer, or equivalent, the acceptable reviewing authority may be a group such as the audit committee, executive committee, board of directors, board of trustees or owners. Contact with people above the immediate superior should normally be initiated only with the superior's knowledge; this assumes of course that the superior is not involved in the dilemma. If the ethical conflict remains unresolved, employees might have no other recourse than to resign from their employer, in order to disassociate themselves from the unethical activity. Consistent with the process described above, the American Institute of Certified Public Accountants (AICPA) (2002) has developed a decision tree (see figure 4.2) to help accountants walk through the process of resolving an ethical issue at work.

## The AAA model //

Although there is no generally accepted formula for ethical decision making that can easily be based on a determinate set of rules, there are important elements that distinguish ethical decision making from routine decision making. These include the careful consideration of the moral values (ethical principles) that are relevant to the myriads of alternatives and an awareness of the range of interests involved in specific decisions. Analysing the elements is best done by breaking up the problem into smaller components to identify the ethical implications of the decision. In this section, we discuss the AAA model of ethical decision making and its various components. The seven steps that comprise the AAA ethical decision-making model are displayed in figure 4.3 and discussed in detail in this section. When reading the commentary below, you should observe the similarities in the AAA model with the process of conventional decision making discussed earlier in this chapter, noting that the key difference between conventional decision making and ethical decision making is the attention given to ethical values and principles.

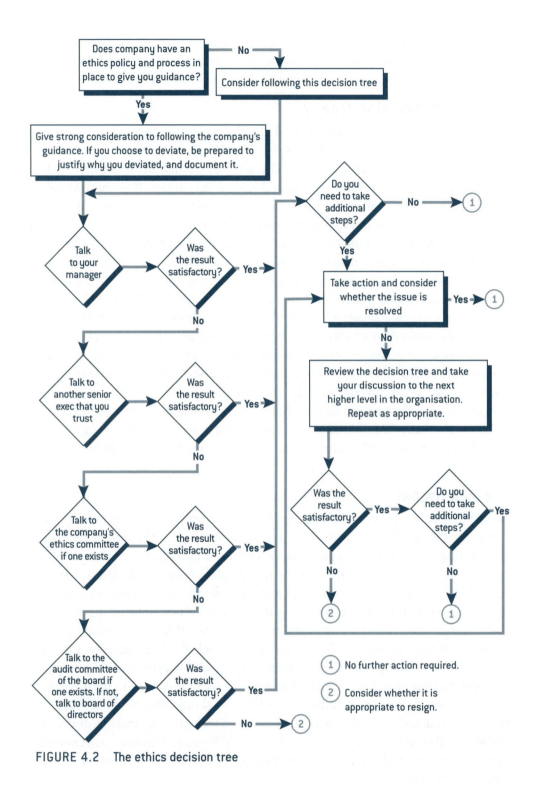

FIGURE 4.2    The ethics decision tree

1. What are the facts of the case?
2. What are the ethical issues in the case?
3. What are the norms, principles, and values related to the case?
4. What are the alternative courses of action?
5. What is the best course of action that is consistent with the norms, principles and values identified in step 3?
6. What are the consequences of each possible course of action?
7. What is the decision?

FIGURE 4.3   The AAA 7-step ethical decision-making model
*Source:* American Accounting Association 1990; Langenderfer & Rockness, 1989, p. 68.

## Step 1: What are the facts of the case?

The first step in the decision-making process is to determine the cause of the dilemma by learning how and why the dilemma occurred. Unlike step 1 of the conventional decision-making model, which aims to define the problem accurately, this model aims to learn as much as possible about the dilemma. Defining the ethical issues is undertaken in step 2. An important part of the problem-finding process is to enquire into the history of the dilemma. Considering the history of the dilemma will more likely determine the root of the issues. In identifying the facts it is important to ask the right questions, otherwise key issues may be overlooked or a decision may be the right answer to the wrong problem. Questions normally asked in this step include Who? What? Where? When? and How? Informed and ethical decisions require full knowledge of the facts; therefore, the purpose of these questions is to assemble as much information as possible. It is not until all the major facts are identified that the dilemma can be clarified and accurately defined.

The reliability of the facts and impartiality are crucial to the quality of the decision. Collecting data should be neutral and not based on loyalties. If personal prejudices, loyalties or other barriers enter at this point, the definition of the issues in step 2 will be distorted and irrelevant information gathered. Impartiality is achieved by collecting as many facts as possible and by viewing the situation from the perspectives of various key stakeholders. By soliciting the opinions of various stakeholders, the decision maker can develop a sense of balance with the issue. In practice, people often avoid gathering information from other parties because they feel it is time consuming, inconvenient or uncomfortable. No matter how difficult, this is an important task that should not be overlooked.

### Step 2: What are the ethical issues in the case?

This question comprises two components. First, the primary stakeholders are identified, and second, the ethical issues must be clearly defined. Each component is discussed separately in this section.

### Step 2a: List the primary stakeholders

**Stakeholders** are defined as people or entities that are affected by the actions or decisions of another. Decisions are seldom made in a vacuum — a number of parties including the decision maker are often involved in the dilemma. In this step, the decision maker is obliged to identify all affected parties. Stakeholders can include shareholders, management, employees and the local community. The analysis of the stakeholders should not be restricted to human beings; the notion of stakeholders extends to the environment as well as institutions such as governments and professional associations.

### Step 2b: Define the ethical issues

The resolution of a straightforward problem is a relatively simple exercise because it is a matter of choosing the right course of action. In contrast, issues or dilemmas do not have a single right answer but a number of competing alternatives without clear resolution. Therefore, an **ethical issue** arises when the alternative courses of action give rise to positive and negative consequences. Identifying and labelling ethical issues and the competing interests of those affected by them is an important part of the resolution process. In this step it is important to think about ethical issues as alternative courses of action with competing interests between the stakeholders in terms of benefits, harms, rights, duties, principles and claims. For example, in accounting, the right to know on the part of investors may conflict with the entity's right to confidentiality. As an ethical issue, this is normally expressed as the investors' right to know versus the entity's right to confidentiality.

### Step 3: What are the norms, principles and values related to the case?

Unfortunately, the terms **norms**, **principles** and **values** are not defined, but in general they represent standards, rules and beliefs that guide acceptable and morally 'good' conduct. The terms norms, principles and values are interchangeable and for the remainder of this chapter they will simply be referred to as values. Examples of values include the profit motive, harm, integrity, loyalty and respect for individuals. The ethical issues identified in step 2 are stated in terms of competing interests, which may not explicitly enunciate the values. In this step, decision makers must consider and identify the values associated with the ethical issues and explain their effect on the individual, company, society and the profession. It is important to identify these items so that they are clearly stated for the comparative analysis required in step 5.

Langenderfer and Rockness (1989) and the AAA (1990) provide little guidance in defining and explaining values, so we turn to other sources to guide us in this part of the decision process. Mary Guy (1990, pp. 14–19) identified 10 core values that provide the benchmarks for ethical decision making. According to Guy (1990), the evaluation of ethical issues in respect of the 10 core values helps clarify the ethics of a dilemma and the implications of alternative actions. Guy's 10 core values (*caring, honesty, accountability, promise keeping, pursuit of excellence, loyalty, fairness, integrity, respect for others*, and *responsible citizenship*) are briefly described in figure 4.4 and can be used to identify the values required in this step of the AAA model. In addition to Guy's 10 core values, the guidance statement (GN 1 Members in Business Guidance Statement) stresses the importance of applying the fundamental principles of professional conduct to resolving ethical issues. To this end, the principles of professional conduct should be considered alongside Guy's 10 core values when dealing with this step of the AAA model. The fundamental principles of professional conduct, discussed in detail in chapter 3, have been reproduced in figure 4.5 for your convenience.

| | |
|---|---|
| **Caring:** | treating people as ends in themselves and not as a means to an end. |
| **Honesty:** | being truthful and not deceiving or distorting. |
| **Accountability:** | accepting responsibility for decisions and their consequences, setting the example for others and avoiding the appearance of impropriety. |
| **Promise keeping:** | keeping commitments and being worthy of trust. |
| **Pursuit of excellence:** | striving to be as good as one can be. |
| **Loyalty:** | being faithful and loyal to those with whom one has dealings. |
| **Fairness:** | being open minded, willing to admit error, avoid favouritism and not take undue advantage of another's adversities. |
| **Integrity:** | using independent judgment, avoiding conflicts of interest, and acting on one's convictions. |
| **Respect for others:** | recognising each person's right to privacy, self-determination, having respect for human dignity, and providing full information so that others can make informed decisions. |
| **Responsible citizenship:** | actions should be in accord with societal values and obey just laws. |

FIGURE 4.4  Mary Guy's 10 core values

*Source:* Guy, M 1990, *Ethical decision making in everyday work situations*, Quorum Books, New York, pp. 14–19.

**The public interest**

Members must at all times safeguard the interests of their clients and employers provided that they do not conflict with the duties and loyalties owed to the community and its laws.

**Integrity**

Members must be straightforward, honest and sincere in their approach to professional work.

**Objectivity**

Members must be fair and must not allow prejudice, conflict of interest or bias to override their objectivity.

**Independence**

Members must be and should be seen to be free of any interest which might be regarded, whatever its actual effect, as being incompatible with integrity and objectivity.

**Confidentiality**

Members must respect the confidentiality of information acquired in the course of their work and must not disclose any such information to a third party without specific authority or unless there is a legal or professional duty to disclose it.

**Technical and professional standards**

Members must carry out their professional work in accordance with the technical and professional standards relevant to that work.

**Competence and due care**

Members must perform professional services with due care, competence and diligence [and] refrain from performing any services which they are not competent to carry out.

**Ethical behaviour**

Members must conduct themselves in a manner consistent with the good reputation of their profession and refrain from any conduct, which might bring discredit to their profession.

FIGURE 4.5   Fundamental principles of professional conduct

*Source:* Section B of the Joint Code of Professional Conduct (CPA Australia and the Institute of Chartered Accountants in Australia, 2002).

### Step 4: What are the alternative courses of action?

In this step, decision makers should list the major alternative courses of action that will resolve the problem, including alternatives that may involve compromise. Many ethical problems normally involve choices. If you cannot list more than two alternatives, you are probably not thinking hard enough. It is important to list more than two options irrespective of the method used to arrive at a decision. This is because two options often represent the extremes. The solution is never black or white and you should think in terms of compromise even if compromise does not conform to your personal notion of what is right.

## Step 5: What is the best course of action that is consistent with the norms, principles and values identified in step 3?

At this point, all alternatives are considered in light of the values identified in step 3. In this step, the decision maker should pause and reflect on the values to determine whether one value, or a combination of values, is so compelling that the proper alternative is clear. For example, correcting a defect in a product that is almost certain to cause a loss of life is paramount if the decision maker is to respect the right to life or health and safety. One problem in this step is that values often conflict. In this situation the decision maker must list the values in the order in which they are to be honoured. Ideally, the decision maker will determine the most important values and in later steps, weigh the probable impact of each alternative on the values and choose the alternative that maximises the essential values. Unfortunately, there is no objective measure for ranking values but with practice a pattern may emerge. Ethical decision making maximises the most important values while acknowledging that trade-offs are inevitable (Guy 1990).

## Step 6: What are the consequences of each possible course of action?

Focusing on the consequences of alternative courses of action can often reveal an unanticipated result of major importance. Therefore, each alternative identified in step 4 should be evaluated not only in terms of its values but also in terms of its short-term, long-term, positive and negative consequences. In effect, this step requires an evaluation of the consequences from two perspectives. First, whether the consequences uphold or violate the values identified in step 3, and second, how the decision is likely to affect the major stakeholders. This question brings to light the potential harm, physical or emotional, that may occur to stakeholders.

Problems arise when the evaluation of the alternatives depends on non-quantifiable outcomes. Consequently, step 6 has been criticised for its lack of measurability (AAA 1990). As stated in chapter 2, not all consequences have an easily determined unitary or monetary value and assessing the outcomes becomes difficult. One solution is to weigh the consequences similar to the method shown in the process of conventional decision making. The AAA (1990) suggest a scoring system ranging from +3 to −3. Numerical weighting is important to give relative significance to outcomes, principles and norms. Additionally, the decision maker must also consider the likelihood that each plausible course of action will succeed or fail. The likelihood of an outcome is a sign of its significance. For example, the loss of a major client is a serious loss. However, if such an outcome is improbable, then its overall importance is diminished.

## Step 7: What is the decision?

The final step requires the decision maker to balance the consequences for each course of action and select an appropriate alternative. If a decision was not reached in step 5, then no principle or value was determinative. Therefore, the alternative that produces the highest overall gain in terms of its consequences should be the choice. Properly identifying and evaluating the consequences in step 6 is critical to selecting a course of action in step 7.

The seven-step model is a useful device for working through a dilemma in an orderly manner and ensuring that the decision maker identifies and considers all of the important issues when analysing the case. In the resolution of an ethical dilemma, it is important to address the seven steps in the order that they are presented. To do otherwise may result in faulty analysis and an inappropriate conclusion. A comprehensive example illustrating the application of the AAA model is presented below in 'In practice: Change the bottom line'. You should read this case carefully to appreciate the difficulties in resolving problems of an ethical nature.

## IN PRACTICE

### Change the bottom line

**Key participants**
Susan Martinazzo — Management Accountant
Harry Fitzsimmons — Divisional Manager

**Facts of the case**
Susan is the management accountant working in the plastics division of a large multinational conglomerate. In accordance with the organisation's decentralised operating model, Susan works for Harry. Harry is the divisional manager for plastics and has a background in engineering.

Susan's responsibilities include the preparation of a monthly management pack that is provided to the divisional manager and forwarded to the organisation's national office together with the divisional manager's monthly review.

The plastics market has reached a mature stage and the division's results have been stable for a number of years. In addition, the industry is under threat from increasing competition as a result of lower barriers to entry and changes in technology. Susan's latest monthly management pack reflects the continuation in the decline in the division's profit margins and no growth in sales.

Harry is anxious about the plastics division's future. For a number of months, the division has failed to meet the organisation's benchmark rate of return. Harry has heard from a reliable source that the national office is seeking to divest the plastics division or, in the absence of a sale, abandon the division. The division employs 35 people.

Harry has reviewed the monthly management pack and instructed Susan to change the accounting treatment of unearned income to bring forward the recognition of sales income, and to increase the useful life of depreciable assets.

Susan has tried to explain to Harry that the national office determines the accounting policies for income recognition and asset depreciation. Harry replies that he is too busy to delve into the accounting 'mumbo jumbo'; Susan is again instructed to make the changes or she may be fired.

What should Susan do?

### Application of the AAA ethical decision-making model

*Step 1: What are the facts of the case?*
- Susan, a management accountant in the plastics division is responsible for the preparation of a monthly management pack that is provided to the divisional manager and the national office.
- The plastics division has failed to meet the organisation's benchmark rate of return for a number of months.
- The plastics division employs 35 people. The division is up for sale, failing which, the division will be abandoned.
- Harry has instructed Susan to change the accounting treatment for unearned income and to lower depreciation expenses.
- The national office sets the accounting policies for income recognition and asset depreciation.
- Susan reports directly to Harry. Harry does not have an accounting background. He has threatened to fire Susan if she fails to change the numbers.

*Step 2a: List the primary stakeholders*
- Susan Martinazzo
- Harry Fitzsimmons
- Directors of the organisation
- Shareholders of the organisation
- Creditors of the organisation
- Plastics division employees

*Step 2b: Define the ethical issues*
- Susan's responsibility to Harry versus her independence and objectivity
- Susan's responsibility to protect the interests of the company and shareholders versus her responsibility to Harry
- Susan's wish to help protect the employment of the division's employees versus her duty to protect the interests of the organisation and shareholders
- Overall, Susan's problem is how to respond to Harry's instructions.

*Step 3: What are the norms, principles, and values related to the case?*

- Integrity (Susan may not supply information that is misleading or false.)
- Objectivity (The interests of Susan's employer should not affect her judgment.)
- Independence (Susan may not bend the rules despite the pressure applied by her superior.)
- Technical and professional standards (Susan should carry out her work in accordance with technical and professional standards relevant to that work, including the national office accounting policies.)

*Step 4: What are the alternative courses of action?*

- Susan can do nothing.
- Susan can try to raise the issue with the accounting staff at the national office as an accounting issue.
- Susan can try to raise the issue with management at the national office as an unresolved issue between Harry and herself.
- Susan can resign.
- Susan can try once more to explain to Harry that accounting policies cannot be changed at a division level.
- Susan can follow Harry's instructions.

*Step 5: What is the best course of action that is consistent with the norms, principles and values identified in step 3?*

- Susan can do nothing — may lead to her dismissal even though to do nothing is consistent with the principles
- Susan can try to raise the issue with the accounting staff at the national office as an accounting issue — may be consistent with the principles but it may not resolve the issue with Harry and may lead to her dismissal
- Susan can try to raise the issue with management at national office as an unresolved issue between Harry and herself — this may be consistent with the principles but may have a detrimental impact on Susan's or Harry's career aspirations.
- Susan can resign — may lead to the required changes being made to the pack to the detriment of the organisation and shareholders.
- Susan can try once more to explain to Harry that accounting policies cannot be changed at a division level — consistent with the principles and affords the opportunity for resolution with Harry (e.g. it may be that the income recognition for sales should be brought forward).
- Susan can follow Harry's instructions — a failure to comply with the principles.

*Step 6: What are the consequences of each possible course of action?*

- Susan can do nothing.
  - may lead to personal costs due to Susan's dismissal. In the interim, Harry's recommended changes may be made to the pack, to the detriment of the organisation and shareholders

- will result in Susan complying with the fundamental principles and with her responsibility to the organisation and shareholders
- if the pack remains unchanged, may lead to the redundancy of staff in the division.

- Susan can try to raise the issue with the accounting staff at the national office as an accounting issue.
  - likely to confirm that Susan can only change the accounting treatment of income and depreciation where there are appropriate grounds to do so
  - will not resolve the issue between Harry and Susan.
- Susan can try to raise the issue with management at the national office as an unresolved issue between Harry and herself.
  - may have a detrimental effect on Harry's career aspirations
  - may result in Susan being rewarded for her objectivity and independence
  - alternatively, may have a detrimental effect on Susan's career aspirations with the organisation.
- Susan can resign.
  - has a personal cost
  - may result in Harry's recommended changes being made to the pack, to the detriment of the organisation and shareholders.
- Susan can try once more to explain to Harry that accounting policies cannot be changed at a division level:
  - may resolve the issue between Harry and Susan
  - may cause Harry to refuse to withdraw the instruction and instigate disciplinary action against Susan.
- Susan can follow Harry's instructions:
  - may cause the pack to be false and misleading
  - may diminish the usefulness of the pack if it is no longer comparable to previous results and the results of other divisions
  - may result in a reduction in organisation and shareholder wealth.

*Step 7: What is the decision?*

In the light of the analysis, Susan could adopt the following plan. First, Susan can try once more to explain to Harry that the national office determines accounting policies and that a change in accounting policy must be disclosed in the statutory accounts. If this fails to resolve the issue, then Susan could explain to Harry that she would need to raise the matter as an accounting issue with the accounting department in the national office. If this fails to resolve the issue and if Harry commences disciplinary action against Susan, then Susan should explain the basis of her actions in writing to Harry and to management at the national office.

*Source:* Guidance Note 1 Members in Business Guidance Statement (CPA Australia and ICAA, 2003)

## The AAA model: a critique //

Some people treat ethical dilemmas as unresolvable conflicts. By giving them irresolvable status, ethical dilemmas are placed in the 'too hard' basket in the hope that they will eventually fade. However, most so-called unresolvable dilemmas can be resolved by employing a model of ethical decision making. To this end, the AAA model helps to dispel the myth that ethical problems are unresolvable. As stated earlier, most ethical dilemmas require a choice among several equally acceptable alternatives. The AAA model assists the decision maker to work through the maze of issues and select the alternative that maximises the values central to the dilemma.

According to Armstrong (1990), using the AAA model to resolve ethical conflicts will increase the likelihood that the decision maker will address moral topics that might have been omitted without this tool. Therefore, the advantage of using a model rather than a decision rule is that it encourages the decision maker to fully analyse the problem and to consider the alternatives and consequences from an ethical perspective. The AAA model achieves ethical analysis by incorporating normative principles of ethics (discussed in chapter 2) in the structure of the model. The AAA model blends **non-consequential** considerations (steps 3 and 5, which deal with norms, principles, and values) with **consequential** considerations (step 6 — utilitarian analysis). Using multiple ethical considerations (consequential and non-consequential) is a strength of the model because taking account of the two systems of ethical analysis provides insights from a number of perspectives, which is generally not achievable from a single theory. As stated in chapter 2, a range of theories provides different perspectives on the problem, which is likely to improve the awareness and understanding of the issues involved in the dilemma. In the end, an ethical outcome is likely.

However, the strength of employing two systems of ethical analysis is lost when the seven-step process lacks synthesis. In step 5, the decision maker is asked to make a decision on the values without consideration of consequences. At this point, the decision process may terminate and the model is essentially non-consequential. If a decision is not reached in step 5, consequences are then added to the process in step 6 to make a final decision in step 7. The alternative with the greatest overall value in terms of its consequences is the preferred course of action. The implication of ending with an assessment of the outcomes is that consequences will ultimately dominate the choice. Therefore, the AAA method of solving conflict is essentially utilitarian. According to Armstrong (1990), one ethical consideration should not dominate another; this is arguably an inherent weakness in the model.

Another strength of the model lies in its ease of application — it is a practical application of normative theories of ethics (Armstrong 1990). Mathison (1988) contends that abstract philosophical concepts such as utilitarianism, rights and justice theories are irrelevant to the needs of managerial decision makers. According to Mathison, these concepts are learned in the classroom but then discarded in real-world applications. The AAA model overcomes the limitation identified by Mathison by presenting ethical considerations in the form of ethical inquiry rather than abstract concepts. Restating the ethical considerations in the form of questions provides a practical approach to ethical problem solving. In this way, theories are no longer abstract concepts but questions used in ethical analysis.

In conclusion, if a problem should arise, evidence of ethical commitment by an organisation could act as a substantial defence against bitter accusations of misconduct. From this perspective, structured ethical decision making and subsequent behaviour is good risk management. In turn, ethical commitment enhances staff morale, which helps an organisation to recruit and retain skilled employees and reduce absenteeism.

## Ethical decision making in practice //

The application of a decision-making model does not guarantee an ethical decision. Decision making is largely a function of individual characteristics and the environment in which the decision maker works and lives. In this sense, rational decision making is constrained by a number of psychological and environmental factors. The purpose of this section is to highlight the forces that shape decisions to provide a better understanding of how and why decisions are actually made. There are two critical factors that shape an individual's choices in the workplace: the ethics of the individual and the environment in which the individual works.

Arguably, the greatest influence on decision making is the individual's personal ethics. **Personal ethics** is defined as the decision maker's level of moral development as measured by Kohlberg's theory of moral reasoning and development. According to Kohlberg (1969), a stage of moral development is a measure of a person's capacity to judge what is morally right. A detailed analysis of Kohlberg's theory is beyond the scope of this chapter (refer to chapter 2 for a discussion of moral development theory). In brief, however, Kohlberg's stage framework consists of three levels of moral development. At level 1, people are likely to act from self-interest, at level 2 they are influenced by peers and organisation policy, and at level 3, they place increased value on the rights of others regardless of general opinion or policy. As a rule, the higher people's moral development, the less dependent they are on outside influences and hence the more likely they are to resolve the problem autonomously.

As employees, individuals must contend with ongoing pressures caused by daily work activities and commitments. The demands of maintaining international competitiveness, improving productivity, and adapting to changes in technology have greatly increased workplace stress and time pressures. Consequently the environment has become a major influence on workplace decisions. In general, questionable decisions can result from an environment clouded by pressure and stress. Such an environment often leads to poor productivity, dissatisfaction, diminished creativity and poor quality decisions that would not have been made under less stressful circumstances. Similarly, the quality of the decision may also be affected by how much time the decision maker has in which to make the decision. Time pressures are significant because the decision maker may consider fewer factors and alternatives, and have restricted the time in which to gather information. The problem with the current environment is that accounting professionals are constantly working under pressure. Rather than simply accept sub-optimal decision making, accountants must learn how to make decisions under difficult conditions.

Although moral cognition provides the initial determination of a right or appropriate action, it is not sufficient to explain or predict behaviour. For example, a stressful work environment may cause a person to abandon their personal values in favour of decisions that are consistent with workplace values. Therefore, the extent to which an individual will make a decision consistent with their personal values will depend on how well they can resist the pressure of the work environment. According to Rest (1986) a person must have sufficient perseverance, ego strength and implementation skills to be able to follow through on his or her intentions.

In conclusion, the application of an ethical decision model does not guarantee a morally sound decision but a structured approach ensures that the decision is reached in a rational manner with coherent justification. Whether the individual adopts the ethical course is a separate issue and will often depend on the ethics of environment in which the individual works. However, if the factors that affect decision making are recognised and understood, then the decision maker is better placed to resist adverse influences.

## Summary //

Ethical decision making is more than a belief in the importance of ethics, it requires an ethical sensitivity to the implications of choices, the ability to evaluate ambiguous and incomplete facts, identify and prioritise moral claims, and the strength of character to implement the decision effectively. The AAA model provides a framework within which ethical issues can be identified, analysed and resolved. Ultimately, however, the application of these steps is often influenced by individual, environmental and contextual factors. In the next chapter, we consider the role of decision making in corporate governance systems — in particular, the roles and responsibilities of the board of directors and senior management.

## Key terms //

AAA model . . . p. 88
Consequential . . . p. 108
Decision rules . . . p. 94
Decision making . . . p. 94

# Questions //

**4.1** Define decision making and describe the difference between routine and non-routine decisions.

**4.2** Outline the steps involved in the process of conventional decision making.

**4.3** Why is defining the problem as important as the decision task itself?

**4.4** Refer to 'In practice: The conventional decision-making process — an illustration' on page 91. Further investigation by David revealed the following information.

| Criterion | Weight | Brand A Rating | Brand B Rating | Brand C Rating |
|-----------|--------|----------------|----------------|----------------|
| Compatability | 8 | 5 | 6 | 8 |
| Price | 8 | 5 | 5 | 8 |
| Warranty | 7 | 6 | 9 | 3 |
| Quality | 6 | 5 | 6 | 8 |
| Portability | 4 | 4 | 7 | 5 |
| Style | 1 | 9 | 7 | 5 |

**Required**

Based on the above information, which computer should David buy? Why?

**4.5** Describe the significance of ethical decision making in accounting.

**4.6** What is an ethical decision? Give an example of an ethical decision and explain why you think it is an ethical decision.

**4.7** Describe the hierarchy of ethical decision making.

**4.8** Why should an individual's personal code of ethics demand more than mere compliance with laws and regulations?

Describe the strengths and weaknesses of the AAA model as a tool for ethical decision making.

**4.10** What are personal ethics and how do they influence ethical decision making?

**4.11** What are the potential implications of stress and poor time management on decision making?

**4.12** Explain the relationship between the normative theories of ethics, principles of professional conduct, the conventional decision-making model, and the AAA ethical decision-making model.

**4.13** Troy, a trainee accountant, discovered that his superior was pilfering funds through the company's petty cash account. His superior is second in charge to the CEO. Assume Troy wants to deal with problem internally. What are his options?

**4.14** Felix Chan, an audit partner, is responsible for six support staff. Felix noticed that Tom, one of his staff, was regularly arriving late for work (up to 30 minutes per day), but was signing his time sheets as arriving at work on time. Felix issued a memo to all staff stating that their hours of employment (9.00 am to 5.00 pm) must be respected at all times and that tardiness would not be tolerated. The next morning all staff, including Tom, arrived at work on time. Felix was pleased with the outcome of his action. That same day, Felix's secretary left the office promptly at 5.00 pm, as did all his staff. However, many tasks that would normally be completed before his secretary went home were left for the next day. When Felix questioned his secretary on this matter, he replied, 'working hours finish at 5.00 pm. Goodbye!' Felix was stunned by his reaction.

**Required**
**a** What problem(s), if any, can you identify with Felix's decision to enforce punctuality?
**b** What would you have done if you were Felix?

**4.15** Gladys, a senior accountant, works with Dan, the CEO's nephew. Due to recent personal hardships, Dan has been drinking regularly at the local hotel. Dan's drinking has not affected his work duties until recently. Gladys has noticed that he has become less diligent in his approach to work, and it is affecting Gladys's performance. When Gladys approached Dan about this problem, he broke down and admitted to Gladys that he has a drinking problem. After some discussion, Dan made Gladys promise not to tell anyone about his drinking problem. Gladys believes that telling the CEO would be the best option for Dan. Should Gladys inform Dan's uncle, the CEO? Justify your answer by considering Guy's 10 core values.

## Half full or half empty

As with many of his audit staff counterparts across the country, Bill Turner spent the last day of the year performing inventory observation procedures. His assignment that 31 December included taking test measurements at a client's grain storage tower in a small regional town. Bill had measured grain inventories on two previous audits and was the in-charge accountant on this audit.

Bill's observations of the quantity of the grain fell 10 per cent below the client's records. Bill's attention was drawn to the discrepancy in the two measurements of what was in the tower because, in his judgment, such a gap was significant enough to be material. The resulting difference between the inventory as reported by the client and the audited amount was enough to cause a significant drop in net income, Bill documented his findings in the working papers and proposed an adjusting entry for the difference.

Upon delving further into the matter, Bill determined that a discrepancy in the grain inventory had also surfaced two months previously. The quantity of grain inventory, as reported by a government inspector at the time was also lower than that on the client's records. The difference on the inventory valuation, however, was not as great as that in Bill's tests. Still no adjustment to the client's records was made. This information was also documented in the working papers.

Prior to discussing the discrepancy with the client, Bill told Greg, the engagement partner, about the problem. Greg, who had substantial experience in the industry, advised Bill that this would be a sensitive issue with the client. He also pointed out that the grain inventories are notoriously difficult to measure, with the potential errors as large as 10 per cent. Greg promised that he would handle the matter personally and therefore told Bill not to discuss the discrepancy with the client. The partner kept the inventory working papers.

After completion of the fieldwork, Bill returned to the office to wrap up his work on the engagement. The inventory working papers were still not in the file. Upon Bill's inquiry, the partner handed him a new set of working papers. These working papers, which had been dated as of the audit date, had been signed off by Greg and substantiated the book amount. Bill's subsequent questioning of the partner revealed that Greg had personally performed additional work on the grain inventory after the client's year-end. Based on his own evidence gathering, the partner had substituted his own work papers for the documentation that Bill prepared. No evidence remained of Bill's proposed adjustments. An unqualified opinion was subsequently issued.

### Required

What should Bill do? Answer this question using the seven-step AAA ethical decision-making model.

## FURTHER RESOURCES AND WEBSITES //

Armstrong, MB, Ketz, JE & Owsen, D 2003, ' Ethics education in accounting: moving toward ethical motivation and ethical behaviour', *Journal of Accounting Education*, vol. 21, issue 1, pp. 1–16.

Bellus, D 1980, *Time management for professionals*, Professional Development Institute, University of North Texas, North Texas.

Bommer, M, Gratto, C, Gravander, J & Tuttle, M 1987, 'A behavioural model of ethical and unethical decision making', *Journal of Business Ethics*, vol. 6, pp. 265–80.

Collins, K & Killough, L 1989, 'Managing stress in public accounting', *Journal of Accountancy*, May, pp. 92–8.

Collins, KM 1993, 'Stress and departures from the public accounting profession: a study of gender differences', *Accounting Horizons*, vol. 7, no. 1, pp. 29–38.

Ford, RC & Richardson, WD 1994, 'Ethical decision making: a review of empirical literature', *Journal of Business Ethics*, vol. 13, no. 3, pp. 205–21.

Josephson Institute of Ethics 2002, *Making ethical decisions*, viewed 15 May 2003, www.josephsoninstitute.org.

Nash, L 1981, 'Ethics without the sermon', *Harvard Business Review*, vol. 59, pp. 79–90.

Reiter, SA 1996, 'The Kohlberg–Gilligan controversy: lessons for accounting ethics education', *Critical Perspectives on Accounting*, vol. 7, pp. 33–54.

St James Ethics Centre, 2003, *Ethical decision making*, viewed 27 September 2003, www.ethics.org.au.

## REFERENCES //

American Accounting Association 1990, *Ethics in the accounting curriculum — cases and readings*, ed. WW May, American Accounting Association, Sarasota, Florida.

American Institute of Certified Public Accountants 2002, Ethics decision tree for CPAs in business and industry, viewed 20 November 2003, www.aicpa.org.

Armstrong, MB 1990, 'Professional ethics and accounting education: a critique of the 8-step method', *Business and Professional Ethics Journal*, vol 9. nos 1 & 2, pp. 181–91.

Brooks, LJ 2004, *Business and professional ethics for directors, executives, and accountants*, 3rd edn, South-Western, Cincinnati, Ohio.

CPA Australia and the Institute of Chartered Accountants in Australia 2002, Joint code of professional conduct, *Members' handbook*, CPA and the Institute of Chartered Accountants in Australia, Melbourne.

CPA Australia and the Institute of Chartered Accountants in Australia, 2002 Joint Guidance Notes, GN 1 Members in Business Guidance Statement, Issued August 2002, *Members' handbook*. CPA and the Institute of Chartered Accountants in Australia, Melbourne.

Guy, M 1990, *Ethical decision making in everyday work situations*, Quorum Books, New York.

Kohlberg, L 1969, 'Stage and sequence: the cognitive developmental approach to socialization', in DA Goslin (ed.), *Handbook of socialization theory and research*, Rand McNally, New York, pp. 347–480.

Langenderfer, HQ & Rockness, JW 1989, 'Integrating ethics into the accounting curriculum: issues, problems, and solutions', *Issues in Accounting Education*, vol. 4, no.1, pp. 58–69.

Mathison, DL 1988, 'Business ethics cases and decision models: a call for relevancy in the classroom', *Journal of Business Ethics*, vol. 7, pp. 777–82.

Rest, JR 1986, *Moral development: advances in research and theory*. Praeger, New York.

# part 2 Ethics in a regulatory environment

Part 2 of this book introduces students to issues commonly facing businesses, accountants, and other professionals in the workplace. The various chapters highlight problems, the ethical issues and potential remedies.

# 5

# Corporate governance

## Learning objectives

After studying this chapter you should be able to:

- Describe corporate governance.
- Identify the parties involved in effective corporate governance.
- Identify and describe the principles of effective corporate governance.
- Explain the importance of culture and values for good corporate governance.
- Explain why corporate governance principles are put into practice.
- Describe the role of the board of directors.
- Discuss the usefulness of remuneration packages in aligning the goals of shareholders and managers.
- Explain the role of equity remuneration.
- Identify and discuss the role of the accountant in the governance of the organisation.
- Discuss the relationship between corporate governance and corporate performance.
- Understand the approach adopted by the rest of the book in addressing the concepts of ethics, corporate governance and accountability as introduced in the ethics framework.

'Public confidence is essential to effective capital markets — and this need for confidence is not limited to the companies listed on the exchange. It must also be reflected in the processes by which the capital market and the wider corporate environment is monitored and regulated . . . Increased disclosure whether it be through the recommendations, legislation or business's own initiative is intended to help investors and other information users understand and compare business performance — so they can be more informed in their decisions on who to punish and reward.'

**Greg Larsen, CEO of CPA Australia, Emerging Issues Work Group (2003)**

# Introduction //

Governance is largely about the decision-making process in a complex organisation. Shareholders (owners) delegate authority to professionals who have the managerial skills to increase their wealth. As a consequence the contributors of a firm's capital base are usually different from the contributors of its management base. This separation of ownership from control has led to organisations establishing a system of corporate governance controls, designed to discourage managers from pursuing objectives that fail to maximise shareholder wealth. These controls constitute the firm's corporate governance framework. Corporate governance controls are designed to monitor managers' behaviour or align the goals of management with the goals of shareholders.

In this chapter, a corporate governance framework is developed that outlines the roles and responsibilities of participants involved in governing the organisation and communicating information to the capital market.

# Corporate governance //

**Corporate governance** refers to the method by which an organisation is governed, administered, directed or controlled, and the goals for which it is governed. Various participants, who have an interest in the organisation, determine the direction and the performance of the organisation. The principal participants are the shareholders, management and the board of directors. As shareholders do not manage most large corporations, managers of the firm are given a considerable degree of decision-making authority. That is, the principal (shareholder) delegates decision rights to the agent (manager) to act in the principal's best interests. This separation of ownership from control implies a loss of effective control by shareholders over managerial decisions that affect the value of their wealth. Problems arise if the managers who initiate and execute decisions also approve and monitor the decisions. Without constraints on their actions managers can pursue their own interests rather than those of the owners, diverting potential profits towards personal pursuits. This action reduces shareholders' gains while raising the managers' total compensation.

As a result of the separation of ownership from control, a system of corporate governance controls is implemented on behalf of shareholders to discourage managers from pursuing objectives that fail to maximise shareholder wealth. These controls constitute the firm's corporate governance framework. The various corporate controls either assist in aligning the incentives of managers with those of shareholders or limit the self-satisfying opportunities for managers. These opportunities are referred to as agency costs — that is, the costs incurred by the firm that are associated with problems such as divergent management shareholder objectives and **information asymmetry**. Information asymmetry occurs when the manager has access to private information about the firm. Corporate governance controls are internal and external controls designed to reconcile manager–shareholder (agency) conflicts of interest that result from the separation of ownership and control (Williamson 1984). These corporate governance controls are used to monitor whether outcomes are in accordance with plans (i.e. the firm attaining planned objectives such as increased profitability); and to motivate the organisation to be fully informed in order to maintain or alter organisational activity (i.e. the organisation is familiar with, and understands, management's future strategies).

Recently there has been considerable interest in the **corporate governance practices** of modern corporations, particularly since the high-profile corporate collapses of firms such as HIH Insurance Group and One.Tel. The results of a corporate collapse impact not only the direct **stakeholders** of the organisations such as employees, shareholders and creditors but also on the economy at large (see 'In practice: The failure of HIH Insurance').

## IN PRACTICE

### The failure of HIH Insurance

The collapse of HIH made professional indemnity, public liability, home warranty and travel insurance policies worthless; placed retirees and disabled people on social security; led to building industry insurance instability; and escalated public liability insurance. About one thousand employees became unemployed immediately, while hundreds of others lost their jobs in the following months. The ramifications of the collapse were far reaching and resulted in public loss of confidence in the insurance industry. Justice Neville Owen, Royal Commissioner, suggested that the failure of HIH was due to the firm not providing adequately for future claims — under-reserving or under-provisioning. This situation arose because the firm was mismanaged and failed to uphold many of the basic corporate governance principles. Ill-informed and extravagant business acquisitions, questionable business transactions, a lack of attention to detail and the CEO's lack of accountability to the board of directors all made the corporate collapse inevitable. Poor business decisions included re-entering the United States insurance market in 1996, expanding the United Kingdom operations in 1997 into areas in which it was unfamiliar, and the acquisition of the already failing FAI Insurance Ltd in 1998. The final doomed business decision was to sell off HIH's profitable businesses to enter a joint venture with Allianz Australia Ltd in 2000. The resulting negative cash flows led to the decision to place the company into provisional liquidation in March 2001.

*Source:* Commonwealth of Australia 2003, *The failure of HIH insurance: a corporate collapse and its lessons,* 3 vols, Commonwealth of Australia, Canberra.

Good corporate governance, however, should be promoted without stifling entrepreneurial drive or impairing competitiveness. Management should have the freedom to drive the company forward, within a framework of effective accountability (Hermraj 2002).

The essential components of corporate governance are the parties involved in governing the entity, the principles of the governance framework, the culture and values of the organisation that support the governance principles, and the tools, or mechanisms, used to apply the governance principles. Table 5.1 has been adapted from the CPA Australia Corporate Governance Task Group discussion paper and further illustrates these concepts.

**TABLE 5.1**

### SOME ESSENTIAL COMPONENTS OF CORPORATE GOVERNANCE

| COMPONENT | EXAMPLES |
|---|---|
| The parties (people with a role to play in the effective governance of the firm) | • Governing body<br>• CEO<br>• Board of directors<br>• Management<br>• Shareholders<br>• Other stakeholders (e.g. customers, suppliers, employees, lenders and the community) |
| The principles (a framework of effective governance) | • Being a good corporate citizen (developing a code of ethics and code of conduct)<br>• Robust, regular performance reporting, monitoring, review and evaluation (using a monitoring system, board assessment, CEO reviews, measuring corporate performance)<br>• Robust compliance and risk management processes<br>• Independent review and verification (through internal audit, external audit, peer reviews, audit committees, board independence, remuneration committees) |
| Culture and values that are supportive of effective governance | • Honesty<br>• Trust and integrity<br>• Openness<br>• Performance orientation<br>• Responsibility and accountability<br>• Mutual respect<br>• Commitment to the organisation |

| The tools, or mechanisms, and means to apply effective governance principles that are suitable for the organisation | • Codes<br>• Charters<br>• Committees<br>• Delegations<br>• Policies and procedures<br>• Key performance indicators (KPIs) etc. |
|---|---|

*Source:* adapted from the Emerging Issues Work Group 2003, 'The essence of corporate governance', CPA Australia Corporate Governance Task Group, viewed 29 September 2003, www.cpaaustralia.com.au/01_information_centre/1_0_0_0_home.asp

## The Sarbanes–Oxley Act and the CLERP (Audit Reform and Corporate Disclosure) Act 2004 //

The Sarbanes–Oxley Act 2002 arose following a succession of high profile corporate collapses in the United States. The Act was designed to review dated legislative audit requirements. The goal of the act was to protect investors by improving the accuracy and reliability of corporate disclosures. The act covers issues such as establishing a public company accounting oversight board, auditor independence, corporate responsibility and enhanced financial disclosure. The Australian counterpart to the Sarbanes–Oxley Act, the Federal Government's *Corporate Law Economic Reform Program (Audit Reform & Corporate Disclosure) Act* was enacted in July 2004. The CLERP Bill proposes a number of reforms to the *Corporations Act 2001* (Cwlth) and is based on the reform proposals contained in the CLERP 9 discussion paper, *Corporate disclosure—strengthening the financial reporting framework*, which was released by the government in September 2002. The CLERP (Audit Reform and Corporate Disclosure) Act 2004 also contains a number of reforms flowing from the recommendations contained in the report of the HIH Royal Commission released in April 2003. Some of the major issues highlighted by this report are discussed later in this chapter. The CLERP (Audit Reform and Corporate Disclosure) Act 2004 proposes three bodies to represent a range of interests: the Financial Reporting Council (FRC) to oversee standard setting for audit and accounting; the Australian Stock Exchange's (ASX) Corporate Governance Council to oversee the development of best practice guidelines for corporate governance within listed companies; and the Shareholders and Investors Advisory Council (SIAC) to provide a forum for the consideration of retail investors' concerns.

The professional accounting bodies — the Institute of Chartered Accountants in Australia and CPA Australia (among others) — commented on the draft of the CLERP (Audit Reform and Corporate Disclosure) Act 2004. It was the responsibility of these bodies to determine whether the legislation was sufficient to promote efficient corporate governance, and financial reporting and assurance. CPA Australia suggested that the legislation should build a framework that not only identifies auditors' conduct and practices but also the conduct and practices of boards of directors, staff who prepare financial reports and the internal and external audit functions. It also suggested including the roles of institutional investors, credit rating agencies, financial analysts and investment banks.

Contrary to the United States experience, the CLERP (Audit Reform and Corporate Disclosure) Act's response to reviewing audit responsibilities states that 'most audits are conducted professionally and competently, with full regard given the interests of shareholders, the need for independence and professional ethics'. The Institute of Chartered Accountants in Australia believes that most audits are carried out this way and suggested that the corporate governance, financial reporting and auditing issues that led to the Sarbanes–Oxley Act are not evident in the Australian market.

## The parties to corporate governance //

The parties involved in the effective governance of the organisation include the governing body (e.g. Australian Securities and Investment Commission, Australian Stock Exchange, Corporate Governance Council, Australian Taxation Office, Australian Competition and Consumers Commission), the CEO, the board of directors, management, shareholders and other stakeholders of the organisation. Other stakeholders include customers, suppliers, employees, lenders and the community at large.

It is the responsibility of the board of directors to formulate the organisation's strategy, develop policy, appoint, supervise and remunerate senior executives and to ensure accountability of the organisation to its owners. The board of directors is a governance mechanism designed to monitor the performance of the organisation on behalf of the owners. This aspect is covered in more detail later in the chapter.

Shareholders are the owners of the entity, to whom the directors are accountable. Under the *Corporations Act 2001* (Cwlth) and the Australian Stock Exchange (ASX) Listing Rules, shareholders have the authority to sanction corporate transactions, appoint directors to supervise management and provide strategic direction, and to sanction other significant acts of listed companies reserved to shareholders (such as a takeover bid). Shareholders rely on continuous disclosure to engage in informed trading and exercise the rights given to them, which they do at general meetings. However, shareholders' participation at general meetings may be impeded because they do not have a clear understanding of the business to be conducted at the meeting or the time and cost involved in attending the meeting. As a consequence of these impediments, shareholders are more reliant on the efficient governance of the corporation. For example, shareholders unable to attend the general meeting are dependent on managers making decisions that will increase their wealth.

Stakeholders (in addition to shareholders) have an interest in the effective performance of the organisation. This interest can be direct or indirect. Customers, suppliers, employees and lenders have a direct interest in the organisation that they buy from, supply to or are employed by. Employees may have a greater stake in the organisation than shareholders because their current and future income depends on the current and future performance of the organisation. As a consequence, the organisation has an obligation to safeguard its employees through ethical and efficient governance. Organisations must ensure that customers' interests are maintained to guarantee the future viability of the organisation. Without customers the organisation will no longer exist. Suppliers of goods and services or funds (lenders) have invested their assets in the organisation and expect a return. Organisations can only guarantee that return if they continue to operate efficiently. Effective corporate governance is a means of providing that guarantee.

## The principles of corporate governance //

In March 2003, the Australian Stock Exchange (ASX) **Corporate Governance Council (CGC)**, which consists of 21 representatives (figure 5.1) of interested groups, set out to develop an industry-wide corporate governance framework.

- Association of Superannuation Funds of Australia Ltd
- Australasian Investor Relations Association
- Australian Council of Superannuation Investors
- Australian Institute of Company Directors
- Australian Institute of Superannuation Trustees
- Australian Shareholders' Association
- Australian Stock Exchange Limited
- Business Council of Australia
- Chartered Secretaries Australia
- CPA Australia
- Group of 100
- Institute of Actuaries of Australia
- Institute of Chartered Accountants in Australia
- Institute of Internal Auditors Australia
- International Banks and Securities Association of Australia
- Investment and Financial Services Association
- Law Council of Australia
- National Institute of Accountants
- Property Council of Australia
- Securities and Derivatives Industry Association
- Securities Institute of Australia

FIGURE 5.1   Corporate Governance Council representatives

*Source:* ASX Corporate Governance Council 2003, *Guidance note 9A: principles of good corporate governance and best practice recommendations*, Australian Stock Exchange, Sydney, p. 3.

The CGC suggests that fundamental to good corporate governance is company management and a board with a mix of skills, experience and independence, and the integrity necessary for ethical decision making. The company must be accountable to attract capital investment, and should therefore meet the information needs of the investment community in a manner that upholds and recognises shareholders' rights.

The CGC recommends ten essential **corporate governance principles**, covering such issues as developing guidelines for the appropriate mix of **executive** and **non-executive directors**; the independence of non-executive directors; the oversight of the preparation of the entity's financial statements, internal controls and the independence of the entity's auditors; the review of the compensation arrangements for the chief executive officer and other senior executives; the way in which individuals are nominated for positions on the board; the resources that are made available to directors in carrying out their duties; and the oversight and management of risk. The principles in the framework presented in table 5.1 are similar to the CGC's principles. However, as the CGC's principles are guidelines to which all listed companies adhere, these principles are discussed in the following section of this chapter.

### 1. Lay solid foundations for management and oversight

Organisations should clarify and make publicly known the roles and responsibilities of board and management to provide shareholders with a level of accountability. Boards should provide strategic guidance and oversee management. The division of roles and responsibilities between the board and management should provide a balance of authority so that absolute power does not rest with any single individual.

### 2. Structure the board to add value

The board needs a range of skills and understanding, to be of sufficient size and have an appropriate level of commitment to fulfill its responsibilities and duties. The board must be able to deal with various business issues and have the ability to review and challenge management performance. The board should consist mostly of independent directors, have an independent chairperson, and the key roles such as chairperson and chief executive officer should not be shared.

### 3. Promote ethical and responsible decision making

Organisations should develop a code of conduct for their directors and executives that promotes ethical and responsible decision making. Organisations should also publish their position on members of the board and employees trading in company shares and associated products.

### 4. Safeguard integrity in financial reporting

Organisations should implement procedures to independently verify and safeguard the integrity of the company's financial reporting. This can be achieved through the formation of an audit committee and the use of skilled, independent external auditors.

### 5. Make timely and balanced disclosure

Organisations should develop written policies and procedures that promote the timely and balanced disclosure of all material matters that concern them. These policies and procedures should ensure that all investors have access to timely information and that the organisation's announcements are clear, factual and balanced.

### 6. Respect the rights of shareholders

Organisations should respect the rights of shareholders and help shareholders to exercise those rights. Organisations can help shareholders exercise their rights by effectively communicating information that is understandable and accessible and encouraging shareholders to participate in general meetings.

### 7. Recognise and manage risk

Organisations should establish a system of risk oversight and management and internal control. Organisations should be continually identifying, assessing, monitoring and managing risk, and informing investors of changes to risk.

### 8. Encourage enhanced performance

Organisations should review and actively encourage enhanced board and management effectiveness. Organisations can facilitate this by providing directors and executives with the information required to assess the company's performance.

### 9. Remunerate fairly and responsibly

Organisations should ensure that remuneration is sufficient and reasonable and that the relationship between remuneration and performance is clear. Organisations should ensure that they are adequately remunerating directors and employees to attract those who have the necessary skills to enhance company performance.

### 10. Recognise the legitimate interests of stakeholders

Organisations should recognise that they have legal and other obligations to all legitimate stakeholders, such as customers, suppliers, employees, lenders and the community. Organisations should recognise the value added to the company by natural, human, social and other forms of capital.

## Culture and values //

For stakeholders to have confidence in an organisation, key elements of the organisation's culture and values must support good corporate governance principles. The key elements include honesty, trust and integrity, openness, performance orientation, responsibility and accountability, mutual respect, and commitment to the organisation.

Fundamental to good corporate governance is how directors and management develop a model of governance that aligns the values of the corporate participants and then test this model periodically for its effectiveness. In particular, senior executives should conduct themselves honestly and ethically, particularly concerning actual or apparent conflicts of interest, and disclosure in financial reports. Establishing a culture where employees feel confident about reporting violations will ensure that the key elements of trust, integrity, openness, responsibility, accountability and mutual respect will be upheld.

An example of an organisational culture that may not have had these fundamental elements is HIH. The CEO/founder continued to run the business as his own, even to the point where company funds were used to pay for senior executives' and executive directors' personal tax advice.

Corporate participants share common goals that shape our policy goals and guide our approach to finding solutions to governance issues. For instance, if the auditor and management share the goal of financial reporting transparency for the investing public, problems relating to failing to disclose relevant information, such as related party transactions, will not arise. This means that investors can be confident that the information flowing into the market fulfils the goal of financial reporting transparency. To ensure effective corporate governance, all participants in the market system must share the goal that financial reporting should provide useful and reliable information that promotes informed investment decisions and confidence in the capital market system.

### The tools, or mechanisms, and means to effect corporate governance //

Financial management and financial reporting are essential to manage and communicate the financial position of the firm at a particular time. There is the potential for the integrity of the result to be compromised through intent or omission to disclose particular information. There have been a number of corporate collapses, such as HIH, One.Tel, WorldCom and Enron, where the corporate governance practices of the company or the absence of an appropriate governance policy has led to information failing to reach the investor. With more than 50 per cent of adult Australians holding shares both directly or indirectly (due to compulsory superannuation), shareholders are no longer a select group and corporate governance responsibilities are far reaching. James McRitchie (2001) poses the following questions: Who controls these assets? Who executes voting rights? How do the workers benefit? Good corporate governance practices are important in determining the cost of capital in a market economy.

# Corporate governance controls //

Managers of publicly listed organisations have more information than investors about the current and future financial performance of the organisation. The information asymmetry that exists between the shareholders and the chief executive officer of a firm is generally considered to be a classic example of a principal–agent problem. In the basic principal–agent model, the agent (the manager) is working on behalf of the principal (the shareholders), who does not observe the actions of the agent. This information asymmetry causes the agency problems of **moral hazard** and **adverse selection**. Moral hazard arises when the manager does not comply with the contractual terms. It can occur when management intends to use capital for their own interests rather than those of shareholders. Managers may adopt financing policies and a capital structure for the firm that can help secure their jobs. For instance, instead of investing in an innovative technology or market, a manager may choose the less risky route of expanding an existing product line that uses known technologies and sells to known markets. Although such a conservative strategy rarely produces large returns, it reduces the chance of a firm-threatening, manager-threatening failure. Forgoing potentially profitable projects reduces shareholders' expected wealth but enhances managers' expected wealth. Adverse selection occurs when the principal makes an inappropriate decision, based on the information available (e.g. selecting managers with inappropriate skills for the task). Adverse selection can also occur because managers are concerned with promoting the sale of the firm's shares to investors and may overstate the benefits of buying shares. Unless the manager can credibly signal the value of the firm, investors will reduce the amount they are willing to pay.

Governance controls are designed to eliminate the danger that managers will not exert maximum effort on the behalf of shareholders, or consume the benefits of the capital raised through excessive abuse of privileges. The inefficiencies that arise from moral hazard and adverse selection can be reduced by either monitoring managers' behaviour or designing compensation contracts that link managers' performance to the performance of the firm. For example, to monitor managers' behaviour, an independent third party attests the accuracy of information provided by management to investors. Thus, the independent auditor assures public investors that financial reporting provides useful and reliable information that portrays the economic realities of the business.

An ideal control system should regulate both motivation and ability. Corporate governance refers to internal and external controls designed to reconcile manager–shareholder conflicts of interest that result from the separation of ownership and control. **Internal corporate governance controls** monitor activities and then take corrective action to accomplish organisational goals. Examples of internal controls include the monitoring of managers by the board of directors, **remuneration committees**, audit committees and incentives designed to align managers' and shareholders' interests. **External corporate governance controls** encompass the controls external stakeholders exercise over the organisation. Examples of external controls include debt covenants, external auditors and government regulations which place restrictions on management behaviour or monitor their actions.

With the significant increase in equity holdings of institutional investors in many corporations, there has been an opportunity for a reversal of the separation of ownership and control problems because ownership is not so diffuse. However, the problems have continued. As institutional shareholders are not privy to managers' private knowledge, they cannot be aware of all the financial and investment opportunities that can be accepted or rejected by management. Hence, the need for corporate governance mechanisms persists. The section entitled 'In practice: Investors willing to pay for well-governed companies' explains that investors are willing to pay more for shares in companies they consider to be well governed.

## IN PRACTICE

### Investors willing to pay for well-governed companies

Coombes and Watson (2000) in three surveys of corporate governance found that investors were willing to pay more for shares of well-governed companies. They defined a well-governed company as one that had mostly outside directors, who had no management ties, undertook formal evaluation of its directors, and was responsive to investors' requests for information on governance issues.

Coombes and Watson found that directors should have significant share holdings in the company and a large proportion of their pay should be in the form of **share options**. The surveys of over 200 institutional investors in Asia, Europe, United States and Latin America demonstrated that 75 per cent of investors consider board practice to be at least as important as financial performance. The premium they were prepared to pay for well-governed companies was a function of the quality of financial reporting in the country where accounting standards were perceived to be higher. The premium investors were willing to pay for a well-governed company in the United Kingdom or the United States was 18 per cent compared to 22 per cent premium for a well-governed company in Italy and 27 per cent for a well-governed company in Indonesia.

## External corporate governance controls //

One example of an external corporate governance control is the Australian Stock Exchange Listing Rule 4.10.3, which requires listed companies to set out in their annual reports a statement of their main corporate governance practices. The statement should disclose:

> the extent to which the entity has followed the best practice recommendations set by the ASX Corporate Governance Council during the reporting period. If the entity has not followed all of the recommendations the entity must identify those recommendations that have not been followed and give reasons for not following them. If a recommendation had been followed for only part of the period, the entity must state the period during which it had been followed.

*Source:* ASX Listing Rule 4.10.3.

The guidelines set out in the listing rule are voluntary only to the extent that listed companies can adopt alternative practices, provided they explain why they did not adopt the ASX guideline. However, investors and information users will ultimately determine whether the adopted alternative practices are acceptable by investing or not investing in the firm.

As mentioned previously, the principles and recommendations for corporate governance are guidelines. The ASX does not stipulate required practices, preferring to state that particular governance mechanisms may not be appropriate for all companies and in some cases may impose unwarranted costs on some listed companies (see figure 5.2).

The best practice recommendations are not prescriptions. They are guidelines, designed to produce an efficiency, quality or integrity outcome. This document does not require a 'one size fits all' approach to corporate governance. Instead, it states aspirations of best practice for optimising corporate performance and accountability in the interests of shareholders and the broader economy. If a company considers that a recommendation is inappropriate to its particular circumstances, it has the flexibility not to adopt it — a flexibility tempered by the requirement to explain why.

Companies are encouraged to use the guidance provided by this document as a focus for re-examining their corporate governance practices and to determine whether and to what extent the company may benefit from a change in approach, having regard to the company's particular circumstances. There is little value in a checklist approach to corporate governance that does not focus on the particular needs, strengths and weaknesses of the company.

The Council recognises that the range in size and diversity of companies is significant and that smaller companies may face particular issues in attaining all recommendations from the outset. Performance and effectiveness can be compromised by material change that is not managed sensibly. Where a company is considering widespread structural changes in order to meet best practice, the company is encouraged to prioritise its needs and to set and disclose best practice goals against an indicative timeframe for meeting them.

FIGURE 5.2  **How to approach adoption of the best practice recommendations**

*Note:* See Appendix A in this chapter for best practice disclosure recommendations of the ASX.
*Source:* ASX Corporate Governance Council 2003, *Guidance note 9A: Principles of good corporate governance and best practice recommendations*, Australian Stock Exchange, Sydney, p. 5.

The report on the failure of the HIH Insurance Group by Royal Commission, tabled in April 2003 provides support for the CGC's recommendations that one size does not fit all regarding good corporate governance practice (Allens Arthur Robinson 2003). The Royal Commissioner Justice Neville Owen stated that:

> By its very nature corporate governance is not something which 'one size fits all'. Even with companies within a class, such as publicly listed companies, their capital base, risk profile, corporate history, business activity and management and personnel arrangements will be varied (Allens Arthur Robinson 2003, p. 2).

## Internal corporate governance controls //

Internal governance controls are designed to monitor the behaviour of managers and provide incentives to align managers' and shareholders' interests. Monitoring by the board of directors and compensation contracts represent two of the many internal governance controls available to organisations.

### Monitoring by the board of directors

Shareholders grant decision control rights to the board of directors. The decisions of managers are monitored and ratified by the board of directors. Shareholders and boards monitor and evaluate managers' actions over time enforcing their ideals of how and what should be achieved. This involves considerable monitoring of actions, direction and intervention, may be very costly and may not totally eliminate information asymmetries.

The board of directors, with its legal authority to hire, fire and compensate top management, safeguards invested capital, and is therefore an important element of corporate governance. Directors have certain legal obligations to shareholders and they can be held liable for damages if they fail to meet these obligations. As a consequence, directors will have some desire to maintain or establish reputations as good monitors and competent business people. The ultimate responsibility for full and fair disclosure to shareholders, and the direct responsibility for the independent audit relationship and the quality of the audit lies with the board of directors and the audit committee. Regulators have suggested that the members of the internal audit committee, responsible for overseeing and liaising with the external independent auditor, should be non-executive directors (i.e. directors who are not employees of the company or directly affiliated with management). This recommendation implies that non-executive directors are better monitors of the auditor.

Researchers have investigated the usefulness of a board of directors as a monitoring device as they communicate the shareholders' objectives and interests to managers. A high ratio of non-executive directors to executive directors is likely to promote decisions that are in the interests of external shareholders. **Board monitoring**, the board's capacity to monitor the actions of management, is jeopardised if executive directors dominate the board.

The CGC suggests that the board should consist of a majority of independent directors. A board is independent if it meets all of the following criteria:

- The director is not a member of management.
- The director is not a substantial shareholder of the entity or an officer of or otherwise associated directly or indirectly with a substantial shareholder of the entity.
- The director has not within the last three years been employed in an executive capacity by the entity or another group member or been a director after ceasing to hold any such employment.
- The director is not a principal of a professional adviser to the entity or another group member.
- The director is not a significant supplier or customer of the entity or another group member, or an officer of, or otherwise associated directly or indirectly with a significant supplier or customer.
- The director has no significant contractual relationship with the entity or another group member other than as a director of the entity.
- The director is free from any interest and any business or other relationship which could, or could reasonably be perceived to, materially interfere with the director's ability to act in the best interests of the entity.

*Source:* ASX Corporate Governance Council 2003, *Guidance note 9A: Principles of good corporate governance and best practice recommendations,* Australian Stock Exchange, Sydney p. 4

The board, in a broader perspective, is devised to limit management and shareholder conflict. In particular, managers receive pecuniary incentives to maximise firm value from share ownership, share option plans and adjustments of salary based on performance. A board of directors is the primary internal corporate governance mechanism responsible for, among other duties, setting management compensation and monitoring senior management. An effective compensation contract provides executives with the incentive to act in the shareholders' best interests. This means that the link between pay and corporate performance should be greater in firms with non-executive director dominated boards and remuneration committees. In addition to compensation monitoring, regular board meetings allow potential problems to be identified, discussed and avoided, and should therefore lead to a superior level of performance.

The combination of incentives for performance and monitoring by the board provide the governance control system for top management. However, different board structures are optimal for different firms, for the simple reason that each firm faces its own management problems, and hence finds their own solution. Forcing companies to have a particular board structure (e.g. non-executive vs executive directors) that is not optimal could be to the detriment of shareholders.

It is therefore likely that in some circumstances it may be more efficient to have a board composed primarily of executive directors. The ability of the board to monitor the firm's executives is a function of its access to information. Executive directors possess superior knowledge of the decision-making process and therefore evaluate top management on the basis of the quality of its decisions that lead to financial performance outcomes, ex ante. In contrast, non-executive directors evaluate managers on the basis of financial performance measures ex post. Therefore, it could be argued that executive directors look beyond the financial criteria.

Even with a board dominated by non-executive directors, the board functions on information provided by the CEO. The CEO can also play a principal role in determining the remuneration and tenure of non-executive directors. In addition, dispersion of ownership and increased powers of senior management have accompanied the evolution of the corporate system. This can result in a decline in the accountability of directors and management, leading to a similar decline in the monitoring role of boards. Hence, these factors can have the effect of weakening the board as a crucial instrument of corporate governance. The section entitled 'In practice: The failure of the board of directors of HIH Insurance' suggests that the HIH collapse was affected by these factors.

## IN PRACTICE

### The failure of board of directors of HIH Insurance

Poor strategic decision making was accompanied by blind faith in an ill-equipped leadership, insufficient independence, and unidentified and mismanaged risks. At the board level there was little analysis of the future strategy of the company. For example, the rationale behind the re-entry into the United States market and the expansion in the United Kingdom market was never discussed or approved by the board. The founder and CEO of HIH, Raymond Williams, did not clearly express the details of his strategy for the company. It is one of the board's key responsibilities to understand, test and endorse the company's strategy; otherwise they will not appreciate the associated risks. The board should measure performance against the company's strategic goals.

There were no clear limits placed on the authority of the CEO with regard to investments, corporate donations, gifts and staff compensation and the board rarely, if ever, rejected or changed a proposal put forward by management. Decisions about the performance and remuneration of senior officers were made by the CEO, who attended all human resource committee meetings (by invitation).

The chairman of the board was ineffective, failing to guide the board to focus their attention on conflicts-of-interest resolution or related-party disclosures. The chairman did not deal with the non-executive directors' concerns about the governance procedures of HIH. The agenda for each board meeting was prepared by the company secretary, approved by the chairman and commented on by the CEO. No other board members were involved. Information was hidden, filtered or sanitised. There were material omissions from information given to the board, even to the point where information was misleading.

*Source:* Commonwealth of Australia 2003, *The failure of HIH insurance: a corporate collapse and its lessons*, 3 vols, Commonwealth of Australia, Canberra.

## Performance-based remuneration

**Performance-based remuneration** is designed to relate some proportion of salary to individual performance within the context of overall company performance. Performance-based remuneration may be in the form of cash or non-cash payments such as shares and share options, superannuation or other benefits that are linked to the firm's performance.

Tying managers' compensation to shareholders' objectives, such as successful firm performance, is likely to motivate managers to behave in a manner consistent with shareholders' interests. Managers who do not maximise their performance level, and who do not act in the best interests of the shareholders, will suffer financially. Linking managerial reward to the price of a firm's shares alleviates the incentive problem of motivating management. In addition, shareholders are able to use the information that is publicly available, the share price, to monitor management. Performance-based incentives may therefore be regarded as a means of reducing conflict between decision makers and shareholders. Thus, performance-related pay is influential in making the interests of managers consistent with those of the shareholders. The compensation system employed by a firm is an important part of the process of controlling both effort and reward, and can ultimately affect the profitability of the organisation.

However, performance-based incentives transfer risk to the manager's compensation. In addition, such incentive schemes are reactive in the sense that they provide no mechanism for preventing mistakes or opportunistic behaviour, and can elicit myopic behaviour. For example, a manager may focus attention on diversified acquisitions with the aim of increasing the share price and hence his or her compensation. However, if the organisation's competitive advantage is specialisation, this approach is in conflict with that strategy.

## Management share ownership

**Management share ownership** can be an important source of incentives and power for managers as well as outside shareholders. It typically bestows voting rights, which can give internal and external shareholders a voice in the governance of a corporation. Distribution of shares among these stakeholders can, therefore, have a significant impact on corporate actions that are dependent on shareholder voting. As managers become shareholders, they have a direct interest in an increasing share price. Better operating performance is one way of achieving this objective.

Two views are expressed regarding the impact of managerial share ownership on shareholder welfare. The first suggests that as managers have already invested their non-diversifiable human capital in the firm, increased share ownership transfers additional risk to managers (compensation) and can lead to risk avoiding behaviour on the part of managers, which may not be in the interest of shareholders.

The second view advocates share ownership as a means of aligning the interest of top managers with that of shareholders. That is, if managers own shares in a company they are less likely to take actions that are not in the interests of shareholders. The more shares management owns, the stronger their motivation to work to raise the value of the firm's shares, which is what the external shareholders want. Consequently, share ownership by board members and executives represents an alignment of goals with shareholders. When insiders own a significant portion of a firm's stock, they have a strong incentive to enhance its value and act in ways that are in shareholders' best interests. Management and board effectiveness depends in part on directors' identification with the interests of a firm's shareholders.

However, problems do not invariably decrease as share ownership by top management increases: large management ownership insulates management from other forces such as the threat of takeovers and the discipline of the board. If managers own substantial shares they may have enough voting power to curb the influence of the market. While share ownership can synchronise the interests of managers and external shareholders in some circumstances, conflicts in agendas and interests of the two groups can result in differences in voting patterns. For example, when efficient corporate policy requires changes in asset and employment structure, management shareholders are interested not only in the value of their equity investment but also in their employment with the firm. In contrast, external shareholders are normally interested only in their equity investment in the firm. As a consequence, managers would prefer to maintain the status quo, avoiding risky investment opportunities and preferring to safeguard their employment, which may be to the detriment of the shareholders.

### Shares options

A share option is an agreement involving the sale or purchase of a share denoting equity in a company. The employee share option is the promise by the company to sell the share to the employee at a specified strike price, which may be greater than or less than the current market price. The employee may decide to enforce the agreement and exercise the options, or let it expire unexercised. Share options may be an efficient way of overcoming the interest divergence between managers and shareholders, especially when the managerial reward is linked to the price of the firm's shares. As share options allow the future purchase of stock at a fixed price they represent deferred remuneration that can be exercised at the manager's discretion. Consequently, share options act as an incentive given the probability that share prices increase. Share options have the potential to align executives' goals with those of the shareholders and therefore represent an incentive for managers to adopt value-increasing projects.

The relationship between owned equity shares and owned share options demonstrates the compensation risk managers are subject to. Share ownership gives the owners voting rights and a **linear payoff** that increases with their firm's performance. In contrast, share options grant recipients the rights to acquire equity at a future date with a **convex payoff**, as they need not exercise the option if the share price has not increased. Options are similar to shares except that they fully benefit from share price increases but do not incur losses if the share price falls below the exercise price. Therefore, options do not have the same risk-bearing properties associated with share ownership. As a consequence, managers who hold more options than shares are able to endure more firm risk, are more likely to invest in riskier assets and have less interest in hedging and managing the risk of the firm (Hutchinson 2003).

Following the corporate collapses mentioned in this chapter, together with excessive option grants in the United States, concern has arisen over the accounting treatment of share options. The issue raised is whether share options should be treated as an expense against profit. Proponents of adopting the expense approach suggest that excluding options understates executives' remuneration and provides the opportunity to overstate profits. The major benefit being that expensing options increases transparency. Opponents of the expense approach suggest that the valuation of executive share options is problematic for two reasons. First, they are not traded, so there is no market valuation to observe. Second, the features of executive share options are such that they bear little resemblance to options on shares or securities in general. It would be difficult to have an international comparable method of valuation, and values move in both directions in line with share values.

There is no mandate on expensing share options to date. However, firms are required to report the number of options awarded to and/or held by directors. Some firms have also chosen to voluntarily report the strike price and exercise date of the options awarded.

## Disclosing remuneration

The Corporations Act requires annual disclosure by listed companies of the details of the nature and amount of each element of the fee or salary of each director and each of the five highest paid non-director executives. The ASX CGC's (2003, p. 52) guidelines for disclosing remuneration include alternatives such as:

- salary
- fees
- non-cash benefits
- bonuses accruing in respect of that year, regardless of payment date
- profit share accruing in respect of that year, regardless of payment date
- superannuation contributions
- other payments in relation to termination and retirement of office
- the value of shares issued and options granted, according to an established and recognised method of valuation
- sign-on payments.

The CGC suggests that the remuneration committee should be comprised of mostly non-executive directors. The responsibilities of this committee will vary among firms but the key functions are to review and recommend remuneration for the CEO and senior management. The committee should obtain independent advice on current remuneration trends. HIH Insurance fell well short of any such independence, as the CEO attended all the remuneration meetings.

# The role of the accountant in the governance of the entity //

Accountants, auditors and the corporate governance structure in which they operate are the primary providers of information to capital market participants. Therefore, directors of the company should be entitled to expect that management prepare the financial information in compliance with statutory and ethical obligations, and rely on auditors' competence on their opinion of the truth, fairness and compliance of the reports. But ultimately it is the directors who make the final decision about the accuracy of the reports on the financial state of the organisation. The reliability of the accounts depends on the integrity of the information on which they are based. Without reliable financial information, the board and auditors are unable to assess the company's financial position and performance and detect any deterioration over time.

One area of concern for accounting and auditing is where the accounting firm acts as both independent auditor and management consultant to the firm they are auditing. This in turn can place the integrity and quality of the financial reports in doubt due to client pressure to appease management. This may lead to certain activities such as concealing bad news. This loss of independence has led to requests that firms have an independent audit committee and mandatory rotation of the audit partner every five to seven years if relief has been granted by ASIC. The CLERP (Audit Reform and Corporate Disclosure) Act 2004 suggests that auditor independence can be strengthened by restricting auditor–client employment relations; mandatory audit partner rotation; disclosure of both audit and non-audit fees; and a statement in the annual reports on how the audit has not compromised audit independence.

In addition to the CLERP (Audit Reform and Corporate Disclosure) Act 2004 guidelines, the ASX Corporate Governance Council recommends that organisations have an audit committee comprising a majority of independent non-executive members to ensure the independence of the committee from management. The audit committee is an essential component of effective corporate governance. The role of the committee is to oversee the financial reports and the audit processes, such as reviewing the external auditor's independence. The major advantage of the audit committee is that the external auditor deals with the board through the audit committee and is therefore not subject to management pressure to comply with their wishes. It is not compulsory to have an audit committee but companies are required to disclose the existence of one. Most Australian companies, however, do have audit committees.

The HIH Insurance and Enron collapses are examples of misleading financial reporting. Justice Owen discussed several issues relating to financial reporting and assurance of HIH, including the interpretation of accounting standards, adoption of international standards and the need for the Australian Accounting Standards Board to provide timely advice on interpretation matters. He emphasised the importance of the audit function for capital markets and the users of financial reports. He suggested that the role of the auditor requires independence equal to that of a judge to avoid bias in preparing the audit reports. As the section, 'In practice: The failure of the accounts of HIH Insurance' shows, it would appear that the HIH audit breached these principles of due care and independence.

## IN PRACTICE

### The failure of the accounts of HIH Insurance

Accounting techniques were used to hide the full extent of the decline. The financial statements were distorted by questionable entries, heavy reliance on one-off end-of-year transactions, and aggressive accounting practices. For example, HIH incurred significant income tax losses in 1999 and 2000 but continued to record the full value of future income tax benefits as assets. The relevant accounting standard states that where a company incurs an income tax loss, unless the future income tax benefits are certain, it is imprudent to record the future tax benefit as an asset.

The HIH audit committee concentrated on the accounts and the numbers contained in them, failing to identify and assess the risk to which the company was exposed. An audit committee should be independent of management, consisting of non-executive directors. However, all directors, both executive and non-executive, attended the HIH audit committee meeting. The audit committee rarely, if ever, preferred the auditor's opinion over management's opinion. Although the auditor had a formal system of quality control and procedures in place, it relied on the valuations of HIH's consulting actuary when conducting its audit, which breached its independence.

*Source:* Commonwealth of Australia 2003, *The failure of HIH insurance: a corporate collapse and its lessons*, 3 vols, Commonwealth of Australia, Canberra.

In addition to the Australian experience, Enron in the United States also provides an example of misleading financial information and lack of audit integrity and independence.

## The failure of the accounts of Enron

The Houston-based energy trading company, Enron Corporation, filed for bankruptcy in 2001. With $62.8 billion in assets, it became the largest bankruptcy in United States history. The *Powers report* of February 2001 was a special investigative committee of the board of directors. The committee suggested that reported transactions were designed to present favourable financial reports, rather than present a bona fide view of the company's operations. Enron concealed huge losses by creating illusions that a third party was contractually obliged to pay the amount of any losses — that is, their risks were hedged. However, the third party was an entity in which Enron had a substantial economic stake. The Andersen partner responsible for auditing Enron was considered to be a client pleaser. Discussions of accounting practices inevitably led to the client's view prevailing. Subsequently, Enron was successful in removing a member of the Andersen's audit team after the member expressed his disapproval of many aspects of Enron.

*Source:* Vinten, G 2002, 'The corporate governance lessons of Enron', *Corporate Governance*, vol.2, no.4, pp. 4–9.

These high-profile failures and the questionable performance of the key players in the financial reporting system place doubt on investors' ability to rely on the oversight of the board of directors and independence of the audit committee. Are the accounting and disclosure standards sufficiently transparent for investors and the public? The range of topics covered by accounting standards has increased substantially throughout the years. In 1980 there were nine accounting standards, by 1990 there were around 26 and by 2000 the number had increased to 43. The CLERP (Audit Reform and Corporate Disclosure) Act 2004 recommends that accounting standards return to the dominance of the true and fair concept in financial reporting. Business has had to improve the nature, volume and quality of information available to shareholders, in response to the loss of confidence facing the market.

Can we rely on self-regulatory corporate governance practices to guide management and ensure auditors perform their role efficiently? If governance controls are efficient there should be a positive relationship between these controls and firm performance.

# Corporate governance and firm performance //

Research investigating the relationship between corporate governance controls and firm performance has been mixed and often weak. The question is whether board monitoring and incentive contracts reduce owner–manager conflict.

# Board composition and firm performance //

Prior research has failed to arrive at a consensus regarding the relationship between board monitoring and firm performance. For example, some researchers have only found support for the relationship between frequency of meetings and profitability. Some researchers have found a negative relationship between the proportion of external directors and firm performance, while others found no relationship between external board membership and performance. Therefore, it is likely that board composition is unlikely to have a direct impact on firm performance. Rather, it is feasible that the relationship between board composition and firm performance is associated with the type of firm and supports the notion that one size does NOT fit all.

# Remuneration and firm performance //

Incentives, both compensation and equity, are governance controls which provide targets, such as financial results, for managers to achieve. The corporation's objective is to construct an incentive contract that aligns the executive's interests with those of the owner.

### Executive compensation and firm performance

The results of previous research on the relationship between firm performance and executive compensation have primarily been insignificant. Researchers have argued that CEOs will pursue their own interests rather than shareholders when their reward does not coincide with that of shareholders. Subsequent research has tested the sensitivity of CEO pay to changes in performance. This argument suggests that an effective governance mechanism that aligns the goals of management with shareholders will be one where a change in shareholder wealth will lead to a significant change in CEO compensation. However, prior research has failed to find consistent and significant relationships between executives' remuneration and firm performance. However, low average levels of pay–performance alignment do not necessarily imply that this form of governance control is inefficient Not all firms experience the same levels of conflict, and external and internal monitoring devices may be more effective for some than for others.

### Share ownership and firm performance

Share ownership can be an important source of incentive and power for executives as well as outside shareholders. Distribution of stock among these stakeholders can therefore have a significant impact on corporate actions that are dependent on shareholder voting. Some researchers have found that the largest CEO performance incentives came from ownership of the firm's shares, while other researchers found that the relationship between share ownership and firm performance was dependent on the level of ownership. They found at levels of ownership between 5 and 20 per cent, profitability increased with ownership. At levels greater than

20 per cent of share ownership profitability decreased with ownership. This result suggests that increases in ownership above 20 per cent cause management to become more entrenched, and less interested in the welfare of their shareholders.

### Share options and firm performance

Research suggests that firm performance is positively associated with share option plans, suggesting that large pay–performance sensitivities were primarily the result of incentives provided by the executives' ownership of shares and share options. Share option plans direct managers' energies and extend their decision horizons toward the long-term, rather than the short-term, performance of the company.

# Does corporate governance work? //

Each firm's governance needs vary with firm-specific and environmental conditions. From the discussion in this chapter it is evident that failures of corporate governance can be devastating. Are the reforms to corporate governance that have arisen primarily from these corporate failures sufficient? Can we rely on corporate governance processes to ensure that management and auditors carry out their responsibilities in an efficient and ethical manner?

Good corporate governance does not necessarily lead to better firm performance; a positive relationship is likely to be dependent on the type of firm. However, from the evidence provided by the corporate collapses we have examined, bad corporate governance is more likely to lead to poor firm performance. Enron and HIH are cases where financial reporting was deliberately distorted with the objective of misleading investors and the public about the underlying economic performance of the firm.

# Summary //

Fundamental to good corporate governance is a board of directors and management with a mix of skills, experience, independence and the integrity necessary for ethical decision making. The company must be accountable to attract capital investment, and should therefore meet the information needs of the investment community in a manner that upholds and recognises shareholders' rights.

The essential components of organisations' corporate governance are the parties involved in governing the entity, the principles of the governance framework, the culture and values of the organisation to support the governance principles and the tools, or mechanisms, used to apply the governance principles.

Shareholders rely on the information provided to the capital market to make decisions about their investments. Accountants, auditors and the corporate governance structure in which they operate are the primary providers of information to capital market participants. The board of directors, as overseers of the company, should be entitled to expect that management prepare the financial information in compliance with statutory and ethical obligations and rely on auditors' competence on their opinion of the truth, fairness and compliance of the reports. The importance of corporate governance is demonstrated by the fact that investors are prepared to pay more for a well-governed entity.

# Key terms //

Adverse selection... p. 127
Board monitoring... p. 130
Convex payoff... p. 135
Corporate governance... p. 118
Corporate Governance Council (CGC)... p. 123
Corporate governance principles... p. 124
Corporate governance practice... p. 119
Executive directors... p. 124
External corporate governance controls... p. 127
Information asymmetry... p. 119
Internal corporate governance controls... p. 127
Linear payoff... p. 134
Management share ownership... p. 133
Moral hazard... p. 127
Non-executive directors... p. 124
Performance-based remuneration... p. 133
Remuneration committee... p. 127
Share options... p. 128
Stakeholders... p. 119

# Questions //

**5.1** Would the economic consequences of poor governance be greater for public or private companies?

**5.2** From your experience, how would you define governance and its implications for companies?

**5.3** Describe the impact of good or bad corporate governance on stakeholders. Refer to the areas of the principles of corporate governance which impact on stakeholders.

**5.4** How do shareholder/investor responses to poor governance practices affect corporate financing?

**5.5** The Corporate Governance Council suggests that corporate governance practices cannot be prescriptive as a one-size-fits-all approach may compromise firm performance. Suggest some instances where imposing a particular governance practice may impede firm performance.

**5.6**  Describe the role of the board and give examples of the activities the board performs.

**5.7**  What are the advantages and disadvantages of appointing non-executive directors to the board?

**5.8**  To what extent should the board be concerned with the ethical conduct of the board and the company as a whole?

**5.9**  Is it the role of the board to promote values and ethics within the company? If it is not the role of the board, whose role is it?

**5.10**  Executives should be paid on the basis of their performance measures. They should not be paid a salary. Do you agree with this statement? Explain your answer.

**5.11**  What is the role of equity remuneration in efficient corporate governance?

**5.12**  What do you think would be the effect of expensing share options remuneration paid to executives or directors?

**5.13**  Examine the corporate governance statement of an annual report. (To do this go to a listed company's website.) For the company you have chosen, answer the following:

   **a**  Do they comply with the CGC principles — in particular, independent directors and shareholders' rights?

   **b**  What guidance is provided by the CGC to address these issues?

**5.14**  A director of the board has borrowed money from the company to invest in property speculation. He plans to pay back the money when he has received the profit from the project. Explain the implications of the director's action and what, if any, disclosure is required.

**5.15**  Assume Harvey Norman's remuneration committee seeks advice from your firm. The committee is interested in the different forms of compensation that can be offered to their executives to motivate them to maximise shareholder value.

   **a**  What types of compensation packages could be used and how would you recommend structuring the compensation to align executives' and owners' goals?

   **b**  What performance measure of the firm could the different forms of compensation be linked to?

**5.16**  You are the executive director of a publicly-listed firm, Extrion Ltd, and you believe that an investment opportunity you have heard about will increase the profits of the firm. The firm operates more like a privately-owned business and does not have the same emphasis on rigorous corporate governance policies as recommended by the CGC.

   This investment opportunity requires funding, which you have arranged through Merchant Securities, an investment firm. You own 5 per cent of the issued shares of Merchant Securities. The board of directors is meeting next week to consider the future of Extrion Ltd.

a You know you have the best interests of the firm at heart. What are your obligations as a member of the board regarding the investment?

b What are your obligations regarding your shares in Merchant Securities?

c Do you see a conflict of interest? Explain.

## FURTHER RESOURCES AND WEBSITES //

### Further resources

Coles, JW, McWilliams, VB & Sen, N 2001, 'An examination of the relationship of governance mechanisms to performance', *Journal of Management*, vol. 27, pp. 23–50.

Dalton, DR, Dailey, CM, Ellstrand, EA & Johnson, JL 1998, 'Meta-analytic reviews of board composition, leadership structure, and financial performance', *Strategic Management Journal*, vol. 19 no. 3, pp. 269–90.

Hermalin, BE & Weisbach, MS 1991, 'The effects of board composition and direct incentives on firm performance', *Financial Management* vol. 20, no. 4, pp. 101–12.

Jensen, MC & Murphy, KJ 1990, 'Performance pay and top management incentives', *Journal of Political Economy*, vol. 98, pp. 225–64.

Kren, L & Kerr, JK 1997, 'The effect of outside directors and board shareholdings on the relation between chief executive compensation and firm performance', *Accounting and Business Research*, vol. 27, no. 4, pp. 297–309.

Treasury Department 2002, *CLERP 9, Corporate Disclosure: Strengthening the Financial Reporting Framework*, Commonwealth of Australia, September.

### Website

ASX Corporate Governance Council website: www.asx.com.au/corporategovernance

## CASE STUDY

### Corporate governance and the collapse of Enron

The failure of the Enron Corporation in 2001 was one of the largest corporate collapses in the history of the United States. The collapse placed in doubt the effectiveness of contemporary accounting, auditing and corporate governance practices.

The chairman of the board, who was also the CEO, reassured investors that the company's core businesses and future earnings growth were stable, while at the same time he was selling his shares and exercising options. In reality, write-offs against losses produced a loss of more than $600 million. This amount included a $35 million loss involving a conflict of interest, where the company's CFO managed the businesses in partnership with Enron. Profits were overstated over a four-year period, primarily due to accounting manipulations. Consumer confidence in the company fell along with the share price, and Enron finally filed for bankruptcy.

The *Powers report* of February 2001 was a special investigative committee of the board of directors. The committee suggested that reported transactions were designed to present favourable financial reports, rather than present a bona fide view of the company's operations. Enron concealed huge losses by creating the illusion that a third party was contractually obliged to pay the amount of any losses — that is, their risks were hedged. However, the third party was an entity in which Enron had a substantial economic stake.

Enron raises the following problems associated with poor corporate governance:
- the strength of the efficient market hypothesis
- the board's capacity to protect the integrity of financial disclosure
- trade-offs in the use of stock options in executive compensation because of the potential to motivate management to commit fraud and prefer risk
- poor fit between stock-based employee compensation and retirement planning.

**The strength of the efficient market hypothesis**
Enron's share price escalated at the same time as earnings fell, demonstrating that markets sometimes ignore evidence about the finances of the firm. Even if Enron actively misled the market about its true financial condition, sophisticated market participants should have had sufficient knowledge of the firm that the efficient market would devalue Enron's shares. Enron's financial structure was highly complex with off-balance sheet entities that were obscured in Enron's disclosure documents. The fact that it was difficult to determine Enron's true financial position should have been sufficient to send warning signals to the market, and the market should have adjusted the share price downwards.

However, Enron's accountants at Arthur Andersen certified that the financial statements 'fairly presented' the overall financial picture of the company. But the credibility of Andersen's certification was compromised. First, because it had permitted its independence to be undermined when the accounting firm cross-sold consulting services, such as tax planning and accounting planning, which made the accountant part of the management team. And second, because the internal governance of Andersen was insufficient to control the behaviour of its Houston partners — the partners responsible for the audit and consulting services supplied to Enron.

Yet all of this is known to sophisticated investors and should have been impounded in Enron's share price. So why was it that there was only a gradual fall in Enron's share price?

### The board's capacity to protect the integrity of financial disclosure — effective board monitoring

The monitoring role of the board is proposed as a remedy for a self-interested or incompetent managerial team. The major features are independent directors, specialised committees (in particular, an audit committee) consisting exclusively of independent directors to perform crucial monitoring functions, and a clear charter of board authority.

On the surface, Enron's board fulfilled many of these corporate governance requirements. Enron had an independent board, of which only two of the 14 were insiders, and an audit committee to oversee the company's reporting process and internal controls. The majority of the external directors had relevant business experience, including accounting backgrounds, prior senior management and board positions, and senior regulatory posts. Most of the directors owned stock and received stock options as part of their compensation packages. The audit committee had direct access to financial, legal, and other staff and consultants of the company and the power to retain other accountants, lawyers or consultants. However, the independence of virtually every board member, including audit committee members, was undermined by related-party payments and compromised by the ties associated with long service and familiarity.

There was a gap between what the Enron board knew and what it could have or should have known. Management effectively portrayed an image of Enron as a well-managed firm. As a consequence, the board did not question a proposal to suspend the corporate ethics code. This suspension permitted conflict-of-interest transactions by a senior executive.

### Trade-offs in the use of stock options in executive compensation because of the potential to motivate management to commit fraud and prefer risk

At the time of the Enron collapse, the grant of a share option was not treated as an expense that reduced earnings, while the exercise of an option created an expense equal to the difference between the market price of the share and the exercise price of the option. There is an incentive for option holders to increase the value of the option as they benefit from increases in firm value. Stock options have value if exercised 'in the money' — that is, the stock price is above the exercise price. If option grants are very large and exercisable in the relatively near term, then a positive swing in the stock price can make the senior executives immediately very rich. As option grants increased, the executives of Enron were confronted with two incentives: fraud and risk taking. Managers with an abundance of options may be motivated to get the stock price high by any means necessary, fraud included. In particular, they may be motivated to increase the risk-taking behaviour of the firm, including accepting projects that offer volatile expected returns. This has the potential to increase the value of managers' firm-related investments, and managers can become risk preferring. Both fraud and costly risk-taking appear to have occurred at Enron. Enron became a hedge fund, taking leveraged bets in exotic markets that, if successful, would have produced a huge jackpot for its executives.

**Poor fit between stock-based employee compensation and retirement planning**
The Enron case exposes the conflict between employee share ownership, used for incentive purposes, with employee retirement planning. The actions of lower level employees are unlikely to have any impact on the share price. For example, improving individual divisional performance is unlikely to influence the share price of a large corporation. It is more likely that only senior management's actions will impact on the share price. However, company shares can achieve organisational goals, such as economic decisions. In addition, company shares can also serve as a form of profit-sharing that does not require a cash outlay by the company and which receives favourable accounting treatment.

However, when shares are considered part of retirement planning it conflicts with their role of an incentive device. In the United States, employee shares are typically placed into a contributory pension plan; for example, a 401(k) plan or an Employee Share Ownership Plan, places strict limits on the employee's ability to sell the shares and ties up the proceeds until the employee's retirement. Thus, the benefits of employee share ownership do not accrue until retirement.

Enron employees were heavily invested in Enron shares in their 401(k) plans. An estimated $1.3 billion of the plan's $2.1 billion in pension assets consisted of now-worthless Enron shares. This investment in Enron shares may be attributable to the accounting and tax incentives that reduced Enron's cost of pension contributions if it used its own shares, combined with the pension plan rules that limited employee sale of Enron-contributed shares until age 50. Therefore, employees' pension funds were typically tied up in an undiversified portfolio.

*Source:* Jeffrey N Gordon. (2002) 'What Enron means for the management and control of the modern business corporation: some initial reflections', *The University of Chicago Law Review*, vol. 69, no. 3, pp. 1233–50.

### Required

1 Why was there no adjustment in Enron's share price when sophisticated investors knew of the complex financial structure, off-balance sheet entities, lack of disclosure, the lack of credibility of Andersen's certification, and loss of independence between the auditors and Enron? Comment on the reasons why you think these factors were not impounded into the share price.

2 Even though Enron had what appeared to be a board structure that satisfied the guidelines for good corporate governance, how did information asymmetry and the board's culture contribute to Enron's demise?

3 As option grants increased, Enron executives were confronted with two incentives: fraud and risk taking. Does this mean that there were no positive effects associated with share options?

4 If employee share schemes are to continue as an incentive to motivate employees to increase firm value, what, if any, restrictions should be placed on them?

5 Enron demonstrates that there are problems that cannot be solved, but can only be contained. Imperfectly fashioned incentives and the lack of self-restraint contributed to the collapse of Enron. Comment on this statement. Are there any other poor corporate governance practices that played a part in the collapse?

## APPENDIX //

### Appendix A: Best practice disclosure recommendations from the ASX

Attachment B

Disclosure

Best practice recommendations

**1.1** Formalise and disclose the functions reserved to the board and those delegated to management.

**2.1** A majority of the board should be independent directors.

**2.2** The chairperson should be an independent director.

**2.3** The roles of chairperson and chief executive officer should not be exercised by the same individual.

**2.4** The board should establish a nomination committee.

**2.5** Provide the information indicated in *Guide to reporting on Principle* 2.

**3.1** Establish a code of conduct to guide the directors, the chief executive officer (or equivalent), the chief financial officer (or equivalent) and any other key executives as to:

    **3.1.1** the practices necessary to maintain confidence in the company's integrity

    **3.1.2** the responsibility and accountability of individuals for reporting and investigating reports of unethical practices.

**3.2** Disclose the policy concerning trading in company securities by directors, officers and employees.

**3.3** Provide the information indicated in *Guide to reporting on Principle 3.*

**4.1** Require the chief executive officer (or equivalent) and the chief financial officer (or equivalent) to state in writing to the board that the company's financial reports present a true and fair view, in all material respects, of the company's financial condition and operational results and are in accordance with relevant accounting standards.

**4.2** The board should establish an audit committee.

**4.3** Structure the audit committee so that it consists of:
- only non-executive directors
- a majority of independent directors
- an independent chairperson, who is not chairperson of the board
- at least three members.

**4.4** The audit committee should have a formal charter.

**4.5** Provide the information indicated in *Guide to reporting on Principle* 4.

**5.1** Establish written policies and procedures designed to ensure compliance with ASX Listing Rule disclosure requirements and to ensure accountability at a senior management level for that compliance.

**5.2** Provide the information indicated in *Guide to reporting on Principle* 5.

**6.1** Design and disclose a communications strategy to promote effective communication with shareholders and encourage effective participation at general meetings.

**6.2** Request the external auditor to attend the annual general meeting and be available to answer shareholder questions about the conduct of the audit and content of the auditor's report.

**7.1** The board or appropriate board committee should establish policies on risk oversight and management.

**7.2** The chief executive officer (or equivalent) and the chief financial officer (or equivalent) should state to the board in writing that:

**7.2.1** the statement given in accordance with best practice recommendation 4.1 (the integrity of financial statements) is founded on a sound system of risk management and internal compliance and control which implements the policies adopted by the board

**7.2.2** the company's risk management and internal compliance and control system is operating efficiently and effectively in all material respects.

**7.3** Provide the information indicated in *Guide to reporting on Principle* 7.

**8.1** Disclose the process for performance evaluation of the board, its committees and individual directors, and key executives.

**9.1** Provide disclosure in relation to the company's remuneration policies to enable investors to understand (i) the costs and benefits of those policies and (ii) the link between remuneration paid to directors and key executives and corporate performance.

**9.2** The board should establish a remuneration committee.

**9.3** Clearly distinguish the structure of non-executive directors' remuneration from that of executives.

**9.4** Ensure that payment of equity-based executive remuneration is made in accordance with thresholds set in plans approved by shareholders.

**9.5** Provide the information indicated in *Guide to reporting on Principle 9*.

**10.1** Establish and disclose a code of conduct to guide compliance with legal and other obligations to legitimate stakeholders.

*Source:* ASX Corporate Governance Council 2003, *Guidance note 9A: Principles of good corporate governance and best practice recommendations*, Australian Stock Exchange, Sydney, pp. 24–5.

## REFERENCES //

Allens Arthur Robinson 2003, 'HIH Report and CLERP 9', *Focus: Corporate Governance*, May, p. 2, viewed July 2003, www.aar.com.au/pubs/pdf/ma/focgmay03.pdf.

ASX Corporate Governance Council 2003, *Principles of good corporate governance and best practice recommendations*, Australian Stock Exchange, Sydney.

Commonwealth of Australia 2003, *The failure of HIH insurance: a corporate collapse and its lessons*, Justice Neville Owen (commissioner), 3 vols, Commonwealth of Australia, Canberra.

Coombes, P & Watson, M 2000, 'Three surveys on corporate governance', *The McKinsey Quarterly*, no. 4, pp. 74–7.

Emerging Issues Work Group 2003, 'The essence of corporate governance', CPA Australia Corporate Governance Task Group, viewed 29 September 2003,
www.cpaaustralia.com.au/01_information_centre/1_0_0_0_home.asp.

Hermraj, M 2002, 'Preventing corporate failure: the Cadbury committee's corporate governance report', *Journal of Financial Crime*, vol.10, no. 2, pp. 141–45.

Hutchinson, MR 2003, 'An analysis of the association between firm risk, executive share options and accounting performance: some Australian evidence', *Review of Accounting and Finance*, vol. 2, no. 3, pp. 48–71.

McRitchie, J 2001, 'Enhancing the return on capital through increased accountability', *Corporate Governance*, viewed July 2003, www.corpgov.net.

Vinten, G 2002, 'The corporate governance lessons of Enron', *Corporate Governance*, vol. 2, no. 4, pp. 4–9.

Williamson, 1984, 'Corporate governance', *Yale Law Journal*, vol. 93, pp. 1197–1230.

# Fraud and forensic accounting

**6**

## Learning objectives

After reading this chapter, you should be able to:

- Describe the development of forensic services as a specialised practice.
- Describe the typical mix of skills within a forensic practice.
- Describe the environment within which the forensic accountant operates.
- Discuss the impact of independence issues on conducting work for clients.
- Describe different types of reactive and proactive services relevant to instances where there are disagreements over facts.
- Describe the different types of reactive and proactive services relevant to instances of inappropriate business behaviour.
- Explain why forensic accountants may be called to investigate fraud, rather than the police.

'Attempt the end and never stand to doubt; Nothing's so hard, but search will find it out.'
**Robert Herrick, *Hesperides—Seeke and Finde***

# Introduction //

Forensic services provided by accounting firms are directed to delivering solutions to clients for issues where there is disagreement about facts, or where business-related behaviour is not in accordance with expectations or standards.

The work under the category, 'Disagreement on facts', traditionally was called 'Litigation support', or 'Dispute advisory services', and included a wide range of services, such as:

- expert opinions
- valuations
- assessments of economic loss and damages
- investigations into accounting information, in the context of a wide variety of claims, for example, contract disputes, regulatory inquiries, professional negligence, and failure of products or services to deliver to specifications.

A significant proportion of work in this area is referred to forensic accountants via instructing solicitors, rather than the entity or individual directly.

Similarly, for many years accountants have been called upon to assist clients in cases of inappropriate behaviour. Most typically, this consists of fraud or corruption within the client organisation, but forensic services have expanded over time to include investigation of almost any situation where the facts need to be clarified for the purpose of some form of legal or disciplinary process.

It is the legal process that differentiates forensic services from other services within accounting firms. Litigation, **arbitration**, alternative dispute resolution, regulatory inquiries in the context of an increasing focus on corporate governance, and adherence to standards and compliance generally, have demanded a level of specialisation in the formulation of evidence, whether on fact or opinion, to assist clients and their legal advisers in dealing with a much more complex business environment.

# History of forensic services //

Forensic services have a long history. It has not been unusual for auditors to receive a call for assistance from an audit client with problems such as those outlined above. In the northern hemisphere, in North America and the United Kingdom in particular, specialist forensic units evolved in the late eighties and early nineties; but, in Australia, it has only been since 1998 that large accounting firms have committed to the development of forensic services in specialised business units.

Prior to 1998, forensic services were provided by accounting practitioners on an ad hoc basis, as requested by clients, and largely without any particular specialisation. In the years since 1998, specialist forensic units have developed a much greater level of expertise, applying knowledge and skills to an extent not possible prior to the development of the specialisation.

The skills within forensic units include specialist accountants, forensic technology, and legal, investigative and analytical skills developed in a different context and, in some cases, outside the accounting profession, and these skills are now applied in a cohesive specialist form of forensic advice.

Investigators have been recruited by the accounting firms from public sector agencies, police agencies, regulators and customs, and their skills have been applied to solving problems in a corporate context. Such public sector agencies have been unable to satisfy the needs of corporations when problems of the kind referred to earlier are encountered, and it is not their role to do so.

The current forensic businesses in the major accounting firms include a significant range of reactive and proactive services designed to deal with the kind of commercial disputes and inappropriate behaviour that have only really evolved over the past few years.

The services requested by clients are driven by a number of factors, including globalisation, an increasing investment by corporations in cultures and jurisdictions with which they are unfamiliar, and an increased risk of fraud, corruption and disputes as a result of those investments. Reductions in overheads, 'de-layering', 'down-sizing' and the increasing use of information technology, have combined to mean that a corporation's transactions receive less scrutiny, but are relied upon for decision-making purposes more automatically than was previously the case. The risk of disputes, corruption and fraud has increased as a result.

Increasingly, many of the disputes and asset-tracing investigations arising from fraud involve multiple locations across diverse geographic and legal jurisdictions. The ability to respond to client needs with a degree of urgency is a quality that public sector agencies are unable to match. Growing signs of organised criminal activity, identity fraud, credit card fraud, loan scams, bond trading scams and the like are all examples of the riskier environment in which corporations operate, and an environment that demands faster, more sophisticated and specialised responses than have previously been available.

# Environment //

The forensic accountant works within an environment in which he or she assists and works alongside the judicial system, regulators and public sector bodies. The nature of the engagement dictates which of these bodies has most relevance to the forensic accountant's work. However, the forensic accountant must have an inherent understanding of his or her role in the context of this environment, and the implications of this for the work performed.

## Court system //

Matters reaching litigation often involve complex or technical financial issues on which **expert witnesses** are called to express an opinion and facilitate the court's understanding. As an expert witness, the forensic accountant must be independent, and owes his or her primary duty to the court.

The expert is often engaged by legal counsel for one particular party, and in doing so, that party will hope that the expert's view is favourable to their case. It is vital that the expert does not see the engagement as an invitation to advocate for his or her client. The expert's duty is to the court, not to the client, and their opinion must be independent and able to stand up to cross-examination, to assist the court arrive at a judgment.

To circumvent misuse of the expert's role, Australian jurisdictions have introduced expert witness guidelines. Some jurisdictions require that the expert's report acknowledge his or her agreement to be bound by these guidelines, for the report to be admitted as evidence.

Examples of such guidelines include:

- Federal Court of Australia Practice Direction, including Guidelines for Expert Witnesses
- The *Supreme Court Rules (NSW)*, Schedule K; the Supreme Court of South Australia, Practice Direction 46A; the Supreme Court of the Australian Capital Territory, Practice Direction 3; and the *Expert Witness Code of Conduct* in the Supreme Court of Victoria
- The Family Court of Australia, Practice Direction 2, 'Guidelines for expert witnesses and those instructing them in proceedings in the Family Court of Australia'.

Generally, the court codes require similar standards of experts, including:

- an overriding duty to assist the court impartially, and not to act as advocate for the client
- a clearly expressed opinion, with all relevant facts and assumptions disclosed within the report
- all appropriate inquiries to be made and a note inserted stating that no significant matters have been withheld from the court to their knowledge (the New South Wales and Australian Capital Territory's codes do not require this specific declaration).

The guidelines also provide that the courts may direct the experts to discuss their opinions, with a view to issuing a joint report on areas of agreement and disagreement. These conferences are useful to the court for identifying the real areas of contention.

## APS 11

Despite court guidelines, judges are still questioning the reliability and objectivity of particular expert testimony before them. Some experts are still seen to be fulfilling the role of advocate rather than independent expert for the court.

In response, and to guide and assist professionals providing expert witness services to courts, joint standard *APS 11: Statement of Forensic Accounting Standards*, and the related Guidance Note 2, *Forensic accounting* (GN 2) were issued by the

Institute of Chartered Accountants in Australia (ICAA) and CPA Australia. APS 11 is a code of conduct for those ICAA and CPA members providing forensic services.

APS 11 and GN 2 reiterate the expert's duty to the court, and their duty to avoid actual or perceived conflicts of interest. These documents reinforce many of the principles underlying the court guidelines, such as the need to set out all facts and assumptions, and the duty to refrain from misleading the court by withholding information.

Guidance Note 2 makes several additional recommendations on the independent expert's role, such as:

- noting that experts' professional fees are based on a fixed fee or hourly rate and are not dependent on the outcome of the case
- making reports as transparent as possible by —
  - setting out all instructions, facts and assumptions
  - noting the methodology employed and the reasons that other methodologies are not appropriate
  - appending the expert's curriculum vitae to illustrate their credentials for the opinion provided
  - providing a summary of a range of opinions, where appropriate.

In summary, the court guidelines and APS 11 are intended to improve and regulate the standard of expert witnesses in judicial proceedings. APS 11 is also intended to promote confidence in the reputation and integrity of accounting professionals, in the context of claims of real or perceived bias.

## Alternative dispute resolution //

As parties recognise the time, effort and cost involved in pursuing a matter to litigation, they often examine alternative means of dispute resolution, such as mediation and arbitration. Where the forensic accountant has the relevant skills as a mediator and arbitrator, he or she facilitates a potentially more cost-effective means of resolution, and one that may help preserve the parties' business relationship.

The decision to go to arbitration may be voluntary or as a result of government or contractual obligation. While the arbitrator's decision is binding, it is useful to note that their decision does not form part of legal precedent.

## Court orders

Due to the nature of the work conducted by forensic accountants, they may become familiar with certain court orders obtained by their instructing solicitors or client. These court orders are sought against defendants to further the investigation process, and are generally obtained ex parte, that is, without the prior notice of the defendant. Such orders include:

- *Anton Pillar* order
  An **Anton Pillar order** is a civil court order providing rights to search property without prior warning, and the main aim of such an order is to prevent the destruction of evidence.

- *Mareva* injunction

  A ***Mareva* injunction** is an order to freeze the defendant's assets, to prevent them disposing of the specified assets during the period of the injunction.

## Role of the regulators //

As noted earlier, the forensic accountant works within an environment that also includes government, industry and professional regulators. The forensic accountant's work may be in conjunction with these entities or with consideration to the rules, regulations and guidelines enforced by them.

The relevant regulator depends on the nature of the engagement. Some of the most relevant and commonly encountered regulatory bodies in Australia include:

- Australian Securities and Investments Commission (ASIC)

  ASIC regulates Australian companies, financial markets and professionals involved in finance, investments, superannuation, insurance, deposit taking and credit. It enforces the relevant laws to protect the public, in conjunction with other regulators and investor and consumer protection groups.

- Australian Taxation Office (ATO)

  The ATO administers and enforces legislation relating to taxation, super-annuation and excise. Of particular relevance to the forensic accountant, the ATO watches for the effects of aggressive tax planning, tax evasion and persistent tax debtors. All of these could lead the ATO to take action, either in or out of court.

- Financial Action Task Force (FATF)

  The Financial Action Task Force is an inter-governmental body formed to develop and promote national and international policies combating **money laundering** and terrorist financing. FATF issued a document entitled *Forty recommendations: a global framework for combating money laundering*, in 1990, and eight special recommendations on terrorist financing following 11 September 2001.

  Forensic accountants are involved in the tracing and investigation of laundered funds, as well as the assessment of anti-money laundering procedures, in the light of FATF's recommendations.

Other notable regulators interacting with the forensic accountant's work include professional organisations such as CPA and ICAA, as well as specialist bodies such as APRA and AUSTRAC, to name but a few. Whenever the forensic expert undertakes an assignment, he or she needs to consider if there is a regulator relevant to this work, and the impact of that relationship on the work to be performed.

## Public sector agencies //

The work of the Australian Federal Police (AFP), state and specialist police, or government task forces also includes areas in common with the forensic accountant. For example, the AFP's current focus includes dealing with major fraud and money laundering.

The forensic accountant may work alongside the police, or as a pre-requisite to police involvement. For example, a forensic investigation into a corporation may uncover significant fraud or misconduct such that the corporation decides to involve the police to pursue a criminal prosecution, or it may be that the forensic accountant's investigation takes place concurrently with ongoing police inquiries.

This raises an interesting issue in relation to the reason for civil forensic accountants being called upon to investigate fraud, rather than the police; particularly when police may have forensic accounting capabilities, as well as additional powers of search and seizure not available to civilians. In relation to the investigation of fraud, such powers can be particularly advantageous to the course of an investigation and in the securing of evidence. For example, if it was believed that false invoices were being created in a suspect's home, the police might be able to obtain a warrant under section 465 of the Crimes Act. Civil forensic accountants are unable to obtain warrants and must rely on *Anton Pillar* orders, which are more expensive and provide fewer privileges. This example alone would suggest that civil forensic accountants would seldom be engaged to conduct investigations; however, this is clearly not the case.

Civil forensic accountants are used instead of the police for a number of reasons. Due to the large volumes of other crimes that police are called to investigate, many of which are violent crimes and are considered to be more serious in nature, resources are not always available to respond immediately to financial problems. In commercial accounting firms, however, resources are often on hand and readily available to respond to requests from clients. The resource constraints that the police have, have also led to value amounts being assigned to frauds to be investigated by the serious fraud groups.

In many circumstances, the decision to appoint civil forensic accountants, rather than police, is solely that of the client. This is often the case when companies want suspected fraud investigated for dismissal purposes, rather than to lay any criminal charges. When this is desired, clients may not want the police involved. Further, some clients may simply want civil forensic accountants to investigate anomalies, because they see this as an extension of other services provided by their accounting firm. In this scenario, the client may find comfort in representatives from their appointed accounting firm conducting investigations, because they know the firm and have the perception that the firm understands their business.

In addition, many forensic accountants can develop specialist skills, given that research and development investments can be made in areas of emerging risk. For example, the private sector has taken the lead role in computer forensics. This is partly because the private sector has greater ability to attract and retain appropriately qualified staff and can supplement their investigation services with fraud prevention strategies.

Because many of the cases that civil forensic accountants investigate are for companies that wish to have the fraudsters prosecuted, it is important that investigations are conducted in a manner that ensures the admissibility of evidence. Forensic accounting work should be conducted to the same standards required by the police when pursuing a criminal investigation; and it is no coincidence that many forensic accountants and investigators are former police officers. Evidence is collated and interviews conducted to the same standards of procedure.

## Independence debate //

The independence of the accounting professional when dealing with clients has been the subject of much debate over the past few years. In particular, forensic practices have been affected by issues concerning conflicts of interest and the provision of non-audit services by audit firms.

### Conflicts of interest

It is vital that the forensic expert gives adequate consideration to conflicts of interest before he or she accepts an engagement. Conflicts of interest may be actual or perceived, and concern the expert's ability to complete an assignment objectively, in the light of past, existing or future relationships with the client or other relevant parties.

Prior to accepting an engagement, procedures should be undertaken to determine if a conflict exists. These should be performed on a firm-wide basis, both local and international, and should not be restricted to the individual expert.

Procedures to determine a conflict of interest should include a search to confirm if a relationship exists with any of the parties involved in the action, whether such relationships arise from professional assignments, share holdings and directorships or personal relationships.

The results of these checks should be considered before the forensic expert agrees to accept an engagement. It is possible for engagements to proceed despite conflicts, provided full disclosure or consent is obtained, but certain safeguards, or **Chinese Walls**, may need to be put in place. These may include:

- ensuring that all work is conducted at a controlled site to which only the current engagement team have access
- ensuring that access to the electronic documents on the firm-wide IT server is restricted to the engagement team
- educating staff on the need for confidentiality
- ensuring all members of the team sign confidentiality agreements in relation to the performance of the work
- monitoring of Chinese Walls for compliance.

### Consulting experts and independent experts

Guidance Note 2, discussed above, also notes the inherent differences in the provision of forensic services by a consulting expert, as opposed to an independent expert. Forensic services may be provided in a consultative or an independent manner, and it is important to note the impact of consulting services on the expert's capacity subsequently to act as an independent expert in the same matter.

A forensic accountant may be engaged to provide a range of services such as investigation; or, as noted in GN 2, 'an assessment of the strengths and weaknesses of the positions of the parties to a dispute, and/or assistance in the development of strategies to resolve the dispute in the best interests of clients'.

In providing these services, the forensic expert is engaged to act in the interests of their client. However, GN 2 notes that this partisan relationship may lead to the perception that the same expert cannot act independently if subsequently engaged as an independent expert for the same matter.

The forensic expert must give this matter due consideration prior to accepting the engagement as independent expert.

## Sarbanes–Oxley Act 2002

On 30 July 2002, the landmark legislation known as the Sarbanes–Oxley Act (S-Ox) was enacted into United States law. Named after its principal authors, Senator Paul D Sarbanes (D-Md) and Rep. Michael G Oxley, the Act sought to restore investor confidence in the United States financial markets, corporate governance and financial reporting.

The Sarbanes–Oxley Act was passed by the United States legislature in the wake of accounting scandals such as Enron, WorldCom and Xerox, all of which had seriously undermined investor confidence. Though strictly United States legislation, its impact on the accounting and financial markets is far-reaching. The Act applies to all Securities and Exchange Commission (SEC) listed companies, and so extends to subsidiary and associated entities of SEC listed companies outside of the United States.

The Enron and WorldCom scandals highlighted the role of the auditor in ensuring the integrity of financial reporting, and in particular, the auditor's independence and objectivity. Accordingly, the Act prohibits professional accounting firms from providing non-audit services to audit clients, with the exception of tax services and specialist management advice. Non-audit services specifically include appraisal or valuation services, and fairness opinions that are traditionally the work of the forensic accountant. Investigation services, often related to audit issues, are not prohibited unless there is a requirement to provide court testimony.

The impact of the requirements of S-Ox is that forensic practices must seek work outside of such traditional sources as existing audit clients, although this potentially opens up avenues into other clients. In turn, clients may lose the benefits of the inherent in-house knowledge and experience obtained from the audit engagement, but they may also benefit from a different expert's perspective.

However, in so far as the nature and performance of the audit engagement was seen to threaten the forensic accountant's independence, the S-Ox provisions go some way to enforcing and promoting objectivity and restoring the accounting profession's reputation.

## Corporate Law Economic Reform Program (Audit Reform & Corporate Disclosure) Act 2004

The CLERP Bill was issued as part of an ongoing government program of business regulation. Specifically, it was in response to the high-profile instances of unacceptable corporate behaviour in Australia, such as the collapse of HIH and One.Tel, and also, the international scandals that prompted the Sarbanes–Oxley Act.

In overview, the CLERP Bill proposes reformed and additional oversight of the audit profession, more effective business reporting and more rigorous internal monitoring of reporting by corporations. The CLERP Bill requirements were effective as law from 1 July 2004.

The impact for forensic assignments stems from the CLERP Bill's proposals on the provision of non-audit services. The CLERP Bill supports the immediate application of the provisions of Professional Statement F1, on Professional Independence[1], which requires that threats to independence be reduced to acceptable levels. Where this cannot be done, Statement F1 prohibits the provision of the non-audit service.

The CLERP Bill also requires the audit committee to disclose in the annual report whether they are satisfied the non-audit services provided are compatible with auditor independence. This includes an explicit statement on why specific services such as valuation services and litigation support services do not compromise auditor independence.

As with S-Ox, this may put pressure on a traditional source of work for forensic services — that of existing audit clients. However, as outlined above in relation to S-Ox, it may also open up other avenues of work from which the expert and the client will benefit.

# Types of forensic services //

As noted previously in this chapter, forensic services can be considered as those addressing disagreements over facts, and those dealing with inappropriate business behaviour. This terminology may differ among forensic practices, as may the terminology used to describe the individual services, but the concepts are consistent. The following sections summarise the types of forensic services that may be offered under these general headings.

It is useful to note that, traditionally, forensic services have been reactive rather than proactive. The forensic accountant has been called upon when a matter is already in dispute, a suspicion of fraud already noted, or misconduct already alleged. It is at that point that the forensic accountant has been called on to conduct an investigation or quantify a claim.

Recently, the profession has identified opportunities to offer proactive services, using the experience gained from reactive engagements. This has recognised the benefits to a company's reputation, as well as the savings in time and money, of addressing issues such as fraud, misconduct and contractual ambiguity before they arise. Accordingly, typical forensic services can be considered as those that are reactive, and those that are proactive.

## Disagreement over facts — reactive services //

### Expert witness services

In any of the services outlined below, the forensic accountant's role may be in the capacity of an expert witness. Specifically, the expert will produce a report that will be filed in court and upon which they will give evidence and be cross-examined.

The expert may also provide guidance to legal counsel on the financial or accounting aspects of particular cases, including the preparation of questions for examination-in-chief and cross-examination, and evaluating and analysing the other party's case.

### Valuation services

Valuation services include the valuation of shares, businesses, trusts and intangible assets — for example, intellectual property — involved in commercial or family law disputes.

The valuer must determine the fair value of the asset or interest, based on the amount a hypothetical purchaser who is willing but not anxious to buy, is prepared to pay a vendor who is willing but not anxious to sell.

Several valuation techniques are used, such as a discounted cash flow method, maintainable earnings, maintainable dividends or an orderly realisation of assets. The method used will depend on the nature of the business and whether the interest held is a minority or controlling interest.

For example, a minority interest has no control over the decisions of the business and the profits generated. Therefore, it is appropriate to discount the value of this interest, compared with a majority interest that provides control of the corporation and its cash flow.

### Economic loss

Forensic accountants are commonly called on to quantify economic loss in disputes arising from areas such as:

- business interruption
- breach of warranty
- personal injury
- professional negligence.

The purpose of assessing economic loss is to determine the amount required to put the plaintiff in the financial position in which it would have been had the incident not taken place, and to leave the plaintiff no worse off as a result of the incident.

In order to quantify the impact of the incident, it is generally necessary to identify a causal relationship between the incident and a change in operations of the business. This usually requires the forensic accountant to identify what the drivers of the business to be analysed were during the relevant period.

**IN PRACTICE**

> ### Economic loss
>
> A retail business within a shopping complex claims it is dependent upon the presentation of the shopfront and passing trade. A key driver of the business is obviously customer numbers; that is, customers passing through the complex, and customers passing the shop and entering the premises.
>
> However, building and renovation works by the managers of the complex disrupted public access to the shop, to the extent that the shop owners claim that customer numbers have fallen, resulting in an alleged loss of profits. The shop owners claim that customers could not easily access the shop; therefore, the usual sales generated from passing trade were lost.
>
> In this example, an economic loss claim assesses how the business actually performed compared to how it would have been expected to perform had the building works not occurred.

## Professional negligence

Professionals, including auditors, accountants and advisors, can find themselves the subject of proceedings questioning the fulfilment of their professional duty of care. Forensic expert witnesses may be asked to provide an expert report assessing the professional's work against the standard expected. In some cases, the forensic expert may also quantify the potential economic loss arising from the alleged breach.

## Post acquisition disputes

Despite the efforts of due diligence procedures prior to a commercial merger or acquisition, disputes can still arise after completion of the deal. The disputes may concern the construction of certain contract clauses, or they may relate to the accounts and alleged financial performance of the subject company, on the strength of which the purchaser made the decision to buy.

It commonly falls to forensic accounting experts to reconstruct or analyse the accounts upon which the deal was made. This process may involve an extensive analysis of the company's financial records and the interviewing of key personnel, as well as a review of the audit and due diligence papers.

The forensic exercise may or may not concur with the accounts relied upon in the sale transaction. This may be due to error, negligence, fraud or misconduct; and may lead to additional causes of actions such as professional negligence or criminal charges.

### Insurance claims

Many forensic accountants' services, such as assessing economic loss for business interruption cases or professional negligence, may be in the context of an insurance claim under a policy of insurance covering loss of fixed assets or profits, arising from natural disaster or professional negligence.

### Intellectual property disputes

Disputes and reviews commonly involve assessing losses suffered by the owners of intellectual property rights, as well as the benefit to the infringer of the use of the rights. A typical engagement may be to quantify the royalties due to the owner of the rights, had the rights been licensed to the infringer in a legitimate manner.

### Class actions

Forensic accountants may also be involved in the provision of independent evidence in relation to class actions, as well as disputes between single parties. Class actions occur when one or more people sue on behalf or a larger group of people all affected by a common issue, but where it is impractical for a large number of complainants to sue.

## Disagreement over facts — proactive services //

### Agreement vetting

Disputes concerning the wording of commercial agreements are common, and can be time consuming and costly to resolve. While each contracting party will believe they understand what has been agreed upon, it is common for that understanding to differ, or for the contract wording to reflect something different to that which was thought to be agreed.

Differences arise for a number of reasons, including:

- imprecise or misused technical terms
- accounting provisions drafted by commercial lawyers unfamiliar with accounting concepts or their application
- confusion or contradiction caused by multiple revisions to the original draft document.

Accordingly, the vetting of commercial agreements prior to signing can provide valuable support to the drafting team, who may have become too close to the document to read it critically and objectively. A review can identify and eliminate problem provisions before they become binding on the parties.

## Agreement vetting

A contract provision states that Party A must pay Party B a fee equal to 5 per cent of its annual profits for the next three years. What is meant by 'profits'? The term is not defined within the contract. Party A may calculate different profits figures, depending on whether the figures are calculated for the management or audited accounts, and the accounting policies used. Under the current contract provision, Party A could interpret the meaning of 'profits' each year to calculate the lowest profit possible.

For example, subsequent to the agreement being signed, Party A changes its depreciation policy on plant and equipment from 10 per cent per annum to 25 per cent per annum. The increased depreciation charge means that Party A no longer makes an accounting profit and therefore argues it does not have to pay a fee to Party B.

Had the agreement been vetted prior to signing, the forensic accountant would have recommended a number of changes to the clause. The meaning of 'profits' should have been defined so that profit was calculated with reference to an established methodology and defined accounting policies, which could only be changed with the written permission of both parties.

### Alternative dispute resolution

As noted above, the time, effort and cost of litigation is prompting some parties to opt for mediation or arbitration as an alternative.

Forensic experts trained as mediators facilitate discussions between the parties. Those acting as an arbitrator must assess each party's case and then reach an assessment that is ultimately binding on the parties.

### Expert determination services

On a similar theme to alternative dispute resolution, some matters, such as contract disputes, provide for issues to be sent to an expert referee for resolution. The forensic accountant may advise a party in making its submissions, or may take the role of the expert referee.

# Inappropriate business behaviour — reactive services //

## Fraud investigations

Fraud investigations involve the discovery of facts on suspected fraudulent activity within or against organisations. This is one of the most well known and common services of forensic accountants; and, with the increase of fraud in the business community,[2] such services are likely to be employed more frequently.

The most common type of fraud within Australia is credit card fraud. Because this is such a significant problem, financial institutions normally have investigation departments and seldom rely on forensic accountants. Forensic accountants not only investigate common fraud types, such as false invoicing, but also atypical types such as identity theft. This range of investigation services is necessary to assist clients in the prevention of threats against the viability and profitability of their businesses.

Fraud can occur anywhere: within the smallest department, across multiple lines of business, during various business cycles, and throughout multinational locations. While this risk is ubiquitous, organisations seldom realise they are vulnerable to fraud until they become victims. Most often, the person behind the deception is a trusted employee, a valued business partner or vendor, or even a member of the management team. Without even knowing it was at risk, a company victimised by fraud can find itself the subject of a criminal or civil investigation, or the defendant in a lawsuit brought by shareholders or other critical stakeholders.

In circumstances where irregularities or anomalies are identified early, forensic accountants can conduct an investigation and eliminate the problems before they grow in magnitude.

## Forensic technology

Modern organisations increasingly depend on technological infrastructure, from email and Internet services, to the management of documents and client records. Such infrastructure can be surprisingly fragile and insecure, and is often open to misuse. Forensic technology specialists are called upon when an organisation's infrastructure is compromised in this manner. Typically, forensic technology is a specialised arm of a forensic practice that identifies, preserves and analyses electronic evidence in a manner that is admissible in court.

Forensic technology specialists assist in determining such information as:

- Where is information stored? — The majority of today's business documents are electronic.
- Who is communicating with whom? — Internet, email and telephone are the predominant means of business communication.
- Where are funds moving? — Large financial transactions can occur in seconds through the use of electronic funds transfers.
- Who knows what? — Business communications such as emails can help establish knowledge and intent.
- Has information been altered? — The authenticity of electronically stored financial data may be challenged.

Forensic technologists can assist in answering these and other questions by performing such techniques as recovering deleted files, copying hard drives, monitoring the history of activity on a computer, locating hidden or disguised files, and reviewing the chronology of computer activity.

Forensic technology services include a technique called **data mining**. Data mining is a method of interrogating electronic data, which may be downloaded from various computers or a network in an organisation, and running queries on the data to identify anomalies or 'red flags' for fraud.

**IN PRACTICE**

> ### Data mining
> As part of an accounts payable review, a forensic technologist performs data mining on Company X's accounts payable system. This is performed by downloading data from the accounts payable system, as well as other organisational data from such sources as payroll, vendor's maintenance system, etc. By running various queries on the data, the forensic technologist identifies a number of red flags, including an ex-employee who is still active on the payroll system and whose bank account details have been changed to match an existing employee, as well as a vendor with the same address as a current employee.
>
> These red flags can then allow a more in-depth investigation into a possible payroll fraud and supplier fraud.

### Asset tracing

Asset tracing uses publicly available information to follow the flow of assets, to determine a current location, whether those assets be in the form of cash, stock, property, vehicles or any other valued commodity. Forensic accountants can be called upon to trace assets following a fraud, to determine where misappropriated funds have been hidden, after an incident of money laundering, or even prior to civil action to determine the extent of a claim.

Forensic accounts often use a technique called Visual Intelligence Analysis (VIA) to determine the location and flow of assets. VIA is a process of charting entities, relationships and commodities to enable a simple, understandable depiction of otherwise complex and ambiguous data. VIA can be used specifically for:

- Link analysis. Depicts associations between entities such as people and organisations, the flow of commodities such as money and property, or complex corporate structures, including ownership, directors, asset holdings and inter-company loans, any or all of which could cover multiple jurisdictions.
- Network and transaction analysis. Extends the concept of link analysis to large datasets, and is particularly useful for analysing high volumes of data such as bank transactions, telephone records and Internet firewall clusters.
- Sequence of events. Reveals how related events unfold over time through arranging data chronologically and recording interconnections between subjects.

- Transaction pattern analysis. Identifies repeated patterns of activity such as a particular sequence of telephone calls indicating a chain of command, or a pattern of account transfers revealing a mechanism for money laundering or other fraudulent activity.

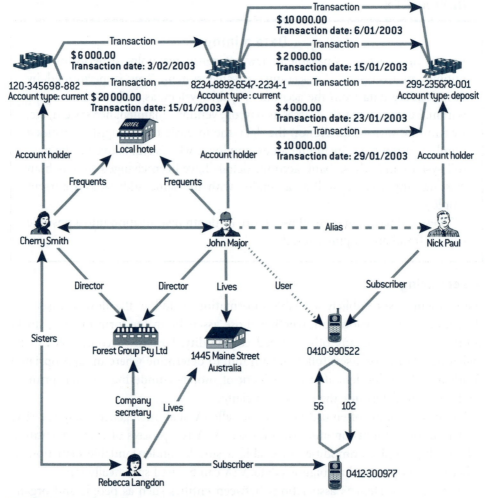

FIGURE 6.1   Example of a typical link analysis chart

## Intellectual property investigations

A company's assets are not always tangible. Indeed, in particular industries such as research and development, and even in consulting, the value of intangible assets can be a significant part of a business. Intangible assets can be stolen just as easily, if not more easily, than physical property. When this occurs, companies will often use the investigation services of forensic accountants to establish theft. This commonly involves a combination of investigators and forensic technologists, particularly if intellectual property is downloaded from company computers or emailed outside the company.

### Investigations for company receivers / administrators / liquidators

Forensic accountants conduct investigations for a number of reasons, including suspicion that a fraud or other form of misappropriation may have contributed to a company collapse. In these circumstances, the receiver, administrator or liquidator may want mismanagement or corporate governance failures investigated to determine whether claims can be made against the directors of the failed company. Similarly, managers and directors can incur excessive expenses in the lead-up to the company going into receivership, administration or liquidation. The investigation of this expenditure can identify instances of fraud or misconduct in the form of kickbacks or the purchase of personal goods.

### Money laundering investigations

A money laundering investigation is a process of tracing transactions for the purpose of seizing and forfeiting funds and assets. The belief that money laundering only relates to illegal drugs, or that it is only prevalent in the Caribbean, South America, Asia and Russia, is a common misconception. Money laundering can occur wherever financial institutions are located, be they banks, building societies, insurance companies, credit unions or bureaux de change.

Predominantly, money laundering occurs for two reasons: to conceal ill-gotten gains or to finance illegal activity. The techniques used to investigate money laundering are the same, irrespective of why funds are laundered, and are similar to those used to trace assets. However, money laundering investigations can be even more complex, due to the number of financial transfers involved. Further, it can be a time-consuming process, as transfers are often made through jurisdictions with bank secrecy laws or which are unwilling to disclose client information. In an effort to force such countries to assist in the fight against money laundering, FATF issues a 'black list' of these countries, called the *Non-cooperative countries and territories list*.

### Integrity investigations

Integrity investigations involve looking into allegations of improper conduct within an organisation. Forensic accountants do not always deal with fraud and illegal activity, because it is often the case at the end of an investigation that no crimes have been committed. Rather, the outcome is proof of misconduct, breach of company policies and procedures, or even discrimination in some form. The experience of dealing with integrity issues as part of fraud investigations results in forensic accountants being well equipped to get to the bottom of integrity issues and concerns.

## Inappropriate business behaviour — proactive services //

In recent years, the profession has identified opportunities to offer preventative services, using experience from investigations, such as the management of fraud risk and integrity risk, anti money laundering and security consulting. In addition to investigation experience, experience with risk management strategies, and research and assisting clients after frauds have been committed, significantly contribute to prevention programs for clients.

### Misconduct and fraud diagnostic

The most common form of fraud and misconduct prevention work is in assessing fraud risk and current controls, and using these to develop fraud prevention strategies. This usually involves implementing three key principles of fraud prevention:

1. Fraud risk assessment — identifying potential risks and ranking them based on their likelihood and consequences, for the purpose of addressing preventative techniques for each risk
2. Fraud control planning — documenting an organisation's strategy for controlling fraud, in accordance with Australian Standard 8001-2003 on Fraud and Corruption Control
3. Fraud awareness training — raising the awareness among staff of the prevalence of fraud in the industry and country in which they are based, as well as methods of detecting, investigating and preventing fraud.

By providing these services, forensic accountants assist their clients to understand and address organisational risks and vulnerability to fraud, while helping them develop the skills needed to identify **red flags**, to help prevent fraud before it happens.

### Corporate intelligence

**Corporate intelligence** is the collection and analysis of public information with strategic value. Forensic accountants use corporate intelligence to research strengths, vulnerabilities and strategies of individuals and organisations engaging in business dealings. Corporate intelligence allows clients to identify whom they are going to do business with, which is particularly important prior to mergers, board appointments and embarking on legal action. Similarly, corporate intelligence can be used for pre-employment screening purposes — to ensure the integrity of information that candidates supply on their résumés.

### Security consulting

Security consulting is a process of addressing physical security issues in the context of enterprise-wide systems. While security consulting is not typically a core service, forensic accounts are often requested to assist with such matters following stock being misappropriated.

## Pre-employment screening

The recruitment of employment candidates often involves fierce competition. Sometimes, a candidate may attempt to gain an advantage over other candidates by falsifying their credentials. Without determining the veracity of the information candidates supply on their résumés, employers are basing their selection on information that may not be correct.

Pre-employment screening may include discussing the candidate with previous employers and referees, conducting bankruptcy searches, directorships and shareholding checks, writs and summonses searches, verifying qualifications and professional memberships, criminal history checks, public profile searches, or work rights status checks.

Undertaking background investigations on candidates through pre-employment screening provides the opportunity to weed out unwanted employees before they join a company.

## Anti money laundering

Given the increased focus on international terrorism and money laundering arising out of the events of 11 September 2001, it is likely that the regulators will have little hesitation in naming and shaming businesses and institutions for their part in money laundering activity. For this reason, forensic accountants assist businesses to assess and enhance internal controls, to prevent money-laundering occurring at the outset. This is typically performed by assisting companies to implement a robust anti money laundering regime, including:

- implementing due diligence procedures to know your customers
- updating client profiles regularly
- using data mining software to alert or indicate certain types of activity or businesses
- obtaining up-to-date training on relevant legislation and obligations
- reviewing procedures regularly, and defining roles and responsibilities clearly
- recognising that doubtful funds can originate, or be routed through, almost anywhere in the world.

## Compliance advisory

Using the experience gained in dealing with regulations and standards relating to fraud and corruption control, corporate governance, risk management and whistleblower protection, forensic accountants are well positioned to advise companies on required changes for compliance.

## Compliance surveys

Compliance surveys act as tools to determine the perception, awareness and acceptance of an organisation's policies and procedures on fraud prevention and integrity promotion. Forensic accountants often use such surveys to determine where intervention is required or where staff may need additional training.

## Culture improvement programs/company code development

Integrity risk management is a process of identifying risks and weaknesses in corporate integrity, developing codes of conduct and integrity programs, and delivering training in ethics awareness and integrity risk management. Companies may seek one or all of these services from forensic accountants, to promote a robust integrity framework. While such services improve the ethical culture of an organisation, they also contribute to the prevention of fraud and misconduct.

## Fraud hotlines

A fraud hotline is an effective tool for capturing information about suspected fraudulent behaviour in a confidential manner. Fraud reporting hotlines can be either internal — going to someone responsible for fraud within the organisation — or external hotlines that are normally received by external parties, such as forensic accountants. External reporting hotlines are encouraged as part of the Australian Standards on Whistleblower Protection (8004-2003) and Fraud and Corruption Control (8001-2003). This is because any inherent risks of recrimination or reprisal for those reporting suspected fraud internally can be avoided by using an external hotline. Forensic accountants typically offer such services, because having experts gathering the facts of the matter can be of significant benefit to clients, and it normally allows the forensic accountants to be well positioned to conduct the ensuing investigation.

## Digital evidence recovery and preservation

Whether forensic accountants are dealing with evidence as part of a civil dispute, or a prosecution for fraud, the importance of having evidence that has been gathered and maintained in an admissible manner is paramount. From a forensic technology viewpoint, the admissibility of evidence is particularly challenging, because digital evidence is continually changing, and changes can jeopardise its admissibility. Forensic technologists adopt techniques to recover and preserve data after it has been deleted or modified, so that courts can rely upon it. This requires consistent recording of the procedures taken to recover the data, recording any changes made and the reasons for them, and securing data during the process so that it cannot be lost or altered in any way.

# Summary //

The development of dedicated forensic services has been driven by the need for specialisation in collating and presenting evidence in commercial disputes and investigations. Forensic practices have developed to encompass a range of services, utilising skills from accounting and technology to investigation and law enforcement.

Much of the development in professional services firms has been in response to requests for assistance from audit clients. In the wake of Enron, and the ensuing independence debate, the provision of non-audit services to audit clients is increasingly prohibited by regulation or increased attention to good corporate governance. Forensic practices must look to a wider market for sources of work.

Forensic practitioners will continue to work alongside law enforcement agencies, the judicial system and regulatory bodies, in addition to working directly with their clients. The ambit of forensic service lines continues to expand, encompassing more traditional reactive and proactive services, as well as new and emerging issues, such as the focus on anti money laundering requirements. Furthermore, given recent commercial and very public scandals such as HIH, Enron and WorldCom, forensic practitioners will continue to investigate and report on instances of creative accounting and the integrity of the underlying financial information.

# Key terms //

*Anton Pillar* order . . . p. 154
Arbitration . . . p. 151
Chinese Walls . . . p. 157
Corporate intelligence . . . p. 168
Data mining . . . p. 165
Expert witness . . . p. 152
*Mareva* injunction . . . p. 155
Money laundering . . . p. 155
Red flag . . . p. 168

# Questions //

**6.1** Explain the development of forensic services as a specialised practice.
**6.2** Describe the typical mix of skills within a forensic practice.
**6.3** Explain the environment within which the forensic accountant operates, giving examples of relevant regulatory bodies and how they may interact with the forensic accountant's work.

**6.4** Describe how accounting scandals such as Enron and WorldCom have impacted upon forensic services, and the positive and negative aspects to that impact.

**6.5** Explain how the different types of reactive and proactive services could be relevant to a prospective client who has the following issues:

> The prospective client company was sold to a third party 12 months ago. The selling price was based on the company's earnings, as disclosed in the audited financial statements for the previous year-end. Since the sale, the company suspects that the results shown in those accounts were overstated and the buyer paid too much to acquire the company.

**6.6** Explain which different types of reactive and proactive services could be relevant to a prospective client who has the following issues:

> A CEO is aware that many of his junior staff members have concerns about middle management, but most of them seem uncomfortable about coming forward to provide him with details of their concerns.
>
> Company A is considering the acquisition of Company B, due to strong synergies between their businesses. A great deal is known about Company B's operations; however, some concerns exist in Company A about the credentials of Company B's directors. A warehouse manager who prides himself on his knowledge of his company's supplier relationships discovers an invoice from an unfamiliar supplier. The invoice has few details on it, but does not appear to be for any material that the company has purchased.

## CASE STUDY

### Forensic accounting

Forensic accountants were asked to investigate the suspected theft of equipment from a major building materials and equipment supplier (the client). The client's business included the supply of equipment to building contractors on a hire basis. The client became suspicious of the level of equipment going missing from major building sites around Australia, and asked forensic accountants to assist in the investigation.

The forensic team set up covert surveillance over certain building sites to monitor activity. As a result, responsibility for the thefts was narrowed down to suspected collusion between a contractor and an employee of the client.

It was alleged that the contractor would simply take the client's equipment from sites where it was being used. He would then either use the equipment himself, rent it out, or sell it. It appeared that the contractor had been doing this for some time.

The forensic team obtained *Anton Pillar* orders to search the premises of the contractor in question, and documents found during the searches were reviewed during the investigation.

In addition, the hard drives of the suspects' laptops and other computers were imaged for analysis. The forensic technology team performed this so that the electronic data could be analysed, but also preserved in a way that allowed it to be still admitted as evidence at a later date.

During searches of the contractor's premises, the forensic investigators found evidence of payments made by the employee of the client, who was also a good friend of the contractor. The employee was a yard supervisor for the client. The employee later denied the allegation that he had assisted the contractor in the theft of the equipment by recording the return of more equipment than had been physically received.

Following the theft of equipment investigation, forensic accountants were asked to produce a loss of profits valuation for the purposes of quantifying an insurance claim in relation to the theft.

Essentially, the economic loss claim had two components. The first component, and the most straightforward to quantify, was the value of the equipment stolen, for which the client was no longer receiving any benefits.

The second component of the valuation was to assess the loss of rental income suffered by the client in relation to the equipment stolen. This was on the premise that, had the equipment not been stolen, the client could have hired it out during the normal course of business and received a rental income thereon.

*Outcome*

The investigation and valuation performed by the forensic team estimated that approximately 500 tonnes of equipment was stolen from the client, resulting in an insurance claim of approximately $3.7 million.

Through the investigation carried out by the forensic team, approximately one-third of the stolen equipment was traced, recovered and returned to the client. The investigation also led to a Supreme Court hearing and a New South Wales police inquiry.

*Further information*

Numerous interviews were conducted during the course of the investigation by the forensic team and the client's management. Though the investigation was concerned with the theft of equipment, the interview team were surprised when one of those interviewed in connection with the thefts admitted to unconnected instances of money laundering via false invoicing on a major building project. These allegations were subsequently passed on and investigated by a royal commission established to look into corruption.

The interviewee admitted he had laundered approximately \$100 000 in funds for a contact at a refurbishment company. He explained that he would generate false invoices, including a 10 per cent commission. He would then return the majority of the cash to his contact and keep the 10 per cent commission for his part. He believed his contact needed the money to pay off union officials.

**Required**

1 Outline the reasons forensic accountants may have been asked to investigate this matter rather than the police.
2 Describe methods that the client could use to prevent similar frauds occurring in the future.
3 Why would an *Anton Pillar* order have been used in this instance, rather than a search warrant?
4 What are the key difficulties in investigating collusive behaviour?

## ENDNOTES //

1. Joint statement issued by ICAA and CPA Australia.
2. KPMG Fraud Survey 2002.

# 7

# Creative accounting

## Learning objectives

After studying this chapter you should be able to:
- Define creative accounting.
- Discuss the various forms of creative accounting.
- Understand the reason creativity is practised in accounting.
- Recognise the consequences of creative accounting.
- Identify and detect creative accounting practices.
- Understand how to reduce creative accounting.
- Consider some possible solutions to the problem of creative accounting.

---

'As with most important issues, the success of Sarbanes–Oxley and the exchanges' proposal in improving the financial reporting process depends on the degree to which the agents involved change their behaviors.'
**April Klein, 'Likely effects of stock exchange governance proposals and Sarbanes–Oxley on corporate boards and financial reporting',** *Accounting Horizons*, vol. 17, no. 4, December 2003, p. 354.

# Introduction //

Accounting is often seen as precise and reliable in nature, because the recording and measurement functions rely on a process that deals with numbers that are allocated to accounts, then simply added up. However, accounting is not a perfect science; the discretion permitted in the calculation and allocation of accounting numbers means that two accountants presented with identical data may not produce identical results. As you read this chapter, you will come to understand that much of what the accountant provides as being precise, objective and reliable may in fact be subjective, and based on a considerable amount of judgment. The flexibility and subjectivity within the rules of accounting enable manipulations, which provide opportunities for unscrupulous accountants to be creative and produce results that serve some particular interest or interests. These activities are known as **creative accounting**.

In this chapter we look at examples of creative accounting and real-life experiences of accountants in businesses, and the related outcomes. We also highlight possible observable areas to detect creative accounting — the key to detecting manipulation is often a questioning mind! We offer possible solutions to the problem of creative accounting by highlighting steps that can be taken or put in place to reduce the phenomenon of creative accounting.

# What is creative accounting? //

A precise understanding of creative accounting can be gained by a description of what it involves.

> It is essentially a process of using the rules, the flexibility provided by them and the omissions within them, to make financial statements look somewhat different from what was intended by the rule. It consists of rule-bending and loophole-seeking. It includes the process by which transactions are structured so as to produce the required accounting outcome rather than allowing accounting to report transactions in a neutral and consistent way.
>
> Jameson 1988, p. 20.

Creative accounting necessarily involves an element of contrivance and a perverse application of the accounting principles so as to secure a deliberately misleading result (Peterson 1995). Creative accounting has also been variously described as fiddling or cooking the books, earnings management, manipulation, deceit and misrepresentation, and as an abuse of the accounting system. Creative accounting can be described as the use of ambiguities in the rules of accounting to convey a different and a desired picture of the business's financial performance.

Despite claims to the contrary, accounting is not an exact science. Accounting is a regulated commodity prescribed by accounting standards. In Australia, accounting standards are backed by the force of law under the *Corporations Act 2001* (Cth), which mandates compliance with accounting standards. Accordingly, the AASB Accounting Standards (accounting standards issued by the Australian Accounting Standards Board) set out the principles and rules that must be observed by companies and other reporting entities that are required to prepare and lodge annual financial statements and accompanying notes. Even though accounting is a prescribed practice, and accounting standards attempt to reduce the diverse ways of recording and presenting financial information, creative accounting continues to occur because it involves making a decision as to which rule is to be applied within the requirements of the accounting standards. Creative accounting relies on the discretion permitted within accounting standards; therefore, breaching rules or regulations is not a condition of creative accounting. While creative accounting may not contravene the letter of the law or the accounting standards, it is clearly in breach of the spirit of such rules. Later in this chapter, we present you with a case entitled, 'In practice: Aggressive but legal', which illustrates how Enron, now bankrupt, aggressively interpreted the rules of accounting for ulterior motives. Creative accounting is a process that takes advantage of the rules in the accounting standards that allow flexibility and subjectivity; which, in turn, allows financial statements to appear different from the true state of an entity's economic affairs.

Creative accounting is a distortion of what actually took place, which can lead to serious allocation problems, both within the business and the economy as a whole. Financial statements are one means by which a company discloses financial information to shareholders and investors. A lack of confidence in the financial reporting resulting from creative accounting may reduce the number of investors, both by amount and number, and in consequence, increase the cost of capital and reduce the productivity in the economy. For some, creative accounting is a serious problem that is widely practised (Elias 2004). Even though the practice of creative accounting is not a new phenomenon, it has become more sophisticated in recent years. Recent business failures involving questionable accounting methods by such entities as Enron, WorldCom, Global Crossing and HIH, to name only a few, are evidence of a growing business culture that fosters creative accounting.

To try and understand why creative accounting occurs is to question the very motive of the business enterprise, and the reason it was created in the first place. Accounting, as with any product, is open to the forces of demand and supply, and accountants, through incentives, may simply be providing what is required by demand. Accounting numbers define relationships between the business, lenders, managers, politicians, employees, customers and suppliers (Whittred et al. 2004); therefore, businesses have incentives to use **accounting methods** that produce the best results possible to attract and retain investors and increase bonuses paid to managers. For example, the more geared a business, the greater its use of creative policies to increase reported earnings, mostly due to the imposition by lenders of restraints on the business (debt covenants), which are frequently expressed in accounting ratios. The motive behind creative accounting is sometimes explained in terms of the 'income smoothing' hypothesis. Rather than having years of exceptionally good or bad profits, companies will try to keep the figures relatively stable by shifting revenues and expenses from one period to another through the use of reserves and provisions. Shareholders benefit from earnings manipulation because reducing the volatility of earnings will improve share value. Accountants are not alone in this process; they are usually a party to the process, often driven by greedy or misguided management. When major corporate CFOs were asked anonymously: 'Has your CEO ever asked you to falsify financial results?' — 68 per cent responded 'yes' (Leib 2002).

To summarise, there is a demand for accounting information that arises from the role of accounting numbers in defining contractual relationships. In order to satisfy and maintain these contractual relationships, management, along with 'creative' accountants, choose accounting methods that distort the events and transactions of the business. According to Shah (1996, 1997), creative accounting is possible for three reasons:

1. judgment and choice within the accounting rules
2. the creation of artificial transactions
3. the creation of new and complex financial instruments.

Mulford and Comisky (2002) illustrate four practical methods of creative accounting:

1. recognising premature or fictitious revenue
2. capitalising expenses and using extended periods for amortising assets
3. classification and disclosure
4. pro-forma earnings measures.

Other common methods used in the creative accounting process include capitalising interest, depreciation, brand accounting and stock valuation (Hussey and Ong 1996). The following sections provide examples to illustrate the practice of creative accounting.

## Accounting systems //

Most accountants acknowledge that, given the same facts, many similar but different accounting treatments are possible for each transaction. The process of keeping accounts for a transaction calls for a number of decisions and judgments between the two competing approaches. Accounting allows flexibility, and this flexibility enables opportunities for manipulation, and maybe a misrepresentation of the economic reality behind the transaction. On a macro accounting level, consider the distinction between cash versus **accrual accounting** (Takatera and Sawabe 2000). It is widely accepted that **cash accounting** is less manipulated because transactions are recorded on the date that they are actually incurred; whereas the accrual basis of accounting recognises transactions in the period incurred, which may not necessarily fall in the same period as the date in which the cash is exchanged. Preparing financial reports on the accrual basis of accounting means that the profits recorded during the year are not the same as the cash that has been received. Thus, it is important to note that profit is not cash. It is equally important to note that accounting is built on assumptions and uncertainties. Changing the assumptions, such as the basis on which transactions are recognised (cash or accrual) can have significant effects on the financial statements.

Separate from this is the great divide between **historical cost** accounting, and current cost accounting. Historical cost accounting records transactions at their original cost. The problem with measuring transactions at their original cost is that they do not consider the value of money. The value of money is not static; currencies erode dramatically, which in turn affects purchasing power. Therefore, adding transaction amounts that have occurred in different periods, particularly assets, is an attempt to add un-addable numbers. This clearly distorts the end results and does not give a 'true and fair' view of the transactions that have occurred. Financial reports may be prepared using the historical cost method of accounting, **current cost accounting**, **general price-level adjusted accounting**, and **continuously contemporary accounting**. It therefore becomes clear that there are different systems of recording transactions, including cash or accrual, each of which may produce vastly different results.

## Assets and estimations //

Asset valuations determined using the historical cost system of accounting outdate with time, therefore amounts shown on the balance sheet may not reflect the asset's current or market value. To counter this problem, assets are regularly revalued. The (re)valuation process is a subjective and contentious issue. In practice, valuations are prepared by qualified chartered surveyors, and it is often the case that businesses may solicit more than one valuation report, and use the valuation report that best suits its purposes. In the event that the asset is constructed within the business, capital expenditure incurred in constructing the asset may be expensed when it should have been added to the cost of the asset or vice versa.

Fixed assets produce economic benefits over many accounting periods; therefore, in order to match the cost of an asset with the revenue that it generates, the asset must be depreciated over its useful life. However, deciding the useful life of the asset and the method of depreciation is often a matter of judgment that lends itself to creative accounting. Common methods of depreciation include the straight line method, the reducing balance method, the annuity method, or the unit-of-production method. This is further complicated with the practice of 'split depreciation'. This method of depreciation uses the original value of the asset to calculate one lot of depreciation, then depreciates a further amount based on the incremental revalued amount of the asset. In the extremes, an entity may permanently reduce the value of an asset, reinstate what was previously written off or no depreciation at all. The method of depreciation will subsequently have an impact on depreciation expense and the carrying amount of the asset.

Provision accounts are sometimes established to cover the permanent diminution in the value of the business. Where a permanent diminution occurs, a provision could be set up and, when it is no longer required, it can be written back. The accountant may argue that conditions have changed and the provision is no longer required. The accounting principle of prudence is used to justify such procedures: better to be prudent and to be proved wrong than to have overstated the profit. Other provisions subject to discretion include provisions for slow-moving or obsolete stocks, product warranties, unfunded pension liabilities, deferred taxes and bad debts. Provision for bad debts affects both the Statement of Financial Position (the value of accounts receivable) and the Statement of Financial Performance (bad debts expense). Companies make approximations and estimates about the amount of debts that can or will go bad. Even though such estimations are normally based on past experience, some may argue that they are nothing more than 'guesstimates' because a bad debt is only known when it actually goes bad. Like depreciation, bad debt allocations can be used to show better than normal earnings.

## Inventory //

Inventory is made up of raw materials, components that are used for subsequent assembly, inventory of partly finished products, and finished products. There are numerous ways of accounting for inventory. Inventory can be valued directly, or through adding other costs that are involved in getting the inventory to its final state before the sale, such as manufacturing overhead, freight, and warehousing costs. For example, manufacturing overhead costs can be suitably included or excluded to the cost of inventory as necessary. Consider the case of labour costs. Labour costs are generally included in the process of adding value to the product. Thus, each unit of product would bear some portion of labour costs. However, in today's manufacturing environment, an increasing proportion of labour costs are becoming fixed in nature and therefore an indirect product (overhead) cost. This allows labour costs, along with items such as general maintenance wages and plant supervision costs, to be added to the pool of overhead costs and eventually allocated to the cost of the product subject to the discretion of overhead cost allocation methods. The valuation of inventory will ultimately depend on how overhead costs are allocated to products.

Freight costs are the costs incurred for getting the raw materials inventory to the place of manufacture, or to a warehouse for use or sale. Where inventories are held for long periods of time, immediately expensing all freight and warehousing costs could be regarded as inaccurate matching because they are expensed in a period different to when the inventory is sold. According to this view, freight and warehousing costs are seen as ongoing costs of running the business and do not add value to the inventory. If freight costs are treated as an ongoing expense of the business, they may not be added on to the cost of inventory.

The way we account for discounts can affect the value of inventory purchases. Suppliers normally offer trade or cash discounts for large orders or early settlement of accounts. Cash discounts can be accounted for distinctly from the cost of the inventory by crediting the cash discounts receivable account. Alternatively, the cash discount may be deducted from the cost of inventory by crediting the purchases account, thus reducing the value of the inventory. Therefore, upon consumption or sale, a smaller amount is written off in the Statement of Financial Performance. This of course results in higher profits, since the cost of purchases are now lower.

## Liabilities and off-balance sheet financing //

The use of new financial instruments, both for restructuring, speculation and for hedging purposes, adds complexity, which allows the accountant and management to find creative ways of either enhancing the Statement of Financial Position or the Statement of Financial Performance. Derivative financial instruments, with their value coming from some underlying financial security, have become common in this regard. Some examples of these are swap agreements relating to interest rates or currency movements, forward exchange contracts, options and futures. To the accountant, the question is whether these new instruments should be recognised, and if so, the method by which they should be measured. The problem is one of recognition and how to account for a transaction when the underlying physical transaction is not yet recognised. A further complication is that these instruments and arrangements are not utilised in isolation but are really used in concert with one another. This gives rise to issues of when and how assets and liabilities may be set-off.

The major advantage of debt finance, as opposed to equity finance, is the taxation benefit derived from the deductibility of interest payments. However, some types of debt finance are arranged to avoid disclosure in the Statement of Financial Position (balance sheet). This type of finance is known as 'off-balance sheet' finance. Typically, the most common way to keep debt off the balance sheet is the use of a **lease**. Operating leases, as opposed to finance leases, allow the lessee to make rental payments for the leased asset. In return, the lessor bears substantially the risks of ownership of the leased asset. In this event, neither the asset nor the liability to pay the rental in the future is shown in the Statement of Financial Position. Thus, the asset and corresponding liability are never shown in the Statement of Financial Position. The only disclosure required in this situation is the rental payments, which appear as an expense in the Statement of Financial Performance. According to *AASB 1008: Leases*, the asset and liability of a finance lease must be disclosed in the Statement of Financial Position. However, friendly finance companies assist in keeping finance leases off the Statement of Financial Position by structuring them so that they become operating leases. One such case is the synthetic lease. Under a synthetic lease, the lessee will pay rental fees on a property for a fixed period, with an obligation to buy the building at the end of the period. However, due to the nature of the lease, the property is not included in the Statement of Financial Position. Problems arise when the business is unable to meet the huge obligation at the maturity of the lease. Some companies disclose the existence of synthetic leases while others do not.

The 'purchase scheme' has a similar effect of keeping liabilities off the Statement of Financial Position. The purchase scheme involves sales of inventory to a finance company or a bank, with the business arranging to repurchase the business's inventory at a later date. The purchase may not be genuine, but it has the effect of replacing the inventory with cash and the obligation to repurchase the inventory may be hidden in the notes to the accounts. The sale is recorded in the Statement of Financial Performance and the value of assets in the Statement of Financial Position is reduced with a decline in inventory. Similarly, long-term work in progress and property may also be used to sell and repurchase, thus improving the Statement of Financial Position.

In a group of related companies consisting of a parent company and a subsidiary or several subsidiaries, a single set of financial statements (**consolidated financial statements**) must be prepared for the entire group of companies, showing them as a single entity. To the creative accountant, this presents an ideal vehicle for keeping borrowings off the consolidated Statement of Financial Position. This is effected by channelling borrowings into a company that is, for practical purposes, controlled by the parent company but is technically not a subsidiary. Therefore, a hidden subsidiary is created, which takes on borrowings that will never have to appear in the consolidated Statement of Financial Position, although the borrowings may be used by the group of companies. Refer to the case of Enron, entitled 'In practice: Aggressive but legal' for an example of such a practice. In other cases involving groups of related companies, loans that have an indeterminate duration may simply be rolled over from year to year. Additionally, when one company is unable to obtain a loan due to insufficient credit history or a poor credit rating, another company from the same group of companies may assist by guaranteeing the loan. In these circumstances the loan should be disclosed as a contingent liability but is often omitted. If it is disclosed, it will probably appear in an obscure part of the notes to the accounts.

## Long-term contracts and revenue recognition //

Accounting for long-term contracts is another opportunity for creative accounting. When a company has long-term contracts and where the outcomes from these contracts are unknown for several periods in the future, determining the timing and amount of revenue to bring to account is problematic. Revenue from long-term contracts may be used to smooth income, particularly when there are several concurrent long-term contracts. When contracts are close to completion, the accountant may suppress turnover in one year, justifying this treatment on the basis of conservatism, and defer the revenue to future years when profit may be lean. The reverse can also be accomplished by enlisting the services of an independent quality surveyor, who will provide a favourable report and add a good deal of credence to the manipulation process.

## Aggressive but legal

Enron Corporation, one of the world's largest companies, filed for bankruptcy in the United States on 2 December 2001. On 8 November, the energy giant announced that, because of accounting errors over a four-year period, changes had been made to its reported earnings: from $105m to $28m in 1997, from $703m to $133m in 1998, from $893m to $248m in 1999, and from $979m to $99m in 2000 (Benston and Hartgraves 2002, p. 2). This should have given a few warning signals that all was not right and, later, instances of creative accounting were found that indicated that aggressive accounting was used; but, at the same time, this was not illegal. This clearly illustrates that the creative accounting was legally achieved, within the rules of accounting.

Among other things, accounting methods were used that played a major role in distorting Enron's financial reality from the reality that was presented. It was a case of bending the accounting rules to the company's advantage. One of these rules was the non-consolidation of Special Purpose Entities (SPEs), which permitted Enron to hide losses and debts from investors.

A question that arises is, when should an entity be included in the consolidated financial statements, and how can this be used to avoid consolidation? According to generally accepted accounting principles, Enron was not required to consolidate the SPEs with its financial statements if independent third parties had controlling and 'substantial' equity interest in the SPE, where 'substantial' was defined as at least 3 per cent of the SPE's assets. To a large degree, the percentage of shareholdings in the subsidiary determined whether control existed and, hence, whether the companies were to be consolidated.

To this end Enron had sponsored SPEs, with whom it engaged in business transactions. They provided fake transaction opportunities, which had a cosmetic effect on Enron's quarterly and annual reports. More damaging was the revelation that half of the transactions came in the final month of a quarter, and nine in the last week of the accounting period. Enron had made transactions with their SPEs in the final weeks of every quarter and reversed them at the beginning of the next quarter. By not fully consolidating these transactions, Enron was able to book huge shares of profits in the SPEs. SPEs were also used to hide liabilities and risks, and such commitments are only mentioned in the footnotes to the financial statements, which are rarely read.

Enron also used SPEs to deposit assets that were falling in value, which effectively meant that their losses would be kept off its books (Thomas 2002, p. 41).

Revenue recognition problems also exist in the extractive industries and the financial sector. The large and highly competitive extractive industry markets means that producers are price takers not price makers. Rather than sell their produce on the open market and risk poor returns, they sell their produce to dealers and brokers at predetermined prices. However, the point at which revenue should be recognised is not clear. Some argue that the extractive business should realise its revenue when it produces the minerals; others take the view that revenue should not be recognised until it has been realised through sales to a third party. A similar problem exists in the financial industry. Banks can either recognise fees and costs received for establishing loans in full when they are paid, or allow them to be spread over the life of the loan by way of an adjustment to the interest rate, or defer them until the loan has largely matured.

## Capitalising and deferring expenses //

Profit is determined by deducting expenses from revenue; therefore expenses are central in the creative accounting process. Reducing expenses can be achieved by deferring expenses to future periods, **capitalising** them or charging them to a provision account or directly to reserves. Expenses such as transport, production, distribution, administrative and storage costs can be deferred to future periods by including them in the valuation of inventory or in work in progress. Alternatively, expenses can be capitalised and included in the Statement of Financial Position as assets. Most costs, including wages, materials, transport, spare parts and overheads, can be capitalised, thereby improving the Statement of Financial Position. For example, many businesses capitalise the interest on money borrowed to finance the construction of new fixed assets, on the grounds that the interest is a legitimate part of the cost of acquiring the asset. Similarly, the uncertainty surrounding the definition of research and development allows the capitalisation of some expenses. The cost of research that does not result in future economic benefits or, where the future economic benefits are unquantifiable, is an expense and should be written off as it is incurred; whereas expenditure on research and development that results in quantifiable future economic benefits is an asset and should be written off over the period in which the benefits are expected to accrue. The blurry distinction between research and development expenditure as an asset, and research and development expenditure as an expense, allows the creative accountant to pass off expenses as assets.

Yet another item that the accountant can use in creating a healthy Statement of Financial Position is goodwill. Goodwill is the store of super profits above and beyond what is to be expected from a particular asset or group of assets. Goodwill comes into existence when one business purchases another and when the real value of the acquired business lies in the reputation of the acquired business. The value of goodwill is calculated by determining the difference between the fair value of the assets acquired at the time of takeover and the consideration price.

Theoretically, goodwill can be written off directly to reserves, written off immediately to the profit and loss account, or written off over the useful life of the assets. According to *AASB 1013: Accounting for goodwill*, the systematic writing off of goodwill should not exceed 20 years. However, consider the case of an intangible asset lasting more than 20 years without continually spending to upkeep the value of goodwill. The asset is written off sooner than its economic life, which can be as much as a few years. Alternatively, an intangible asset that has an economic life of only a few years may be written off over 20 years. Refer to the case entitled, 'In practice: Innovative tools for creativity' for an example involving the amortisation of goodwill.

**IN PRACTICE**

### Innovative tools for creativity

Shah (1997) provides evidence of a new financial instrument that was issued through a special purpose finance subsidiary, which was created in a tax haven. As the instrument was classified as preference shares, it escaped the need to be classified as debt and did not adversely impact on the leverage ratio. By doing this, the subsidiary was able to combine tax and accounting benefits in one instrument and also give the issuing companies a significant head start in making acquisitions.

United Biscuits was the first company to issue this instrument, which was invented by a major investment bank. United Biscuits was about to make an acquisition for a price of £335m, giving rise to goodwill of £190m. Had this goodwill been capitalised and amortised over 20 years, the annual income would have been reduced by £9.5m every year, as a result of this acquisition alone. The accounting treatment preferred by management was to minimise any adverse impact on reported profits and earnings per share, and therefore write off goodwill against reserves. To write off goodwill against reserves, United Biscuits had to have adequate reserves, which it did not have. To get around this, the offshore convertible preference share was structured in such a way as to have a nominal value of £1 and an issue price of £5000. This created a substantial reserve, which was later used for goodwill write-off. It had bolstered its reserves and cushioned the impact of goodwill write-off, and had created a reserve for goodwill write-off. From a tax perspective, as the issue was an offshore issue, the loan from a subsidiary based overseas was therefore a deduction. Thus, it was a case of accounting and tax benefits rolled into one issue. It was a convenient instrument, designed to meet a particular need. The offshore convertible preference share provided issuers with a potential to show improved profits and at the same time improved the leverage position.

## Mergers and take-overs //

Typically, in the area of mergers and takeovers, the accountant of the acquired company may apply creative accounting practices to show that the company is a healthy and viable going concern. This favourable impression is sometimes extended to the periods after the takeover has occurred, to present a case that shows that the promises that were made before the takeover have been delivered. However, the acquiring company may examine the accounts of the newly acquired company and write off all of the under-performing assets. Such actions are justified on the basis that the business has been mismanaged and has been acquired in the nick of time. When profits take a big hit, also known as the 'big bath', analysts will look beyond a one-time loss and focus on future earnings. As far as the acquiring entity is concerned, future performance is assured, because the write-offs have reduced the carrying amount of the assets, lessening the amount of future depreciation and amortisation charges. Improvements in future financial reports are attributable to the new management. The big bath phenomenon is not restricted to mergers and acquisitions, it also occurs when companies are making large losses. In a year where losses are expected, managers will seek to maximise the loss with large write-offs so that future years will look better.

An acquiring company normally records the assets of the acquired business at fair values. If the amount paid for the assets varies from its fair value, the difference is recorded as goodwill. A suitable alternative is to treat the takeover as a merger, in which case fair values do not come into play. The accounts are presented as if the businesses have merged, which now produces values according to their current carrying values, and no fair value assessment has to be made. This also means that the assets can be depreciated at the pre-merger carrying values, which are likely to be less than if the depreciation were carried out under acquisition accounting.

## Foreign currency translations //

Businesses with overseas operations face two accounting problems: transaction and translation exposures. In the first problem (transaction exposure), businesses are exposed to risks that arise from exchange rates that differ at the beginning of the transaction to those at the end. This difference in exchange rates results in a gain or a loss. For the creative accountant, the gain or loss from the transaction exposure is a matter of where they show up in the Statement of Financial Performance and whether they affect important ratios. The accountant may elect to include the gain in normal revenue, since this could have an advantage on the calculation of the gross margin.

In the second problem (translation exposure), the parent company must recast (translate) the financial statements of their offshore entities using the domestic currency of the parent company. The translation process raises questions in the selection of an exchange rate. Accounting standard *ASRB 1012: Foreign currency translation* prescribes the use of the temporal method or the current/closing rate method, depending on the kind of overseas operations. The current or closing rate method is used when the overseas operation is self-sustaining and the temporal method is used when the overseas operation is integrated. Accountants are also permitted to rely on average exchange rates but ASRB 1012 does not specify how the average exchange rate is to be calculated. Some companies use the weighted daily rate and others use the monthly average. By the time the creative accountant has finished choosing currencies, exchange rates, and deferring gains and losses—a great deal of which is open to choice—the financial statements are likely to reflect the desired position rather than the true position.

## Transfer pricing //

Transfer pricing is the price used to determine the value of a transaction (usually a buy–sell transaction) between related entities. The transfer pricing process is a method that can shift profits from one entity to another by simply adjusting the transfer price. The important thing to observe is that there are no rules for determining the transfer price, and there is no universally agreed upon method that is appropriate in all circumstances. Transfer pricing is about putting the costs and profits of an organisation wherever the business wants them to be. The aim may be to minimise group-wide tax charges by transferring taxable income to a region where the rate of tax is lowest. To do this, the accountant must provide good reasons for adjusting the price charged against the cost of goods or services transferred (transfer price) to other entities. In some cases, the transaction has no real business substance such as management service fees, commissions, rebates, and discounts. Refer to the case entitled, 'In practice: Creative accounting' for an example of a profit shifting arrangement between related entities as well as other misdeeds.

Joint ventures and the cost-plus contracts are two other vehicles that can be used to shift profits from one entity to another. Techniques that are normally used include the allocation of the highest cost staff or equipment to the venture or contract, or allocating common corporate costs on the basis that the venture or the contract gets more than its fair share. It is also possible to use the business's goods and services to the venture or the contract at market value, rather than at cost. A similar situation is possible with labour. In the event that the labour charges attract an overhead recovery rate, then the more labour that is chargeable to the venture or contract, the more the business's fixed overhead is paid for by the other party to the venture or someone else.

### Creative accounting

Investigations into Astra brought out some classic examples of creative accounting. Creative accounting was used to cover up losses over a five-year period by stretching accounting standards to their very limit. Methods used in the process were:

1. The inclusion in Astra's profits of an invoice for an amount that was 70 per cent of the group's consolidated reported profits as a fee for services and not for the supply of goods, so that substantially all of it represented profit in Astra's subsidiary's accounts, which it controlled and settled through a Swiss bank to conceal the payers' identities.

2. By the group targeting a company, Richard Unwin International, which was insolvent but was owed moneys by a government ministry. In order to include the profit on this contract into Astra's accounts, Astra needed to use merger accounting. Astra could not do this because it did not meet the requirements of the accounting standards. To get around this, a new company was created. The new company would purchase Richard Unwin's shares in Unwin, in consideration for issue of shares and a medium-term loan note at a commercial rate of interest. The new company would account for the acquisition of Unwin and, as a result, the profit on the contract with the government ministry, which was to be completed after the acquisition, would be brought into the new company's profit and loss account, while Unwin's losses would be excluded because they would have been incurred prior to the new company's acquisition. Once the contract was fulfilled, Astra would buy the new company's shares from Richard Unwin in exchange for its own shares and could then treat the acquisition as a merger for accounting purposes.

3. To use an off-balance sheet finance scheme so that Astra would not have to consolidate the results and liabilities of another target company to which it had lent substantial sums in the hope of a turnaround. To facilitate this, a new off-the-shelf company was acquired and kept separate from Astra, although the group injected funds into the company until it was large enough to absorb the new off-the-shelf company's net liabilities without a material adverse effect on its group balance sheet (Irvine 1993).

## Budgeting //

Internal reports such as budgets can be manipulated to meet specific targets. The managers' performance is often monitored on the basis of the budgets that they prepare. By padding the budget, management provide themselves with easily achievable targets setting themselves up for an impressive performance. One common way to pad the budget is to understate the estimated revenue so that the target sales figure is easily achieved, if not exceeded. In the expense side of the equation, budgeted expenses are increased using the most pessimistic assumptions, double counting, and by simply overstating the estimated amount. In these circumstances, spending within the budget constraints becomes a comparatively easy exercise. However, this form of padding the budget can have undesirable side effects such as inefficient spending based on a 'fat' budget, then having greater amounts approved in the budget for the following year. This encourages overspending and over-budgeting, both real and fictitious.

Moving costs from one budget to another, charging costs to other budgets, and moving costs from one year to another are additional methods of creative accounting. Costs from budgets are moved around from what seems like overspent budgets to those that are underspent. A particularly common technique relates to the allocation of periodic fixed charges. By altering the method of allocation, a higher proportion of fixed costs can be charged to underspent budgets and a smaller proportion charged to overspent budgets. It is also the case that one manager may charge costs to another manager's budget. Where a business operates a complex network of cross-charging, deliberate manipulation may never be known. In regard to budget variances, favourable variances are explained in terms of the manager's superior performance, and unfavourable variances are rationalised on the basis that the budget is too tight or that outside circumstances intervened in a way that made it impossible to achieve.

In capital budgeting, a desired position can be supported with accounting numbers that have been reworked starting from the required answer. This is then supported with a set of assumptions and parameters that are plausible, to ensure that the required amounts for the projects are approved. A common area of manipulation in capital budgeting is the determining of the cost of the project, which uses the discounted cash flow (DCF) calculation. The project may be made to look more attractive if the estimate can be reduced. A complementary method is to use the net present value (NPV) of the project and to defer some of the forecast capital expenditure into the second or subsequent years of the project. Applying a higher discount factor will improve the NPV and make the project more attractive. Another method is to trim back the operating costs or to rephrase them to later years. Similarly, income forecasts in the proposal can be increased, with the effect on the revenue being quite dramatic and the NPV enhanced further. Advancing revenue from later to earlier years can transform the economics of the project significantly. A lower discount for evaluating capital budget proposals can also be used, based on the argument that the project finance uses that particular discount rate.

## Creativity in presentation

With the accounting technique complete, the creative accountant now turns to the presentation of the business's financial position. Accounting is a process that records the transactions that the business undertakes, categorises them, summarises them, and eventually produces three statements: the Statement of Financial Position, the Statement of Financial Performance and the Statement of Cash Flows. In the process of writing up these statements, other opportunities exist for the creative accountant to distort the real picture of the business. Take, for instance, administrative costs, which are normally intended to show the efficiency of the business in conducting its affairs. A large administrative expense would imply that the business is overly bureaucratic and inefficient, and perhaps overstaffed. One way to avoid this impression is to reclassify part of this cost and transfer it (e.g. head office administration costs) to the cost of sales. Other examples of reclassification include the incorporation of intangible costs, such as legal costs, expenses, interests and overheads into the tangible fixed asset items of expenses.

The inclusion or exclusion of associated companies from the consolidated financial statements is a creative accounting method affecting the presentation of the reports. The accounting standards prescribe 'control' as the criterion for consolidation purposes, which implies dominance in decision making. However, there is sufficient flexibility in this criterion to allow choices as to whether or not the subsidiary should be included. Further, if the subsidiary is making losses, the creative accountant can exclude the subsidiary from the group of companies by claiming that the parent company has lost control. The parent company should not suffer as a result of continued losses from one subsidiary. The reverse is also true, when the subsidiary begins to make profits, the control of the subsidiary may be restored.

In conclusion, the methods and techniques described above are tools available to the accountant to manipulate the accounting numbers so that a picture emerges that is different from the 'economic reality' of the business. It may increase the numbers that make the business look better, or it may reduce the numbers so that the business appears to look worse than it actually is. The purpose of this discussion is to describe some of the ways and means available to the accountant to achieve this kind of distortion. The accountant has in his or her means the ability to make the business look any way that the interests of people in power dictate. Thus, power and wealth are closely related, and accounting is a tool that transforms power into wealth (Alagiah 1997).

# Creative accounting in practice //

Creative accounting is widely practised by companies. Smith (1992) reports that 208 of the largest quoted companies in the United Kingdom applied accounting manipulations that had an impact on the Statement of Financial Position and the Statement of Financial Performance. The techniques used were:

1. writing down of assets before an acquisition
2. disposals—profits on sales of assets taken 'above the line' and deconsolidation of subsidiaries in anticipation of sale

3. deferred consideration on acquisition
4. extraordinary and exceptional items
5. off balance sheet finance
6. contingent liabilities
7. capitalisation of costs such as interest, and research and development
8. brand accounting—capitalisation of assets
9. changes in depreciation policy—both in method and in the period
10. convertibles, with premium put options or variable rate preferred stocks
11. pension fund surplus, used to reduce annual charge
12. currency mismatching between borrowing and depositions.

Of the twelve listed here, it was found that seven of the techniques had an effect on the income of the entity.

Changes in accounting policy provide further possibilities for manipulation of accounting numbers. In Australia, Smith et al. (1997) found that 274 companies had made 185 policy changes over the period 1987/1988 and, further, that 78 of these changes had an effect on company income and 60 of these had an income-increasing effect. In a more recent study, Smith (1998) found 437 manipulations with an income impact, with the use of extraordinary and exceptional items the predominant technique used. In the case of Enron, the dominant technique was the use and misuse of off-balance sheet transactions (Chaffin 2003).

Davis (1999) reports how WR Grace & Co in the United States, along with Price-waterhouseCoopers LLP, had been accused of earnings manipulation through creative accounting techniques. Grace & Co had apparently created corporate reserves to create the illusion of consistent profits. It was alleged that Grace & Co stashed profits from good years in all-purpose reserves and later tapped them in a way to mask slowing earnings (p. 2). Further evidence from the audit firm's records and internal company documents showed that internal controls had broken down and there were far more significant distortions to the earnings. The auditors had discovered the profit stockpile in early 1990, and had repeatedly warned that what the executives were doing was wrong. Nonetheless, the external auditors gave Grace's financial statements a clean bill of health. They had used a fundamental assumption in accounting: the question of materiality. In accounting, an amount is deemed to be material if it is more than 10 per cent of the relevant base amount. Any amount that falls below 5 per cent is deemed immaterial and is therefore of no consequence. The materiality of amounts between 5 and 10 per cent will depend on the circumstances that gave rise to the misstatement. In this case, Grace and Co and their external auditors had used this accounting principle to manipulate the profits in good years and use these reserves in less profitable years.

In the software industry, companies sign long-term contracts to supply and service their products. Companies can take a conservative approach to these contracts and record revenue over the life of a contract. Others may record the bulk of the revenue in the first or second year of the contract, justifying this by saying that the bulk of the services were delivered in those years. Brown (2002) reports that Microstrategy Inc is a company that prematurely recorded revenue from software sales, by recording sales before determining the full extent of services it would have to provide in connection with those sales. Sunbeam Corporation and Bausch & Lomb Inc also used a similar tactic, but with a twist. Both of these companies cut deals with customers to take more inventory than they needed, and further suggested that they not pay for them immediately. Other customers were promised unlimited rights to return goods. This practice will boost sales revenue at the time of the deal, only to have the goods returned after the balance date.

If accounting regulators wish to curb creative accounting they must reduce the number of permitted accounting methods and minimise the use of judgment. When accounting policies are selected, they must be consistently applied from one period to another. To date, regulators have only addressed issues associated with presentation and disclosure, but not recognition and measurement. Until such time as these kinds of issues are dealt with, opportunities for creative accounting are rife. This is not to suggest, however, that when one loophole is blocked, another will not be sought. It appears that there is a multiplicity of rules that the accountant can choose from, and to this extent, what is reported in the Statement of Financial Position and the Statement of Financial Performance is at the discretion of the accountant, along with management. Empirical evidence suggests that choices in accounting methods is not totally arbitrary; they appear to have been directed to maximise the value of the firm.

# Detecting creative accounting //

In order to detect the presence of creative accounting or to determine if some form of creative accounting practice has taken place, it is important to understand why accountants would stoop to manipulating the accounts. Reasons for manipulating the accounts might include, to:

1. enhance the earnings and the profit figures
2. improve the appearance of the Statement of Financial Position
3. be seen as successful in a political and social climate
4. show a steady gradual annual increase in their annual profits
5. avoid failure
6. satisfy investor demands.

If we understand that these are the reasons why an accountant, in collaboration with others, might undertake activities like creative accounting, then it is useful to follow that lead to establish where and how creative accounting may occur. Consider each one of the following cases.

## Capitalising interest //

Capitalising interest is a method of removing interest charges from the Statement of Financial Performance and including them as part of the Statement of Financial Position. Interest paid on borrowings to purchase an asset is normally charged against profits, but interest is sometimes capitalised when it is considered a cost of acquisition. Problems arise when the purchase of the asset is funded from the general borrowings rather than from a specific loan. Can the interest from general borrowings be linked to the asset and, if so, how much of the interest should be capitalised? Given these unregulated questions, the accountant has ample opportunity to manipulate profit, asset values, and related ratios by varying the amount of interest that is expensed or capitalised.

To look out for this practice, you should peruse the Statement of Financial Position for capitalised borrowing costs and compare the previous year's borrowing costs with the current year. Excessive increases in borrowing costs may indicate aggressive capitalisation policies. You should also look out for new additional borrowings and determine whether borrowing costs have been capitalised. Details of assets being used as security for borrowings may indicate the acquisition of new loans. You should also be wary of entities using general borrowings rather than specific loans to fund new assets. New loans hidden in general borrowings may go unnoticed and are less likely to raise questions on borrowing costs. This practice is prevalent in the construction and property development industries.

## Depreciation //

Depreciation is an expense recognised systematically for the purpose of allocating the cost of a depreciable asset over its useful life. As stated above, entities may use a number of methods to depreciate assets. They include:

1. the straight line method
2. the reducing balance method
3. a method based on the expected yield to the business, such as the estimated units of production, operating hours or distance travelled
4. a method based on measurement of the specific wear that has occurred in each financial year.

Any of the above methods are permissible, with businesses generally using the reducing balance method or the straight line method. To detect creativity in depreciation, you should observe changes in the method of depreciation, which must be disclosed in the notes to the accounts. Also, watch out for depreciation methods that write off smaller amounts of depreciation at the beginning of the asset's life than in later years. Changes in the level of depreciation as a percentage of the fixed assets from one period to another may also indicate creative accounting. You should also look for changes to the estimated useful life of the asset.

## Accounting for goodwill //

Goodwill is the result of future economic benefits from unidentifiable assets. These may take the form of healthy relationships between the employer and the employee, market penetration, effective advertising and a superior operating team. Remember that only purchased goodwill must be reported and the reported amount must represent the future benefits that are expected to flow to the purchaser. According to *AASB 1013: Goodwill*, only the straight line method of amortisation may be used, and the amortisation period must not exceed 20 years from the date of acquisition. Therefore, you should consider the motivations of an entity using the maximum period of time to amortise goodwill. You should also observe the method used to amortise goodwill. The business may argue that the reducing balance method, and even the inverted sum of years digits method, is a more appropriate method. Some firms will identify goodwill as 'brands', which are not affected by AASB 1013, and therefore place it in the Statement of Financial Position as an asset, and leave it there unless there is a permanent diminution of the firm's value.

## Revenues //

According to generally accepted accounting principles, revenue is recognised when it is earned, not when the cash is received. Therefore, credit sales are legitimately recognised as revenue even though cash has not been exchanged. However, companies may artificially increase their sales revenue by signing long-term contracts to supply and service their products, and subsequently recognise the revenue from the contract in early years, rather than record the revenue over the term of the contract. Companies justify this practice by claiming that the bulk of the services were delivered in those years. The level of services supplied in later years often is not clear until the end of the contract. To detect this practice you should observe the company's accounts receivable accounts. If the amount of accounts receivable is growing faster than the rate of sales, it may be a sign that there are large amounts of sales on credit, and the method in question is being used to artificially inflate revenue. The practice of improving sales performance using this method is particularly common in the information technology industry.

In closing, the places to detect creative accounting activities are to look for them in the notes to the accounts and work from there. You should look for sudden changes of accounting policies, a sudden or frequent change of auditors, and transfers between the Statement of Financial Performance and the Statement of Financial Position. You should also compare the percentage of tax paid against the stated profits to see if the profits are real or just 'paper' profits.

# Possible solutions to 'creative' accounting //

From their extensive study entitled, *Rebuilding public confidence in financial reporting: an international perspective* (2003), the International Federation of Accountants (IFAC) make a number of recommendations that may reduce the possibility of creative accounting. In general, if all the participants in the accounting and reporting process were held accountable, then attitudes towards business ethics would change, and instances of creative accounting would diminish. In actual terms, the IFAC recommends ten steps that may reduce 'creative' accounting. The steps are:

1. Effective corporate ethics codes need to be in place and actively monitored.
2. Corporate management must place greater emphasis on the effectiveness of financial management and controls.
3. Incentives to misstate financial information need to be reduced.
4. Boards of directors need to improve their oversight of management.
5. Threats to auditor independence need to receive greater attention in corporate governance processes and by the auditors themselves.
6. Audit effectiveness needs to be raised primarily through greater attention to audit quality control processes.
7. Codes of conduct need to be put in place for other participants in the financial reporting process and their compliance should be monitored.
8. Audit standards and regulation need to be strengthened.
9. Accounting and reporting practices need to be strengthened.
10. The standard of regulation of issuers needs to be raised.

A secondary solution to the process of discouraging and preventing creative accounting is to dispel, through education, the notion that accounting is objective, precise, and reliable because of its arithmetical neatness. The alert user may be in a better position to make a judgment if they are aware of what the figures actually represent.

A further method to reduce 'creative' accounting is applying a single accounting standard globally, based on a single global currency (Alagiah 2001).

# Summary //

In this chapter we have introduced the concept of creative accounting and illustrated its practice with various examples. It appears that there are a number of ways in which businesses are able to recognise a transaction, which leads to vague and questionable accounting treatments. Businesses are permitted to use a considerable amount of discretion in the way that they account for some transactions, which could easily mislead the unsuspecting user of financial reports. Due to the increasing complexity in the ways particular transactions are accounted for and the numerous accounting standards that have evolved, financial statements are becoming increasingly complex, and readable only by the expert. We have also examined the possible motives for creative accounting and indicated anomalies in the financial statements that represent possible instances of creative accounting. Some suggested remedial steps to reduce creativity or eliminate them have also been suggested.

## Key terms //

Accounting methods...p. 177
Accrual accounting...p. 178
Capitalise...p. 184
Cash accounting...p. 178
Consolidated financial statements...p. 182
Continuously contemporary accounting...p. 179
Creative accounting...p. 176
Current cost accounting...p. 179
General price-level adjusted accounting...p. 179
Historical cost...p. 179
Lease...p. 181

## Questions //

**7.1** What is creative accounting?

**7.2** List and describe three methods of creative accounting.

**7.3** Provide three examples of ways by which the accountant can be creative.

**7.4** Provide three ways to detect creative accounting.

**7.5** Based on the 'In practice' case studies presented in this chapter, is it possible to detect creative accounting?

**7.6** What are the consequences of creative accounting?

**7.7** What are the reasons that businesses undertake creative accounting?

**7.8** What methods can be used to reduce or eradicate creative accounting?

**7.9** What are the essential elements for detecting creative accounting?

**7.10** Will increasing regulation reduce creative accounting?

**7.11** In your opinion, are all businesses carrying out some form of creative accounting?

**7.12** Are financial statements reliable? Can they be used for making informed decisions? Discuss.

## FURTHER RESOURCES //

Briloff, A 1972 *Unaccountable accounting*, Harper & Row, New York.

Griffiths, I 1986, *Creative accounting: how to make your profits what you want them to be*, Unwin Hyman, London.

Mulford, WC and Comisky, EE 2002, *The financial numbers game: detecting creative accounting practices*, John Wiley & Sons, New York.

Naser, K 1993, *Creative financial accounting: its nature and use*, Prentice Hall, London.

## CASE STUDY

### Enron—the creative accounting issues

On 2 December 2001, Enron, one of the largest corporations in the world, filed for bankruptcy under Chapter 11 of the United States Bankruptcy Code. In mid-2000, the price of Enron's shares were as high as $90 per share, but had declined to under $1 by the end of 2001. With assets of $63.4 billion, this is the largest United States corporate bankruptcy.

Enron's bankruptcy is of particular interest to accountants for illustrating how creative accounting was partially responsible for the company's failure. It shows how Enron sought to stretch accounting rules to its advantage.

Of the numerous accounting issues that Enron had used in creating a perception that was different from how things were within the company, nothing could be more glaring than the recording of fees for services rendered in future periods as current revenues.

Enron had sponsored several special-purpose entities (SPEs) to shelter foreign-derived revenues from United States taxes with some domestic SPEs with whom Enron had done business. Some of the SPEs had paid Enron fees for guarantees on loans made by the SPEs. Typically, in recognising revenue for a period, under the Australian accounting standard, AASB 1004, an entity may recognise revenue by reference to the stage of completion of the contract when, and only when, all the following conditions have been satisfied.

(a) The entity controls a right to be compensated for services rendered.
(b) It is probable that the economic benefits comprising the compensation will flow to the entity.
(c) The amount of revenue can be reliably measured.
(d) The stage of completion of the transaction can be reliably measured.

(AASB 1004, paragraph 7.1)

According to the matching concept, Enron should have recorded as revenue portions of the revenue as they were earned. However, in December 1997, Enron had recorded as revenue a $10 million up-front payment from one of its SPEs for a guarantee that was outstanding for the next 12 months.

//

Enron also entered into a partnership that contracted to pay Enron an annual 'management fee', which Enron then converted into a 'required payment' in March 1998. This allowed Enron to record its present value through June 2003 (net of reserve) of $25.7 million as revenue.

More revenues were recorded when Enron sold forward gas commodity contracts to a Channel Islands company connected with a bank, and simultaneously purchased a comparable and offsetting forward gas commodity contract from another Channel Islands company, which was connected with the first-named company and the first-named bank. Enron immediately collected the discounted present value of the sales contract, which was recorded as sales revenue. It had failed to recognise the purchase contract as an offsetting expense, since it did not have to be paid until the contract delivery date (Eichenwald 2002, p. 1).

## QUESTIONS

1 What was Enron doing to enhance its revenue?
2 What accounting principle was Enron violating when it recognised revenue and did not recognise a related expense?
3 Why did the auditors, Andersen's, accept these transactions as valid when they were in violation of generally accepted accounting principles?
4 Under Australian accounting standards, what are the rules that must be observed when recording revenues when rendering services?
5 Do you think that the accountant at Enron was acting on his own or in consort with management? Discuss.

## REFERENCES //

Alagiah, R 1997, Accounting implications in social security payments: a Foucaultian analysis. Unpublished PhD thesis, the University of Wollongong.

Alagiah, R 2002, Theory leading practice: world order and uniform accounting standards worldwide, American Accounting Association, International Section Conference, Fort Lauderdale.

Benston, GJ and Hartgraves LA 2002, 'Enron: what happened and what we can learn from it', *Journal of Accounting and Public Policy*, vol. 21, issue 2, Summer, pp. 105–27.

Brown, K 2002, 'Creative accounting: how to bluff a company', *Wall Street Journal* (Eastern Edn), New York, 21 February, p. C.1.

Chaffin, J 2003, 'Enron Chief found "negligent"', *Financial Times*, 25 November.

Davis, A 1999, 'SEC and WR Grace are near accord over alleged earnings manipulation', *Wall Street Journal* (Eastern Edn), New York, 25 June, p. B.5.

Eichenwald, K 2002, *New York Times*, 2 February, p.1.

Elias, RZ 2004. 'The impact of corporate ethical values on perceptions of earnings management', *Managerial Auditing Journal*, vol 19, no. 1, pp. 84–98.

Institute of Chartered Accountants and CPA Australia 2003, AASB 1004 *Revenue, Accounting Handbook 2003, Volume 1 of the Accounting and Auditing Handbook*, pp. 123–37.

International Federation of Accountants 2003, *Rebuilding public confidence in financial reporting: an international perspective*, International Federation of Accountants, New York.

Jameson, M 1988, *A practical guide to creative accounting*, Kogan Page.

Lacy, C 2002, 'Telstra takes writedown on old debtors', *Australian Financial Review*, 13 May, p. 15.

Leib, B 2002, 'Forensic accounting: from innocent, fraud can grow quickly'. *Financial Executive*, vol. 18, no. 93, p. 36.

Mulford, WC and Comisky, EE 2002, *The financial numbers game: detecting creative accounting practices*, John Wiley & Sons, New York.

Paterson, R 1995, 'New creative accounting', *Accountancy*, vol. 116, issue 1227, November, p. 88.

Shah, AK 1996, 'Creative compliance in financial reporting', *Accounting Organizations and Society*, vol. 21, issue 1, pp. 23–40.

Shah, AK 1997, 'Regulatory arbitrage through financial innovation', *Accounting, Auditing and Accountability Journal*, vol. 10, issue 1, p. 85.

Smith, M 1998, 'Creative accounting: the auditor effect', *Managerial Auditing Journal*, vol. 13, no. 3, pp. 155–8.

Smith, M, Fiedler, B and Kestel, J 1997, 'Structure versus judgment in the audit process: a test of Kinney's classification', *University of South Australia Seminar Series*, Adelaide, SA.

Smith, T 1992, *Accounting for growth*, Century Business, London.

Takatera, S and Sawabe, N 2000, 'Time and space in income accounting', *Accounting Organizations and Society*, vol. 25, issue 8, p. 787.

Thomas, CW 2002, 'The rise and fall of Enron', *Journal of Accountancy*, vol. 193, issue 4, p. 41.

Whittred, G, Zimmer, I, Taylor, S and Wells, P 2004, *Financial accounting: incentive effects and economic consequences*, 6th edn, Thomson.

# Social responsibility accounting

## Learning objectives

After studying this chapter you should be able to:

- Describe the development of social accounting.
- Explain the relationship between social accounting and ethics.
- Evaluate the advantages and disadvantages of the provision of social information.
- Explain accountability, and its relationship with stakeholder and legitimacy theories.
- Describe the 'logics' that link stakeholder accountability and ethical considerations.
- Discuss the relationship between social accounting and sustainability.
- Identify methods of social reporting.
- Discuss the effects of social accounting on corporate decision making.

'People are understandably frustrated and angry at what they see as a lack of corporate transparency and accountability. It is of no surprise that a company's level of governance and responsibility has emerged as a significant indicator of its overall health as a business. After all, companies such as Westpac need more than a legal licence to operate – we require a community licence as well. For us, this means having a set of decent values that underpin our everyday activities'.

**Leon A. Davis, Chairman, Westpac, p. 2,**
*Westpac 2003 Social Impact Report*

# Introduction //

Chapter 2 provided a brief discussion of normative and descriptive theories, and introduced us to the normative ethical theories of utilitarianism, rights and **justice**, from a philosophical perspective. In this chapter, we will consider the practical application of these concepts and their relationship with corporate social responsibility, and the role played by social accounting in providing the transparency of reporting upon which ethical decisions can be made.

# Social accounting //

The efficient allocation of resources, through the operation of the market system within the western capitalist environment, is credited with providing opportunities for people to improve their 'standard of living'. This concept of 'living standards', which is measured in economic terms of national productivity, also implies that social benefits are a concomitant advantage of economic growth. **Capitalism** and ethics have been similarly intertwined in commentaries about growth and development, as, in a utilitarian sense, capitalism has been credited with providing a greater benefit, to the greatest number of people, than any other economic system.

Some of the economic benefits of the development and growth of capitalism have been accompanied by social and environmental costs. While environmental issues are the subject of the next chapter, it should be borne in mind that many social and environmental effects of economic growth are inseparable, and often have a causative relationship. For example, the growth of large plantations in developing countries may have a detrimental effect on environmental biodiversity, but may improve social conditions for the local population. However, the issues are complex because, should market demand for the plantation products fall, local populations may no longer be able to support themselves without their previous subsistence farms or foraging options.

While financial reporting is generally aimed at providing economic information to the providers of finance, such as shareholders and lenders, social accounting and reporting is concerned with the voluntary identification and disclosure of information about the relationship of an organisation with its employees, its local community and society in general.

Gray et al. (1987, p. ix) defined corporate social reporting as:

the process of communicating the social and environmental effects of organisations' economic actions to particular interest groups within society and to society at large. As such, it involves extending the accountability of organisations (particularly companies), beyond the traditional role of providing a financial account to the owners of capital, in particular, shareholders. Such an extension is predicated upon the assumption that companies do have wider social responsibilities than simply to make money for their shareholders.

Thus, social responsibility accounting encourages commercial organisations to consider the effects of their operations on communities, and to disclose information about their social performance. Disclosure can be made in the organisation's annual report, although many large companies and government organisations now publish separate social and/or environmental reports. Social accounting is a component of the 'triple bottom line' of economic, environmental and social responsibility, often referred to as 'profit, people and planet'.

Social accounting does not, however, require that social effects and their implications be measured in financial terms. Some social aspects of a firm's operations can be valued, such as financial contributions to community organisations. Other social contributions or effects can be quantified, but not valued, and these may include, for example, 'in-kind' donations such as time or information to assist community projects. Still other social contributions, such as expertise used in assisting community developments, may not be able to be quantified, and these can be described in narrative terms.

While strong growth has occurred in corporate social disclosure in recent times, the relationship between economic activities, accounting and society is a very ancient one. It is therefore useful to consider some of the historical aspects, in order to place the more recent social accounting and reporting developments within the context of a very long time continuum.

## Social accounting: the history //

Beginning with Europe's awakening from the early days of feudalism, western economic development from the tenth century onward was characterised by productivity increases that enabled large population growth. In these early days there was an energy of invention, trade, finance and risk-taking, and Michelman (1994, p. 53) describes the establishment of 'craft guilds, arsenals, ships, factories, town halls and cathedrals, all elements of civic pride, fed by ambition and competition'.

Economic surpluses, which were the early forms of capital, enabled voyages of discovery, the establishment of trade routes for commodities such as silks and spices, and the development of international trade. The Italian city-states, established on the shores of the Mediterranean, and with long sea-going traditions, were early leaders in the development of trade and free-market transactions. Goods were sent overseas to be sold, and the proceeds were not realised until the ships returned, often months or years later, so merchants sought better ways of recording economic transactions that were beginning to occur over longer periods of time. Double entry bookkeeping developed in response to this need, and it is this system that was recorded by Luca Pacioli in 1494.

As accounting and recording methods developed in response to the needs of traders at the time, and have continued to evolve to meet the needs of modern business organisations, it is often suggested that accounting is **socially constructed**. This means that the discipline and its methods are the result of social, economic and political events, reflected in economic transactions. An alternative approach, however, suggests that accounting may be **socially constructing**, in that the use of accounting information plays a role in decision making that affects relationships within society, and societal development itself. There are many examples of the way in which accounting affects economic transactions, such as the introduction of AASB 1012, relating to foreign currency transactions, which resulted in the restructuring of offshore and domestic debt by many large corporations. The effects of accounting on social interactions, and its implications for social equity and justice, are not always so clearly visible. As a result, people may remain unaware of them until the effects become so great that they are impossible to ignore, or until attention is particularly drawn to them, such as by whistleblowers or the media.

An idea of the power of accounting can be gained from Sombart's (1924) suggestion that double entry bookkeeping was the catalyst for the development of the new social and economic system that we now call capitalism. Michelman lends support to Sombart's position in his comment that, 'maritime insurance, collective syndicates for raising funds, new credit instruments such as bills of exchange, and the art of double-entry bookkeeping hastened the acquisitive process'. It was this process of acquisitiveness that led to massive social changes, such as those described by Lane (1973, p. 151):

> The Venetian doges, in effect merchant princes, cut their eyeteeth on the relentless Arab raids preceding the Iberian reconquest of the Mediterranean. Combining diplomacy with sea power, they captured the Byzantine market and became the pivot of exotic trade flowing overland through the Alps to northern Europe, whose somnolent, war-ravaged countries would eventually succeed the Italian city-states as centres of early capitalism. Meanwhile, between four wars with Genoa, the calculating Venetians seized upon the Crusades as a commercial opportunity. Contracting with Popes and naïve knights, they built prodigious fleets for transporting the warriors of the Fourth Crusade and their giant horses to the Holy Land. En route, they argued over payment, abandoned the quest and instead conquered and looted Christian Constantinople for themselves in 1204.

Historically, therefore, there are very strong links between economic activities, facilitated by the accounting process, and social effects. The consequentialist approach of utilitarian ethical principles, discussed in chapter 2, considers outcomes beyond the decision maker and seeks to maximise the net benefit to all people affected. Let us consider how this might apply to events that followed the looting of Constantinople mentioned above.

Visitors to St Mark's Cathedral in Rome are impressed by the four bronze horses, representing masterpieces of Roman sculpture, which were transported from the Hippodrome at Constantinople and installed during the building of St Mark's. Looting and the transfer of such treasures was commonplace in those days, and the fact that the stolen horses were installed in a cathedral is a clear indication that ethical norms in society were far different then than they are today. While such acts may be regarded as reprehensible nowadays, how much more disturbing would be the records indicating that, between 1414 and 1423, about 10 000 slaves, mostly female, were sold in Venice alone, and that slavery was just another bookkeeping item for the builders of St. Mark's Cathedral (Michelman 1996)!

While we have no comprehensive records of the treatment of the Venetian and Roman slaves, we do have detailed records of the American slave system, which was only terminated by the thirteenth Amendment to the Constitution in 1865. This was clearly an economic issue, reflecting a preference for the use of coerced human beings as the labour factor of production in order to create more economic wealth, and plantation accounting records list slaves as assets on the balance sheets. Utilitarian arguments have historically been made in defence of slavery, and remind us of the moral ambiguities that have been faced in the past, and, to a different extent and for different issues, still exist today. The arguments in regard to the plantation slaves were paternalistic in nature. Not only was slavery a profitable choice over free labour, enabling an increased standard of living for white Americans, but also the slaves themselves were said to be better fed, healthier and better housed than would have been the case had they been allowed to remain in their own countries.

It is clear that such utilitarian arguments would be unacceptable today, and the rights-based, non-consequential view of ethics would condemn such practices. However, circumstances and events identified through social accounting indicate that, although to a lesser degree, injustices still exist in the global market place.

To finalise our review of slavery and its economic and moral implications, it is perhaps salutary to consider what happened to the Roman slaves as the empire fell. Finley (1996, p. 54) explained that:

> As the decadent Empire disintegrated over the centuries, it created its own underclass of serfs and peasants, discriminated against both legally and economically, making slavery unnecessary.

Today, social accounting is concerned with the modern equivalent of this 'underclass', and with the equity and social justice that may be denied to some members of society who do not have economic or political power. Large corporations, often more powerful than national governments, spread their operations throughout the world, in the way that the Italian merchants once did with their trading vessels, and social accounting is aimed at providing information about, for example, their relationships with employees, working and safety conditions, the people affected by their activities, such as customers and suppliers, and local communities.

## Social accounting: recent developments //

Gray, Owen & Maunders (1987, p. 1) began their first text on social accounting with the observation that, twenty or thirty years ago:

> There appeared to be a fairly general, if implicit, view that business and non-business organisations alike were essentially beneficial and well-intentioned entities which, guided by a presumed 'enlightened self-interest', strove to fulfil an essential and desirable role in Western societies.

They went on to explain that problems that arose were usually narrowly construed, normally with regard only to their economic effects, and there was little recognition that the activities of business organisations could be socially harmful. In the utilitarian environment in which companies were regarded as meeting the needs of the majority of people, problems such as dangerous products, corruption, fraud, and unsafe labour practices were regarded as 'financial' problems affecting profitability, which had wider implications only insofar as the financial viability of the enterprise might be threatened.

This began to change with the development of **corporate social reporting** in the early 1970s. The response to the Vietnam War, and the peace movements that were very active at that time, are credited with beginning the move towards satisfying public demands for increased corporate social responsibility. People wanted to know, for example, the extent of company involvement in the manufacture of weapons or military ordnance, and university students were refusing to consider careers with companies that they considered socially or ethically irresponsible. Churches were also considering their investment options, and refusing to support companies that were promoting tobacco or alcohol, or that were perceived to be exploiting their employees, and the first ethical investment funds were offered as an alternative strategy for investors seeking to support socially responsible organisations.

A major catalyst of the increased interest in the relationship between business and society during the 1970s was the publication of Milton Friedman's (1970) ideas that the only social responsibility of business was to increase profits for shareholders. During the 1970s corporate social reports were developed, and their adoption by established accounting firms such as Ernst and Ernst helped promote them as a practical method for discharging corporate social accountability. More recently, the concept of triple bottom line reporting has developed to address public concerns about the broader effects of business activities and decisions.

## IN PRACTICE

### Du Pont

Included in the Corporate Mission Statement of the Du Pont company is the intention that the company 'will conduct its business affairs with the highest ethical standards and work diligently to be a respected corporate citizen worldwide'.

Transparency is a major aspect of this goal, and the company publishes its *Business Conduct Guide* in eighteen languages, aimed at guiding employees and improving understanding of the company's ethical standards among customers, suppliers and the general public. On the first page is an ethics hotline number, so that any ethical violations can be reported directly, and anonymously if desired.

> The Chairman of the Board, in his message to employees at the beginning of the guide, says:
>
> We currently operate diverse businesses around the globe under a wide range of competitive situations and subject to a variety of local laws, regulations and cultures. The future holds the promise of even greater complexity and diversity. In this type of global environment, the foundation of our long-term success will be business excellence consistent with the highest ethical standards and compliance with the law. As we watch other companies face the loss of business and possible extinction because of ethical and compliance crises, we are reminded yet again of the value of ethical conduct and compliance with the laws as not only the right thing to do but the smart business thing to do.
>
> Du Pont's commitment is to conduct its business in such a fashion as to be a respected corporate citizen throughout the world.
>
> Du Pont (2002)

# Accountability //

The issues of professional ethics discussed in chapter 3, and the importance of good corporate governance practices discussed in chapter 5, are part of a broader concept of **accountability**. The discharge of accountability by organisations operating in society has been identified as a key area of focus for accounting and the use of accounting information. Herbohn & Herbohn (1999, p. 412) described the modern concept of accountability as a holistic concept that represents 'something beyond responsibility'.

This concept of accountability requires that organisations be accountable for the often unintended and unacknowledged moral, social and environmental consequences of the pursuit of economic objectives. Stakeholder theory, organisational legitimacy and the idea of the political economy of accounting have developed from this broader view, and attempt to explain why companies are engaging in the provision of social information.

## Stakeholder theory //

Within the stakeholder perspective, the success of an organisation depends on its ability to balance the conflicting demands of its various **stakeholders**. Stakeholder theory is a descriptive theory that attempts to justify the provision of social information in an attempt to gain stakeholder support and thus minimise the costs of dealing with complaints and actions that might otherwise affect them. Corporate stakeholders have traditionally been identified as those parties with a direct financial interest in an organisation, such as shareholders and other finance providers. Since the publication of the *Corporate Report* (ASSC 1975), however, the concept of a stakeholder group has been broadened to include not only equity investors and creditors, but also employees, analysts, business contacts, the government and the public. Thus, companies may be accountable to any person or organisation affected by their activities or otherwise having a right to information about them.

Stakeholder rights can be considered in terms of three different 'logics', or moral viewpoints, that form a link between the descriptive notions of stakeholder accountability and the normative ethical considerations. These three viewpoints are interest-based, rights-based and duty-based (Werhane & Freeman 1997).

An interest-based analysis assesses the consequences of actions and policies solely in relation to parties with a direct interest in those actions. It thus encompasses self-interest, group interest, and the concept of utilitarianism. The central idea of the second 'logic', rights-based analysis, is that rights protection should supersede interest satisfaction, and that the most important rights to be protected are the rights to a fair distribution of opportunities and wealth, and rights to basic freedoms or liberties. The third strand of logic in stakeholder theory, the duty-based analysis, is governed by the ethical concept of duty or responsibility to communities rather than individuals. It is thus concerned with the ideals of fidelity and loyalty.

It is perhaps appropriate at this point to mention that there is a fourth moral viewpoint discussed by Werhane & Freeman (1997), which, while not stakeholder-oriented, is nevertheless relevant to social accounting. This is a virtue-based analysis, concerned with prudence and justice, which is more able to concern itself with issues such as environmental awareness than the other three viewpoints that are dependent upon (generally human) stakeholder preferences. Environmental degradation and loss of biodiversity has an inevitable effect upon human stakeholders, and virtue-based analysis is very relevant to the issue of triple bottom line reporting.

In terms of the above four 'logics', economic power is greatest for the interest-based stakeholders and least for those whose interests are virtue-based. For this reason, companies have traditionally concerned themselves with providing relevant information for the more powerful, interest-based, groups, and other groups have been regarded as less important to corporate interests.

BHP's experience at Ok Tedi in Papua New Guinea, discussed in the case study at the end of the chapter, demonstrated very clearly that such an attitude can be unwise. In operating the Ok Tedi mine, BHP was very careful in considering the interest-based stakeholders, including the Papua New Guinea and Australian governments, and the World Bank. To a large extent, they were also concerned with the needs of their employees, their shareholders and the local landholders, and as a result, the mining operations were able to progress. However, the duty-based stakeholders, comprising the local government leaders and villagers who were not employed at the mine, were not considered to be particularly important. It was these stakeholders, however, who took political action, which delayed the mining operations and proved costly to the company. The fourth, virtue-based group was not considered in the strategic planning and operation of the mine. This group included the communities down river, the women, and the environment, and, ultimately, it was this group that was instrumental in the closure of the mine. The environmental effects of pollution from the mining operations affected the livelihood of the downstream communities, and they took action in the Australian courts to force BHP to take remedial action. The company eventually realised that the effects on these virtue-based groups were too large to remedy, and BHP was compelled to withdraw from mining operations.

From this example, it is clear that the provision of information and communication with all stakeholders is of utmost importance to corporations, so that problems can be addressed before they become insoluble. Social accounting has a major role to play in this communicative process.

## Legitimacy theory //

The **legitimacy** theory perspective is based on the notion of a social contract, express or implied, between an organisation and the community (Frost & Wilmshurst 1999). A proposition of legitimacy theory is that companies are granted privileges, such as limited liability and perpetual succession, through the mechanism of corporations legislation. This legislation is enacted in parliament by the elected representatives of the public, and there is thus an indirect social contract between a company and the general public. If a sufficient number of people are opposed to the activities of a corporation they can, through their elected representatives, lobby for more stringent controlling legislation.

Organisational legitimacy thus depends on social and political support, and the survival and growth of corporations is dependent on their delivering some socially desirable ends. Moreover, it is expected that corporations will deliver benefits to the groups from which they derive their power, and that their activities will not be socially harmful. One of the ways in which companies can 'legitimise' their operations is to provide information on their broader social effects, and to adopt a broader concept of accounting and accountability.

## Political economy //

Proponents of the third perspective, the political economy of accounting, argue that the economic domain cannot be considered in isolation from the environment within which economic transactions are undertaken. Thus, accounting reports are considered to be social and political, as well as economic, documents.

### Charities and organisational legitimacy

Companies aiming to establish their legitimacy often form associations with community and charitable organisations that are already highly respected. Canon, for example, has an effective association with the World Wide Fund for Nature, in which the WWW Panda emblem is used in Canon's advertising. There is synergy between the organisations, as people use cameras to film wildlife and nature, Canon gains social legitimacy from the implication that the WWF would only be associated with a socially responsible organisation, and the WWF gains funding from Canon. Most people would regard this a socially beneficial relationship.

Other companies, however, may attempt to gain legitimacy from associations in which such synergy does not exist. An example of this is the sponsorship of sporting events by cigarette or alcohol manufacturers. In the past, charities were willing to accept any funding to support their operations, but many are now realising that associations with some industries are a threat to their own legitimacy.

This was a dilemma facing the Salvation Army when it was offered a $5 million donation from the gambling company Tattersall's (Charles 2003). The donation was rejected, with the Salvation Army pointing out that 43 per cent of Tattersall's income from electronic gaming machines came from problem gamblers, and that they are called on to offer help to 40 000 people a year in Victoria alone with problem gambling addictions. The Salvation Army's finance manager pointed out that the question of ethics versus practicalities is a very difficult one facing not-for-profit organisations, and many people believe that all available funding should be accepted to support the work that they do. He asked, however, how the Salvation Army could justify the acceptance of such funding while helping the people affected by the products of those organisations. The decision was made that it was not possible to accept the funding and maintain the credibility of the organisation within the greater community.

## Power and accountability //

While the socially constructing nature of accounting has deep historical roots, the effects of accounting information continue to affect society in indirect and often unacknowledged ways, and at many levels of complexity. Traditional financial reports are not regarded as 'neutral' documents by social activists, but as a reflection of corporate power over society. Social reporting is aimed at providing a broader range of information, so that the power provided by the possession of information is more equitably distributed. This is important because, as Hines (1988) explained, the communication of organisational information constructs a picture of that organisation, and the picture becomes the reality to information users who cannot see the actual organisation and its activities for themselves.

The idea of an 'organisational picture' is not new, as accountants are familiar with the notion of a balance sheet being referred to as a 'snapshot'. To carry the photography analogy further, accountants, in preparing the financial statements, choose the way in which items will be measured through the adoption, for example, of different depreciation methods. In this way the size of the photographic image is determined. Accountants also choose those items that will be disclosed separately, and those that will be summarised, or those that will be included or excluded, and this determines the photographic frame and focus. More recently, research into earnings management (for example, Holthausen et al. 1995) proposes that managers are able to choose the level of profit that will be disclosed, and this could represent the substitution of an altogether different photograph. Information users respond to the image in the photograph to make their investment or consumption choices, and can therefore be unaware of the corporate activities that they are supporting. These activities may well be detrimental to society, or to certain sections of it, and it is for this reason that information users are demanding a more broadly based information set that includes social information.

Perks (1993) explained that power and accountability are intertwined, and that attempts to impose accountability are attempts to restrict power. However, the way in which accountancy operates tends to mirror and enhance existing power relationships by providing information that supports the status quo of corporate importance to economic growth. He believes that the extent to which accountants can change these power relationships is limited; but other writers, such as Gray et al. (1996) would suggest that the provision of information is an empowering act, which gives the ability to information receivers to take social and political action aimed at achieving change. Such information, however, must use language that can be readily understood by a wide range of users.

### Language, culture and equity

Since Pacioli first recorded the method of double entry bookkeeping in 1494, accounting, previously developed by merchants for their own purposes and therefore generally well understood, has adopted special terminology by defining certain words to have special meanings, and has thus developed into a special medium of communication that is used as the 'language of business'.

In anthropological terms, the possession of language is a major factor that has led to the dominant position of the human species on earth (Craig 1994); while, in economic terms, 'dominance' is the result of success in the market. Accounting, as the language of business, has therefore played a major role in facilitating the economic dominance of powerful groups, including large corporations. As the accounting language is exclusive of information that cannot be measured in financial terms, much of the information that is important to communicating the social effects of business activities has not been provided. This means that those most affected by corporate practices have been unable to monitor their effects until it is too late to have any input into business decisions, even those which may affect them in a negative way. The result has been that

> a lot of business enterprise now goes on products that can create a demand admittedly, but which are rather trivial or even destructive in terms of the actual problems that face society. (Self 1992, p. 46).

Historically, a great deal of information has been excluded from accounting reports, because it fails the criteria of 'reliable measurement' specified in Statement of Accounting Concepts (SAC) 4. Glautier (1983, p. 57), however, reminded us that in the world of antiquity the absence of money transactions 'did not impede the development of complex and effective accounting control systems'. Glautier's description of accounting as the 'mother of literacy' indicates the extent to which accounting concepts have been narrowed from their ancient broad communicative purpose to the current accounting paradigm, which 'frustrates the ability of the accounting process to deal with problems which cannot be encompassed within an ambit defined by monetary measurement'.

## Alternative societal structures

The effects of business activity, facilitated and supported by accounting information, can fall unequally on different societal groups, and it is in these circumstances that issues of equity and justice arise.

Experiences such as those of the first nations tribes in Canada and North America, and the Aboriginal people in Australia are currently being revisited on local hunter-gatherer societies around the world, as the search for increased supplies of resources to fuel economic growth continues. The experiences of these people are a stark illustration of the effects of power imbalances when colonisation seeks to impose the western ideals of economic capitalism upon a hunter–gatherer social economy. Gibson (2000) discusses the way in which the accounting language prevents a clear acknowledgment of alternative societal values. In Australian Aboriginal communities, for example, to possess a resource is to have an obligation to share it with others. Thus, the accounting concept of assets, with its requirement for exclusive control of the service potential of a resource, represents an opposing idea to the obligations of such traditional societies, whose understanding of assets would be similar to the accounting definition of liabilities.

Miscommunication on such fundamental issues resulted in dispossession when Aboriginal tribal elders exchanged their land for trinkets. They believed that they were agreeing to share the land, in accordance with their tradition, and were unaware of an economic paradigm in which private property rights superseded the interests of the community, even into future generations. They had no concept of a kind of land ownership that conveyed a right to exclude others from it.

This is another example of the way in which the western neoclassical economic paradigm, supported by the language and practices of accounting, can disadvantage particular societal groups. It illustrates the breadth of opportunities that exist for accounting to reconsider its role, and to take on the mantle of catalyst for social equity, rather than an exclusive focus on economic growth.

## Justice //

The political philosopher John Rawls (1971) developed a theory of **justice** applicable to economic institutions that involved moral judgments about the distribution of social goods. Rawls noted that the free market capitalist system depends on the unequal rewards and privileges that are inherent in profits and competition. Rawls is described (Michelman 1996) as an advocate of contingent inequality who advocated a property-owning regime. He set out to demolish the moral and social theory of utilitarianism, which he perceived as having an inability to accommodate personal preferences because of its value-free attachment to results or consequences.

Rawls (1982) proposed two principles for the guidance of political, economic and social institutions:

1. Each person has an equal right to a fully adequate scheme of equal basic liberties which is compatible with a similar scheme of liberties for all.

2. Social and economic inequalities are to satisfy two conditions. First, they must be attached to offices and positions open to all under conditions of fair equality; and second, they must be to the greatest benefit of the least advantaged members of society.

The second principle thus deals with the fair distribution of society's resources, and it is this that is also the concern of social accounting. While large corporations necessarily have control over a large part of society's resources, the principles of justice and fairness require that they be used in society's best interest, and not in the self-interest of corporate managers and shareholders. Social reporting enables companies to discharge this social accountability in the same way as financial reports are aimed at discharging economic accountability to stakeholders.

## Sustainability //

The concept of **sustainability** was introduced in 1987 in a report commissioned by the United Nations, the *Brundtland Report*. Brundtland defined sustainability as

Development which meets the needs of the present without compromising the ability of future generations to meet their own needs.
(see www.brundtlandnet.com/brundtlandreport.htm)

---

### Who cares?

One of the world's largest accounting firms, PricewaterhouseCoopers (PwC 2003), recently posed the question: 'If a company is generating profit from its activities, does anyone care if the board has any interest in good governance? Still less, does anyone, beyond a small group of activists, care if the board is taking into account wider social issues?'

PwC have carried out corporate and business surveys over many years, and provide evidence that 'increasingly, the world does care'. They suggest three main reasons for this. First, communications technology, such as the Internet, has led to greater scrutiny of corporate performance from a wide range of stakeholders. Second, social expectations have changed, and global investors are seeking a broader range of information. The third reason is the evolution that has occurred within the investment industry, aimed at providing investors with niche products. This had led to the growth of socially responsible investing, and the investment industry is busily developing funds and indices to meet the needs of ethical investors.

The financial markets are also beginning to care. The Dow Jones Sustainability Index is now a permanent feature of the United States capital markets, and in the United Kingdom an index of leading ethical companies, called 'FTSE4Good' is being developed. Analysts and investors are now asking about sustainability-related performance issues, and corporate boards are being questioned about social performance at their annual meetings. Coca-Cola, for example, faced questions about recycling its bottles and cans, and BP was asked to explain how it was adapting its products to climate change.

The PwC research demonstrates that investors now expect boards of directors to have in place governance processes for monitoring and reporting on how the business is responding to community issues and social change. It seems that even investors care!

---

The concept of sustainability was originally proposed as environmental sustainability, and was concerned with the use of environmental resources in such a way as to deprive future generations of them. Thus, it has been very closely linked with environmental accounting, and is discussed in greater detail in chapter 9. Business organisations have more recently adopted the term 'sustainability', and it has become the basis of a great deal of corporate promotion and advertising. In business organisations, however, the concept has been transformed into the notion of 'corporate sustainability' or 'corporate social responsibility', and this term has become more closely linked with economic sustainability, or financial viability.

Many companies have now adopted **triple bottom line** reporting, as they believe that it provides an opportunity to demonstrate to their stakeholders that they are introducing sustainable business practices. In many of the 'sustainability' reports that are published, however, social performance is closely related to its economic effects. For example, benchmarks of reduced employee accidents are related to savings in insurance premiums or work days lost. The *Mays Report* (2003), in discussing sustainability, points out that

> While transparency is an important aspect of sustainability, embedding the concepts internally in order to add shareholder value is the most important issue (see www.deh.gov.au/industry/finance/publications/mays-report/footnotes.html).

It is interesting to note that, in defining sustainability in terms of shareholder value in this way, Mays has demonstrated very clearly the business position that social and environmental concerns are not considered to be of importance in their own right, but only insofar as they affect financial performance. Social accountants such as Gray have expressed disappointment at what appears to be a corporate capture of the sustainability agenda. Issues of justice, morality and ethics are subverted in this economic paradigm. Mays discusses 'embracing opportunities and managing risks derived from social, environmental and economic factors'. In this philosophy, market solutions are sought to social and environmental 'problems', and the possibility that free market operations may in fact be the cause of some of society's problems is not acknowledged. This clearly embraces Friedman's position that the only ethical responsibility of business is to maximise shareholder wealth.

It is perhaps encouraging, however, that business, for whatever reason, is reporting social information, as it does assist in increasing the transparency of corporate operations, and it could be suggested that any social information is better than none. There is a counter-argument, however, that partial information is less useful than no information at all. The danger is that, given partial information and not knowing how much is concealed, information users may make decisions that, in the light of more complete information, may not be achieving the results that they desire. If no information is provided, actions may be postponed or changed, because the risk of taking action without information is perceived to be too high. This potential problem may be exacerbated by the fact that the provision of social information by business organisations is entirely voluntary, and research has shown that only 'good news' is provided. Writers such as Collison (2000) have suggested that such reporting could be considered a form of corporate propaganda.

Collison explained that propaganda is not about truth, but rather about power, and it is characterised by an intention to achieve the adoption of attitudes and beliefs that are determined in advance by the supplier of the propaganda information. The danger is that information users may not realise that they are being exposed to propaganda, and they may be unwitting agents, who pass on the information to other contacts. This leads to an acceptance of the information as 'true' by an increasing number of people, who then take their own actions based upon it. In this way, social effects that they might otherwise consider undesirable are unwittingly supported.

Social accountants seek ways to minimise the potential for information about the social effects of business or government operations to be misleading. One of the ways in which this can be done is for the information provided to be the subject of a social audit, in the way that the integrity of accounting information is attested to by means of a compliance audit. Several organisations, including large accounting firms such as KPMG and PricewaterhouseCoopers, are providing social audit services, as are specialist organisations such as the United Kingdom-based SustainAbility.

# Social accounting methods //

Mathews (1993) has been active for many years in proposing methods for improving the provision of social information. In particular, he has reviewed socially responsible accounting studies from around the world, and has developed a series of social accounting classifications. These classifications include:
- total impact accounting
- socio-economic accounting
- social indicators accounting.

## Total impact accounting //

Mathews describes the term **total impact accounting** as referring to attempts at measuring, in monetary terms, the total cost of running an organisation in its existing form. The total organisational cost may be divided between private and public costs. The private costs, which are also called internal costs, are those that are traditionally recorded and measured by the accounting system, such as raw materials, labour costs and overheads. Public costs are also known as external costs, or externalities, and these costs are borne by the community. In terms of social accounting, externalities include costs such as health problems caused by emissions from industrial processes that result in increased demands on medical and social services.

Mathews explains that the difficulties faced in attempting to introduce total impact accounting are related to the identification, measurement and valuation of externalities, to enable their disclosure in financial statements. There are also additional difficulties in that these costs are borne by people outside the entity, and to include them would contravene the entity concept of generally accepted accounting principles. Some companies have in the past attempted to place a financial value on social costs, and a notable example of this was the Dutch company, BSO Origin. This company produced an annual report in which waste products and emissions were measured and valued on the basis of, for example, market prices for carbon dioxide and waste disposal costs for those emissions for which no market currently exists. The company also measured the value of actions taken to minimise social effects, and these amounts were offset against the costs in a value added statement. This was then combined with the profit and loss statement to produce a 'net value added' result. While the preparation of this annual report was a one-off exercise performed in 1990, it provides an example of how total impacts can be reported.

## Socio-economic accounting //

Mathews (1993) described **socio-economic accounting** as being concerned with a micro approach to the problems of project selection, operation, control and evaluation, and explained that it is a method more suitable to the public sector than the private sector. It can be closely related to the concept of cost–benefit analysis. Once a cost–benefit analysis has been performed and a project has been accepted, it will be easier to use socio-economic accounting to evaluate the performance of the project, as the cost and benefit data will already be on record. Mathews provides the following example:

> If changes are made to an educational programme, as a result of an analysis of objectives, costs and benefits, the costs may be expressed in financial terms, but the benefits may be given in terms of greater teaching effectiveness or a lower dropout rate for students.

Clearly, some of the measurements will be very difficult to obtain, but there are social valuation models in the economics literature, such as contingent valuation and option pricing, that offer some guidance. These models can be used to provide a financial estimate of, for example, the costs that people are willing to pay to visit a particular area of social significance, or how much people are willing to pay to protect social assets such as heritage sites or national parks. It is important, however, to understand that the values obtained are social values, and not financial ones, and to include them in financial statements could be very misleading to users.

Socio-economic accounting models can be very complex, as Mathews is careful to point out, as they are used to assist in making decisions about the effectiveness and efficiency of publicly funded activities in the absence of market prices for outputs. He explains the difficulties in that inputs may be valued in financial and non-financial terms, but output will often be limited to non-financial values, such as the numbers of employable school leavers, reformed prisoners, discharged patients or university graduates.

## Social indicators accounting //

**Social indicators accounting** is identified by Mathews as the macro approach that corresponds with the micro approach taken by socio-economic accounting. Social indicators accounting can be applied where the objectives of a social system are to have a healthier, wealthier and better-educated population, where progress towards the objectives is capable of measurement. Performance indicators are developed in relation to the goals to be achieved, and performance is measured against them.

# Current reporting practices //

The triple bottom line reports currently being provided by many companies include a combination of financial information, quantified non-financial information and narrative descriptions. A potential problem with placing financial values on social resources is that users often regard financial information as being objective, without recognising that judgment is often involved in calculating the reported amounts. This can lead to sub-optimal results from the use of that information by people who are not fully informed of its nature. Quantified, non-financial information may be more objectively reported, but there is often difficulty in comparing quantities of different social resources. For example, a comparison between a health outcome and an educational achievement would be extremely complex and difficult to make. Narrative can be very useful in describing issues and effects, but may be subjectively reported and the difficulty of comparison remains.

Useful reporting is nevertheless achievable. Accountants, when they calculate financial ratios, are aware of the shortcomings, in that a single ratio is not useful for decision purposes, but a trend over time can provide a meaningful indicator. In the same way, accountants are very careful in comparing financial ratios of different companies, and especially of companies in different industries. Social information can work in a very similar way.

Many of the more recent social reports published by companies and government organisations provide benchmark indicators against which performance can be assessed. For example, a water company can set a benchmark for the level of organisms present in local waterways, and set targets for reduced concentrations over a number of years. In this way, a trend is established and reported against, and a performance trend can be identified in a similar way to financial ratio trends. While intrinsic measurements cannot be compared across organisations, percentage improvements can, and this can provide a useful basis for community decision making.

As an example of the kinds of social indicators or benchmarks that are in use, the *Westpac 2003 Social Impact Report* includes financial measures of institutional lending with a high social benefit and male/female salary comparisons. Examples of quantitative information include the number of employees accessing paid parental leave, an index of employee morale and complaints resolution rates. These are all plotted over time, so that improvement or deterioration is clearly and transparently communicated. In terms of narrative, Westpac describes the expansion of services to rural and regional Australia and Indigenous partnerships.

The best social impact reports are acknowledging areas in which performance is falling, or not meeting planned levels, and, while a measure of healthy scepticism is a wise accompaniment to digestion of most corporate social reports, the fact that such reports are increasingly provided is a good basis from which to move forward. Current debates are concerned with whether or not social information provision should be subject to legislation. Arguments in favour of regulation include comparability, required provision of 'bad' news, and the monitoring that regulation may facilitate. Opponents of regulation, however, argue strenuously that, in a regulated environment, companies will only provide the basic minimum of information required. This may be a spurious argument in light of the current levels of information voluntarily provided by some organisations, and for businesses that are not yet reporting social information, the incentive provided by regulation could yield positive results.

## Summary //

Social accounting is one of the components of the 'triple bottom line' of economic, social and environmental performance. It is closely linked with environmental performance, as often there is a direct relationship between the effects of business activities on society and the environment.

Social accounting is based on a broad concept of accountability, in which businesses are required to discharge their responsibility for the social resources that are necessary to their operations. The social aspects of business operations include the people who work for them, communities that are affected by them or their products, and the use of public goods, such as infrastructure or education and training.

In this chapter we discussed the historical and more recent developments in social accounting, and considered both the socially constructed and socially constructing nature of accounting information. We considered the power of the accounting language, and its implications for culture, equity, justice and sustainability. The fact that the concept of sustainability continues to evolve was also discussed.

Finally, examples of how social accounting might be achieved were considered, and the issue was raised as to whether regulation might result in the provision of improved social accounting reports.

## Key terms //

Accountability . . . p. 206
Capitalism . . . p. 201
Corporate social reporting . . . p. 205
Justice . . . p. 212
Legitimacy . . . p. 208
Social indicators accounting . . . p. 216
Socially constructed . . . p. 202

## Questions //

**8.1** What is meant by 'standard of living'?

**8.2** What were the major economic activities that contributed to the development of double entry bookkeeping?

**8.3** What were the social and political activities that contributed to the development of double entry bookkeeping?

**8.4** What social conditions encouraged the development of corporate social reporting in the early 1970s?

**8.5** Describe in your own words the meaning of 'accountability'.

**8.6** Explain the three 'logics' of stakeholder theory and provide an example of each.

**8.7** Briefly describe the theories that attempt to explain why corporations have an incentive to provide social information. Which do you find most persuasive, and why?

**8.8** Provide an example of the way in which accounting may be socially constructed.

**8.9** What is meant by the suggestion that accounting is socially constructing?

**8.10** What are the social implications of considering accounting as a language?

**8.11** In what way has the concept of sustainability changed during the past few years?

**8.12** What are the main differences between Mathews' three proposed methods of social accounting?

**8.13** Do you believe that the reporting of the social effects of corporate operations should be required by law? Why or why not?

**8.14** Discuss the implications of companies being required to consider the social impacts of their operations on virtue-based stakeholders.

**8.15** It may be said that efforts to persuade companies to provide information about the social effects of their operations are based on political ideology, rather than sustainability. Give your opinions on this suggestion.

### FURTHER RESOURCES AND WEBSITES //

*Accounting, Auditing & Accountability Journal*, MCB University Press, Bradford, UK.

Centre for Social & Environmental Accounting Research: www.gla.ac.uk/departments/accounting/csear/

*Corporate Social Responsibility and Environmental Management*, John Wiley & ERP Environment, UK and www.interscience.wiley.com

Corporate Social Responsibility Forum: www.csrforum.com/

Corporate Social Responsibility Newswire Service: www.csrwire.com

Elkington, J 1998, *Cannibals with forks; the triple bottom line of 21st century business*, New Society Publishers, Canada.

Global Reporting Initiative: Sustainability Reporting Guidelines: www.globalreporting.org/guidelines/2002.asp

Quarter, J, Mook, L & Richmond, BJ 2003, *What counts: social accounting for nonprofits and cooperatives*, Pearson Education, New Jersey.

SustainAbility: www.sustainability.com/home.asp

Sustainable Investment Research Institute: www.siris.com.au/index.asp

## CASE STUDY

### OK Tedi Mining Limited

The Ok Tedi gold and copper mine is located in the upper catchment of the Ok Tedi River, which is a major tributary of the Fly River in the western highlands of Papua New Guinea. It is approximately 18 kilometres from Papua New Guinea's border with Irian Jaya, which is controlled by Indonesia.

The Ok Tedi area has a very high rainfall, with eight to ten metres of rain falling over an average 339 days of the year. Seismic activity further contributes to geological instability. The result is local land movement and massive run-off into the major rivers such as the Fly. The population of the 76 000 square kilometre Fly River catchment is approximately 40 000 people who, prior to the development of the mine, lived in separate communities and were mainly dependent upon hunter gathering and fishing for their livelihood.

The mine is situated at Mt. Fubilan, and an idea of the size of the operations can be gained from the fact that this mountain, originally 2053 metres high, would be reduced to a height of only 800 metres at the end of the mine's 18-year life. The mountain is a sacred site of local communities.

BHP was encouraged by the Australian government to consolidate economic links with Papua New Guinea following political independence and the Papua New Guinea government was also very keen to encourage successful development and operation of the mine.

The Papua New Guinea government passed special legislation for the project, which, while including a requirement for the construction of a tailings dam, placed limits on the expenditure that BHP was required to commit. While, legislatively, Papua New Guinea is the most advanced country in the South Pacific, the two major environmental Acts, covering planning and contamination, specifically exempted mine development and operation from their conditions.

BHP was not acting alone, but was heading a consortium of public and private sector interests, including the Papua New Guinea government, who were all shareholders in Ok Tedi Mining Limited (OTML). The World Bank also had an indirect interest in the project, as the country's indebtedness was placing the government under pressure to increase exports as part of a financial restructure.

It was known at the outset, because of the topography, geology and meteorology of the region, that there were potential environmental problems, but the Papua New Guinea central government took a utilitarian view that the economic benefits to the country as a whole would outweigh the detrimental local impact. It was believed that the economic benefits would also bring social advantages to the local villagers, but there were potential problems in that the relationships between different clans of local people were extremely fragile.

The main environmental problem at Ok Tedi was the disposal of tailings. These are waste products, including rock powder, silt, water, some metals, and chemical residues such as hydrogen peroxide and cyanide from the extraction process. The building of a tailings dam, to prevent mine tailings entering the river system, began in 1983. The dam, however, was destroyed by massive landslips in 1984, which followed rainfall of almost seven metres in one month. This resulted in a financial loss of $64 million to OTML, and it was estimated that replacement of the dam and associated delays would cost more than $460 million. Following this, the Papua New Guinea government agreed that tailings from the mine could be disposed of either directly into the river system, or into tailings dumps. To enable this, exemptions from environmental legislation were granted, and these have been maintained by succeeding Papua New Guinea governments. Under these exemptions, 20 000 tonnes of tailings were dumped each day into the river system until 1989, when public concern about environmental degradation caused the government to take action to limit pollution levels.

The Ok Tedi and Fly Rivers were unable to flush these massive amounts through their system, and the resulting environmental changes in the catchment area destroyed traditional lifestyles and caused ill health among the local villagers. This further exacerbated the disagreements between the various clans, as many of the people to suffer the impact of the mine were not those making economic gains through direct or indirect employment. The sediments reduced the gradient of the river and completely changed its flow behaviour, habitat value and use to local villagers. As a result, greatly increased flooding occurred in an area of extremely high rainfall, and deposition of sediment widened the valley floor, burying riverine vegetation and causing forest dieback over a 30 square km area. According to Rosenbaum (1993, p. 41) the first 70 km of the Ok Tedi (is) biologically dead, and species diversity in the next 130 km . . . has been dramatically reduced.

The International Water Tribunal became involved in 1992, and from that time pressure from western environmental groups, including the Australian Conservation Foundation, began to increase.

In terms of legal accountability, OTML operations, through exemptions from relevant legislation, have always been in compliance with the law, and remained within the legal requirements for the dumping of waste. Nevertheless, in May 1994 a $4 billion writ was lodged against BHP through the Melbourne law firm Slater and Gordon, acting for 550 village leaders representing 30 000 villagers of the Ok Tedi/Fly River region. Their claim was that the mine had ruined the river system and destroyed their traditional way of life. The villagers were, however, not intending to obtain closure of the mine, but attempting to enforce the construction of a tailings dam and rehabilitation of the area. Shortly after the writ was lodged, the Papua New Guinea government insisted on the building of a tailings dam, regardless of the outcome of the claim.

BHP's response was to negotiate a $110 million compensation package, payable over 15 years, from which it was agreed that the cost of tailings dam construction could be deducted (BHP 1995, p. 6). The agreement also contained provisions aimed at ending the legal action, and BHP liaised with the Papua New Guinea government to draft a Bill aimed at making the lodging of compensation claims a criminal offence, punishable by fines up to $100 000. These provisions drew criticism, particularly from environmental groups who had also involved sections of the international media. One result was a call by the Australian senator Bob Brown for the federal government to apply Australian environmental laws to Australian companies operating overseas. BHP was possibly protected by its relationship with the Australian government, as no action was taken in response to this appeal. Further, the then Minister for Foreign Affairs, Senator Evans, 'vigorously defended the agreement between BHP and the PNG Government'. He said that Papua New Guinea needed development and international investment, and that the Papua New Guinea government 'had to ensure that it "crunched" actions' such as this (Barker 1995, p. 3). The Australian government stance was, however, not supported by the International Commission of Jurists, who condemned BHP for its involvement in the preparation of the legislation (Stevens 1995).

The Victorian Court hearing the villagers' original claim considered these defensive actions of BHP, and held them in contempt on the grounds that they interfered with the administration of justice. Mr Justice Philip Cummins ruled that BHP had acted criminally to interfere with the processes of the Victorian Supreme Court. The Papua New Guinea government, however, supported BHP, signifying that the economic relationship with the company was of greater importance to them than the social responsibility to their local villagers.

BHP was nevertheless forced to respect the legal jurisdiction of the Victorian court, and, in attempting to rebuild its public legitimacy, argued that it was committed to best practice environmental management.

While OTML has contributed to the development of local infrastructure, which has achieved improved health and educational outcomes, it has been reported (Jackson et al. 1995) that little of the current economic activity in the region would be sustainable following closure of the mine, predicted to occur in 2010. Jackson et al. also discovered gross wastage of financial and other benefits, and pointed out that 46.5 per cent of the village development funds provided by OTML remained unaccounted for. In this way, there has been a deficiency in accountability of the Papua New Guinea government to the local villagers, partly because both they and OTML were more interested in satisfying the demands of shareholders and other powerful economic interests.

A stark response from the duty-based stakeholder group included the throwing of dead fish by Ok Tedi villagers at the BHP 1995 Annual General Meeting in Australia. While BHP admitted to poor managerial handling, which had led to damaging publicity, the company believed that the main problem was their failure to convey a balanced story, rather than any failure to act in an accountable manner (BHP 1997). Accountability was finally acknowledged in response to the villagers' Australian legal action, which, although eventually settled out of court, achieved much of what the villagers sought, including a tailings containment program, rehabilitation and compensation (BHP 1996).

The downstream villagers have suffered many of the detrimental effects of livelihood and amenity loss suffered by those closer to the mine, without the offsetting employment opportunities and financial benefits of royalties or lease payments. As these villagers were outside the traditional OTML stakeholder group, activism and increased public awareness were necessary to fight their case as 'economic outsiders'. Their situation was eventually acknowledged by OTML, who then established the Ok Tedi/Fly River Development Trust to assist in developing village infrastructure, including social, educational, health, and recreational services, and providing opportunities for business development.

Women in particular were affected by the mine development. Rosenbaum (1995, p. 37) pointed out that

> The labour force draws on men from other regions of PNG, resulting in cultural tensions and problems such as sexual harassment of local women. The employment of men at mine sites, while bringing with it the ability to participate in the cash economy, increases the burden of agriculture and child care on women who remain in the villages. The extra workloads, domestic violence and alcohol abuse mean that the quality of women's lives often seriously deteriorates as a result of mining activities.

The issue of tailings containment was entirely related to financial constraints, and not to environmental impacts. Government approval was given to continue operations without a tailings dam, after a report indicated that it would not only be technically difficult, but that it might also jeopardise the economic viability of the mine. Mining operations also continued in spite of a report to the Papua New Guinea Cabinet by the Mines Minister that an acknowledged 70 per cent margin of error in the prediction of sediment impact meant that 'fish losses could be as little as nothing or as high as everything' (Davis 1994). Although an environmental monitoring and management program had been implemented by OTML, environmental legislation placed the onus on the company to monitor its own discharge and inform the government of the results.

The importance of accountability was not recognised until the harm had been done, and BHP became the subject of public condemnation. Even then, damage control in terms of boosting corporate image was the initial response. A public relations campaign was launched in Australia, mostly in the form of paid advertisements, and BHP expressed a willingness to 'spend whatever funds were required to fix the waste problem if the economics of the solution fit within the fiscal regime of the project' (Frith 1995). Prior to his departure, a former managing director identified Ok Tedi as simply 'an organisational failure', saying that the mine 'was run from the San Francisco base of BHP Minerals and was out of touch with the resonance of issues in Australia' (Kohler 1996, p. 80).

Since then, the financial costs have continued to rise, and BHP has been forced to respond in a more substantive manner. A special package of benefits has been developed for the most affected area, and negotiations have taken place for the implementation of a $38 million compensation package for the people of the Lower Ok Tedi River (Kirsch 1996). Dredging of the riverbed is also required to reverse the effects of aggradation (BHP 1996).

An analysis of the Ok Tedi case reveals that higher levels of accountability were accorded to the economically powerful interest-based stakeholders, and that accountability was steadily reduced as the spectrum through rights-based and duty-based stakeholders to the virtue-based groups was traversed. It is clear that, in this case, when it became difficult to achieve both strong financial returns and protection of the interests of the local people and natural environment, good intentions came second to commercial considerations. Ethical errors were made in dismissing the interests of the virtue-based groups, including the decision to proceed without a tailings dam, and the attempt to criminalise further compensation claims.

BHP has since acknowledged that it should not have become involved in mining at Ok Tedi, and it has now ceased operations there. However, in an address to an ethics forum before the withdrawal decision was made, the managing director identified the ethical dilemma in which the company was by then embroiled.

If BHP continued the mining operations, environmental damage and ongoing health and welfare effects on the downstream villagers would also continue. Further, the unequal wealth in the hands of local people working at the mine would continue to cause social disruption, and the accompanying problems of alcohol and violence.

If BHP withdrew from mining operations, local people, whose traditional lifestyles had been destroyed, would no longer be able to gain employment at the mine to support their families. The many families indirectly supported by the mine, for example in making uniforms or providing catering and cleaning services, would also lose their livelihoods. If an operator with a lower level of corporate social responsibility took over the mine's operation, the health and welfare infrastructure and services provided by BHP might be discontinued.

To add to this, a further ethical dilemma faced the BHP Board of Directors. According to Friedman (1970) their only ethical responsibility was to increase the wealth of shareholders. It is debatable whether this was being done when company funds were used to provide health and welfare services to the villagers in Papua New Guinea.

This case illustrates the complexity of ethical decision making in a corporate environment, and the question is raised as to whether the use of social accounting and reporting could have contributed to a better outcome. An argument is that by providing information that enables a wide range of users, including community groups, special interest groups and the media to be aware of the occurrence of social problems resulting from corporate activities, governments can be pressured into taking action to protect the less powerful stakeholders. A further argument is that companies will reconsider activities that are socially risky if they know that a full account has to be given on an ongoing basis. From Friedman's perspective, however, it may act to prevent companies from entering into activities that may be economically beneficial,

// ─────────────────────────────────────

and thus act to financially disadvantage the shareholders. The economic argument could also be that if corporate operations that would otherwise be economically viable are discouraged in this way, the market will be less efficient and the costs of finance could be increased. This in turn would increase the cost of products or services to consumers, including higher prices for the copper utensils that would have been produced from the Mt Fubilan copper ore.

Ultimately, the solution may correspond with the arguments of social accountants that, if full information is provided, decisions will be made that are likely to be more just and equitable to less powerful stakeholders, but that may be at the expense of the more economically wealthy. In global issues, such as the Ok Tedi case, this may, for example, translate into everyone in Australia paying more for their copper products, so that expensive tailings treatments can be put into place to at least protect the livelihoods of the villagers downstream. With full information, however, including transparent reporting of the social effects, those decisions can at least be made on an informed basis.

### QUESTIONS

1 If you were a member of the board of directors during the time of the Ok Tedi operations, would you have been in favour of implementing a social accounting and reporting regime in the company?

2 What would have been the advantages to BHP in making full disclosure of the conditions and events at Ok Tedi at the time the mine was in operation?

3 Discuss whether the provision of health and education infrastructure and services is a reasonable requirement of companies operating in remote areas.

4 Can social reporting be justified in cases where it results in a decline in market efficiency? Why, or why not?

5 Should the social standards of one country (such as Australia) be imposed on another country (such as Papua New Guinea)? Give reasons for your answer.

## REFERENCES //

ASSC 1975, *The corporate report*, Accounting Standards Steering Committee, London.

Barker, G 1995, 'Dead fish, ethics and Ok Tedi', *Financial Review*, 9 October, p.15.

BHP 1995, *BHP and Ok Tedi: the facts*, The Broken Hill Pty Ltd, Melbourne.

BHP 1996, *Resolution of Ok Tedi litigation*, Press Release, unpublished, 11 June.

BHP 1997, 'Guiding business conduct', Proceedings of *Forum on Corruption in International Procurement*, Institution of Engineers Australia, Canberra, March.

Brennan, G 1992, 'Competition: the double life of econospeak and the limits of human values' in Harris, JW (Ed), *Competing for good—human values in a competitive Australia, Ethics and contemporary issues, no. 4*, New College, UNSW, pp. 21–31.

Charles, E 2003, 'A bit of give and take', *Australian CPA*, December, pp. 26–7.

Collison, DJ 2003, 'Corporate propaganda: its implications for accounting and accountability', *Accounting, Auditing & Accountability Journal*, vol. 16, no. 5, pp. 853–86.

Craig, D 1994, Environmental science, Environmental Science Project Committee, Australian Academy of Science, Canberra.

Davis, M 1994, 'PNG presses for Ok Tedi tailings dam, *Business Review Weekly*, 16 May.

Du Pont 2002, *Du Pont business conduct guide*, E. I. du Pont de Nemours and Company, www.dupont.com, January.

Finley, MI 1980, *Ancient slavery and modern ideology*, Viking Press, New York.

Friedman, M 1970, 'The social responsibility of business is to increase its profits', *The New York Times Magazine*, 13 September, pp. 122–6.

Frith, D 1995, 'BHP digs deep for Ok Tedi solution', *The Australian*, 27 September.

Frost, GR & Wilmshurst, TD 1999, 'Corporate environmental reporting: a test of legitimacy theory', Working Paper 02/99, University of Newcastle.

Gibson, K 2000, 'Accounting as a tool for Aboriginal dispossession: then and now', *Accounting, Auditing & Accountability Journal*, vol. 13, no. 3, pp. 289–306.

Glautier, MWE 1983, 'Searching for accounting paradigms', *The Accounting Historians Journal*, vol. 10, No. 1, pp. 51–68, Spring.

Gray, R, Owen, D & Adams, C 1996, *Accounting & accountability*, Prentice Hall, London.

Gray, R, Owen, D & Maunders, K 1987, *Corporate social reporting*, Prentice Hall, New Jersey.

Herbohn, KF & Herbohn, JL 1999, 'Accounting for forests in social, economic and political contexts', *Accounting Forum*, vol. 23, no. 4, p. 408.

Hines, R 1988, 'Financial accounting: in communicating reality, we construct reality', *Accounting, Organisations and Society*, vol. 16, no. 4, pp. 251–61.

Holthausen, R, Larcker, D & Sloan, R 1995, 'Annual bonus schemes and the manipulation of earnings', *Journal of Accounting & Economics*, vol. 19, pp. 29–74.

Jackson, R, R Peterson and O Stanley 1995, *Towards sustainable development in the Ok Tedi impact area*, Consultancy report to OTML, Melanesian Studies Centre, James Cook University, Cairns.

Kirsch, S 1996, 'Return to Ok Tedi', *Meanjin*, vol. 55, no. 4, pp. 657–66.

Kohler, A 1996, 'How BHP's System Works', *The Independent Monthly*, March, pp. 80–3.

Lane, FC 1973, *Venice: a maritime republic*, Johns Hopkins University Press, Baltimore.

Matthews, MR 1993, *Socially responsible accounting*, Chapman & Hall, London.

Mays, S 2003, *Corporate sustainability—an investor perspective*, Department of the Environment & Heritage, Commonwealth of Australia.

Michelman, IS 1996, *The moral limitations of capitalism*, Ashgate Publishing, Aldershot, England.

Perks, RW 1993, *Accounting and society*, Chapman & Hall, London.

PwC 2003, *Corporate social reporting—who cares?* www.pwcglobal.com, accessed 4.7.2003.

Rawls, J 1971, *A theory of justice*, Harvard University Press, Cambridge, Mass.

Rawls, J 1982, Tanner Lecture, reprinted in Rawls, J 1987, 'The idea of an overlapping consensus', *Oxford Journal of Legal Studies*, vol. 5.

Rosenbaum, H 1993, 'Ok Tedi—undermining PNG's future? *Habitat Australia*, November, pp. 39–44.

Rosenbaum, H 1995, 'Partners push for sustainable PNG mining', *Habitat Australia*, February, pp. 36–7.

Self, P 1992, 'Competition: Is it Consistent with Human Values?' in Harris, JW (Ed) *Competing for good—human values in a competitive Australia, Ethics and contemporary issues*, no. 4, New College, UNSW, pp. 44–53.

Sombart, W 1924 'Der moderne kapitalismus', cited in Mathews, MR & Perera, MHB 1991, *Accounting theory and development*, Nelson, South Melbourne.

Stevens, M 1995, 'BHP The tarnished Australian', *The Weekend Australian*, 30 September, pp. 21–2.

Werhane, PH & Freeman, RE 1997, *The Blackwell encyclopaedic dictionary of business ethics*, Blackwell, Cambridge, Mass.

# Environmental responsibility

# 9

## Learning objectives

After studying this chapter you should be able to:

- Explain the major issues relating to environmental responsibility.
- Evaluate the free market and regulatory arguments in terms of environmental outcomes.
- Discuss the relationship between ethics and sustainability.
- Discuss corporate responses to environmental responsibility.
- Discuss the potential effects of environmental issues on corporate decision making.

---

'At Orica we manage our operations with concern for people and the environment. We strive to conduct our business sustainably, so that the current benefits to society do not come at the cost of the quality of life of future generations.'

**Malcolm Broomhead, Managing Director and CEO,
Orica Limited *Annual Report 2003*. Taken from www.orica.com.au/BUSINESS/
COR/orica/COR00254.NSF/Page/GovernanceCodeofEthics.**

'AGL believes ensuring a sustainable future . . . is an ongoing journey. As part of this journey AGL is undertaking work to refine its knowledge of the company's environmental footprint and how we manage it. We are doing this to ensure we meet the needs and expectations of AGL's stakeholders, consistent with the company's commitment to corporate sustainability.'

**M John Phillips, Chairman,
The Australian Gas Light Company, *Annual Report 2003*.**

# Introduction //

> Economics and ethics do have something in common: historically neither of them has taken environmental concerns seriously.
>
> Enteman 1990, p. 218.

Some two centuries ago, John Stuart Mill, in contemplation of free market economic development and political economy, addressed the question: 'What about the earth itself, and its forests and waters that are the inheritance of the human race?' This led to a consideration of what rights a person should be able to exercise over this common inheritance, and under what conditions.

To follow Mill's arguments, environmental policy is concerned with distribution, as is economic policy. In granting environmental rights, however, and in determining conditions under which they can be exercised, ethical questions are raised as to who gains and who loses. The gainers and losers may well live in the same local area, but the gainers are often the more economically wealthy members of the community, and the losers the less wealthy. For example, if a local company pollutes its environment, the company gains from the use of such **free goods** as clean air and water. By using these free resources, the company gains reduced costs of production, and its consumers gain through paying lower prices. In this instance, the losers may well be members of the community who live close to the factory but who cannot afford to, or choose not to, consume its products. They may still support the company indirectly, for example through paying the costs of pollution clean-up, in reduced aesthetic values, increased council rates for cleaning up public buildings or waterways, or even the increased health costs of asthma and respiratory illness.

On a broader scale, the losers may well be citizens of another country; for instance, when pollution entering the Rhine River in Germany washes up in Holland, or gases from America's power stations affect tree growth in Canada, or radioactive fallout from a Russian power station affects farms in the north of England, making their produce unsaleable. Broader still, the losers may be the members of society who are least able to protect themselves: unborn children, or non-human species with no voice to command attention. This introduces us to a consideration of **intergenerational** and **inter-species equity**, which can cause the traditional utilitarian ethical approaches to become unserviceable, as the 'greatest number' for which an optimal outcome is sought does not include the overwhelming numbers of future generations of our own species, and the present and future generations of all the other species on earth.

# Language //

In chapter 8, you will remember that we referred to the possession of language, and the social power that it can confer. Let us now consider some further aspects of language, and its implications for the use of environmental resources. In particular, business activities are concerned with **wealth**, **assets** and the **equity** of share-holders, and corporate managers are rewarded according to their success in maximising the economic measures of these. Importantly, when we extend these concepts to environmental issues, the possibility of different meanings, and therefore the capacity for misunderstanding, becomes apparent.

## Wealth //

Most dictionaries define wealth in terms of riches, prosperity, abundance, or 'well-offness', and the utilitarian basis of present-day economic activity is to increase the wealth of nations as a whole, so that increased wealth for individual members of society will follow. We have international league tables that measure comparative national wealth based on Gross Domestic Product (GDP) or Gross National Product (GNP), and most of us, if asked, could easily identify several of the wealthiest and least wealthy nations: the 'winners' and 'losers' in the GDP stakes. The relative measure of GDP is adopted universally, as it traditionally represents the prosperity or increase in 'well-offness' of a country, and we refer to the measure that it presents as our 'standard of living'. When a government measures a country's GDP, or standard of living, the statistics are an aggregation of individual incomes from the production of goods and services throughout the country, but they do not deduct the expenses to society of pollution or contamination of the environment, biodiversity loss or species extinction.

Thus, while the measure has gained international acceptance and may be very useful as an economic indicator, it is less useful, and sometimes harmful, when applied to the use of environmental resources. For example, if a manufacturing process contaminates land, water or air, the value of production is added to GDP. If the contamination is not cleaned up, then GDP does not account for any detriment. However, if the contamination is so bad that a clean-up is required, then the cost of clean-up is recorded as a further increase in GDP. In this way, both the production cost and the environmental remediation are added together to calculate national wealth, or standard of living. It follows that those nations that pollute the most are likely to show the highest rate of growth in national wealth and living standards. This is paradoxical, because if we were measuring standard of living in terms of clean land, fresh air and drinkable water, pollution would be counted as a reduction in wealth. This demonstrates the potentially mischievous effect of the power of language. Because we define wealth in terms of GDP and identify specific measurement rules, increases in economic wealth are inevitably gained at the expense of environmental wealth, and perhaps more insidious, perverse incentives are provided for increased levels of environmental degradation.

## Assets //

The assets of a business or an individual are defined in terms of the resources that are controlled by that business or person, from which they can exclude other persons. Assets are a major factor in economic wealth accumulation, as prosperity is often measured according to the amount of resources controlled. In economic terms, assets are good to have. In environmental terms, natural assets such as clean air, oceans and forests are also good to have. In terms of language, therefore, there appears to be commonality in the concept of assets. Once again, there is a difference in understanding, which can be illustrated by considering the two issues of **private property rights** and the balance between **man-made** and **natural assets**.

## Private property rights

The nature of control is fundamental to the recording and measurement of assets in a business environment. Australian and international accounting regulations require that, to account for a resource, an organisation or individual must have exclusive rights to its use. It is clear, therefore, that environmental resources such as air and water can never be considered as assets within these definitions. It is often argued that, because they are not the property of any individual, there is no incentive for individuals to minimise their use of them, or to take care of them.

Historically, for example in medieval Europe or in Australia prior to white settlement, land boundaries were not in place, and land areas were used by whole communities for food gathering or production. In Europe, land areas around villages were called commons, and were available to the entire local community to graze their cattle and sheep, and produce food for their families. Gradually, in what has become known as 'the tragedy of the commons', some individuals became greedy and brought larger herds of grazing livestock onto the common land. This reduced the amount of grass available for their neighbours' cows, which then produced less milk, and the gap between the wealthy and the less wealthy steadily widened. The government's solution to this was to pass legislation, known as the Enclosures Acts, which provided for the fencing of parts of the commons for the exclusive use of individuals. Very few commons now survive, but you may have heard of Wimbledon Common or Clapham Common, which remain as community areas, even though cattle grazing is no longer a permitted use.

The 'commons' argument is often referred to in environmental debates, where it is argued that if individuals were given ownership rights over parts of oceans, forests and rivers, for example, they would be better taken care of, as the owners would have an economic incentive to maintain or improve their financial value. The counter-argument, in terms of equity and social justice, is that these environmental resources are truly owned by the whole community, who should not be excluded from enjoying them. This leads to a third argument, which proposes that the **anthropocentric** view, of environmental resources existing for the use of the human community, ignores the rights of non-human species. If common wilderness areas are open and available to all, then, with human populations increasing, the 'tragedy of the commons' may be repeated, to the detriment of all other species of flora and fauna, and the whole of nature. Many people who are concerned about the environment argue that this is already the case.

### Insurance Australia Group (IAG)

IAG was the overall winner of the *Ethical Investor* magazine's Sustainability awards for 2003/2004 and has been named 'Sustainable Company of the Year'. The company's CEO, Michael Hawker, believes that the link between insurance and environmental risk is very clear, when it is considered that 19 out of 20 of Australia's major insurance claims have been related to weather events such as bushfires, floods and hailstorms. He identifies a strong relationship between rising global sea temperatures and the ferocity and frequency of storm events, and believes that, as IAG is in the business of risk mitigation, the company itself has a responsibility to minimise its own environmental footprint.

Internally, the company has introduced an energy efficiency program, and uses green power whenever possible. Double-sided printing and paper recycling programs are part of a three-to four-year strategy for cultural change towards a true sustainability-sensitive company.

The company has a major external influence on supply chains through its purchasing power influence. Hawker says that 'by replacing insured household white goods with similar items that carry higher environmental ratings, and by using generic recyclable parts instead of one-use branded parts for car repairs, and insisting that contract mechanics dispose of toxic chemicals properly, the insurer can leverage environmental improvements into the wider community, using a market-based process'.

The company has implemented sustainability goals as part of ongoing management processes in its business groups, and reports that 'recognition of stakeholders and environmental goals is part and parcel of what's considered good business'.

*Source:* Kendall (2004)

## Man-made and natural assets

The issue of man-made and natural assets is at the heart of intergenerational equity, and arguments in relation to this, as with many environmental discourses, are polarised.

One potential argument is that, if we use up natural assets such as forests or mineral reserves, and replace them with man-made assets such as highways and bridges, then the asset equation is still in balance. Well-constructed roads and bridges will last for several generations, so community infrastructure could be considered an alternative form of wealth to the minerals or vegetation that would otherwise be left in the earth. But what of consumer goods, which are used and converted to waste within one generation? In relation to these, it is argued that intergenerational equity is not achieved. This will be discussed briefly in the next section.

Some of the arguments about man-made and natural assets concern issues of costs and values. When a man-made asset is used by a business to produce goods and services, the cost of its use is accounted for as one of the costs of production. This is called **depreciation**. The more valuable an asset, the higher the depreciation cost, and the lower the profit made from the goods that it produces. This provides an incentive for businesses to use valuable assets to their maximum extent, thus spreading the cost over ever-larger quantities of goods and services. If production cannot be increased, high prices must be charged for the goods that are produced. High prices in turn reduce demand for the goods; so, ultimately, the extremely valuable assets become too costly to use, and are conserved. This, of course, is the classic argument in favour of private property rights in environmental resources. The argument is that if whales, for example, were in private ownership, the last whale would never be killed; because, in the marketplace, scarcity drives up price and the whale would become an extremely valuable asset. The faulty logic in this argument is clear; because, for a species to survive there needs to be sufficient numbers to reproduce, and habitat and food sources need to be conserved.

Let us consider other environmental resources, such as the logging of publicly owned old-growth forests. Because the community owns these forests, they do not represent an asset in the balance sheets of logging companies. Therefore, when the trees are logged, there is no cost to the forestry company in terms of asset loss or depreciation, as no original cost has been recorded for them. The only cost of using these environmental resources is the cost of cutting them down, converting them to sawlogs or woodchips, and transporting them. The environmental cost of forest growth over several hundred years is not accounted for. More importantly, the price of a tree as a piece of timber takes no account of its value as a living organism, a mechanism for preventing soil erosion, a home for birds and insects, a store of carbon dioxide, or its role in maintaining biodiversity. The question is raised of whether the resulting man-made asset, such as a piece of furniture, is of equal value to the natural asset, the old tree.

Yet another argument about the use of natural assets concerns the use of clean air and water. If these are taken freely from the environment and used in the production process, they form part of the input into manufactured products, but at no cost to the producer. In a competitive market, if one producer installs costly equipment to prevent environmental pollution, and another producer does not, the 'dirty' producer will be able to sell products more cheaply; therefore, more polluting products are likely to be sold. Highly competitive markets are price-sensitive, and in a situation such as this, there is a strong possibility that the 'clean' producer will be unable to sell sufficient products to stay in business. In this way, the market can reward those producers who use the most 'free goods', and drive out those who do not. The result is an increasing loss of environmental assets, and once again, the tragedy of the commons is recalled.

## Equity //

In the economic language of business, equity is synonymous with wealth. This rarely corresponds with the ethical notion of equity as 'fairness', and it can be seen that once again we are faced with a large conceptual gap between economic and environmental definitions and understanding.

In corporate balance sheets, equity is determined as the ownership interest of the shareholders in the assets of the business. It is measured as the difference when the value of total **liabilities**, which are amounts owed to other people, is deducted from the value of the total assets. Thus, if all a company's assets were sold, and all its debts were paid, the money remaining would be the equity of the owners or shareholders. It is for this reason that equity is used as a measure of wealth. As discussed in chapter 8, it has been proposed that a company's main purpose is to maximise the wealth or equity of its shareholders.

To do this, a company attempts to maximise its income and minimise its costs. You will remember from our previous discussion that one way that costs can be minimised is to use 'free goods' such as clean air, water, and other environmental resources, as much as possible.

# The anthropocentric balance sheet

'In the beginning God created the heaven and the earth. And the earth was without form and void; and darkness was upon the face of the deep' (Genesis 1: 1: 2).

From that zero base, God built up a budget, which was his master plan for the earth. Then he put his program into action.

On the first day, he created light. This was a debit to the asset account, and a credit to equity.

On subsequent days he created the dry land and the seas; vegetation; the sun, moon and stars; and all living creatures — all of which in turn increased the assets and equity of the earth.

In this way, the opening balance sheet was formed.

Then God created man to fulfil a stewardship function, to 'replenish the earth ... and have dominion over the fish of the sea, and over the fowl of the air, and over every living thing that moveth upon the earth' (Genesis 1: 28).

However, man was not an imaginative accountant, and, having been given the opening balances, was confused by the debit and credit entries necessary to account for the self-generating and regenerating assets, such as plants and animals, which had been entrusted to him. So, he consulted his financial adviser, the serpent, to see how he could manage these to maximise his personal wealth.

The serpent advised man that if he consumed all the new plants and animals that grew from the original stock of these assets, the balance sheet would remain in balance. This pleased man, as he was very happy to transform these natural assets into goods and other products that he enjoyed using. To ensure that he received sufficient reward for his advice, the serpent offered his services as bookkeeper, and took his commission from the natural assets that man had not consumed.

On the further advice of his financial adviser, the serpent, man converted more of the natural assets, which God had provided, into man-made consumables, such as jewellery and luxury goods. The balance sheet was still in balance, and, as long as he continued to consume the growing renewable assets, his recorded assets and equity remained the same, and his standard of living was greatly improved.

One day, the serpent introduced man to leverage. The serpent explained that if man were to borrow funds from future generations, he could consume the earth's non-renewable assets, as well as the renewable ones. By making simple entries to a 'liability' account, man could increase both his consumption and his total wealth. This was very appealing to man, particularly as the serpent offered to do the accounting entries in exchange for a very small share of the increased wealth.

Man was then able to invent technology, and, by converting and consuming more of the natural resources that God had provided, was able within a very short time to manufacture exciting man-made assets, such as motor cars, industrial machinery and electronic equipment. Later, by borrowing additional amounts of liabilities, he was able to develop even more attractive assets, such as nail polish, pesticides and nuclear bombs. His manufactured assets continued to grow, and the annual reports produced by the serpent assured him that his standard of living was continuing to increase.

The balance sheet revealed a wonderful array of assets, which the serpent now classified into two categories: natural and manufactured. Man was particularly proud of the ones he had made himself, and wanted to convert more and more of the assets into this category.

So, the serpent introduced him to the futures market. The serpent taught him that by taking a small quantity of assets such as timber and metal ores, and leveraging the benefit through the use of 'free goods' such as clean air and water and forest resources, the returns, measured by growth in manufactured assets, could be exponential. The serpent showed him a smart accounting trick. By not accounting for the pollution and contamination, or the loss of natural habitat produced from this process,

(*continued*)

the equity in the original balance sheet could remain intact and God, the main shareholder, would be none the wiser.

But then man learnt about margin calls. When the value of the liabilities started to exceed the value of the equity, some of the assets had to be sold to pay the debts owed to the futures traders. Man was reluctant to reduce the manufactured assets of which he was so proud, so he relinquished more and more of the natural ones; he cut down more forests and killed more wildlife, he polluted more air, and contaminated more land and water. The serpent had failed to tell him about joint assets and biodiversity: that he could not destroy one without also losing the other. So, he did not realise that, in clearfelling the forest, not only was he losing the future service potential of the trees to cleanse the air and provide food and shelter for the earth's creatures, he was also forgoing the unidentified future benefits of biodiversity, such as medicines from plants and herbs, and the raw materials of evolution. The result was, that in exchange for a small increment in manufactured assets, a large deficit in natural assets, together with a huge increase in liabilities, was created as a legacy to future generations. This meant that equity was shrinking rapidly; but man, not wanting to reduce his consumption, and trusting his financial adviser, paid no heed.

Until one day God walked in the garden...

God saw that the natural resources over which he had given man stewardship had been depleted and misused. Whole forests were destroyed; whole species extinct; degradation was upon the land, and oil slicks upon the waters.

And God called upon man to be accountable for what he had done. The serpent slithered away, and man was left to balance his books alone. It seemed that the natural assets with which he had been entrusted were exceeded by the liabilities which he had incurred. Try as he might, he could not balance the assets such as the cars, bombs and consumer goods that he had manufactured with the liabilities of pollution and contamination that he had caused. And the renewable assets that he had inherited were degraded and could no longer regenerate. As man laboured over the balance sheet, it became obvious to him that his liabilities were many times larger than his assets. And the equity was gone...

So God placed him into liquidation.

Article adapted from Gibson (1996) with kind permission of CPA Australia.

This brings us to a consideration of intergenerational equity; because, if environmental resources are used to the maximum by the present generation, the likely result is fewer resources remaining to future generations.

## Intergenerational equity

> Fresh water, like the oceans' fish, is generally thought of as a common property. Theoretically fresh water could be extracted and sold like oil; in fact, most countries believe it should be used freely by all. As a result, a growing number of countries are reaching the point where the availability of water will become a serious constraint to agricultural expansion and industrial development. For example, India is already using half the rain that runs off land into rivers and lakes, and half as much again from underground wells and springs. By the year 2025, India is likely to use 92 per cent of its available fresh water.
>
> Cairncross, 1995, p. 9.

In the previous section, we posed the question of whether the man-made asset, furniture, might be of equal value to the old tree used in its manufacture. In other words, are these assets substitutable? As with most ethical arguments, there are no clear answers to questions such as these, and many of the arguments are centred around the degree to which environmental resources are renewable. Trees can be replaced, but perhaps ecosystems cannot, and current business arguments emphasise the economic aspects of equity, and not the connotations of fairness that an ethical discourse would consider.

The question becomes one of whether the maximisation of wealth for current shareholders is consistent with fair or equitable treatment of future generations, and this raises the concept of **sustainability**, which is fundamental to intergenerational equity. Sustainable development has been defined as development that:

> meets the needs of the present without compromising the ability of future generations to meet their own needs.
>
> Bruntland, 1987.

Pearce et al. (1990) explained that there are two interpretations of the idea of intergenerational equity. The first interpretation is that the next generation should inherit a stock of wealth, comprising man-made assets and environmental, or natural, assets, no less than the stock inherited by the previous generation. This is based on the idea that man-made and environmental assets are substitutable, and that, provided that minerals are used in building long-term infrastructure and durable goods, intergenerational equity is maintained.

The second interpretation is that the next generation should inherit a stock of environmental assets no less than the stock inherited by the previous generation. This interpretation does not regard manufactured and natural assets as substitutable, and means that present-day business activities should use only those environmental resources that are renewable, such as regenerating plants and animals. Pearce explains that, in practical terms, this is difficult to achieve, because the effects of some current activities will already affect many generations into the future, including the storage of radioactive waste or biodiversity that has already been lost. Moreover, harvesting practices of renewable resources would need to ensure that no collateral environmental effects are caused.

If man-made capital is destroyed, it can usually be quickly rebuilt, as has been demonstrated following natural disasters, although some heritage assets such as monuments and architectural treasures cannot be regained, as modern equivalents are not substitutable for them. Many environmental resources, however, are non-renewable, and close substitutes are not available to replace the ozone layer or the climate-regulating functions of ocean currents, or pollution-cleaning and nutrient-trap functions of wetlands. Requirements that these assets should not be used may well increase the level of intergenerational equity, but may simultaneously result in inequitable outcomes for some members of the present generation, as the effects can be felt more heavily by poor people rather than the rich. An example of this is found in developing countries, where rural livelihoods, in particular, depend on the free availability and use of natural resources. Achievement of equity requires a redistribution of wealth that is difficult to realise even within nations, but particularly between nations; the level of **altruism** that it would require may be unacceptable to the present beneficiaries of environmental resource consumption.

## IN PRACTICE

### Solar Energy Systems (SES)

A common problem among rural and Aboriginal communities is a lack of infrastructure to provide the services that urban residents take for granted, including electricity and clean water supplies.

Anthony Maslin, the Managing Director of SES, co-founded the company so that he could 'take water to the developing world in the cleanest way possible whilst still making a buck out of it'. The company produces a solar-powered water pump and a solar-powered water purification unit, which can rid brackish water of all bacterial diseases, metals and salts. Together these products can bring clean drinking water to isolated communities in areas of dirty ground water or drought conditions. For small populations, dispersed over wide areas, the equipment overcomes the major costs of clean water provision, which are the costs of transport.

Although environmental concerns were not paramount when the company was formed, Maslin now says that 'having a social and environmental ethos makes economic sense, whether you are prepared to acknowledge it or not'.

*Source:* Kendall (2004)

Murphy & Bendell (1997, p. 21) reported at the time of the Rio Earth Summit that:

The rich societies of the industrialised North want everyone to begin being sensible about the environment; the people of the Southern latitudes maintain that those who polluted the environment en route to great prosperity are really asking the less well off to take steps that will keep them that way.

In spite of government aid donations and the efforts of non-government organisations, the present inequities between developed and developing nations persist. It is difficult to imagine what incentives will persuade business corporations to change their mission voluntarily, from the maximisation of shareholders' equity to a voluntary conservation of natural resources and positive steps towards both intragenerational equity in developing nations, and intergenerational equity for future generations. However, as we shall see in later sections, some companies are making the attempt.

# Preserving the commons //

One way of preserving the environmental commons — in a similar way to the effects of the Enclosure Acts — is, as previously discussed, the granting of private property rights to individuals or companies over certain sections of land, air, or water, so that they have a private interest in conserving those resources through sustainable use. This has been done in certain countries and for certain industries such as forestry and water supply; but, in terms of the natural environment, there is perceived inequity that certain wealthy parties could use that wealth to prevent access to areas and benefits that were formerly considered to belong to everyone.

In chapter 8 we discussed the notion of the social contract, and the expectation that political representatives would act to ensure that the rights of the community and society in general were protected. In many cases, the government has chosen to ensure this protection through enacting environmental protection legislation. In other cases, governments have considered the use of market mechanisms in a modified system of private property rights. Both alternatives have advantages and disadvantages, and some of these are discussed briefly below.

## Regulation //

What is the appropriate role of government? Is it, as Adam Smith urged, to construct a system of natural liberty in which people are free to pursue their own ends, in which the invisible hand will lead people who seek to pursue only their own interests to promote the social interest? Or is the appropriate role of government ... to serve as a benevolent parent to ensure that its wards act in a way that is in their own best interest?

Friedman 1981, p. 4.

Once governments or other regulatory bodies establish regulations, issues of compliance become legal rather than ethical. There is, however, an expectation that the law will reflect society's ethical standards to the extent that they are generalisable, and there are expectations that, in some circumstances, action will be taken that exceeds the basic minimum required by law. In particular, this is the case with environmental issues, which have broad and wide-ranging effects, as legislation addressing particular aspects may fail to take into account the combined effects of activities taking place in different areas. Examples of these effects include regulations to protect endangered species that fail to take account of habitat destruction, or regulations to control motor vehicle emissions that do not take into consideration the effects of other emissions, such as those from factories or power stations in particular local areas. Regulation is still, however, often regarded as the fairest means of achieving desired environmental outcomes, and much environmental lobbying today is aimed at achieving more restrictive regulation.

## Legislation

One of the major forms of regulation is direct legislation, and examples of this include the various types of environmental protection laws enacted in many countries throughout the world. Increasingly, large fines are being imposed for environmental damage caused by business organisations, and company officers are being held accountable for environmentally harmful activities that are in breach of the law. This can only occur when a comprehensive monitoring and enforcement system is in place, and the costs of such policing and audit can be very high. While this does force businesses to internalise some of the costs of environmental protection, which are then incorporated into the cost of their products to consumers, some of the development, monitoring and enforcement costs of legislation are borne by the general public.

In addition, the legislated level of protection differs between countries, and even between different parts of the same country. An example of this is Australia, where environmental protection, although having many common requirements, differs between the individual states. This makes environmental protection more difficult to achieve, as business operations are able to be located in whichever geographical area has the most supportive legislative environment. On an international basis, the problems become very clear, for example, see the case of the Ok Tedi mine in Papua New Guinea, at the end of chapter 8.

Apart from direct environmental legislation, other protection is also offered by legislative requirements that have indirect effects on the use of environmental resources and the way in which companies are required to report on the environmental effects of their operations. The Australian Corporations Act, for instance, requires (s 299(1)(f)) that companies whose operations are subject to environmental regulation must provide details of their compliance with such regulations. Other legislation, such as the Financial Services Reform Act and the Pensions Act, requires investment managers to provide a declaration as to the extent that environmental and social considerations are taken into account in business investment decisions.

Regulations developed by such non-government bodies as professional organisations can also play subsidiary roles. The Association of Professional Engineers, for example, has an environmental code with which its members are required to comply, and the accounting profession has accounting standards that require reporting of provisions for mine site remediation, and contingent liabilities for environmental incidents such as oil spills or site contamination events.

It can be argued that increased information reaching the public domain in this way provides a higher level of public knowledge, which then empowers communities to make more informed decisions about the companies with which they wish to conduct business. It is at this level that ethical decision making has a strong role to play.

### Taxation

Various forms of taxation and tax concessions offer an alternative regulatory approach to issues of environmental protection.

In the United Kingdom, for example, tax reductions are available to farmers who agree to 'set aside' a proportion of their land to allow the regeneration of natural vegetation and provide wildlife habitat. In addition to sections of general income tax legislation, however, there have been suggestions from time to time in relation to the introduction of special taxes aimed specifically at achieving environmental outcomes. An example of this is a proposed **carbon tax**.

When fossil fuels such as coal or oil are burnt, for example in motor vehicles, carbon dioxide, which is an important **greenhouse gas**, is emitted into the atmosphere. Proposals have periodically been made that motor vehicle emissions of carbon dioxide could be metered and measured, and a tax paid, based on the emitted quantities. Such a carbon tax is an example of the **polluter pays principle**, aimed at providing a financial disincentive to pollution of the atmosphere. The argument is that, if tax is levied at a sufficiently high level, this will provide an incentive for polluters to invest in cleaner, less polluting motor vehicles. Economic theory suggests that users would act to reduce their emissions as long as the cost of doing so did not exceed the penalty imposed for continuing to pollute. One of the clear difficulties, therefore, is to identify a level of taxation that would discourage pollution, but without disadvantaging those less wealthy members of the public who could not afford to upgrade their vehicles. Further, research indicates that poorer people spend a higher proportion of their total income on energy and transport than higher-income groups, and they would therefore bear a greater relative burden of any carbon tax imposed. However, it is possible that revenues from the tax could be redistributed to poorer householders as part of a tax benefit package aimed at achieving fairer socio-economic outcomes or spent on providing free public transport.

There are further suggestions that any tax collections aimed at environmental protection or improvement should be **hypothecated**, or set aside specifically, to be spent on environmental improvements.

Another tax variation with similar proposed effects is the Tobin tax (Tobin 2004), originally proposed by James Tobin at Yale University, and since refined. This proposal is to impose a simple sales tax on international currency trades at a low level of 0.1 to 0.25 per cent of volume (about 10 to 25 cents per $100). As a result of the high volumes of trading in international currency markets, the estimated revenue to be generated from this would be between $100 billion and $300 billion per year. The intention is that this would go into earmarked trust funds to fund urgent international priorities, some of which have been identified as global climate change, deforestation, population growth, declining fisheries and pollution that threatens communities worldwide.

## IN PRACTICE

### Origin Energy

Origin Energy gained an award in 2003 for its environmental performance. The view of the judges was that the company 'has not only given strong support to renewable energy, and faced a real business risk in the process, but has also made strong inroads into running its core business of natural gas extraction and provision, and energy generation, in an increasingly transparent and sustainable way'.

According to Green Energy Watch, a group of 17 environmental advocacy organisations, Origin is not only the largest renewable energy provider, but also the best. Its green energy products are sourced 100 per cent from wind and solar energy, and, as well, the company produced its first annual sustainability report in 2003.

The company has a stated mission to use its positioning in the industry to 'engineer a path towards more renewable energy use'. It is also 'keen to use this position to win energy customers with a concern for clean energy and greenhouse gas abatement'.

*Source:* Kendall (2004).

## Market mechanisms //

For economists such as Milton Friedman (1981), environmental interests can best be served through the free operation of an efficient market, where commodity prices will reflect the purchasing preferences of the community. In order to include environmental concerns within the market mechanism, private property is assumed to be a fundamental right, in which the buying and selling, costs and benefits, of environmental positives and negatives reflect community preferences. Issues of corporate legitimacy, discussed in chapter 8, are very relevant to this, as companies aim to convince the public that they are acting in an environmentally responsible manner. Industry and professional bodies have introduced a wide range of environmental awards such as those won by Origin Energy and IAG, and many companies now compete for these in order to demonstrate their commitment to environmental responsibility and to maintain legitimacy.

Other market mechanisms are more direct in granting private property rights to organisations and permitting them to transfer those rights, if required, to other organisations, both nationally and internationally. The buying and selling of such property rights has been a major recent development, and a current example of this is the market created for **tradeable emission permits**, or **pollution permits**.

## Pollution permits

Within a tradeable emissions permit system, permits are granted to commercial and industrial organisations that will allow them to emit up to a maximum level of particular pollutants, such as carbon dioxide or sulphur dioxide. If a firm emits less than the permitted level of pollutants, it can sell its excess permits to other organisations, who are either unable to reduce their own pollution emissions, or who want to expand their operations and therefore expect to create additional pollution above their own permitted level.

One of the most significant tradeable permit systems in operation is that of sulphur dioxide emission allowances in the United States, which were introduced as part of the country's acid rain program under the 1990 Clean Air Act Amendments. The purpose of the 1990 legislative amendments was to shift the focus of acid rain control away from the monitoring and prosecution of individual organisations, to controlling the aggregate emission level across the whole country. The goal is to reduce the level of permits that are issued over time, and so reduce the total pollutant load of sulphur dioxide that companies can emit.

Evidence (AGO 1999) indicates that companies prefer a market-based system such as this to a 'command and control' system based on government legislation and monitoring. Within their permit levels, companies can decide for themselves whether it is beneficial to costs to reduce their emissions or to purchase further permits from other companies. Further incentives for emissions reduction include the fact that the permits themselves become valuable commodities, and profits can be made from selling them on the open market. While such a market solution is popular with some industrial organisations, optimal outcomes depend very heavily upon the operation of an efficient market, and there are acknowledged difficulties in terms of enforcement and the costs of trading, which introduce inefficiencies. There are also other economic issues, such as access to information, and potential abuse of market power by large organisations, that can act to erode market efficiency and the potential benefits of the trading system.

However, non-market effects on people and organisations that are not part of the trading process are a matter of potential concern from an ethical standpoint. As Lehman (1996) pointed out, an emissions trading system arises from modern economic theory that defines nature as a market problem, and proposes that the current environmental crises can be solved through micro-economic reform, financial incentives and pricing. There are many ethicists who would disagree.

---

### International Accounting Standards Board (IASB)

The International Accounting Standards Board's interpretive committee has released proposals for new accounting requirements for companies participating in schemes aimed at reducing greenhouse gas emissions.

The chairman of the interpretation committee, Kevin Stevenson, has said that 'emission control schemes that utilise marketable allowances are becoming widespread as a result of the Kyoto agreement and companies are looking for timely guidance. At present, some companies are not accounting for the assets, liabilities or government grants involved, or at least are very uncertain about the appropriate accounting treatment.'

Sir David Tweedie, Chairman of the IASB, is of the opinion that it is vital for the board to respond to emerging issues like gas emission schemes, as the accounting matters involved are very challenging.

This interpretation is part of the IASB's stated commitment to developing, in the public interest, a single set of high quality, global accounting standards that require companies to provide transparent and comparable information.

*Source:* IASB (2003)

---

While few would argue that there is not an urgent need to reduce environmental pollution on an international scale, use of the 'blunt instrument', which the market represents, can cause considerable inequity in where and by whom the effects of pollution are felt. If we take sulphur dioxide emissions as an example, the greater the concentration of emissions, the more harmful they are likely to be. In a market-based system, those polluters who can more easily reduce their emissions and profit from the sale of permits are those that are operating within a system or location in which access to new technology is available and affordable to them. This means that older factories in older industrial areas, or in developing countries, may find it less easy to switch to new production processes that are less polluting. These older or poorer factories are therefore the ones that will need to purchase permits to continue their operations, and the incurrence of this cost may prevent their investment in new technology. People living around these factories are the ones who will be forced either to tolerate the pollution, or suffer the economic hardship of job losses.

Sulphur dioxide is also synergistic in combination with smoke or other pollutants in the atmosphere, which greatly increase its harmful effect. These compounded effects are not taken into account in the distribution and sale of single-pollutant allowances, and are more likely to be present in the air around industrial, economically disadvantaged suburbs, which multiplies the effects on local residents. In an international market, this becomes even more of an issue for developing nations, who do not have the baseline protection of environmental protection legislation.

It could be argued, however, that the economic trading of pollution permits at least presents a serious attempt to incorporate the previously 'free goods' of clean air use into the costs of production. The opposing view to this is that these permits do not reflect the economic cost of pollution, but only the cost of permission to pollute, and that the economic costs of the pollution itself remain, to be added to the environmental and social costs to society.

Although there was a proposal in 1999 that Australia might adopt such an emissions trading system, it has not yet been introduced, and this is possibly a result of government acknowledgment that the market mechanism does not have all the answers to our social and environmental problems.

## Alternative economic systems and the environment //

The above discussion was concerned with potential solutions arising from the present economic environment, and to a certain extent, a political system that is based on capitalist concepts. Had capitalism continued as Adam Smith conceived it, we may have been facing fewer environmental problems today. This is because Smith's idea was of a multitude of small firms competing to satisfy consumer demands, and such small firms may have had a lesser aggregate impact on the environment. Although his concern was not environmental, he foresaw with little enthusiasm the possible growth of large corporations, and was opposed to the granting of corporate privileges such as limited liability and perpetual succession. Smith's lead was not followed by subsequent economists, however, and we now have corporate power of such a high order that writers such as Enteman (1990) have proposed that it is no longer appropriate to use the term 'capitalism' to describe our current ideology, but that the term 'corpocracy' is more descriptive. The connotations for democracy are clear from this.

An alternative, socialist, system, could not, however, be relied on to be more sensitive to environmental issues than capitalism. While capitalism is an economic ideology with the consumer at its centre, socialism is an economic ideology focused on the worker, in which society is free to use the natural environment in whatever way will improve his or her situation. In both socialist and capitalist concepts, the concern is with existing people, rather than an acknowledgment of the trade-off between present and future generations, and between human and non-human species.

# Ethics and the environment //

Since environmental concerns involve both economics and ethics, it is perhaps useful at this stage to contemplate some of the broader ethical issues to which we were introduced in the earlier chapters, and relate them to matters of the environment considered in this chapter so far.

## Utilitarianism //

In terms of ethical teleology, or utilitarianism, acts are right if they maximise community happiness. However, as mentioned earlier, this depends upon how the community is defined over time. If we include future generations within our community, then the magnitude of the number of future community members overwhelms the numbers of the present generation, and ensuring the happiness of the greatest number will affect the happiness of the current generation. Enteman (1990) considered the idea that our current liveable environment is bought at the expense of the environmental quality of future generations. Consequently, the utilitarian approach would require that the present generation live at a level approaching subsistence, and this would apply to each succeeding generation. He points out that, to maintain our environment, utilitarianism leads to the curious conclusion that the attempt to achieve maximum happiness actually results in its minimisation.

## Determinism //

At the narrow end of the deterministic spectrum, since people have no real choice in what they do, they should not be held morally responsible for effects such as environmental deterioration. At the broader end, however, moral responsibility is independent of whether or not the agent has a choice, but in the absence of free choice it is difficult to justify responsibility. For example, in relation to the environment, we cannot hold a tidal wave morally responsible for the environmental damage that it causes, but we would assign responsibility to company directors who failed to prevent an environmental disaster such as an oil spill. Determinism and environmental responsibility appear to be at odds, and the ethical concept of determinism is thus not helpful to the environmental responsibility debate.

## The ontological argument //

The ontological argument for the preservation of the natural environment is primarily aesthetic and ethical, and begins with a consideration of the relationship between duty and good. The object of duty — what we ought to do — is the achievement of good, or what ought to be (Hargrove 1989). In this context, the duty to preserve beauty comes from the recognition that beauty is a good. Hargrove argues that the duty specifically to promote and preserve natural beauty arises out of the recognition that not only artistic beauty, but also natural beauty, constitutes an aesthetic good that makes up part of the general good that exists, and ought to exist, in the world. He points out that there are two possible objections to this. First, some might claim that nature is not beautiful; or, second, that its beauty is so inferior to artistic beauty that the duty to preserve it does not exist. Most people, however, would refute these objections, and claim that the loss of natural beauty would represent a loss in the total beauty of the world.

This argument does not necessarily mean that we always have a duty to promote and preserve everything in nature, beautiful or not, so the ontological arguments are also deficient in providing grounding for complete environmental protection.

This short review of economic systems, utilitarianism, determinism and ontology indicates that the economic and ethical conceptual structures of the nineteenth century are no longer sufficient to deal with some of the economic and environmental realities of the twenty-first century. Enteman (1990, p. 226) warned us that 'the old ways will not do'. In his words:

> We must conclude . . . that any economics carries with it ideological, moral and value-laden assumptions. The assumptions of determinism, the calculus, and zero cost of environmental use are all value laden and anti environmental. Once determinism is abandoned, discretion is possible, and ethical judgements make a difference. Under those conditions, the economists and the philosophers can join in an effort to bring rigorous understanding to these problems in the context of an ideology relevant to us as we enter the twenty-first century.

The charting of a new course is required.

# What is being done? //

While the ethical and philosophical debates are set to continue, as travellers on this planet together, we all acknowledge, although to differing extents, that current levels of natural resource exploitation and environmental damage cannot continue. In many instances, the blame for environmental harm is placed on business and industry, and in particular, on the large corporations. To an extent, this may be justified, as the activities of large companies are of such magnitude that a small environmental mistake becomes a major environmental disaster. You will recall that, in the Ok Tedi case, a simple decision was made in relation to a tailings dam, but the consequences were suffered by a very large local community, and the effects will be felt by many future generations.

On the other hand, corporations are simply a nexus of contracts, and exist merely to provide goods and services that are demanded by the community. The community is not bound by determinism. People have choices, and companies must either respond or go out of business, so to simply blame 'business' for our environmental situation is an abrogation of personal responsibility, which is probably itself unethical.

Irrespective of the ethical debates, companies are themselves beginning to take action to reduce their environmental effects. Cynics would recognise that it is in their economic self-interest to do so, but for whatever reason, recent developments in corporate environmental responsibility can be viewed in a positive light.

The provision of higher levels of information is improving the ability of communities to be aware of the operations and environmental effect of business organisations, and a fifteen-year longitudinal study has shown that, by the end of the twentieth century, the number of firms reporting environmental information had increased to 94 per cent, from a base level of 27 per cent in 1986 (Gibson & O'Donovan 2000). Moreover, firms are enthusiastically adopting the principle of the **triple bottom line**, and reporting their performance in terms of economic, environmental and social outcomes. Further, many large organisations are voluntarily beginning to incorporate triple bottom line principles into their management systems. The mining company WMC, for example, publishes an annual *Sustainability Report*, in which it plots its progress along a pathway from reporting its performance on the triple bottom line to complete integration of environmental and social principles into its decision-making processes. Its performance is also independently assessed, and environmental and social audit reports are included as a demonstration of the company's commitment. In a clear reference to the social contract and corporate legitimacy, the CEO, Andrew Michelmore, has reported that

> Incorporating sustainable development principles into all aspects of our activities remains a work in progress for WMC Resources. We have travelled a long way since our first environment report in 1994–95. We acknowledge the need for such broad-based reporting, and recognise its value to our reputation in relation to securing and maintaining our public licence to operate.
>
> WMC Resources, *Sustainability Report 2002*, p. 3.

Many other large companies are taking similar action, including major banks, oil companies, and transport groups. In a further example, Leon Davis, Chairman of Westpac has said that

> People are understandably frustrated and angry at what they see as a lack of corporate transparency and accountability. It is of no surprise that a company's level of governance and responsibility has emerged as a significant indicator of its overall health as a business. After all, companies such as Westpac need more than a legal licence to operate — we require a community licence as well.
>
> Westpac, *Our Social Impact Report 2003*, p. 3.

The indications are, that if large corporations fail to behave in an environmentally and socially responsible way, they may well lose their licence to operate, or at the very least be diminished, as the community turns to alternative providers of services, who are believed to be more aligned with community values. A good example of this is the success of local credit unions in competition with the major banks, and one of these, the Maleny Credit Union, is the subject of the case study that follows. Such a transition to smaller institutions reminds us of Adam Smith's early ideas that, in engaging in fair competition, improved environmental and social outcomes may be achieved, as well as the economic successes to be gained in the free market. Perhaps Smith's 'invisible hand' will then be recognised as the benign force that he intended, and not the symbol of corporate rapaciousness that it became during the last century.

# Summary //

This chapter represents a continuation of the social considerations discussed in chapter 8. The concepts of stakeholder and legitimacy theory are as relevant to corporate environmental performance as they are to the effects of corporate activity on society. The social and the environmental are inseparable, and cannot be considered in isolation. Their ethical underpinnings are shared, and they are both components of the biodiverse universe upon which we, future generations, and other species depend.

In this chapter we continued the theme of language, and the power that its possession conveys, particularly in the accumulation of economic power or wealth. We noted how the 'free goods' provided by the environment bestow wealth upon individuals and organisations, often in direct proportion to the level of environmental harm that they cause. The use of free goods means that the pricing mechanism in a free market is unable to regulate the demand for goods and services in a manner that considers the environmental effects of production and use. We saw that, in many cases, the greater the level of environmental harm, the cheaper the product, and the more of it that is demanded, in a cycle of pollution that acts to drive out the companies that voluntarily engage in cleaner production processes.

The issue of the 'environmental commons' is an important concept in understanding the market mechanism, and private property rights are discussed as an alternative to regulation and 'command and control' systems. Ultimately, however, the decisions are ethical ones, and although our review of some of the ethical concepts identifies shortcomings in the traditional philosophical positions, it is perhaps heartening to know that many major companies are adopting ethical positions that appear to extend beyond their traditional economic imperatives.

# Key terms //

Altruism ... p. 238

Anthropocentric ... p. 231

Assets ... p. 230

Carbon tax ... p. 241

Depreciation ... p. 233

Equity ... p. 230

Free goods ... p. 229

Greenhouse gas ... p. 241

Hypothecation ... p. 241

Intergenerational equity ... p. 229

Inter-species equity ... p. 229

## Questions //

**9.1** What is the relationship between corporate social reporting and environmental responsibility?

**9.2** Provide two examples in which the use of language has been implicated in environmentally harmful activities.

**9.3** Why might it be suggested that GDP is not an optimal measure of 'standard of living'?

**9.4** What is the 'tragedy of the commons', and how did it occur? Describe a present-day environmental equivalent.

**9.5** What are the implications for intergenerational equity of the substitutability of man-made and natural assets?

**9.6** Explain the links between the social contract and government regulation.

**9.7** What are the differences between a carbon tax and a Tobin tax?

**9.8** How might a carbon tax be hypothecated?

**9.9** Explain how a system of tradeable emissions permits operates.

**9.10** Explain some of the disadvantages of an emission permit trading system.

**9.11** Explain why the concepts of utilitarianism and determinism are not very helpful in contributing to the environmental debate.

## FURTHER RESOURCES AND WEBSITES //

ACCA Sustainability Awards
www.acca.co.uk/sustainability/awards/asra

Centre of Excellence for Cleaner Production
http://cleanerproduction.curtin.edu.au

Earthscan Publications
www.earthscan.co.uk

Environment Australia
www.environment.gov.au

Green Tourism Eco-labelling system
    http://europa.eu.int/comm/environment/ecolabel

Greenhouse Challenge Program
    www.greenhouse.gov.au/challenge

Greening of Industry Network
    www.greeningofindustry.org

Greenleaf Publishing
    www.greenleaf-publishing.com

World Business Council for Sustainable Development
    www.wbcsd.ch

World Resources Institute
    http://newsroom.wri.org/wrifeatures.cfm

## CASE STUDY

### Maleny and District Community Credit Union

The mission statement of the Maleny and District Community Credit Union
(MCU) states:

> Our reason for being is to offer appropriate and ethical financial solutions to
> our members in ways which are:
> • Socially just
> • Environmentally responsible
> • Empowering to the local community and individuals
> • Based on the belief in people, honesty and goodwill.

The company, based at Maleny in South-East Queensland, began its
operations in a rented room, but has grown steadily since its inception in
1984 to its current size of 4000 members and $22 million in assets.

In its *Sustainability and Financial Annual Report 2003*, the company
explains (p. 5) that its agenda is much broader than 'profit maximisation for
shareholders'. Its triple bottom line approach has an emphasis on sustainability with commitment to financial, environmental and social issues for the
benefit of its members and local community.

While many companies produce a triple bottom line report that reports on
the positive aspects of their performance, Maleny's governance policy is
aimed at 'embedding the philosophy of sustainability integrally with the way
MCU is governed and managed'. In other words, the company aims to
include triple bottom line concerns in all of its operations, not just at the end
of the year when a report has to be produced.

//

This is incorporated in the credit union's basic rules of operation. Section 1.15 of its *Governance Policies* states:

The General Manager shall not allow the environment and social impact of the credit union to be inadequately maintained and managed.
Accordingly, they may not:
(a) Operate without an environment and social impact management plan
(b) Operate without considering the environmental and social impacts of any management decisions
(c) Fail to pay an 'Eco-tax' of 50c per ream of paper purchased to a local environmental association
(d) Fail to report the major environment and social impacts in the Annual Report
(e) Fail to meet the environmental and social target outlined in the performance targets.

The organisation's environmental and social impacts are monitored on an annual basis by means of both internal and external social audits. These audits assess performance in relation to a series of environmental indicators, including:

*Ecological impact and resource consumption indicators*
• Reduce paper consumption per 1000 members
• Achieve a decrease in electricity consumption per 1000 members
• Maintain Earth's Choice electricity supply for greenhouse gas reduction
• Pay an eco tax to Barung Landcare on each ream of paper
• Achieve a decrease in water consumption per 1000 members

*Ecological and sustainable building and landscaping practices indicators*
• Provide sustainable loans
• Enhance and maintain MCU gardens to encourage sustainable practices
• Sponsor the development of the Earth Benefits Club

*Ecological restoration projects indicator*
• Sponsor annual tree planting day.

Each year, Maleny reports its performance against its key indicators, and shows the change from the previous year, even if performance against that indicator has deteriorated. This gives a firm impression of an organisation that is ethically committed to reporting its failures as well as successes, and in this way it affirms a strong commitment to ecological sustainability.

MCU is a financial institution owned by its members, and its *Sustainability and Financial Annual Report* reflects its focus on community, to the extent of including the comments of staff and community members on its performance. This is an unusual focus in the world of high finance and competitive financial institutions.

In addition to the credit union's internal resource conservation efforts, it has a 'green loan' portfolio, which includes a Cool Home Loan. This loan

//

is offered at a special low interest rate to members who want to buy, build or upgrade their home to become more energy efficient. The idea is to achieve financial savings and a reduction in greenhouse gas emissions, as a condition of the low-interest loan is that the home financed will incorporate features such a solar hot water heating, water efficient fittings, wall and ceiling insulation and overhanging roof eaves. As part of its extended services the credit union also offers information on achieving the best energy efficiency, aimed at making it easy for homeowners to take better care of their environment.

MCU has reported that over 34 per cent of loans made in 2002–2003 were for environmentally friendly purposes such as these. It is expected that this percentage will increase as more members take advantages of their Cool Home Loan and Green Car Loan financial products.

One of the problems faced by this relatively small, locally based organisation in developing its triple bottom line reports is that there were very few suitable guidelines available to it. The Global Reporting Initiative, for example, offers guidelines that are very useful to big organisations with large financial resources, but are less useful for small, community-based ones. Maleny, therefore, has had to pioneer many of its reporting practices, but in the tradition of its community engagement vision, it is sharing the knowledge gained with other credit unions and mutual organisations. Its general manager describes the 'Maleny Model' as a living document embedded with community values, which provides room and scope for change and development as values and community needs change. He also sees it as a social contract of a business within its community.

## QUESTIONS

1 What might affect the decisions of ethical investors when considering investment in an organisation such as the Maleny Credit Union?
2 Is it likely that larger financial institutions, such as the big banks, might emulate the actions of the Maleny Credit Union? Why or why not?
3 What are the main advantages to be gained by organisations such as the Maleny Credit Union acting in an ethically responsible manner?
4 Access the website of the Maleny Credit Union (www.malenycu.com.au) and scan the latest issue of its *Sustainability and Financial Annual Report*. Access a similar report from one of the major Australian banks and scan its most recent triple bottom line report. Apart from scale, what are the major differences?

## REFERENCES //

AGO 1999, *National emissions trading*, Discussion Papers 1–4, Australian Greenhouse Office, Canberra.

Bruntland, GH 1987, *Our common future*, World Commission on Environment and Development.

Cairncross, F 1995, *Green, Inc*, Earthscan Publications, London.

Enteman, WF 1990, in Hoffman, WM, Frederick, R & Petry, ES (Eds) *The corporation, ethics, and the environment*, Quorum Books, New York.

Friedman, M 1981, *Taxation, inflation and the government*, Occasional Paper 4, Centre for Independent Studies, Sydney.

Gibson, K 1996, 'God created the accountant...', *Australian Accountant*, February, pp. 38–9.

Gibson, K & O'Donovan, G 2000, 'Environmental disclosures in Australia: a longitudinal study', *Accounting for the environment*, Seminar Series 2000, RMIT Business, Melbourne.

Hargrove, EC 1989, *Foundations of environmental ethics*, Prentice Hall, New Jersey.

IASB 2003, *Proposed new accounting interpretation — greenhouse gas emissions*, Press Release, International Accounting Standards Board, London, 15 May.

Kendall, R 2004, 'Inside out on sustainability culture', *Ethical Investor*, Issue 29, December/January, pp. 6–10.

Lehman, G 1996, 'Environmental accounting: pollution permits or selling the environment', *Critical Perspectives on Accounting*, vol. 7, No. 6, December, pp. 667–80.

Murphy, DF & Bendell, J 1997, *In the company of partners*, The Policy Press, Bristol, UK.

Pearce, D, Markandya, A & Barbier, EB 1990, *Blueprint for a green economy*, Earthscan Publications, London.

Pearce, D (Ed) 1991, *Blueprint 2*, Earthscan Publications, London.

Tobin, J 2004, www.ceedweb.org/iirp/factsheet.htm.

Westpac 2003, *Our 2003 social impact report*, Westpac Banking Corporation, Melbourne.

WMC 2002, *Sustainability report*, WMC Resources Ltd, Melbourne.

# Professional independence

**Learning objectives**

After studying this chapter you should be able to:

- Explain agency theory and the role of professional independence.
- Describe the historical development of professional independence.
- Define 'professional independence' and distinguish independence in fact from independence in appearance.
- Explain the significance of professional independence to investors, the accounting profession, and capital markets.
- Describe some of the threats to professional independence in relation to employment relationships, financial relationships, and the provision of non-audit services.
- Explain the role of an auditor independence supervisory board.
- Explain the benefit of audit committees to auditor independence.

'the collapse of the moral order; the disintegration of value systems over the last decades; the lack of moral orientation. We are now living with these consequences. These events came to pass precisely at the time when the emergent world society is in need of a global ethic, a universal standard of values, ideals and goals.'
**Udo Schaefer 1994, Ethics for a global society,**
*Bahá'í Studies Review*, **vol. 4, no. 1.**

# Introduction //

Professional independence is so fundamental to accounting that it is the key to maintaining the respect and trust of investors and government regulators. Without independence, the opinions of accountants — in particular, auditors — are of little value. The purpose of this chapter is to examine critically the concept of professional independence and its significance to accounting, including to users of financial statements, the accounting profession, and efficient capital markets. We also review the history of professional independence, the meaning of its various facets, and the factors that threaten its existence.

The notion of professional independence has existed since the inception of auditing; but the recent corporate collapses, such as those of HIH and Enron, and the role played by their auditors, have prompted government, professional, and regulatory agencies to revisit this principle. Much of the information presented in this chapter is based on recent investigations and developments in auditor independence. These include: Professional Statement F.1: 'Professional independence', revised and reissued in 2002 by CPA Australia and the Institute of Chartered Accountants in Australia; a report to the Minister for Financial Services and Regulation by Ian Ramsay entitled, *Independence of company auditors, review of current Australian requirements and proposals for reform*, also known as the Ramsay report (Ramsay, 2001); and the proposals contained in the CLERP (Audit Reform and Corporate Disclosure) Act (2004), which in turn are based on the CLERP 9 Discussion Paper, *Corporate law and economic reform program—corporate disclosure strengthening the financial reporting framework*.

# Agency theory and the rise of independence //

The notion of professional independence evolved from the formation of shareholder-owned companies and the consequent separation of owners from the managers of the business. As businesses grew into conglomerates and owners lacked the skill to manage their businesses effectively, they hired managers. The practice of hiring managers and separating the owners from the business gave rise to issues of agency. **Agency theory** is a structure in which managers (agents) are employed by the owners (principals) to manage the assets of the organisation for the benefit of the owners (principals). In this sense, the economic resources of the corporation are entrusted to the managers, who have an obligation to act on behalf of, and for the betterment of the shareholders.

Issues of agency gives rise to unique problems. With management remuneration packages based on short-term performance measures such as profit, agents are tempted to maximise their self-interest at the expense of the long-term interests of the shareholders. Therefore, in order to protect owners' interests and to ensure an adequate return on their investment, mechanisms are put in place to monitor the agent's performance. This is normally achieved through the Statement of Financial Performance and the Statement of Financial Position. A well-managed company will have healthy financial reports; but, can the integrity of the reports be trusted when the agents who prepare the reports have a vested interest in the outcome? One purpose of accounting standards is to reduce the flexibility in financial reporting and ensure that financial statements are consistently prepared and presented fairly so that shareholders can evaluate the performance of those entrusted with the assets of the company. However, in today's environment many shareholders are unlikely to have the skill, expertise and access to the underlying records to assess the accuracy of the financial statements. To overcome this problem, owners employ external auditors to verify the assertions made by management in the financial reports. The cost of the audit function is known as a **monitoring cost**.

The ultimate purpose of an **audit** is to express an opinion on the truth and fairness of the audited financial statements of the client company. If shareholders are to accept the auditor's opinion, the auditor must be independent of the client company. Without independence, the auditor's opinion is questionable. Consider an analogy involving the acquisition of a secondhand car. The quality of the car is important to your decision, but relying on the word of the sales clerk is risky, particularly when the sales clerk's primary goal is to maximise sales, which may not coincide with your best interests. If you are unable to assess the quality of the car yourself, you commission a vehicle assessment report from a qualified vehicle tester. However, if the report is prepared by an assessor who is related to the sales clerk, for example a motor mechanic employed by the saleyard, the assessor's objectivity is doubted and the report is untrustworthy. In order to accept such a report, it must be prepared by an *independent* assessor, for example a person employed by a motor vehicle club or association. This analogy is equally applicable in accounting. In order to accept an auditor's opinion on the veracity of the financial statements, the auditor must be independent of the client company and its officers. If the auditor is inappropriately linked to the company or its officers, the auditor's opinion will hardly appear credible.

## The historical development of professional independence //

The audit function and thus, the notion of independence, has existed since commercial life itself, and over time it has evolved alongside the development of accounting and the growing need for documentary evidence. Evidence of auditing first surfaced in Great Britain during the middle of the nineteenth century, with the emergence of the corporate form of business. The separation of ownership from control provided a natural stimulus for auditing. The role of the auditor was an evolving one, with a variety of statutory requirements arising from the growth of 'public interest' organisations such as banks and railways, and the growth of professional accounting associations in response to the state's demands for corporate control, mostly due to company collapses and insolvencies. From this base of insolvency work grew the increased demand for audit services.

In the beginning, auditors were drawn from the ranks of the shareholders themselves. This selection process was fraught with problems. Auditors selected from the shareholder group colluded with managers to systematically deceive other shareholders. As these problems became apparent and shareholders learned of the dangers of appointing auditors from the cohort of shareholders, the need to appoint an auditor external to the company, its shareholders, and management, became clear. This marked the beginning of the external auditor. The modern audit is now described as an independent audit because it involves an independent examination of the financial statements of an entity by a qualified and independent external auditor. The importance of independence in auditing has become such that the terms 'independent' and 'audit' can no longer be separated (Ramsay 2001, p. 113).

It was always assumed that if an accountant exercises professional skill honestly, applies best judgment without fear or favour, and expresses an opinion impartially and objectively, he or she is independent. However, these qualities are subjective, and as tests of independence, they are immeasurable. As the concept of independence evolved, objective tests for determining the existence of independence emerged. They included:

1. Does the accountant hold a financial interest in the client's business?
2. Is the accountant connected with the client as promoter, underwriter, voting trustee, director, officer or employee?

A positive response to either of these two questions meant that the accountant failed the test of independence. Stempf (1942, p. 226) states: 'serving both as director and independent auditor, or as internal accountant and external auditor . . . is functionally incompatible and impossible for an accountant to serve in two conflicting roles'. Noyes (1959, p. 28) similarly states: 'the accountant must have no financial or other interest in a client's business which might colour his or her judgment'.

The tests of independence have now evolved into a complex framework of law, professional pronouncements, and personal conscience. The rules and standards that govern audit independence will be discussed in detail later in this chapter.

# What is professional independence? //

Many definitions of **independence** have been proposed, and while differences in definitions exist, there are two common threads. The concept of independence implies first that the auditor has the ability to act impartially, and secondly, the auditor will not be influenced by others in matters of opinion (Ramsay 2001, p. 110). To this end the auditor must avoid any financial or other interest in the audit process that threatens the proper exercise of integrity and objective judgment. Professional independence is not based on a set of defining rules, but is an overarching concept, based on interest, objectivity and integrity. An accountant is independent when he or she has no financial stake or other interest in the person on whose statements he or she has expressed a professional opinion (Kohler 1975, p. 254). Independence is important because a lack of independence might impair objectivity or impartiality, or otherwise interfere with the free exercise of the auditor's professional judgment.

Ramsay (2001, pp. 111–12) further explores the notion of independence by distinguishing the independence of the individual auditor from the independence of the profession. Independence of the individual auditor refers to the freedom of the auditor to develop an audit program and perform duties without interference or prejudice. Whereas, independence of the profession refers to the trust afforded by the public in the independence and integrity of the entire audit profession. Without such trust in the profession, the opinions of individual auditors become questionable, irrespective of actual independence and how well auditors perform their work. Currently, the profession relies on a system of self-imposed standards and peer-group surveillance to maintain its honourable reputation and public acceptance of the auditors' status. This system of self-regulation and discipline is discussed in chapter 3. The distinction between the independence of the individual auditor and the independence of the profession is acknowledged in Professional Statement F.1, discussed in the next section.

## Independence in fact and independence in appearance //

The joint code of professional conduct defines independence as being free, in fact and appearance, of any interest which might be regarded, whatever its actual effect, as being incompatible with integrity and objectivity (Section B.4). Professional independence manifests itself in two forms — independence *in fact* and independence *in appearance*. **Independence in fact** is concerned with the performance of the individual auditor's work as described by Ramsay in the above section. Independence in fact is the auditor's ability to plan and perform their duties without pressure or bias. Mautz and Sharaf (1961, p. 205) refer to independence in fact as **practitioner independence** — 'the ability of the individual practitioner to maintain the proper attitude in the planning of his audit program, the performance of his verification work and the preparation of his report'. Professional Statement F.1, paragraph 14, refers to independence in fact as **independence of mind**, and defines it as a state of mind that permits the provision of an opinion unaffected by influences that compromise professional judgment, allowing an individual to act with integrity, and to exercise objectivity and professional scepticism. The problem with independence of mind is that there is no demonstrable way that an auditor possesses it, and even if the right attitude is proven, it will not necessarily result in correct behaviour (Ramsay 2001, p. 110). Therefore, the appearance of independence takes on greater significance because of its demonstrable existence.

**Independence in appearance** is concerned with apparent independence and the image of the community of accountants (Mautz and Sharaf 1961). Ramsay, as discussed in the above section, refers to this as the independence of the profession. Investors trust auditors because they appear to be independent: it is not enough that the financial reports are accurate; investors must perceive the financial reports as accurate. Audit firms have tremendous market incentive to maintain independence in fact, but the significance of independence in appearance cannot be denied. Consider a situation where the auditor is independent in fact but does not appear to be so. Without the appearance of independence, the credibility of their work and the financial statements they audit is diminished significantly.

Professional Statement F.1 defines independence in appearance as the avoidance of facts and circumstances that are so significant that a reasonable and informed third party, having knowledge of all relevant information, including any safeguards applied, would reasonably conclude integrity, objectivity or professional scepticism of the accounting firm or of its members had been compromised (paragraph 14). This definition relies on the reasonable person argument to determine consistency with the principle of independence. The reasonable person, having all the facts, must be convinced of the accountant's impartiality and freedom of bias. In a time when corporate fraudulent practices are common, a criteria based on the reasonable person argument is testing the profession's apparent independence.

# Why is professional independence important? //

The significance of professional independence in auditing should be viewed on three levels:
1. survival of the audit profession's very existence
2. protecting the interests of users
3. improving market efficiency.

The auditing profession has a long history of contributing to the effective and efficient functioning of business operations, the capital markets, and the economy by adding credibility to financial statements. So important is independence to the auditing profession that it is often referred to as the cornerstone of the profession. The very nature of an audit enhances users' confidence in the veracity of the financial statements, because the auditor is an independent, objective expert in accounting and auditing procedures. The auditor's independence, integrity and objectivity encourage users' faith in the audit function so they may confidently use and rely on the audited financial statements and therefore place faith in the entire accounting profession. For some, independence in appearance is so important that the basis of the profession's existence rests on the public's acceptance of the profession appearing independent. Without the appearance of independence and public faith in the profession, the demand for external auditors will become redundant, leaving the audit function to internal auditors or other examiners.

One important goal of an audit is to provide users with reasonable assurance that an entity's financial statements give a true and fair view and are devoid of material error and fraud. Even though the company being audited is a client of the auditor, the auditor has an overriding responsibility to the users of the audit report and not to the client. Therefore, the auditor is expected to rise above the interests of the client and accept responsibility for those of third parties who, although often unknown, might have a material interest in the financial statements upon which the auditor is reporting (Simon 1982, p. 105). In performing the audit function, professional independence imposes an obligation on auditors to be fair, intellectually honest, and free of conflict of interest in relation to their clients (*Auditing and Assurance Handbook*, 2004). Therefore, professional independence protects users' interests because it avoids clouded judgment caused by pressures from inappropriate relationships or financial interests in the client.

On a macro-economic level, audited financial statements play a key role in maintaining efficient capital markets. The role of the external auditor is the principal check by which the financial statements can be relied upon for economic decision making. Independently verifiable information encourages public investments in listed companies; a lack of confidence in the auditor's opinion engenders a fear or reluctance to invest in listed companies, ultimately affecting security prices. Without confidence in financial reporting, market efficiency will erode, resulting in a higher cost of capital. The *Ramsay report* (2001, p. 21) recognises the following four functions of an independent audit in relation to capital market efficiency:

1. add value to financial statements by improving their reliability
2. add value to the capital markets by enhancing the credibility of financial statements
3. enhance the effectiveness of the capital markets in allocating valuable resources by improving the decisions of users of financial statements
4. assist to lower the cost of capital to those using audited financial statements by reducing information risk.

In conclusion, independent audits add justified credibility to the financial statements, which enables users, especially investors, to make better and more informed decisions. You should now refer to the 'In practice: Xerox Corporation' for a case highlighting the significance of professional independence in practice.

### Xerox Corporation

When the interest of the client and the accountant becomes so closely aligned, the accountant's role as a public watchdog becomes secondary. Such is the case of Xerox Corporation reported by Pulliam and Bandler (2003, p. A.3).

The Securities and Exchange Commission (SEC) is set to file civil-fraud charges against KPMG LLP for the audit of Xerox Corporation. The SEC is expected to charge several KPMG employees, including one former auditor and two current employees, for their role in the accounting scandal at Xerox.

The cause of the SEC's actions is twofold. First, Xerox had improperly booked revenue amounting to $3 million increasing to $6.4 million over five years. Second, KPMG, as auditor, had become so closely aligned with Xerox that its role as a public watchdog had become largely secondary when it objected to particular transactions, but then allowed them to pass without amendment. A lack of independence is cited as one reason KPMG partners are under threat of legal action.

The SEC were also concerned that KPMG had signed off on Xerox's 2000 annual report after Xerox made only minor restatements, in spite of the SEC turning up evidence of massive overstatements of profits from 1997 to 2000.

The SEC's case against KPMG is exceptional because it signals a view by regulators that the auditors played an active role in misleading the public as to the company's financial position. KPMG was eventually succeeded by PricewaterhouseCoopers LLP as Xerox's auditor.

# Threats to independence and safeguards //

The auditing process, which involves the auditor providing a service to a client in exchange for a fee, creates a potential conflict of interest between the auditor's obligation to the users of audited financial statements and pressures from management to compromise the quality of an audit. This threat to practitioner independence is ever present, but the ability to resist such pressures is limited. Some difficulties arise from the political influences from within the client entity and others are created by auditors themselves. Professional Statement F.1 on independence was issued in 2002, and is based largely on Section 8 of IFAC's (International Federation of Accountants) *Code of Ethics for Professional Accountants*. The statement advocates a conceptual framework approach that requires the identification and evaluation of threats to independence and the application of safeguards to reduce any threats to an acceptable level. Table 10.1 lists the threats to independence identified in Professional Statement F.1.

TABLE 10.1

## THREATS TO INDEPENDENCE

| THREAT | DEFINITION | EXAMPLES |
|---|---|---|
| Self-interest | Occurs when the firm or member of the assurance team could benefit from a financial interest in, or other self-interest conflict with, an assurance client. | (a) a direct financial interest, or material indirect financial interest, in an assurance client<br>(b) a loan or guarantee to or from an assurance client, or any of its directors or officers<br>(c) undue dependence on total fees from an assurance client<br>(d) concern about the possibility of losing the engagement<br>(e) having a close business relationship with an assurance client<br>(f) potential employment with an assurance client<br>(g) contingent fees relating to assurance engagements |
| Self-review | Occurs when:<br>1. any product or judgment of a previous assurance engagement or non-assurance engagement needs to be re-evaluated in reaching conclusions on the assurance engagement, or<br>2. a member of the assurance team was previously a director or officer of the assurance client or was an employee in position to exert direct and significant influence over the subject matter of the assurance engagement. | (a) a member of the assurance team being, or having recently been, a director or officer of the assurance client<br>(b) a member of the assurance team being, or having recently been, an employee of the assurance client in a position to exert direct and significant influence over the subject matter of the assurance engagement<br>(c) performance of services for an assurance client that directly affect the subject matter of the assurance engagement<br>(d) the preparation of original data used to generate a financial report or preparation of other records that are the subject matter of the assurance engagement |
| Advocacy | Occurs when a firm, or a member of the assurance team, promotes, or may be perceived to promote, an assurance client's position or opinion to the point that objectivity may, or may be perceived to be, compromised. | (a) dealing in, or being a promoter of, shares or other securities in an assurance client, and<br>(b) acting as an advocate on behalf of an assurance client in litigation or in resolving disputes with third parties |

| THREAT | DEFINITION | EXAMPLES |
|---|---|---|
| Familiarity | Occurs when, by virtue of a close relationship with an assurance client, its directors, officers or employees, a firm or a member of the assurance team become too sympathetic to the client's interests. | (a) a member of the assurance team having an immediate family member or close family member who is a director or officer of the assurance client<br>(b) a member of the assurance team having an immediate family member or close family member who is an employee of the assurance client, is in a position to exert direct and significant influence over the subject matter of the assurance engagement<br>(c) a former partner of the firm being a director, officer of the assurance client or an employee in a position to exert direct and significant influence over the subject matter of the assurance engagement<br>(d) long association of a senior member of the assurance team with the assurance client<br>(e) acceptance of gifts or hospitality, unless the value is clearly insignificant, from the assurance client, its directors, officers or employees |
| Intimidation | Occurs when a member of the assurance team may be deterred from acting objectively and exercising professional scepticism by threats, actual or perceived, from the directors, officers or employees of an assurance client. | (a) threat or replacement over a disagreement with the application of an accounting principle, and<br>(b) pressure to reduce inappropriately the extent of work performed in order to reduce fees |

*Source:* Professional Statement F.1: 'Professional Independence', Appendix 1, paragraphs 1.22 – 1.27.

When threats are identified, appropriate safeguards should be applied to eliminate such threats or reduce them to an acceptable level. The nature of the safeguards to be applied will vary depending upon the circumstances, but consideration should always be given to what a reasonable and informed third party having knowledge of all relevant information (Professional Statement F.1, paragraph 1.29). Table 10.2 below lists the different safeguards that mitigate threats to independence. Later in this chapter we examine specific issues in auditing and identify threats to independence and the potential safeguards to reduce such threats to an acceptable level.

**TABLE 10.2**

## SAFEGUARDS THAT MITIGATE THREATS TO INDEPENDENCE

| SAFEGUARDS | TYPES OF SAFEGUARDS |
|---|---|
| Safeguards created by the profession, legislation or regulation | (a) educational, training and experience requirements for entry into the profession<br>(b) continuing education requirements<br>(c) professional standards and monitoring, and disciplinary process<br>(d) external review of a firm's quality control system<br>(e) legislation governing the independence requirements of the firm. |
| Safeguards within the assurance client | (a) when the assurance client's management appoints the firm, persons other than management ratify or approve the appointment<br>(b) the assurance client has employees competent to make managerial decisions<br>(c) policies and procedures that emphasise the assurance client's commitment to fair financial reporting<br>(d) internal procedures that ensure objective choices in commissioning non-assurance engagements<br>(e) a corporate governance structure, such as an audit committee, that provides appropriate oversight and communications regarding a firm's services. |
| Safeguards within the firm's own systems and procedures | 1. Firm-wide safeguards:<br>(a) firm leadership that stresses the important of independence and the expectation that members of assurance teams will act in the public interest<br>(b) policies and procedures to implement and monitor quality control of assurance engagements<br>(c) documented independence policies regarding the identification of threats to independence, the evaluation of the significance of these threats and the identification and application of safeguards to eliminate or reduce the threats, other than those that are clearly insignificant, to an acceptable level<br>(d) internal policies and procedures to monitor compliance with firm policies and procedures as they relate to independence<br>(e) policies and procedures that will enable the identification of interests or relationships between the firm or members of the assurance team and assurance clients<br>(f) policies and procedures to monitor and, if necessary, manage the reliance on revenue received from a single assurance client<br>(g) using different partners and teams with separate reporting lines for the provision of non-assurance services to an assurance client |

| SAFEGUARDS | TYPES OF SAFEGUARDS |
|---|---|
| | (h) policies and procedures to prohibit individuals who are not members of the assurance team from influencing the outcome of the assurance engagement |
| | (i) timely communication of a firm's policies and procedures, and any changes thereto, to all partners and professional staff, including appropriate training and education thereon |
| | (j) designating a member of senior management as responsible for overseeing the adequate functioning of the safeguarding system |
| | (k) means of advising partners and professional staff of those assurance clients and related entities from which they must be independent |
| | (l) a disciplinary mechanism to promote compliance with policies and procedures |
| | (m) policies and procedures to empower staff to communicate, to senior levels within the firm, any issue of independence and objectivity that concerns them; this includes informing staff of the procedures open to them. |
| | 2. Engagement-specific safeguards: |
| | (a) involving an additional professional accountant to review the work done or otherwise advise as necessary. This individual could be someone from outside the firm or network firm, or someone within the firm or network firm who was not otherwise associated with the assurance team |
| | (b) consulting a third party, such as a committee of independence directors, a professional regulatory body or another professional accountant |
| | (c) rotation of senior personnel |
| | (d) discussing independence issues with the audit committee or others charged with governance |
| | (e) disclosing to the audit committee, or others charged with governance, the nature of services provided and extent of fees charged |
| | (f) policies and procedures to ensure members of the assurance team do not make, or assume responsibility for, management decisions for the assurance clients |
| | (g) involving another firm to perform or re-perform part of the assurance engagement |
| | (h) involving another firm to re-perform the non-assurance service to the extent necessary to enable it to take responsibility for that service |
| | (i) removing an individual from the assurance team when that individual's financial interests or relationships create a threat to independence. |

*Source:* Professional Statement F.1: 'Professional Independence', Appendix 1, paragraphs 1.28 – 1.37.

The auditor's role should always be one of absolute independence. The auditor's usefulness, source of authority, integrity and professionalism stems from his or her ability to be independent. Independence in absolute terms is an ideal, and to achieve it, he or she must constantly strive to be independent of all interests. If the services provided by auditors were free, selected from a pool of government sponsored qualified auditors, then we could demand that auditors be absolutely independent. But they are not free, they are hired by companies and paid a fee for their service. This contractual relationship may cause conflicts with the auditor's obligation to protect the interests of users of audited financial reports. Thus, there are degrees of independence, and translating an ideal state such as professional independence into a measurable quality requires a set of criteria that will adequately capture the phenomenon. What follows in Professional Statement F.1: 'Professional Independence', is an attempt to codify an abstract idea into a measurable form and to list the criteria that define the practice of professional independence.

The *Ramsay report* (2001, p. 230) identifies three key issues to be addressed when considering whether accounting firms are independent of their audit clients:
1. employment relationships
2. financial relationships
3. the provision of non-audit services.
These issues are discussed below along with the criteria established in Professional Statement F.1.

## Employment with audit clients //

Employment relationships between an accounting firm and an audit client are such that they can give an impression that an auditor is not independent of the client. When such relationships exist, it is difficult for an auditor to adopt an unbiased approach to his or her work. Professional Statement F.1 sets out the principles guiding employment relations with audit clients. The independence of the audit firm may be threatened if an employee of the audit client is a former member of the audit team or partner of the firm. Such circumstances may create self-interest, familiarity and intimidation threats particularly when significant connections remain between the individual and his or her former firm (F.1, paragraph 2.41). The significance of such threats will depend upon the following factors (F.1, paragraph 2.42):
- the position the individual has taken at the assurance client
- the amount of any involvement the individual will have with the assurance team
- the length of time that has passed since the individual was a member of the assurance team or firm
- the former position of the individual within the assurance team or firm.

Where the significance of the threat is clearly other than insignificant, safeguards should be considered and applied as necessary to reduce the threat to an acceptable level. This might include, for example, assigning an audit team that is of sufficient experience in relation to the individual who has joined the audit client (F.1, paragraph 2.42). In all cases, the following safeguards are necessary to reduce the threat to an acceptable level (F.1, paragraph 2.42):

- The individual concerned is not entitled to any benefits or payments from the audit firm unless these are made in accordance with fixed predetermined arrangements. In addition, any amount owed to the individual should not be of such significance to threaten the firm's independence.
- The individual does not continue to participate or appear to participate in the audit firm's business or professional activities.

A self-interest threat may also arise when a member of the audit team may knowingly join the audit client some time in the future. This type of threat can be reduced to an acceptable level by policies and procedures to require the individual auditor to notify the firm when entering serious employment negotiations with the audit client; and removal of the individual auditor from the audit engagement (F.1, paragraph 2.43).

An additional threat to independence identified by Ramsay (2001, p. 39) occurs when retired audit partners join the boards of their audit clients. The threats arise because of the employment relationship with the audit firm and also of the financial arrangements that may exist with the audit firm after retirement. The threats to independence are threefold. First, the retiring partner may not have exercised an appropriate level of scepticism during the audit process prior to their retirement. Second, the retiring partner may be so familiar with the audit procedures that he or she is able to circumvent them. Third, the partner is likely to have personal relationships with the remaining members of the audit team, who may in turn be reluctant to challenge the decisions of the former partner. Ramsay (2001) recommends that there be a mandatory period of two years following the partner's resignation before they can become a director of a former client company. However, the extent to which this problem exists in Australia is probably very small. A survey by ASIC (2002), found that only 3 per cent of the top 100 companies had a director or senior executive who was previously employed by their external audit firm.

### Recent service with audit clients

A former employee of the audit client who currently serves as a member of the audit team may create self-interest, self-review and familiarity threats. This is particularly true if this person reports on the subject matter that he or she had prepared as an employee of the audit client (F.1, paragraph 2.44). In general, such individuals should not be assigned to the audit team (F.1, paragraph 2.45). Alternatively, additional auditors could review the work done by the individual and discuss the issue with those charged with governance, such as the audit committee (F.1, paragraph 2.46).

## Serving as an officer or director on the board of audit clients

If a partner or current employee of the audit firm serves on the board of an audit client, the self-review and self-interest threats created would be so significant that no safeguard could reduce the threats to an acceptable level. It is difficult to remain unbiased when auditing a company in which the auditor holds a significant position. Consequently, if such an individual were to accept such a position, the only course of action would be to withdraw from the audit engagement (F.1, paragraph 2.47). Routine administrative services to support a company secretarial function are generally not perceived to impair independence, provided client management makes all relevant decisions (F.1, paragraph 2.48).

## Long association of senior personnel with audit clients

Using the same senior personnel on an audit engagement over long periods may create a familiarity threat. The close relationship that develops between the auditor and client is such that the auditor establishes empathy for the client, which may compromise objective judgment. You should now refer to 'In-practice Tyco International' for an example of an auditor whose judgment appeared to be swayed by his relationship with the client. To counter the effects of long-term relationships, audit firms should rotate senior personnel off the audit team after a pre-defined period (F.1, paragraph 2.50). In response to this recommendation, the CLERP (Audit Reform and Corporate Disclosure) Act (2004) proposes mandatory partner rotation every 5 years, including a mandatory period of two years following rotation before a partner may participate in the engagement of the same client. Exceptions to the mandatory rotation rule may apply in some circumstances. For example, when the audit client undergoes a restructure that would otherwise coincide with the rotation of the lead partner; or the size of the audit firm prohibits rotation, or rotation does not constitute an appropriate safeguard (F.1, paragraph 2.52). In these circumstances, the audit firm should apply other safeguards to reduce the threat to an acceptable level, such as involving an additional non-related accountant to review the work done (F.1, paragraph 2.53). One limitation of the mandatory partner rotation rule is that the incoming partner may not fully understand the company's operations. This is important if you consider that audit failures or errors occur in the early years of an audit relationship. In Australia only 43 per cent of the top 100 companies were aware of their external auditors having a policy of rotating partners and senior staff. Of the known policies, the period of rotation varied from 2 to 7 years. In regard to the rotation of audit firms, the vast majority (93 per cent) of companies advised that they did not have a policy of rotating their external auditors. Of the few companies that did rotate their auditors, the most common period was every three years (ASIC 2002).

## Tyco International

The role of an independent auditor is to keep a watchful eye on the books of the companies that they oversee and protect shareholders from fraud or intentional misstatements. Investors feel betrayed when auditors fail to conduct diligent audits. Morgenson, (2003, p. C1) reports that professional independence was overlooked in the audit of Tyco International when Richard P Scalzo, a partner at PricewaterhouseCoopers, turned a blind eye to improper accounting practices at Tyco.

Mr Scalzo missed a number of signs at Tyco. He spotted improper accounting treatments, but allowed them to continue and did not inform the audit committee of Tyco's board. For example:

- From 1998 through 2001, Mr Scalzo was aware that Tyco maintained a general reserve used to offset unanticipated expenses. Such a reserve is prohibited under generally accepted accounting principles, because it can mask the true state of a company's operations and artificially improve the company's profit.
- During the 1999 audit, Mr Scalzo learned that L Dennis Kozlowski, Tyco's chief executive officer, had borrowed $35.5 million from the company, interest-free. He also knew that Mark H Swartz, the company's chief financial officer, had taken $8 million in no-interest loans. Although the PricewaterhouseCoopers audit team recommended that Tyco disclose the loans, Mr Swartz argued that the loans were not required to be disclosed because they were not material. Mr Scalzo agreed, and the loans remained under wraps.
- In 2000, Tyco completed an initial public offering of its stake in TyCom Ltd and Mr Kozlowski granted $96 million in bonuses to 51 Tyco officers and managers, including Mr Swartz himself. Together, Mr Kozlowski and Mr Swartz received almost $50 million in bonuses. The bonuses were not disclosed. When Mr Scalzo discussed the need for disclosure of the bonuses, Mr Swartz assured him they were not material to merit disclosure. Mr Scalzo again relented.
- In 2001, Tyco paid Frank E Walsh, a director, an undisclosed finder's fee of $20 million in connection with the $10 billion acquisition of a finance company, CIT. When Mr Scalzo discussed the details of the fee with Tyco's management, he was advised that it was immaterial. Mr Scalzo concurred, and did not inform the audit committee.

Clearly, Scalzo's response to these events and transactions raises questions about his independence of mind and whether his relationships with senior staff at Tyco influenced his judgment in these very important matters.

# Financial relationships //

Financial relationships between the audit firm and the client are incompatible with auditor independence, because auditors may be tempted to protect their financial interests (self-interest threat) ahead of their responsibility to third-party users of audited financial statements. Financial relationships cover a broad range of transactions between the audit firm and an audit client. In general, they include an investment in the client, a business relationship, and other financial interests such as loans, insurance, and savings products (Ramsay 2001, p. 45). In Australia, almost all of the top 100 companies (97 per cent) claim they have no financial interest or business relationship with their external audit firm (ASIC 2002).

## Financial interests

A financial interest in a client includes such things as having shares in the client company or joint venture projects. This type of financial interest is generally prohibited because the auditor's judgment might be swayed by their investment. The significance of the self-interest threat arising from a financial interest in a client will depend on the nature of the financial interest. This includes the materiality of the financial interest and whether it is a direct or indirect financial interest. An indirect financial interest exists when the individual has no ability to exercise control over the financial interest (for example, a mutual fund or unit trust) and a direct financial interest exists when the individual has control over the financial interest (for example, as a trustee) or is able to exert influence over investment decisions (F.1, paragraph 2.4).

If an auditor, or their immediate family member, or the firm, has a direct financial interest, or a material indirect financial interest in the audit client, the only safeguards available to eliminate the self-interest threat are to (F.1, paragraphs 2.5 and 2.12):

- dispose of the direct financial interest;
- dispose of the indirect financial interest in total or in sufficient amount to reduce the threat to an acceptable level; or
- remove the auditor from the engagement.

Similar safeguards must be applied when the auditor or close family member receives a direct financial interest by way of an inheritance, gift or as a result of a merger. During the period of sale, the auditor should also discuss the matter with the audit client or involve an additional accountant to review the work performed by the auditor (F.1, paragraph 2.6). In the case of a close family member, the disposal of the direct financial interest should occur at the earliest practical date after the auditor learns of the direct financial interest (F.1, paragraph 2.7).

When the financial interest is held in the client as a trustee, the financial interest is acceptable only when the auditor, close relative or firm, are not beneficiaries of the trust; the trust is not able to exercise significant influence over the client; and the auditor or the firm does not have significant influence over any investment decision involving a financial interest in the client (F.1, paragraph 2.8).

An inadvertent violation of independence resulting from a financial interest would not ordinarily impair independence, if the firm has established policies and procedures that require all members of the audit firm to promptly report violations and the disposal occurs at the earliest practical date (F.1, paragraph 2.11).

### Loans and guarantees

A loan or a guarantee by an audit client that is a bank or a similar institution to the audit firm would not create a threat to independence provided the loan is made under normal lending procedures and is immaterial to both the firm and lender. If the loan is material to either the audit firm or client, safeguards must be applied, such as a review of the work performed by an external accountant (F.1, paragraph 2.25). Ramsay (2001) recommends an amendment to the Corporations Act so that an amount exceeding $10 000 will breach independence. A loan on normal lending terms to an individual member of the audit team, or close family member, such as a home mortgage, would not create a threat to independence (F.1, paragraph 2.26). In cases where an audit firm or an individual member of the audit team makes a material loan to a client, the self-interest threat to independence is considered so significant that no safeguard could reduce the threat to an acceptable level (F.1, paragraphs 2.28 and 2.29). Therefore, no such arrangements must ever be entered into.

### Close business relationships with audit clients

A close business relationship between an audit firm and a client company includes such things as joint venture projects, and other arrangements such as distribution and marketing activities that combine one or more services of both parties. Close business relationships create self-interest and intimidation threats (F.1, paragraph 2.31). In such cases, the audit firm should:
- terminate the business relationship;
- reduce the magnitude of the relationship so that the financial interest is immaterial; or
- refuse to perform the audit engagement.

The purchase of goods and services from an audit client would not generally create a threat to independence, provided the transaction is in the normal course of business and on an arm's length basis (F.1, paragraph 2.33). In Australia, only 3 per cent of the top 100 companies offer discounts to audit staff for the purchase of goods and services (ASIC 2002).

## Provision of non-audit services to audit clients

Ramsay (2001, p. 55) defines non-audit services as all services not coming within the scope of the audit contract. These include such things as taxation, information technology, finance, and human resource management. The dynamics of change within the audit profession have transformed audit services from a profitable core product to its current by-product status, compared to non-audit services. The growth of non-audit services is derived from the demand from clients for specialised services, and the corresponding revenue growth for large accounting firms has been substantial. As a consequence, audit firms now collect more fees from non-audit services than audit services. In America, more than 80 per cent of the fees collected by the large accounting firms in 2000 were, on average, collected for non-audit services (Zabihollah 2004). The ratio of auditing revenue to consulting revenue reduced from 6 to 1 in 1990 to 1.5 to 1 in 1999 (Ramsay 2001, p. 64). In Australia, the top 100 companies paid, on average, 47 per cent of their total fees for non-audit services. Interestingly, the majority of companies indicated that there were no rigorous processes employed in appointing auditors for non-audit services. Usually the Chief Financial Officer was the person responsible for engaging the external auditor in these roles. The level of non-audit services provided by external auditors was not normally a consideration for the board or the audit committee (ASIC 2002).

Audit firms have traditionally provided to their audit clients a range of non-audit services that are consistent with their skills and expertise. Clients benefit from non-audit services provided by audit firms that have a good understanding of the business. The provision of non-audit services may, however, create self-interest and self-review threats to independence because the audit team may be reluctant to self-criticise the non-audit services provided by their colleagues. However, according to Ramsay (2001, p. 65) there is no solid evidence of any specific link between audit failures and the provision of non-audit services. When the non-audit service is not related to the subject matter of an audit engagement, the threats to independence will generally be insignificant (F.1, paragraphs 2.24 and 2.55).

Some activities such as authorising and executing a transaction on behalf of the client and determining which recommendation should be implemented are considered so significant that no safeguard will reduce the threat to an acceptable level (F.1, paragraph 2.55). However, threats coming from other activities, such as having custody of a client's assets, can be reduced to an acceptable level with appropriate safeguards (F.1, paragraph 2.57); for example, making arrangements so that personnel providing such services do not participate in the audit engagement. Innovative developments in business make it impossible to draw up an all-inclusive list of all situations involving the provision of non-audit services, the potential threats to independence, and the different safeguards that might eliminate these threats or reduce them to an acceptable level. In general, however, a firm may provide services beyond the audit engagement, provided any threats to independence have been reduced to an acceptable level (F.1, paragraph 2.59). Table 10.3 below provides a list of safeguards that are particularly relevant in reducing to an acceptable level threats created by the provision of non-audit services to audit clients.

TABLE 10.3

## SAFEGUARDS AGAINST THE PROVISION OF NON-AUDIT SERVICES

- Policies and procedures to prohibit professional staff from making management decisions for the assurance client, or assuming responsibility for such decisions;

- Discussing independence issues related to the provision of non-assurance services with those charged with governance, such as the assurance committee;

- Policies within the assurance client regarding the oversight responsibility for provision of non-assurance services by the firm;

- Involving an additional professional accountant to advise on the potential impact of the non-assurance engagement on the independence of the member of the assurance team and the firm;

- Involving an additional professional accountant outside of the firm to provide assurance on a discrete aspect of the assurance engagement;

- Obtaining the assurance client's acknowledgment of responsibility for the results of the work performed by the firm;

- Disclosing to those charged with governance, such as the assurance committee, the nature and extent of fees charged; or

- Making arrangements so that personnel providing non-assurance services do not participate in the assurance engagement.

*Source:* Professional Statement F.1: 'Professional Independence', Appendix 2, paragraph 2.60.

Professional Statement F.1: 'Professional Independence' goes into some detail about the types of non-audit services provided to audit clients and their implications for auditor independence. In Table 10.4 we identify the types of non-audit services discussed in Professional Statement F.1, their corresponding threats and potential safeguards.

**TABLE 10.4**

### NON-AUDIT SERVICES, THREATS AND SAFEGUARDS

| NON-AUDIT SERVICE | THREAT | SAFEGUARDS |
|---|---|---|
| Preparing accounting records and financial statements | Self-review | Threat cannot be reduced to an acceptable level by any safeguards; however, some discretion is allowed in the case of non-listed entities. |

| NON-AUDIT SERVICE | THREAT | SAFEGUARDS |
|---|---|---|
| Valuation services | Self-review | Where the valuation involves matters material to the financial report, the threat cannot be reduced to an acceptable level by any safeguards. In other cases, safeguards include:<br>• Involving an additional professional accountant who was not a member of the audit team to review the work done or otherwise advise as necessary;<br>• Confirming with the audit client their understanding of the underlying assumptions of the valuation and the methodology to be used and obtaining approval for their use;<br>• Obtaining the audit client's acknowledgment of responsibility for the results of the work performed by the firm; and<br>• Making arrangements so that personnel providing such services do not participate in the audit engagement. |
| Provision of taxation services to audit clients | Nil | Taxation services comprise a broad range of services, including compliance, planning, provision of formal taxation opinions and assistance in the resolution of tax disputes. Such assignments are generally not seen to create threats to independence. |
| Provision of internal audit services to audit clients | Self-review | Services involving an extension of the procedures required to conduct an audit would not be considered to impair independence. When the firm provides assistance in the performance of a client's internal audit activities or undertakes the outsourcing of some of the activities, or performs a significant portion of the audit client's internal audit activities, safeguards include:<br>(a) The audit client is responsible for internal audit activities and acknowledges its responsibility for establishing, maintaining and monitoring the system of internal controls; |

| NON-AUDIT SERVICE | THREAT | SAFEGUARDS |
|---|---|---|
| | | (b) The audit client designates a competent employee, preferably within senior management, to be responsible for internal audit activities; |
| | | (c) The audit client, the audit committee or supervisory body approves the scope, risk and frequency of internal audit work; |
| | | (d) The audit client is responsible for evaluating and determining which recommendations of the firm should be implemented; |
| | | (e) The audit client evaluates the adequacy of the internal audit procedures performed and the findings resulting from the performance of those procedures by, among other things, obtaining and acting on reports from the firm; and |
| | | (f) The findings and recommendations resulting from the internal audit activities are reported appropriately to the audit committee or supervisory body. |
| Provision of IT systems services to audit clients | Self-review | Threats derived from services involving the design and implementation of financial information systems technology are likely to be too significant to allow the provision of such services to an audit client unless appropriate safeguards are put in place: |
| | | (a) The audit client acknowledges its responsibility for establishing and monitoring a system of internal controls; |
| | | (b) The audit client designates a competent employee, preferably within senior management, with the responsibility to make all management decisions with respect to the design and implementation of the hardware or software system; |
| | | (c) The audit client makes all management decisions with respect to the design and implementation process; |

| NON-AUDIT SERVICE | THREAT | SAFEGUARDS |
|---|---|---|
| | | (d) The audit client evaluates the adequacy and results of the design and implementation of the system; and<br><br>(e) The audit client is responsible for the operation of the system (hardware or software) and the data used or generated by the system. |
| Temporary staff assignments to audit clients | Self-review | The lending of staff by a firm to an audit client may create a threat when the individual is in a position to influence the preparation of a client's accounts or financial statements. Safeguards include:<br><br>(a) The staff providing the assistance should not be given audit responsibility for any function or activity that they performed or supervised during their temporary staff assignment; and<br><br>(b) The audit client should acknowledge its responsibility for directing and supervising the activities of firm, or network firm, personnel. |
| Provision of litigation support services to audit clients | Self-review | Litigation support services include activities such as a threat may be created when the litigation support services include the estimation of the possible outcome of litigation or other a legal dispute. Safeguards might include:<br><br>(a) Policies and procedures to prohibit individuals assisting the audit client from making managerial decisions on behalf of the client;<br><br>(b) Using professionals who are not members of the audit team to perform the service; or<br><br>(c) The involvement of others, such as independent experts. |
| Provision of legal services to audit clients | Self-review and advocacy | The provision of legal services is not considered to create an unacceptable threat to independence. However, legal advice may create self-review threats. Safeguards include:<br><br>(a) Members of the audit team are not involved in providing the service; and |

| NON-AUDIT SERVICE | THREAT | SAFEGUARDS |
|---|---|---|
| | | (b) The audit client makes the ultimate decision or, in relation to the transactions, the service involves the execution of what has been decided by the audit client.<br><br>The threats arising from acting in an advocacy role when the amounts are material in relation to the financial statements are so significant that no safeguard could reduce the threat to an acceptable level. |
| Recruiting senior management | Self-interest, familiarity and intimidation | The firm could generally provide such services as reviewing the professional qualifications of applicants, provide advice on their suitability for the post, or produce a short-list of candidates for interview in accordance with criteria specified by the audit client. In cases where threats are significant, the firm should not make management decisions and the decision as to whom to hire should be left to the client. |
| Corporate finance and similar activities | Self-review and advocacy | Services such as promoting, dealing in or underwriting an audit client's shares is not compatible with providing audit services. They create a threat to independence so significant no safeguard could reduce the threat to an acceptable level. Other services such as assisting a client in developing corporate strategies, assisting in identifying or introducing a client to possible sources of capital, and assisting a client in analysing the accounting effects of proposed transactions are acceptable with appropriate safeguards:<br>(a) Policies and procedures to prohibit individuals assisting the audit client from making managerial decisions on behalf of the client;<br>(b) Using professionals who are not members of the audit team to provide the services; and<br>(c) Ensuring the firm does not commit the audit client to the terms of any transaction or consummate a transaction on behalf of the client. |

*Source:* Professional Statement F.1: 'Professional Independence', Appendix 2, paragraphs 2.63 – 2.101.

# Audit committees //

A well structured and well functioning **audit committee** (a sub-committee of the board) can play a very important role in ensuring that the auditor is independent of the company. An audit committee assists the board in overseeing its responsibilities in relation to its audit by regular communications with the auditor regarding relationships and other matters that might reasonably be thought to bear on independence (F.1, paragraph 1.33). Facilitating auditor communication to the board through the audit committee rather than management is an important benefit of audit committees. Serious disagreements with management during the audit process, undue delays by management in providing information, and other major problems experienced by the auditor are now reported directly to the audit committee. As an independent body, the audit committee can follow up difficulties encountered by the auditor and, above all, it ensures that management does not exert undue influence on the auditor (Knapp 1987).

According to Ramsay (2001, p. 85), there may be insufficient incentives for companies to form audit committees and, when they are formed, they might not be formed for the right reasons, and in the absence of specific requirements they may suffer through a lack of consistency. In Australia, the Corporations Act and the Listing Rules of the Australian Stock Exchange (ASX) do not require companies to establish an audit committee; but the Listing Rules do require companies to disclose the existence, or non-existence, of an audit committee. If no audit committee exists, the company is required to disclose the reasons it has not formed an audit committee. Audit committees are widespread in the Australian corporate environment. According to a survey of Australia's top 100 companies, 97 per cent of the companies have an audit committee (ASIC 2002). However, having an audit committee and having an effective audit committee are separate issues. Audit committees might merely impose an additional layer of bureaucracy on an organisation motivated by the desire to satisfy due diligence requirements. If members of the audit committee lack expertise or the mandate to ask probing questions, the likelihood of audit committees improving the governance of a company is limited. The financial competence of committee members and their independence is important if they are to withstand pressure from management. Ramsay (2001, p. 89) recommends that the ASX Listing Rules be amended to require all listed companies to have an audit committee. The CLERP (Audit Reform and Corporate Disclosure) Act (2004) makes audit committees mandatory for the top 500 listed companies.

# Independent oversight of auditor independence //

Ramsay (2001, p. 75) recommends the establishment of an independent oversight board as a means of strengthening compliance with standards on audit independence. The Auditor Independence Supervisory Board (AISB) would serve the public interest and protect and promote investors' confidence in Australia's capital markets. The functions of the AISB would include the monitoring of:

- international developments in auditor independence and the adequacy of Australia rules
- the nature and adequacy of systems and processes used by Australian audit firms to deal with issues of auditor independence
- compliance by companies with the new auditor independence regime
- the adequacy of teaching professional and business ethics by the professional bodies and universities.

The CLERP (Audit Reform and Corporate Disclosure) Act (2004) supports Ramsay's recommendation for an independent supervisory board to address the challenge of implementing new auditor independence requirements in Australia; but it proposes that the role be carried out by the Financial Reporting Council (FRC) and not a new independent body. In addition to the roles recommended by Ramsay (2001), the CLERP Bill (2003) recommends that the FRC should also monitor fee dependence for all audit firms auditing listed companies. Issues associated with fee dependence are discussed in chapter 11. Houghton and Jubb (2002) go further and suggest that the larger audit firms should establish their own Auditor Independence Board (AIB). A board with internal access will be more effective than an arrangement imposed externally. An external board such as the AISB or the FRC would only consider extreme or crude independence issues; whereas an internal board such as the AIB can deal with threats to a firm's independence more swiftly and diplomatically.

## Summary //

Professional independence is a multifaceted concept that evolved from a need to monitor the performance of opportunistic managers. Professional independence is vital to the practice of auditing, and to the people who rely on audited financial reports for their economic decision making. Without independence, confidence in the auditor's opinion is limited, and capital market efficiency will erode, causing an increase in the cost of capital. To ensure a robust regime of auditor independence, the revised Professional Statement F.1 sets out detailed guidelines on activities and relationships that threaten independence, and safeguards that might reduce such threats to an acceptable level. The *Ramsay report* (2001) made a number of recommendations consistent with Professional Statement F.1 that are now largely adopted in the CLERP (Audit Reform and Corporate Disclosure) Act (2004). The new regime is designed to both safeguard independence and allow accountants to engage in new services as part of an evolving global economy (Hayes 2002).

To act as arbiter and interpreter, to be beyond suspicion, to exercise professional skill honestly, to apply the best judgment without fear or favour, and to apply and express an opinion impartially and objectively, calls for a personal ethic that is just short of exemplary. While a self-enforced personal code of conduct may fall short of such a high ideal, compliance with a regime of auditor independence that focuses on avoiding relationships, transactions and services that compromise objective judgment, aspires to this high standard of service.

## Key terms //

Agency theory ... p. 256
Audit ... p. 257
Audit committee ... p. 279
Independence ... p. 258
Independence in appearance ... p. 260
Independence in fact ... p. 259
Independence of mind *see* independence in fact ... p. 259
Monitoring cost ... p. 257
Practitioner independence ... p. 259
Professional independence ... p. 258

## Questions //

**10.1** Describe the role of independence in agency theory.

**10.2** Define professional independence and distinguish independence in fact from independence in appearance. Which is more important? Why?

**10.3** Why is professional independence important in accounting?

**10.4** List are the types of threats to independence and at least three safeguards in relation to:
   **a** employment relationships
   **b** financial relationships
   **c** the provision of non-audit services to audit clients.

**10.5** Explain the rationale for rotating senior audit staff off audit engagements.

**10.6** Why should a retiring audit partner be precluded for two years from accepting a position on the board of an audit client? Explain.

**10.7** What should an auditor do if he or she discovers a close family member:
   **a** has a direct financial interest in an audit client?
   **b** has a material indirect financial interest in an audit client?

**10.8** Discuss whether the principle of independence is violated in each of the following circumstances.
   **a** An audit client loans money to its audit firm.
   **b** An audit client loans money to an individual member of the audit team.
   **c** An audit firm loans money to an audit client.

**10.9** What are the arguments for and against an audit firm providing non-audit services to an audit client?

**10.10** Compare and contrast the threats and safeguards in each of the following non-audit services. Why are the threats and safeguards different?

  **a** Preparing accounting records and financial statements.

  **b** Provision of taxation services.

**10.11** Explain how an audit committee enhances auditor independence.

**10.12** What are the benefits of an independent oversight board?

## CASE STUDY

On 16 October 2001, Enron, one of the world's largest corporations, announced a write-down of its after-tax net profit of $544 million and share-holders' equity by $1.2 billion. On 8 November 2001, Enron announced a restatement of its previously reported net profit for four years. Accounting errors were cited as the reason for the restatement. Within a month, Enron's equity lowered by $1.7 billion, approximately 18 per cent of the previously reported $9.6 billion. On 2 December 2001, Enron filed for bankruptcy — the largest corporate bankruptcy in United States history at that time.

Arthur Andersen, a respected international accounting firm, audited Enron and issued unqualified opinions throughout this entire period. Arthur Andersen consulted and participated in the setting up of special-purpose entities (SPEs) which conformed to accounting regulations but failed in substance. In effect, the activities of SPEs such as the related-party transactions were excluded from Enron's financial statements (Benston & Hartgraves 2002, p. 15).

Arthur Andersen received $52m in fees from Enron in 2000, and between $50m and $55m in 2001. Almost 50 per cent ($25m) of the fees received in 2000 was received as remuneration for audit services, and the remaining $27m was paid for non-auditing services. The Securities and Exchange Commission (SEC) has since proposed regulatory actions, including forbidding public accounting firms from offering their clients non-audit services such as tax preparation, internal auditing, systems analysis, litigation support and financial planning.

David Duncan, the Andersen partner in charge of the Enron account said:

> the auditors in charge of the Enron audit may have overlooked or supported their client's overly "aggressive" accounting, misleading and possibly fraudulent accounting practices in order to protect their very salaries and bonuses. Or, as many critics have charged, the gate keepers may have been corrupted by the sizeable audit, and possibly, the non-audit fees paid by Enron (Reported in Benston & Hartgraves 2002, p. 127).

### QUESTIONS

**1** Discuss the rationale for the SEC's regulatory actions against the provision of non-audit services by public accounting firms.

**2** Under what circumstances does Professional Statement F.1 limit the ability of public accounting firms to offer non-audit services?

## FURTHER RESOURCES //

Knapp, MC 1985, 'Audit conflict: an empirical study of the perceived ability of auditors to resist management pressure', *The Accounting Review*, April, pp. 202–11.

Malan, MR 1986, 'Traps on the path to audit credibility', *The Internal Auditor*, June vol. 43, no. 3, pp. 29–36.

Power, M 1997, *The audit society, rituals of verification*, Oxford University Press.

## REFERENCES //

Australian Securities & Investments Commission 2002, *Audit independence survey*, ASIC, Melbourne.

Benston, JG, and Hartgraves, LA 2002, 'Enron: what happened and what we can learn from it', *Journal of Accounting and Public Policy*, vol. 21, issue 2, pp. 105–27.

CLERP (Audit Reform and Corporate Disclosure) Bill (2003), Commonwealth of Australia.

CPA Australia and the Institute of Chartered Accountants in Australia 2002, Professional Statement F.1: 'Professional independence', *Members' handbook*, December 2002.

CPA Australia and Institute of Chartered Accountants in Australia 2004, *Accounting and Auditing handbook 2004*, vol. 2, Pearson Education.

Hayes, C 2002, 'The *Ramsay report* and the regulation of auditor independence in Australia', *Australian Accounting Review*, vol. 12, no. 2, pp. 3–11.

Houghton, KA and Jubb, C 2002, 'An Australian response to recent developments in the market for audit services', *Australian Accounting Review*, vol. 12, no. 2, pp. 24–30.

Knapp, MC 1987, 'An empirical study of audit committee support for auditors involved in technical disputes with client management', *The Accounting Review*, July, pp. 578–88.

Kohler, LE 1975, *A Dictionary for accountants*, 5th Ed, Prentice Hall, p. 254.

Mautz, KR, and Sharaf, AH 1961, *The philosophy of auditing*, American Accounting Association, Sarasota, FL.

Morgenson, G 2003, 'SEC puts ban on accountant over his work on Tyco's books', *New York Times* (Late Edn (East Coast)), New York, 14 August, p. C.1.

Noyes, E. C. 1959, 'Professional independence', *Journal of Accountancy*, June, p. 28.

Parker, C, and Hopp, E 1998, 'Professional standards', *Australian Accountant*. February, vol. 68, issue 1, pp. 51–2.

Pulliam, S, and Bandler, J 2003, 'Leading the news: KPMG is likely to face fraud charges—SEC set to file civil action against accounting firm for role in Xerox audits', *Wall Street Journal*, (Eastern Edn), New York, 23 January, p. A.3.

Ramsay, I 2001, *Independence of company auditors, Review of current Australian requirements and proposals for reform*, Report to the Minister for Financial Services and Regulation, Commonwealth of Australia.

Simon, BE 1980, 'Can the auditor be truly independent?', *Accountancy*, June, vol. 91, issue 1042, p. 105.

Stempf, HV 1942, 'Professional independence', *Journal of Accountancy*, September, p. 226.

Zabihollah, R 2004, 'Restoring public trust in the accounting profession by developing anti-fraud education, programs, and auditing', *Managerial Auditing Journal*, vol. 19, no. 1, pp. 134–48.

# Client-centred conflicts of interest

# 11

## Learning objectives

After studying this chapter you should be able to:
- Identify and describe the elements that comprise conflicts of interest.
- Discuss the conflicts of interest and the accountant's professional responsibilities in each of the following situations:
    - tax evasion and tax avoidance
    - setting and collecting professional fees
    - accepting new clients
    - giving second opinions
    - referring clients to specialists
    - engaging in incompatible activities.
- Describe how accountants can avoid conflicts of interest.

'It is not the greatness of man's means that makes him independent,
so much so as the smallness of his wants.'
William Cobbett, 1763–1835, Politician and journalist

# Introduction //

Conflicts of interest are central to many of the problems faced by practising professionals. For example, in medicine, pharmaceutical companies offer gifts to doctors such as free samples and travel, to try to influence their decisions on the kinds of drugs they prescribe to their patients. In business, share options offered to senior management as part of their compensatory package provide powerful incentives to boost the short-term share prices at the expense of the long-term interests of the company. In accounting, auditors charged with independently reviewing the financial reports of their clients are sometimes found to be overly complicit with management. Leung and Cooper (1995) conducted a study of ethics in the Australian accounting profession, to examine the type and extent of ethical problems experienced by accounting professionals. The ethical issues encountered most frequently were conflicts of interest. Therefore, if accountants are to avoid the adverse consequences that arise from conflicts of interest, they must be able to identify conflicts when they occur, and deal with them in accordance with their professional responsibilities.

# Conflicts of interest //

**Conflicts of interest** happen when the interest of the professional, or their family or friends, conflicts or has the potential to conflict with the interests of another party (Carson 1994). In accounting, conflicts of interest involve a clash between the interests of the accountant (or the firm of accountants), and the interests of the client or employer to which the accountant has an obligation. The meaning of the phrase 'conflicts of interest' has been widely debated and discussed by many commentators. In summarising the different interpretations, Carson (1994) and Gaa (1994) identified the following important elements in the definition of 'conflicts of interest'.

## Fiduciary relationship //

The professional is in an official or **fiduciary relationship**. As a fiduciary, whether in a client or employer relationship, the professional has a primary duty to act in the best interests of the other party over their own interests. The client or employer relies on the professional to use their superior knowledge and skill with integrity and objectivity for the betterment of the client or the employer.

## Proper exercise of duty //

The nature of a conflict means that the professional is divided between two or more loyalties, obligations or interests. This divided loyalty can sway judgment, which makes it difficult for the professional to exercise sound, independent, and objective judgment. Therefore, one attribute of a conflict of interest is that it interferes with the professional's ability to discharge their fiduciary duties properly. It is not necessary for the professional to have failed in their duties, only to experience difficulty.

## Self-interest //

Conflicts of **self-interest** is broadly defined to include not only the interests of the professional, but also the interests of the professional's friends and family or other related parties—including clients. Therefore, conflicts of interest can arise from the professional's desire to promote his or her own interest, as well as the interests of other related parties.

## Real or imaginary conflict of interest //

It is not necessary for an actual conflict of interest to exist, there need only be the perception that it does. It is sufficient that the professional believes that there is a conflict between the interests of the various parties. Whether the conflict is real or imaginary is irrelevant. A professional is just as likely to be hindered in the performance of their duties because they mistakenly believe that their actions are contrary to their interests or the interests of those they have an obligation to advance.

## Actual or potential harm //

Harm resulting from poor decision making is not a necessary condition for the existence of conflict of interest, there need only be the potential for the harm from a decision that is compromised by a real or imaginary conflict of interest.

In summary, a professional, for instance an accountant, occupies a special fiduciary role—one that involves making judgments that affect others. When an accountant fails to adhere to their fiduciary duties and favours self-interest ahead of the interests they are obligated to serve, the result is some winners and some losers. Consider the actions of an accountant who overlooks a reporting entity's decision to alter its accounting policy, causing the deferral of revenue to future periods. Altering the financial position and shifting profit to future periods will disadvantage existing shareholders and benefit future shareholders. It is not only those reliant on the accountant's judgment who are affected by conflicts of interest; conflicts of interest can also detract from the reputation and credibility of the accountants involved. A conflict of interest can arouse resentment and undermine the trust held by clients and the public in the entire accounting community. Those who do the most for others and not for themselves most readily win public trust and recognition. Trust is vital to the professional–client relationship, and should never be taken lightly. Public trust and its significance to the accounting profession was discussed in chapter 3. Take, for example, the case of PricewaterhouseCoopers (PwC) and the Ansett Australia Group (refer to the section, In practice: Ansett Australia Group, elsewhere in this chapter). The apparent conflict of interest was enough to force PricewaterhouseCoopers' (PwC) to resign as administrator of the Ansett Australia Group. The mere existence of a conflict of interest signifies that accountants may fail to act in accordance with the duties owed to others; duties which are implicit in their role as accountants. Therefore, avoiding conflicts of interest, whether they are real or imaginary is integral to the professional's duties.

**IN PRACTICE**

### Ansett Australia Group

In 2001, Ansett Australia, one of two domestic Australian airlines, collapsed because of liquidity problems caused by ill-performing investments and market downturns. On 17 September 2001, PricewaterhouseCoopers (PwC), an international accounting firm, was appointed by Ansett's controlling entity, Air New Zealand, as the voluntary administrator of the Ansett Australia Group. Within days, and after a little more than 100 hours on the job, PwC resigned from this engagement. The resignation followed discussions with the ACTU and major unions, who maintained that PwC had a conflict of interest as administrator due to the existing relationship between PwC and Air New Zealand. Air New Zealand, which itself was battling financial distress, was rumoured to have stripped Ansett of money and resources immediately prior to the company's downfall. Because of their pre-existing relationship, Air New Zealand appeared to be acting on advice from PwC. The extent to which PwC approved of these actions (note, they were only rumours) or offered such advice is irrelevant; the appearance of a conflict was enough to force their resignation. In order for PwC to act in the best interests of Ansett's creditors, the vast majority of whom were the company's own employees, PwC needed the support of the unions. Without their confidence, PwC had no choice but to resign from the engagement. PwC proposed a cessation of further work for Air Zealand in order to remove itself from the apparent conflict of interest, but this was not enough to restore the unions' confidence.

# Types of conflict of interest //

In this chapter we distinguish two types of conflict of interest: client-centred conflicts of interest and employer-centred conflicts of interest. **Client-centred conflicts of interest** are conflicts between the client and the accountant or the firm of accountants, which impair the accountant's ability to exercise properly his or her professional obligations. For example, **public accountants** have great incentives to avoid giving bad news to the client managers who hire them and pay their fees. The mere fact that public accountants receive a fee causes a perception of possible bias or conflict of interest. Conflicts of interest are not restricted solely to public accountants. For example, **accountants in business** or **salaried accountants** face a conflict of interest when their employer seeks liberal interpretations of accounting standards. Conflicts confronting accountants in business (also known as **employer-centred conflicts of interest**) are examined in chapter 12. In this chapter, we examine the conflicts that are faced by accountants in public practice (public accountants), and **client-centred conflicts**.

The most prominent conflicts facing public accountants are client-centred conflicts, which threaten their independence. Issues relating to professional independence, for example the conflict with audit and management advisory services, were addressed in chapter 10. In this chapter, we examine the conflicts of interest associated with:

- clients who evade tax
- accepting and setting professional fees
- potential clients seeking second opinions
- accepting new clients
- referring clients with special needs
- accountants engaging in more than one activity.

For each of the conflicts addressed in this chapter, we describe the nature of the conflict, the ethical issues, and the responsibilities of the accountant when faced with such conflicts. In discussing the accountant's responsibilities, we rely on the official pronouncements espoused in the *Joint Code of Professional Conduct* issued by CPA Australia and the Institute of Chartered Accountants (ICAA), and the revised code of ethics issued by the International Federation of Accountants (IFAC).

## Conflicts in taxation //

Taxation services are a major contributing factor to the rapid growth of the accounting profession. The revenue derived from taxation services is the mainstay of many accounting practices, and a major source of ethical conflict. For example, the fear of losing clients, with a consequent loss of professional fees, can lead to aggressive interpretation of the tax laws — conduct that contravenes the public's expectations of the professional's ethical behaviour. The accountant's responsibilities when dealing with clients' taxation affairs are outlined in APS 6: *Statement of Taxation Standards* of the *Members' Handbook* issued by the professional accounting bodies. Professional responsibilities will differ, depending on whether the accountant is faced with clients implicated in tax evasion or tax avoidance. Therefore, before discussing the accountant's professional responsibilities, we must first distinguish tax evasion from tax avoidance. **Tax evasion** is defined as the deliberate falsification of information, and deceit for the primary purpose of escaping tax liability. In general, schemes designed to evade tax are unlawful and are considered a criminal offence. On the other hand, **tax avoidance** is the process of arranging one's affairs, events and transactions to secure a tax advantage by legal, albeit sometimes contentious, means. The test that distinguishes tax evasion from tax avoidance is the legality of the taxpayer's conduct: tax avoidance is legal; tax evasion is not.

## Tax avoidance //

Tax avoidance is the process of legally arranging one's affairs, events and transactions to secure a tax advantage. There is nothing improper in an accountant assisting clients to minimise their tax liability by legal means. Where there is reasonable legal support for a position that will result in a lower tax liability for the client, the accountant may not only advance the solution that is most favourable to the client, they have a duty to do so. Therefore, the primary role of the accountant is to minimise the client's tax liability by arranging their affairs to ensure the lowest possible tax burden (APS 6, paragraph 23). If the legitimacy of the client's tax position is uncertain, the accountant should only resolve in favour of the taxpayer if there is reasonable support for that position. It is also important to make clear to the client the repercussions of an adverse assessment. At no time should the accountant claim that the tax position is beyond challenge from the taxing authority. In the following commentary, we discuss schemes or arrangements that have no commercial merit other than avoiding tax liability.

**Tax avoidance schemes**, or arrangements that comply with the 'letter of the law', but are not within the spirit of the law, allow some taxpayers to avoid their taxation responsibilities. Such schemes, although legal, are generally regarded as unethical because they enable taxpayers to receive an unfair or unintended tax advantage. Nevertheless, the accountant has a professional obligation to do all that is possible to ensure that client taxpayers do not pay more tax than is necessary, even though accountants have a competing ethical obligation to society to ensure that a taxpayer does not pay less than is fair. The decision to enter into a tax arrangement must always be that of the taxpayer, but the accountant must ensure the taxpayer is fully informed of the current and future ramifications in relation to changes in the law (APS 6, paragraph 24). While the accountant must not devise or promote such schemes or arrangements (APS 6, paragraph 26), this does not preclude them from advising clients of such matters. However, the accountant has an overriding responsibility to avoid association with any scheme or arrangement that involves documents or accounting entries that intentionally misrepresent the true nature of the transaction or event (APS 6, paragraph 25).

Tax avoidance schemes are often the result of legal loopholes created by an absence or an inconsistency in the law. The responsibility for dealing with legal loopholes resides with the parliament, not the accountant (Lynch 1987). Until such time as the legislature deals with the loophole, accountants can and should advise their clients on the benefits of such matters. In spite of the ethical implications of giving such advice, it is not the accountant's responsibility to act as a moral agent for the client. The morality of such decisions is up to the taxpayer. The accountant's responsibility is only to inform the client of the alternatives and the potential repercussions.

## Tax evasion //

The taxation return is primarily the taxpayer's representation of the facts. However, before an accountant signs as the preparer of the tax return, he or she must take all reasonable steps to obtain from the taxpayer the information needed to answer all questions on the return. The accountant has a responsibility to make all reasonable inquiries as to the accuracy and completeness of the financial information provided by the taxpayer (APS 6, paragraph 10). While it is permissible for the accountant to rely on the information provided by the client without verification, the accountant should question such information if it appears incorrect, incomplete or inconsistent. It is important to encourage the taxpayer to provide supporting documentation, to allow the accountant to consider thoroughly the legitimacy of the claims. Carelessness can unwittingly involve the accountant in tax evasion, by a failure to notice discrepancies that should have been detected.

Similarly, it is not prudent to accept unsatisfactory explanations from the client without further inquiry. Accepting unsatisfactory information or explanations is tantamount to contributing to the tax evasion. The accountant has a primary duty to ensure, as far as practicable, that he or she has not contributed to the evasion of tax (APS 6, paragraph 11). If, upon further inquiry, the accountant learns that the information is deficient, he or she should not sign the preparer's declaration. The declaration states that the tax return has been prepared in accordance with the information supplied by the taxpayer, who in turn declares that the information provided is true and accurate. If the accountant has reason to believe that the information supplied by the taxpayer is not true and correct, then the preparer's declaration should not be signed.

In general, tax evasion occurs when a taxpayer intentionally or accidentally under-declares assessable income or declares an expense that is not allowable for tax relief. In these circumstances, the accountant must do nothing to assist the client to commit a criminal offence (APS 6, paragraph 16). The accountant must ensure that unlawful client behaviour is entirely of the client's own volition. If the accountant becomes aware that the client is evading tax, he or she should endeavour to persuade the client to correct the misstatement and submit a correct taxation return (APS 6, paragraph 17). In persuading the client, the accountant should point out the risks and related penalties of such behaviour. The accountant has a subsequent responsibility to refuse further association with that taxation return until the misstatement is rectified. If the misstatement is considered material, the accountant should carefully consider withdrawing their services and cease to act for the client in all matters, not just those relating to the client's tax affairs (APS 6, paragraph 20).

When an accountant withdraws their services, they should inform the taxing authority that they no longer act for the client. Regrettably, this is the extent of the information that may be communicated to the taxing authority. The accountant is bound by client confidentiality and cannot inform the taxing authority directly (APS 6, paragraph 14). The accountant can only notify the taxing authority with the taxpayer's permission. In cases of accidental error, obtaining authority from the client to notify the taxing authority is not normally a problem; however, sometimes the client may not cooperate. If the taxpayer refuses to give the accountant permission to disclose the error to the taxing authority, and fails to do so voluntarily, the accountant should consider withdrawing and discontinuing the relationship with the taxpayer.

## Taxation ethics and the law //

The law is often regarded as the minimum requirement for ethical behaviour, and it is generally agreed that breaking the law is morally wrong. However, the problem faced by accountants is that some taxpayers do not have the same respect for the tax law as they do for the law generally. The mindset of many taxpayers is that the tax law is a special case. There appears to be a 'catch me if you can' attitude or an opinion that non-compliance with tax law, or bending it a little, is not really breaking the law. We suggest that those who take the greatest risks with non-compliance least understand the connection between ethics and the law.

The rationale supporting the evasion of tax stems from an attitude that claims, 'the government can afford it', and 'no one is being hurt'. If this were only true! Widespread tax evasion has a number of adverse effects. First, it places a disproportionate burden on other taxpayers, who are committed to paying their fair share of taxes. If one citizen escapes their just tax, others must pay more. Second, increasing the tax burden to compensate for the tax evasion will reduce disposable incomes and consumption expenditure, which will hamper economic and employment growth. Third, government expenditure on public services might be reduced as an alternative to increasing the tax rates, which will have adverse consequences on those reliant on such services. Clearly, evading tax is not in the interests of the community.

In this section, we briefly examine the ethics of the taxpayer, by looking at the extent of taxpayer compliance with tax laws. Taxpayer compliance is becoming an increasingly voluntary activity, with the onus on the taxpayer to justify their taxation claims. According to Pilkington (1998), taxpayer compliance is directly related to the threat of a tax audit and the perceived threat of detection from the taxing authority. Not surprisingly, the level of compliance is greatest when the source of taxable income is perceived to be readily and independently verifiable, such as bank interest. The type of taxpayer is another indicator of compliance. For example, older taxpayers, female taxpayers, and taxpayers with middle to higher-level incomes are inclined to overestimate the probability of detection from taxing authorities, and are therefore more compliant. Evidence also shows that self-employed taxpayers, compared to wage and salary earners, have greater opportunity to evade tax and are more likely to do so. In summary, it appears that taxpayers are more likely to comply with the tax laws when the details are verifiable and the threat of detection is high. However, it appears that when these factors are absent, tax-payers are influenced by their own situational needs and perceived opportunities.

In the one-year period to 30 June 2003, the Australian Taxation Office (ATO) received 51 000 reports on suspected incidences of taxpayers defrauding the tax system. The most common reports were about the cash economy, undeclared business income, overstated expenses, and goods and services tax (GST) collected from customers but not remitted to the ATO (Commonwealth of Australia, 2003). Some examples of actual tax frauds emanating from these reports are presented in the section, In practice: Tax evaders.

## IN PRACTICE

### Tax evaders

The following is a list of examples that typically represent fraud perpetrators.

- An employer was ordered to pay over $13 000 in tax and penalties when they failed to provide an employee with a payment summary, did not account for GST, and failed to remit to the ATO taxes deducted from employees' wages.
- A company was ordered to pay approximately $6 million in tax and penalties for falsely claiming GST refunds.
- A takeaway food retailer was ordered to pay an extra $2.5 million in tax and penalties for not declaring business income and not remitting to the ATO the GST collected from customers and tax withheld from wages.
- A manufacturer was ordered to pay $170 000 in tax and penalties. The case involved private expenses against tax, GST-related offences and failure to pay employee superannuation contributions.
- A company was ordered to pay $150 000 in tax penalties when it failed to ask employees to complete employment declaration forms and paid them cash in hand.
- The owner of a hairdressing business was alleged to refuse to give receipts, had high living expenses, yet boasted of receiving benefits from Centrelink. The taxpayer paid $8000 in tax and penalties.
- At the time of this publication, a software company was being investigated by the ATO for promoting software designed to hide transactions.

*Source:* Commonwealth of Australia 2003.

## The roles of the tax accountant //

The tax accountant's responsibilities, when dealing with tax avoidance and tax evasion, entail a multiplicity of roles. The accountant has a primary duty to the client, but must also recognise an obligation to the government and to the public it represents. In this sense, tax accountants play a dual role: enforcer and exploiter of the taxation system. Accountants enforce the tax law when the law is clear and unequivocal, but exploit the tax laws when they are ambiguous. The degree to which accountants exploit the law depends on the situation and the integrity of the particular accountant. In general, the accountant is not an agent of the government and has a primary responsibility to the client, to legally minimise the client's tax liability and avoid unnecessary overpayment of tax. The accountant also owes a duty to keep their clients out of trouble and to advise them against underpayments of tax that may attract penalties.

## Contingent fees and taxation services //

Setting and collecting fees is an area of major concern for tax accountants. We discuss establishing appropriate charges, rates and commissions later in this chapter, in the section entitled 'Professional fees'. In this section, we discuss the ethical implications of setting a fee that is contingent on the amount of 'tax saved', or the size of the tax refund. Before we discuss the problems associated with tax-related contingency-based fees, we must first explore the notion of 'tax saved'. A properly prepared tax return will result in an appropriately determined tax liability; therefore, there is no basis for computing a tax saving. If there is no basis for computing tax saved, then there is no basis for setting a fee on the amount of tax saved.

A **contingent fee** is a fee for performing any service in which the amount of the fee depends on the outcome of a transaction or the result of the service. The problem with contingency based fees in taxation, regardless of whether they are based on the amount of the tax refund or some arbitrary notion of tax saved, is that they unwittingly produce optimistic interpretations of the tax law, motivated by the desire to maximise the amount of the tax refund and hence the size of the fee. Therefore, linking the fee to the amount of the tax liability is improper. In general, an accountant should not accept a contingent fee for the preparation of an original or amended tax return, or a claim on a tax refund. This prohibition ensures potential conflicts of interest are avoided and the accountant's objectivity is preserved.

It is common practice for tax accountants to deposit their clients' taxation refund cheques into the firm's trust account, then pay the client the balance after deducting the accountant's fee. This method of collecting fees is a contentious issue, and it is a common complaint confronting the profession's disciplinary machine. Depositing client moneys into the accountant's trust account threatens the accountant's integrity, particularly when prior approval has not been obtained from the client. A taxation cheque payable to the client belongs to the client and cannot be negotiated without the client's authority. Fees due from a client can only be drawn from the client's taxation cheque provided the client, after being notified of the amount of the fee, has agreed, preferably in writing, to such an arrangement.

# Conflicts with professional fees //

Establishing compensation arrangements is one of the most troublesome issues facing accountants. In this section, we rely heavily on the official pronouncements of the accounting profession. They include Professional Statement F.1: 'Professional Independence' and Professional Statement F.6: 'Professional Fees' from the *Joint Code of Professional Conduct*, and the *Proposed Revised Code of Ethics for Professional Accountants* issued by IFAC in 2003. As discussed in chapter 3, the *Revised Code of Ethics for Professional Accountants* adopts a conceptual framework approach for applying the fundamental principles of professional conduct. This approach requires accountants to identify, evaluate, and address the threats to compliance with the fundamental principles of professional conduct. If the identified threats are significant, accountants should take appropriate action to eliminate them or reduce them to an acceptable level. This conceptual framework approach, as proposed in the revised code of ethics, will form the basis of discussion in this section.

## Undue dependence on one client //

At the centre of many conflicts is the desire to earn ample income while trying to uphold the high ethical standards advanced by the profession. However, the pursuit of greater income may at times jeopardise the appearance or reality of ethical propriety. A client is important to the wealth of the firm and the success of all the accounting staff involved. If a single client represents a significant part of the firm's overall revenue, pursuing issues or concerns that may jeopardise that relationship becomes risky. On the other hand, if a client's total contribution to the firm's overall revenue is relatively small, the firm and its management are more likely to stand fast on ethical principles.

When the receipt of recurring fees from a client or group of connected clients represents a large proportion of the total gross fees of an accounting firm, or the individual **partner**, the extent of dependence on that client (or group) will inevitably raise doubts as to the accountant's objectivity. The economic dependence of that client on the firm can create revenue or career related pressures that might threaten the partner's objective and professional judgment. Under pressure, whether real or perceived, the partner may be tempted to err in favour of the client. For example, the partner may accept marginal accounting practices from an audit client because of subtle suggestions that the engagement may be lost. In addition to lost fees, threats of resignation from clients can have serious impacts on the careers of individual partners, which in turn can compromise their objectivity. For example, the partner could be concerned that the client will ask the firm to appoint a new partner because of a disagreement. Arthur Andersen's technical partner was removed from the Enron audit because he was giving answers that Enron considered too harsh (Siegel and McGrath 2003).

The problem with fees is that they create a **self-interest threat**. According to Professional Statement F.1: *Independence*, a self-interest threat occurs when a firm, or a member of the firm can benefit from a financial interest, or other self-interest conflict, with a client (F.1, paragraph 1.23). Undue dependence on total fees from a client and concern for the possibility of losing an engagement are two examples provided in Professional Statement F.1 that create a self-interest threat. Precise guidance on the proportion of fees from one client that would constitute a self-interest threat is difficult to measure accurately. However, in Professional Statement F.1, 'Appendix 2, Application of principles to specific situations', recurring fees that exceed 15 per cent of the firm's revenue may bring to account independence issues. In general, if the fees in question are the only income or a substantial part of the firm's gross income, the firm should carefully consider its position.

When faced with such conflicts, what should the firm or partner do? Two types of safeguards are available that can reduce the significance of the self-interest threat to an acceptable level. First, accounting firms can reduce the amount of fees and subsequent dependence on the client, by either declining to provide some services or subcontracting part of the engagement to another accounting firm. In some cases, the fees could be so large that no amount of lowering could reduce the threat to an acceptable level. If these steps are inadequate, and maintaining objectivity is impossible, the firm should withdraw or decline the engagement.

Second, the firm should create a supportive culture with a track record of doing the right thing. Partners must stand up to clients who threaten their self-interest and believe that they can count on their firm and colleagues for support. The firm should adopt a supportive culture by not tolerating clients who use intimidation to persuade the partner. The firm should encourage partners to consult with other partners or members of the firm on difficult issues, and ensure that everyone understands that the firm views consultation as a strength, not a weakness. According to the Task Force on Rebuilding Public Confidence (IFAC 2003, p. 34), the firm needs to have in place a process for consultation which is robust enough to deal with cases, ensuring that decisions are the firm's decisions and not those of the individual partner. The consultative process should ensure that quality related decisions that may have a negative impact on the firm's short-term revenue are not affected by the partners' concerns about the impact on their own remuneration. The process must support the partner in communicating problems and in making the right decisions.

## Low-balling //

In general, there are two compensatory methods for charging clients: agreement to a specific fee (quotation), or arrangement of a charging basis calculated by reference to hourly rates. In regard to charging, Professional Statement F.6: *Professional Fees* of the *Joint Code of Professional Conduct* does not set charge rates nor does it prescribe the basis for calculating fees; it sets out the criteria upon which fees should be based. In principle, **professional fees** must reflect fairly and equitably the value of the work performed for the client (F.6, paragraph 1). As a matter of practice, accountants should inform the client in writing, prior to commencement of the engagement, of the basis upon which the fee will be calculated. If there are any changes to the fee structure, the client must be advised without delay.

Fees are normally determined by using appropriate rates per hour, based on factors such as the skill, knowledge, and time of all persons engaged on the work performed (F.6, paragraph 1). However, estimated fees or quotations are becoming more common. According to paragraph 5 of Professional Statement F.6, quotations are permissible so long as the quote is based on a reasonable estimation of the time, skills, and resources required to complete the job competently and diligently. Quotations are prohibited when, at the time of the quotation, it is thought the actual fee is likely to be substantially more than the estimated fee.

When entering into negotiations with prospective clients, accountants may quote whatever fee they deem appropriate. The fact that one accountant may quote a fee lower than another accountant is not in itself unethical. However, self-interest threats may arise that will compromise the principle of **competence and due care** if the fee quoted is so low that it may be difficult to perform the engagement satisfactorily. For example, the firm may eliminate or reduce the number of audit procedures, without a corresponding change in the assessed level of audit risk, in order to meet tight budgets resulting from an abnormally low quotation. The practice of undercutting, also known as **low-balling** in the vernacular, is practised by some accounting firms to get a 'foot in the door' and eventually secure more lucrative management advisory or other consulting services. Today's public accounting industry is big business, and consulting services comprise a significant portion of a firm's total revenue. While low-balling is a profitable marketing strategy, accountants have a responsibility to perform services with integrity and objectivity, and in accordance with appropriate technical standards. Low-balling that creates undue pressure and compromises professional standards is inconsistent with these responsibilities.

However, low-balling can be acceptable when safeguards are in place to reduce the self-interest threat to an acceptable level. Clients should be made aware of the terms of the engagement and, in particular, the basis on which fees are charged and quoted. This includes the services that are covered by the quoted fee, and assigning appropriate time and qualified staff to the task. In rendering professional services, the firm must ensure it complies with all applicable assurance standards, guidelines, and quality control procedures (F.6, paragraph 5). Fee quotations should be made only after proper consideration of the nature of the client's business, the complexity of the operation, and the work performed.

## Commissions //

**Commissions** are generated for recommending or referring a product or service, usually for the purchase or sale of a financial product supplied by a third party. For example, accountants may receive commissions from third parties in connection with the sale of goods or services to a client, such as insurance or investment products. Accepting such commissions may give rise to self-interest threats, because sound judgment may be influenced by the fee dependency. That is, a commission bias arises when an adviser favours one product over another in order to earn a higher commission. Consequently, commission-based advisers are more inclined to offer poor financial advice compared to fee-based peers. This is not to say that fees based on hourly charge rates are without a potential bias. It is possible for a fee-based adviser to drag on the time of the consultation to earn more fees. In practice, however, many accountants use commissions to subsidise their clients' fees. Setting fees entirely on hourly charge rates might mean a higher fee charged to clients, compared with commission-based fees.

In general, accountants may accept commissions that are disclosed to clients, except in situations where accountants perform traditional audit and assurance functions. Commissions are acceptable only when performing non-audit related services such as personal financial planning. This is because audit-related services are directly linked to the public interest. Third party users may lack confidence in financial reports that are audited under a fee arrangement carrying a self-interest threat. Furthermore, third party users are at risk of loss from poor professional judgment caused by commission-based fees. This risk is considered unfair when users must shoulder the burden of potential losses without express or implied consent to the fee arrangement. Refusal to accept and perform the audit engagement is the only acceptable safeguard against threats created by commissions (F.1, paragraph 2.110).

Unlike audit engagements, non-audit related services offered by accountants affect only the client. Therefore, commission-based fees in non-audit situations are acceptable when the client is aware, and agrees to the risks and burdens. The most important safeguard in relation to commissions is transparency. Accountants must disclose the details of the commission in writing to the client, including its basis and terms (F.6, paragraph 8). Clients need to understand how much they will pay if they are to feel comfortable with the pricing arrangement and the potential risks. If the client feels threatened by the commission-based arrangement, disclosure of the commission will provide the non-audit client with the opportunity to refuse this service. This rationale is the basis for the Australian Securities and Investments Commission (ASIC) decision against RetireInvest, whose advisers failed to disclose their commissions (ASIC 2003). Refer to 'In practice: RetireInvest' for further detail.

### RetireInvest

An investigation by ASIC into RetireInvest, a financial services provider and licensed securities dealer, found that some authorised representatives (advisers) failed to:

- fully disclose the fees, commissions and benefits they received, so that investors were not fully informed of the incentives that might have tainted their decisions
- obtain all necessary information to ensure clients were placed in investments consistent with their needs and risk profile.

ASIC expressed concern that the breaches occurred because the compliance systems and processes were inadequate and the internal complaint handling rules were not always followed. As a consequence, RetireInvest and ASIC entered into an 'enforceable undertaking' — a voluntary undertaking by RetireInvest, enforceable by ASIC in court. Details of the enforceable undertaking include:

- posting a notice in its client newsletter and on its website providing details of the enforceable undertaking to encourage grieved clients to come forward
- engaging an independent consultant to review the practices and ensure ASIC's concerns are addressed
- implementing all the recommendations made by the independent consultant
- providing remedial training to authorised representatives who do not understand their responsibilities
- providing formal training to all relevant employees in the operations, practice, and procedures of the complaints handling system.

According to ASIC, the enforceable undertaking aims to improve the compliance standards within RetireInvest and to provide redress for clients who may have been adversely affected by the company's poor compliance standards.

*Source:* ASIC 2003.

## Unpaid fees //

Unpaid fees create a self-interest threat that may impair independence because such fees are tantamount to having a financial interest in, or making a loan to a client (F.1, paragraph 2.105). A financial interest in a client has the potential to impair, if only in appearance, objective judgment, in order to protect the collectibility of the outstanding fees. The self-interest threat may be reduced to an acceptable level if, at the time of the current engagement, a definite commitment is made by the audit client to pay delinquent fees before the current engagement is completed. Alternatively, an arrangement may be entered into for the client to make periodic payments for remittance of the delinquent fees. Depending on the significance of the threat and the likelihood of payment, the firm should consider whether it is appropriate to be reappointed for future engagements.

# Conflicts with changes in professional appointments //

Professional Statement F.3: 'Changes in Professional Appointments' describes the accountant's responsibilities in dealing with new and potential clients. Respecting the wishes of the client when choosing their professional adviser is the foundation principle underlying the structure of Professional Statement F.3. Clients have an indisputable right to choose their professional advisers and to change to others should they so desire (F.3, paragraph 2). Accordingly, a public accountant must not attempt to restrict in any way the client's freedom to change to another accountant or to obtain specialist advice. When an accountant is approached by a potential client, the accountant is free to discuss a possible engagement, even though the client is presently served by another accountant. However, it is considered professional etiquette to defer acceptance of the appointment until the proposed accountant has formally communicated with the existing accountant.

When an accountant is asked to provide services or advice, inquiries should be made to determine whether the prospective client has an existing accountant. Communicating with the existing accountant enables the proposed accountant to properly ascertain if there are any professional reasons, such as a self-interest threat, for not accepting the appointment (F.3, paragraph 3). For example, the information provided by the existing accountant may indicate that the reasons given by the client for the change in appointment are not in accordance with the facts obtained from the existing accountant. Communication may also disclose that the client's proposal to change their accountant was made because the existing accountant stood their ground and properly carried out the duties of professional accountants, in spite of the opposition or evasion from the client. Therefore, communication between accountants serves as a safeguard to protect the proposed accountant from accepting an appointment in circumstances where all the pertinent facts are unknown.

Before accepting a new client relationship, the accountant must consider whether acceptance poses any threats to their independence or integrity. For example, clients may have a personal or financial relationship with the accountant, or the client could be involved in illegal activities such as money laundering or questionable financial reporting activities. Ascertaining reasons for accepting the appointment cannot be done effectively without direct communication with the existing accountant; but before communication occurs, the prospective accountant must receive the client's permission to communicate with the existing accountant (F.3, paragraph 7). In turn, the existing accountant is also bound by a duty of confidentiality and must not volunteer information on client affairs without the client's permission.

With client consent, the existing accountant should be honest, unambiguous and provide all the information needed to enable the proposed accountant to decide whether or not to accept the appointment. If permission is not granted, the existing accountant should report that fact to the proposed accountant, and the proposed accountant should consider declining the appointment. If the proposed accountant does not receive a reply from the existing accountant within a reasonable time, the proposed accountant should send a letter confirming the assumption that there is no professional reason why the appointment should not be accepted and that there is an intention to do so (F.3, paragraph 9). After a change of appointment has been effected, the existing accountant must make available for collection to the proposed accountant all books, papers and documents belonging to the client (F.3, paragraph 10).

The fact that there may be fees owing to the existing accountant is not a professional reason for another accountant not to accept the appointment. It is the existing accountant's responsibility to take reasonable steps to resolve any disputes relating to the fee. The rules pertaining to changes in professional appointments are not designed to resolve fee disputes but to reduce delays that can exist where existing accountants are owed money and are not prepared to sue for their fees.

# Conflicts arising from referring clients with special needs //

Accountants may sometimes feel they are stuck between the proverbial rock and a hard place as clients request more one-stop shopping. As the variety of services offered to clients broadens in response to clients' needs, the demand for special skills also increases. Accountants are forced either to expand their services or refer some services to other professionals. When a firm lacks the required skills, **referrals** to specialists become increasingly common. However, in accounting, referrals may not occur in the same way as commonly practised in other more mature professions such as medicine. The reluctance on the part of accountants to rely on referrals is due in part to a fear that the specialist may replace the accountant and render the recurring services originally provided by the referring accountant. As a result, clients may be deprived of receiving the expert advice that they are entitled to receive.

The reluctance to rely on referrals is unfortunate, because accountants, like all professionals, must be in a position to competently perform whatever engagements they undertake. When accountants lack the necessary skill or knowledge required for a particular task or engagement, there is a clear threat to their ability to perform the required services with competence and diligence. A self-interest threat arises when accountants accept an engagement without having the necessary specialist knowledge for the competent performance of that engagement. In general, accountants should only undertake such services when they have the requisite skill and can expect to complete the task with professional competence. If the required skill or knowledge is absent, it is essential for the client that the accountant seeks advice and assistance from those who are competent to provide it.

In order to protect the referring accountant and maintain confidence in the system of referrals, paragraph 5 of Professional Statement F.4: 'Referrals' states that the receiving accountant must comply with the instructions received from the referring accountant, and limit the services provided to the specific assignment received by the referral. The receiving accountant also has a duty to take reasonable steps to support the referring accountant's current relationship with the client, and should not express any criticism of the professional services of the referring accountant without giving the latter an opportunity to provide all relevant information.

# Conflicts with giving second opinions //

**Opinion shopping** begins when a client is displeased with the auditor's judgment on the application of accounting or auditing standards. Suppose the client has a difference of opinion with the auditor as to the propriety of a particular accounting or auditing treatment. In this situation, the client may seek a second opinion from the auditor's competitors about the disputed treatment. If the second opinion does not meet the client's expectations, then the client could continue seeking further opinions, possibly on the basis of massaged facts, until they obtain an opinion that supports their desired position.

Seeking second opinions is not in itself a troublesome practice. For example, second opinions are common in medicine when a patient is faced with a major surgery, or in business when a valuable asset is being appraised. However, in auditing, problems arise when the client succeeds in obtaining a view favourable to their position and uses this opinion to apply pressure on the existing auditor to give way, in the knowledge that if the auditor fails to be persuaded, the firm will lose the audit. Similarly, the client may decide to change the auditor, safe in the knowledge that a more favourable opinion is in their back pocket. Conflicts of interest may also arise for the second auditor if they accept an engagement and once involved in the engagement, they find the facts and circumstances to be different to those they were originally led to expect.

In the commercial and competitive business of accounting services, clients have learned to shop for accounting and audit opinions. The pressure of playing one accounting firm or partner against another is one way clients can persuade accountants into submission on disputed accounting issues. According to paragraph 1.27 of Professional Statement F.1, **intimidation threats** arise when an auditing firm is threatened with replacement over a disagreement about a client's application of accounting principles, or if an auditor believes that the client's expression of dissatisfaction will damage the partner's career within the firm. In these circumstances, accountants have a responsibility to remain objective and not allow the client to influence their professional judgment. Accountants should select the accounting principles that best depict the economic facts of a transaction, or the principles that give the fairest most balanced financial position. To do otherwise could impair the credibility of the financial statements and the quality of subsequent investment decisions.

Professional Statement F.5: 'Opinion Requests', sets out the issues and professional responsibilities for dealing with second opinions. When a second auditor is asked to provide an opinion, the threat of intimidation can be mitigated by seeking the client's permission to contact the existing auditor. Before the second auditor offers an opinion, they must communicate with the existing auditor and request access to all relevant information to ensure the second opinion is based on the same facts and circumstances available to the existing auditor (F.5, paragraph 1). Communicating with the existing auditor will bring to light any relevant facts that should be considered in preparing the opinion, and ensure a fully informed second opinion. It is important that the existing auditor, with the permission of the client, provides the second auditor with all the relevant information about the client. With client consent, the second auditor should also provide a copy of their opinion to the existing auditor. If the client seeking the opinion will not permit communication with the existing auditor, the second auditor should consider whether it is appropriate to provide the opinion that is being sought (IFAC 2003, paragraph 5.3). If at any time the second auditor believes that the request for an opinion will have an adverse impact on the auditor's professional responsibilities, the request for an opinion should be declined (F.5, paragraph 2).

# Conflicts created by incompatible activities //

The profession has no desire to unduly restrict business or investment activities in which members may engage outside of their professional activities. However, accountants should not concurrently engage in any business, occupation or activity that impairs objectivity or independence, or the good reputation of the profession (F.7, paragraph 1). Any simultaneous engagement or activity that prohibits the accountant from the proper conduct of services is regarded as incompatible with the rendering of professional services.

According to paragraph 3 of Professional Statement F.7: 'Incompatible Duties', **incompatible activities** are any activities, including a business, job or service, that create conflicts of interest, impair the good reputation of the profession, and impair the ability to provide an objective and competent service to clients and the public. For example, many new public accountants building their practice often work as salaried accountants to supplement their income until their own practice is self-sustaining. In such circumstances, accountants have a right to work as employees and provide professional accounting services to willing clients. However, conflicts of interest arise when the accountant is unable to perform both tasks competently, and the quality of services rendered is impaired. In some cases, the time constraints imposed from over-commitment restricts the level of diligence applied to individual tasks. When the drive for income results in activities that threaten the principle of competence and due care, accountants should stem the amount of work for each activity undertaken (salary or public practice) or, alternatively, focus on only one activity. Accountants must never subordinate their professional responsibilities to their commercial interests. Self-interest must always be secondary or equal to the responsibility of providing quality service, never greater than.

# Avoiding and resolving conflicts of interest //

Some conflicts of interest are inevitable, and individuals have no responsibility for the conflicts of interest in which they are involved. For example, a judge does not act wrongly when a friend or relative appears before him or her in court. However, how the judge responds is critical to maintaining integrity and objectivity, and the confidence of those reliant on the judge's opinion. In this situation, the judge should eliminate the conflict of interest by stepping down and allowing someone else to try the case.

Accountants have a responsibility to take reasonable steps to avoid circumstances that could pose a conflict of interest between the client and themselves. Like judges, accountants need to be vigilant in identifying relationships and situations that could be viewed by others as presenting a conflict of interest. For example, auditors must not audit the financial statements of an entity owned by a close relative. When confronted with a conflict of interest, the accountant has three options, to:

1. remove themselves from the conflict
2. resign from their position or client
3. seek consent from all interested parties to continue in the position or relationship in spite of the conflict of interest.

Each of these options is discussed below.

## Remove themselves from the conflict //

Accountants can avoid conflicts of interest by removing themselves from the situation in which the conflict arises. As with the judge trying the case of a related party, conflicts of interest can often be avoided if the accountant asks someone else to assume their professional responsibilities. The accountant should not reveal the existence of the conflict, but simply turn over the decision to some other party. The accountant should consider withdrawing full explanation of the circumstances because, if the other party were aware of the nature of the conflict, then this itself may create a conflict of interest. The other party may feel pressured by having knowledge of the existing conflict (Carson 1994).

## Resign from the position or relationship //

Sometimes conflicts of interest can be avoided only if the accountant resigns from their position or client. For example, PwC had no choice but to resign as administrator of the Ansett Australia Group (see 'In practice: Ansett Australia Group', elsewhere in this chapter). The disadvantage with this option is that it often constitutes a serious hardship for the accountant or firm in question, and it might also be harmful to those they serve.

## Disclosure of conflict to all interested parties //

In cases in which an accountant becomes a party to a conflict of interest that cannot be avoided by withdrawing or resigning from their position, he or she may consider informing all interested parties and obtaining their informed consent to continue the relationship. This would allow clients to judge for themselves the likelihood of damage, if any, and by giving consent, the interested parties agree to bear the risk of the adverse effects from the conflict of interest. In some cases, however, disclosure is precluded due to constraints imposed by the principle of confidentiality. In situations where there is a conflict of interest between two clients, such as divorce or a company takeover, the accountant must not advise both clients on the matter, unless consent to do so is received from both clients. If consent from both parties is not received, the accountant should continue to advise only one client. However, in cases of divorce, there is the potential for more subtle consequences that are not immediately visible, such as the feeling of handicap by the estranged spouse in a hostile settlement.

# Summary //

Accountants face a conflict of interest when their personal interest interferes with the proper exercise of professional judgment. In this chapter we examined various conflicts of interest in which the economic needs of the firm or the accountant are at the core. Conflicts of interest that cause accountants to favour their own self-interest often come at the expense of their client or the public. The duties of an accountant when faced with a conflict of interest will vary depending on the circumstances; however, the guiding principle is simple: an accountant should withdraw or refuse to act in any engagement when there is likely to be a significant conflict of interest between themselves and the client. In a world in which we cannot assume high ethical standards, there must be strategies that will aid in reducing unethical behaviour. The professional requirement to avoid conflicts of interest between the accountant and the client, both in reality and appearance, is to be honoured at all times. In the next chapter, we examine conflicts of interest that are typically faced by accountants in business.

# Key terms //

Accountants in business ... p. 288
Client-centred conflicts of interest ... p. 287
Commissions ... p. 297
Competence and due care ... p. 296
Conflicts of interest ... p. 285
Contingent fee ... p. 293
Employer-centred conflicts of interest ... p. 288
Fiduciary relationship ... p. 285
Incompatible activities ... p. 303
Intimidation threat ... p. 302
Low-balling ... p. 296
Opinion shopping ... p. 301
Partner ... p. 294
Professional fees ... p. 296
Public accountants ... p. 287
Referrals ... p. 300
Self-interest ... p. 286
Self-interest threat ... p. 295
Tax avoidance ... p. 289
Tax avoidance schemes ... p. 289
Tax evasion ... p. 288

# Questions //

**11.1** Define 'conflicts of interest', its various elements, and the potential problems arising from conflict of interest situations.

**11.2** Distinguish a client-centred conflict of interest from an employer-centred conflict of interest. Illustrate your answer with an example.

**11.3** How does tax evasion differ from tax avoidance? What are the ethical responsibilities of the tax practitioner in dealing with tax avoidance?

**11.4** Describe the ethics of a tax evader. What is the typical rationale used by taxpayers to support tax evasion?

**11.5** A bookkeeping company has asked Gabriele, a tax accountant, to prepare tax returns on the basis of worksheets provided by the bookkeeping company. There would be no direct contact between Gabriele and the customers of the company. Gabriele asks you if he may enter into such an agreement. How should you respond?

**11.6** How can the fees from a single client constitute a self-interest threat? What should the accountant do when faced with such a threat?

**11.7** What are the threats from the practices of low-balling and opinion shopping that give rise to a conflict of interest? How can accountants mitigate such threats?

**11.8** What are the ethical implications of unpaid fees from an assurance client? Assume the client offers to pay the fees in instalments over a period of three years. Is this acceptable?

**11.9** Bill, a public accountant, earns revenue from commissions on the sale of insurance and investment products, and fees for the provision of auditing and taxation services. Is Bill facing a conflict of interest? Why?

**11.10** What is the purpose of seeking ethical clearance from an accountant before accepting a new appointment? You have asked the principal at Forma Accountants & Co for professional clearance in relation to a change of appointment. The principal is refusing to comply because she says that her firm is owed money. How would you respond?

**11.11** What are the advantages of referring clients to another accountant? What if a referral is made and the client requests an extension of the service beyond the specific engagement?

**11.12** List and describe the options available to an accountant in dealing with conflicts of interest.

## A taxing client

Jay Mackintosh is a public accountant in the suburbs of Perth. He specialises in accounting and taxation services for small businesses, and his practice relies primarily upon the businesses in the local area. Jay employs Amanda Lang, a part-time university student in her final year of an accounting degree program. Amanda has worked for Jay for five years while attending classes in the evenings. Amanda requires only four subjects to graduate, one of which is taxation.

Picture Perfect Pty Ltd (PP) has been a client of Jay's practice for four years. Picture Prefect's taxation return was initially prepared by Jay but, from the second year onwards, this responsibility fell to Amanda. Amanda is in the process of preparing the current year's tax return. In reviewing the previous working papers, Amanda discovers an error that understated PP's tax liability by $19 000. The total amount of tax liability reported on the previous year's return is $250 000.

Amanda brings the error to the attention of Julie Wong, the owner of Picture Perfect. Julie's response is terse, 'you caused it, you fix it'. She further states, 'I am not paying you until it's fixed'. Amanda is stunned by Julie's reaction and is unsure of how to deal with it. She raises the issue with Jay, and Jay tells her to review the working papers carefully to determine the cause of the error. If the error can be attributed to Julie furnishing erroneous information, then Jay will threaten to inform the Australian Taxation Office unless Julie promptly pays her account in full.

**Required (Answer each questions independently unless otherwise stated.)**

1 Is it appropriate for Jay to inform the ATO about the error discovered in PP's taxation return? Why? As a professional accountant, what are Jay's responsibilities now that the error has been discovered?

2 Assume the error was an oversight on Amanda's part. Has Amanda and/or Jay breached their professional responsibilities? If so, how?

3 Assume the error was the result of Amanda's reluctance to seek expert advice on a unique transaction. How would you explain to Jay the significance of seeking expert advice?

4 Assume Jay informs Amanda that the amount of the error is immaterial and he will compensate the error by overstating Julie's tax liability in the current year by $19 000. Discuss the ethical issues of this behaviour.

5 Jay discovers that the error was an intentional misstatement by Julie. He subsequently decides that Julie, as a client, is more trouble than she is worth. So, he deposits her tax refund cheque in his trust account, retains an amount equal to his fee and remits the balance to Julie. He also terminates his professional relationship with Julie, but agrees to speak glowingly of Julie to her next accountant. Discuss the ethical propriety of Jay's behaviour.

## FURTHER RESOURCES AND WEBSITES //

Brooks, LJ 2003, *Business and professional ethics for directors, executives and accountants*, 3rd edn, South Western, Ohio.

CPA Australia, 2003, *Public practice program*, CPA Australia, Melbourne.

Gaa, JC 1994, *The ethical foundations of public accounting*, Vancouver, CGA–Canada Research Foundation.

Leung, P and Dellaportas, S 1997, 'Conflicts of interest: an analysis of the concept in relation to auditors', *Perspectives on Contemporary Auditing*, vol. 20 no. 2, pp. 48–61.

Ponemon, LA and Gabhart, DRL 1993, *Ethical reasoning in accounting and auditing*, Vancouver, CGA–Canada Research Foundation.

Ramsay, I 2002, *Disclosure of fees and charges in managed investments: review of current Australian requirements and options for reform*, Report to the Australian Securities and Investments Commission.

### Websites

Australian Securities and Investments Commission, viewed 3 December 2003, www.asic.gov.au

Commonwealth of Australia 2003, Australian Taxation Office, Reporting Tax Evasion, viewed 3 December 2003, www.ato.gov.au

CPA Online 2003, CPA Australia, viewed, 3 December 2003, www.cpaaustralia.com.au

The Institute of Chartered Accountants 2003, viewed 3 December 2003, www.icaa.org,au

The International Federation of Accountants 2003, New York, viewed 3 December 2003, www.ifac.org

## REFERENCES //

Australian Securities and Investments Commission, 2003, 'Enforceable undertaking ensures redress for RetireInvest clients affected by poor compliance', *Media release 03-074*, Issued Thursday, 27 February 2003.

Carson, TL 1994, 'Conflicts of interest', *Journal of Business Ethics*, vol. 13 no. 5, pp. 387–404.

Commonwealth of Australia 2003, Australian Taxation Office, Tax evasion and the community — recent results and observations of the tax system in operation, viewed 17 November 2003, www.ato.gov.au.

CPA Australia and the Institute of Chartered Accountants in Australia, *Joint Code of Professional Conduct, Members' Handbook*, December 2002.

CPA Australia and the Institute of Chartered Accountants in Australia, APS 6 Statement of Taxation Standards, *Members' Handbook*, December 2002.

CPA Australia and the Institute of Chartered Accountants in Australia, Joint Guidance Notes, GN1 Members in Business Guidance Statement, Issued August 2002, *Members' Handbook*.

International Federation of Accountants, 2003, *Proposed Revised Code of Ethics for Professional Accountants*, IFAC, New York.

International Federation of Accountants, 2003, *Rebuilding public confidence in financial reporting: an international perspective*, The task force on rebuilding public confidence in financial reporting, IFAC, New York.

Leung, P and Cooper, B 1995, 'Ethical dilemmas in accountancy practice', *Australian Accountant*, May, vol. 65, no. 4, pp. 28–33.

Lynch, T 1987, 'Ethics in taxation practice', *The Accountant's Magazine*, November, pp, 27–8.

Pilkington, C 1998, 'Taxation and ethical issues', in *Ethical issues in accounting*, Gowthorpe, C and Blake, J eds, Routledge, New York, chapter 5, pp. 82–97.

Siegel, A and McGrath, S 2003, 'Recognising and addressing conflicts of interest', *The CPA Journal*, vol. 73 no. 4, pp. 6–11.

# Ethics in a corporate environment

# 12

## Learning objectives

After studying this chapter you should be able to:

- Describe the significance of truth in financial reporting.
- Describe the ethical issues and responsibilities when an accountant is faced with pressure from an employer to collude in deceptive financial reporting.
- Explain why a financial interest in an employer creates a self-interest threat.
- Explain the phrase 'whistleblowing' and its implications for the notions of loyalty and confidentiality.
- Describe the typical reactions to a whistleblower and the conditions that justify blowing the whistle.
- Describe the circumstances that determine whether an accountant should accept or reject a gift.
- Discuss the ethical problems that can arise from conducting business cross-nationally.
- Describe benefits and limitations of cultural relativism and universalism.
- Define the term 'corporate culture' and explain its influence on employee behaviour.
- Explain how corporate leaders can manage the ethics of an organisation.

'All that is necessary for evil to triumph is for good men to do nothing.'
**Edmund Burke, 18th-century English political philosopher**

# Introduction //

Client-centred conflicts of interest and related issues were discussed in chapter 11. In this chapter, we continue the theme, conflicts of interest; but, rather than client-centred conflicts, we focus on employer-centred conflicts of interest. We pay particular attention to the problems faced by accountants in business, their professional responsibilities, and potential remedies in dealing with such problems. Discussion in this chapter is based on five distinct themes. The first three themes deal directly with the accountant and employer-centred conflicts. First, we examine the conflicts created by employers who seek liberal interpretations of accounting standards. Second, we examine the personal and professional dilemmas that accountants and other professionals face when they consider blowing the whistle. Third, we draw attention to the factors that accountants should consider before they accept or reject business-related gifts and hospitality.

In the last two themes of this chapter, we focus on the problems and issues facing organisations, rather than individual accountants. The fourth theme examines the challenges created by the internationalisation of business and the impact of nationally defined culture on business ethics. In the final theme, we examine corporate culture and the influence of management on the ethical behaviour of their employees.

# Accountants in business and financial reporting //

A **public accountant** is one who renders professional services to clients for a fee such as assurance and taxation services. An **accountant in business** is one who is employed in commerce and industry or the public sector and earns a salary rather than a fee. Accountants in business are also known as salaried accountants, employed accountants, and internal accountants. Accountants in business have many responsibilities, but they usually fall within two broad categories: the preparation and reporting of financial and other information; and providing effective financial management and competent advice to senior managers on a variety of business-related matters. In this section, we focus on the role of accountants as preparers of financial information.

Efficient capital markets depend on reliable, relevant, understandable, and comparable financial information in allocating scarce resources. The company's financial statements are normally the primary source of financial information from which users make investment or other decisions. The public, including investors, lenders, and government agencies all rely on the financial representations and disclosures prepared by accountants. Distorted financial information released to the public will ultimately result in sub-optimal decisions, to the detriment of the users. Accurate recording and reporting of financial information is arguably the most essential job responsibility of accountants, because the welfare of users is vitally affected by the competence and quality of information prepared by accountants in business. Therefore, the services performed by accountants in business bear significant value to society; and the level of competence with which they function, or how responsibly they conduct themselves, is important.

Accountants must recognise the importance of professionalism in carrying out their different roles. Like public accountants, accountants in business are held to be publicly accountable, not just accountable to their private conscience. In a competitive environment in which individuals and organisations are trying to survive, conflicts of interest may arise that result in the erosion of professional attitudes. Money, power, prestige, pride, and position have always put pressure on truth, fairness, humility, and honesty. Unfortunately, with businesses such as Enron and WorldCom fostering a culture of aggressive and creative accounting, the battle for truth and fairness appears to be losing to deception and lies. Companies like Enron and WorldCom are now infamous for engaging in complex creative accounting transactions that deliberately obscure their true financial position and performance.

In this section, we discuss two potential conflicts of interest facing accountants in business. First, we consider the demands of the employer at odds with the accountant's professional responsibility to report fairly and accurately. Second, we consider conflicts that arise from having a financial interest in the employing entity. The following discussion draws heavily on the *Proposed Revised Code of Ethics for Professional Accountants* issued by the International Federation of Accountants (IFAC 2003).

## Pressure to collude //

Accountants in business have a professional responsibility to support the legitimate and ethical objectives established by their employers (IFAC 2003, paragraph C.1.5). However, there are times when the accountant's responsibilities to the employing organisation conflict with their obligations to comply with the fundamental principles of professional conduct. The external financial reports, which are ultimately management's responsibility, are the representations of the company. A conflict arises when management propose an accounting policy or directive that may affect the faithful representation of the company's financial performance or position. In response, the accountant may either comply with management's proposals and face possible sanctions by the relevant professional body, or they can challenge the employer's position and face possible repercussions from their employer, such as delayed promotion or termination. In such cases, there is enormous pressure on the accountant to go along with the employer's demands — particularly when success within an organisation is judged on the basis of employer satisfaction.

Accountants in business must be alert to such pressures so that they are not exploited by management for window dressing the accounts. Like public accountants, accountants in business have a responsibility to ensure the financial reports are not misleading or inaccurate, and that no material items are omitted. Professionalism calls for accountants to respond to the community interests and not their own. It is important that the public regard internal accountants as persons of integrity and objectivity. Users are unlikely to believe accountants who put personal rewards ahead of services to the public. Therefore, accountants must ensure that they are not pressured by their employers to put a positive spin on the company's position.

The problem with such pressures is that they often lead to **intimidation threats**. An intimidation threat arises when there is a threat of dismissal or replacement of the professional accountant in business, or of a family member, over a disagreement about the application of an accounting principle, or the way in which financial information is to be reported (IFAC 2003, paragraph C.1.14). Consequently, the accountant may be deterred from acting objectively. In response to such threats, internal accountants must, in the first instance, refuse to collude in such matters. If management continues to apply pressure to collude, the accountant should then raise the issue with a party, usually a higher authority within the employing entity, for example, the audit committee. Alternatively, the accountant may draw on the formal dispute resolution process within the employing organisation. If the dispute remains unresolved, the accountant may seek advice from an independent professional adviser or the relevant professional accounting body. Ultimately, the accountant may consider resigning from the employing organisation. If the option to resign is pursued, accountants should give their reasons for resigning, but their duty of confidentiality precludes them from communicating their reasons to external parties. In circumstances where the accountant believes that unethical behaviours or actions will continue to occur after their resignation, they may consider seeking legal advice.

## Financial interest in the employer //

In previous chapters we learned that the concept of independence is vital to the roles and existence of the accounting profession. Without at least the appearance of independence, the public will lose faith in the reports prepared and audited by accountants. Members of the public accounting profession maintain independence by avoiding relationships — such as a financial interest in clients — that could be viewed by others as presenting a conflict of interest. However, the situation is different for accountants in business. Accountants in business cannot maintain the appearance of independence, due to the contractual nature of their relationship with their employer. In this sense, the concept of independence has no direct relevance to the employed accountant.

Even though the nature of the relationship between an employer and an accountant in business precludes them from maintaining the appearance of independence, this does not absolve accountants from their professional duty to report accurately and fairly. The form of the relationship with the employing organisation has no bearing on the ethical responsibilities incumbent on accountants in business. According to Professional Statement F.1: 'Professional Independence', an accountant in business has a duty to be objective in carrying out his or her professional work, whether or not the appearance of professional independence is attainable. Thus, an accountant performing professional work in commerce, industry or the public service, must be alert to the problems created by employer–employee relationship that might threaten their objectivity.

The problem with a financial interest in the employing organisation, such as owning shares or share options, or eligibility in a profit-related bonus, is that it creates a **self-interest threat**. Self-interest threats can obscure objective judgment when accountants have motive and opportunity to manipulate price-sensitive information in order to gain financially (IFAC 2003, paragraph C.5.1). This issue is becoming increasingly important, with many large organisations offering their employees, including accountants, the opportunity to participate in company share participation plans. Such plans allow employees to purchase shares in their employing organisation, usually on favourable terms. If the financial interest in the employer is significant, accountants have a responsibility to disclose all relevant interests, and any plans to trade in relevant shares to those charged with the governance of the employing organisation. Disclosing the financial interest allows senior personnel to consider the nature of the conflict and potential consequences. In effect, the company is in a position to manage the risk of the adverse effects from the conflict of interest and give consent to continue or change the nature of the relationship.

# Whistleblowing //

Blowing the whistle normally occurs in sport to indicate foul play. In business, **whistleblowing** occurs when one or more employees disclose, without authorisation, information about an unethical or illegal act by the employing organisation, to a party external to the employing organisation that owns the information. Two important conditions are necessary to satisfy the definition of a **whistleblower**. First, the information is disclosed without permission from the employing organisation, and second, the information is released to an external party rather than an internal party. In this context, an external party could be the public, media, or an appropriate government agency. When information is reported within the organisation, the whistleblowing is internal; when it is reported to an outsider, it is external. **Internal whistleblowing** is discussed in the section entitled 'Internal whistleblowing' on page 319 of this chapter. For the remainder of this section, the term 'whistleblowing' is synonymous with **external whistleblowing**.

The issue of accountants acting as whistleblowers is extremely complex; involving economic, social and emotional conflicts at personal and professional levels. As with the previous topic in this chapter, whistleblowing is a conflict of interest: a conflict between protecting the public interest and the duty of loyalty and confidentiality to their employer.

## A duty of loyalty //

Whistleblowing raises important questions about the loyalties of employees. At the core, the issue is whether accountants should blow the whistle on their employing organisation to protect the public from its harmful acts. As employees, accountants enter into a contractual agreement to act on behalf of the employer in all matters pertaining to the business. The question is whether this agreement imposes an unlimited obligation to turn a blind eye to immoral conduct by the employer or colleagues.

To some, employees have a prima facie duty of **loyalty** to their employers (Corvino 2002). Since employers rarely approve of whistleblowing and generally feel it is not in their best interests, it follows that whistleblowing is an act of betrayal (Larmer 1992). According to this view, the silent loyalty overrides the individual employee's sense of moral or social duty. In this context, whistleblowing cannot be justified, even on the basis of a higher duty to the public good. Whistleblowing is thus an act of disloyalty and is morally wrong, because employees have a moral obligation to their employer.

The issue raised here is whether the employee's duty to the employer outweighs their obligation to society. The problem with having a prima facie duty of loyalty to the employing organisation is that it sometimes conflicts with other duties, such as the duty to blow the whistle in response to dangerous or unethical practices by the employer. Loyalty is a valued trait, but it does not imply that employees have a duty to refrain from reporting the immoral actions of those to whom they are loyal. This is particularly important for accountants, who have a professional duty — possibly more than any other profession — to protect the public interest ahead of their loyalty to the employer. Commentators argue that an employee who blows the whistle is demonstrating greater loyalty in protecting the public interest than the loyal employee who ignores the immoral conduct (Larmer 1992, p. 127). Therefore, maintaining silence and allowing the violation to continue unabated is unethical. In fact, silence might even suggest an implication in the malpractice.

Although it is reasonable to claim that employees have a loyalty to their employing organisations, the loyalty is not absolute. Just as an employee can resign from an organisation when participation is no longer beneficial, an employee can speak out when serious moral costs are at stake. Similarly, just as an employer who is acting immorally is not acting in the best interests of the company, an employee who blows the whistle is not acting disloyally. Loyalty is only a virtue when the object of that loyalty is good (Corvino 2002).

## A duty of confidentiality //

The position of the would-be whistleblower accountant is complicated by the accountant's duty of **confidentiality** (*Joint Code of Professional Conduct*, section B.5) on the one hand and the **public interest** (*Joint Code of Professional Conduct*, section B.1) on the other. Accountants are required to act in the best interests of the public, while also keeping the concerns of their employment confidential. Unfortunately, whistleblowing occurs because it is sometimes impossible to achieve both, and in order to ensure the public interest is upheld, the principle of confidentially must be breached.

The principle of confidentiality precludes an accountant disclosing information obtained in the course of his or her employment, without express consent from their employer. Treating such information with the utmost confidentiality is a fiduciary obligation. However, problems arise when the employer is acting illegally or unethically. Unfortunately, the ethical guidelines of the professional accounting bodies offer little support to would-be whistleblowers. The *Joint Code of Professional Conduct*, section C.5, provides exemptions to the principle of confidentiality. They generally include a requirement by law, or a professional requirement such as a formal investigation by the professional accounting bodies (refer to chapter 3 for a detailed discussion of the confidentiality principle and its exemptions), but they provide little assistance in whistleblowing situations. Even when accountants have a legal responsibility to blow the whistle, they reman reluctant to do so (see the section, 'In practice: Whistleblowing failures', elsewhere in this chapter).

In the end, whistleblowing is a complex balancing act of duties and consequences. The whistleblower must weigh the responsibility to serve the public interest against the responsibility to their colleagues and the employing organisation. The whistleblower's dilemma is further complicated when we consider typical reactions to the whistleblower.

## Reactions to whistleblowers //

Initially, whistleblowers are applauded by the public as heroes for having the courage and moral maturity to stand up to their corporate bullies. However, within the company, the whistleblower is vilified as a traitor who has been disloyal to the company and colleagues. In Australia, whistleblowers are colloquially referred to as 'dobbers'. Most whistleblowers undergo serious penalties for their commitment to the truth. Unfortunately, history is littered with examples of whistleblowers penalised for their actions. They suffer some form of harassment, lower performance evaluations, demotions, punitive transfers, and dismissal (Martin 1992). Whistleblowers are ostracised by management and colleagues as troublemakers, which in turn hinders future employment opportunities. Regardless of whether attitudes toward whistleblowers are changing, many people still disagree with blowing the whistle because of the loyalty they feel is owed to their employers.

### Whistleblowing failures

Under the *Superannuation Industry (Supervision) Act 1993* (Cwlth) (SIS Act), auditors have a responsibility to watch over the fund's financial and compliance status. Where there are potential contraventions of the SIS Act, and the trustee fails to take appropriate remedial action, the auditor must advise the regulator, the Australian Prudential Regulation Authority (APRA). As prudential regulator, APRA's mission is to ensure, to the extent reasonably possible, that financial promises to Australia's depositors, policy-holders and super fund members made by regulated entities have been fulfilled (APRA 2003). If APRA is to protect super fund members, they must be informed promptly of any improprieties so that appropriate action can be taken. In effect, the SIS Act empowers the auditor to act as a whistle-blower. However, according to Venkatramani (2002), auditors appear to be reluctant to use the whistleblowing provision when they have grounds for blowing the whistle. This is in spite of the profession's increasing support for strengthening the position of whistleblower (ICAA 2003; CPA Australia 2002). Failure by the auditor to alert the regulator calls into question the role assigned to auditors under the law. A perceived conflict between their obligations to clients and legislative responsibilities could impact on the auditor's ability and willingness to exercise fully whistleblowing powers.

Unfortunately, employees contemplating blowing the whistle can expect retaliation and overwhelming personal and financial hardship. Herein lies the personal dilemma: accountants are people as well as professionals. In addition to the right to pursue their careers, accountants have personal obligations, for example, to their families, as well as others, and these personal obligations can be met only if they have an income. For some, the personal cost that comes with blowing the whistle is too high and should be avoided. According to this view, some may feel that the safest option for the would-be whistleblower is to resign from the organisation rather than blow the whistle, especially when the whistleblower can expect to gain nothing from revealing improper behaviour. However, the problem remains that the whistleblower is likely to suffer emotional and financial pressures by resigning, while top management remain unchallenged.

Given the plight of the whistleblower, why blow the whistle? Contrary to popular opinion, whistleblowers are not acting out of self-interest, but because of perceived concerns about the public being defrauded or endangered. Most whistleblowers do so because of their strong moral values and the belief that their inaction could result in tragedy and unbearable guilt. Whistleblowers are conservative and committed employees, motivated by the imperative to change organisational practice. They are primarily concerned for their colleagues, the organisation, or the public (Jones 1996).

## Conditions justifying blowing the whistle //

Ideally, the employing organisation should have procedures in place that deal with ethical or legal transgressions and make it unnecessary for an employee to blow the whistle. However, in circumstances where the internal procedures are unsuccessful, blowing the whistle is seen by the employee as the only option. The following discussion sets out the minimum criteria that justify an act of whistleblowing.

### Preventing harm to the public

Whistleblowing is justified when it is done from an appropriate moral motive, in particular, to protect the public from serious harm. If harm is not likely to result by remaining silent, the whistleblower must seriously question whether the public has a right to know. When deciding whether to blow the whistle, the whistleblower must assess whether going public will give rise to an investigation that will lead to a resolution that will prevent harmful consequences to the public. Without a reasonable chance for resolution, the whistleblower should not expect to put themselves at personal risk (De George 1999, p. 256). In this sense, whistleblowing should be regarded as an unavoidable tragedy.

### Reliable evidence

The employee must be satisfied that they can support their allegations of foul play with evidence that would convince a reasonable person (De George 1999, p. 255). The whistleblower must be absolutely confident of the reliability of the information, and under no illusions as to the extent and strength of pressure that they will encounter. If the evidence is dubious, considerable harm can be done to the reputations of those who are innocent, but accused by the whistleblower.

### Internal procedures

There is an expectation that top management is responsible for resolving ethical issues raised within the company. Informing management of the problem is viewed as a display of loyalty to the company, which provides management with every opportunity to redeem their behaviour. If the employee blows the whistle without first following the recommended internal procedures, they are likely to be branded troublemakers. Therefore, whistleblowers should exhaust all internal channels of dissent before taking their information outside the organisation.

If appeals within the organisation are not successful, then the employee should determine their next course of action, in consultation with independent and outside advisers such as the professional accounting body. When the adviser and whistleblower clearly conclude that public awareness of the circumstances will prevent harmful consequences, then the employee has a moral responsibility to go public with the information. Unfortunately for the whistleblower, if they have followed the rules and raised their concerns internally without success, their ultimate whistleblowing act is likely to be seen as malicious by fellow employees. Due to the far-reaching consequences that whistleblowing has for all parties, blowing the whistle should always be considered a last resort.

## Internal whistleblowing //

Corporations pay a high price when an employee blows the whistle externally. The negative effects of external whistleblowing include bad publicity, declining reputations, lawsuits, diminished profitability, and the demoralisation of the workforce. The most effective way to avoid external whistleblowing is to encourage employees to blow the whistle internally, and to resolve the problem before it becomes a public scandal. Internal whistleblowing occurs when the employee discloses violations within the organisation rather than outside the organisation. Disclosures within the organisation can be made directly to a higher authority, a designated officer, or anonymously via a whistleblower hotline.

Currently, blowing the whistle, whether it is internal or external is seen as a negative act and disloyal to the organisation. Combined with the personal and professional reprisals afforded to whistleblowers, few employees are ever likely to blow the whistle. If employees are to blow the whistle internally, management must establish a culture that supports whistleblowing as a positive act—one that is loyal, and in the best interest of the employing organisation. A loyal employee should be defined by the culture as one who recognises illegal or unethical acts as running counter to the best interests of an organisation. Remaining silent in these instances could be read as condoning the behaviour and, by extension, disloyalty. Therefore, internal whistleblowing should not only be permissible, but expected. An ethical corporate culture that encourages internal whistleblowing is discussed in the section entitled, 'Developing an ethical corporate culture' on page 330 of this chapter. In brief, however, making external whistleblowing unnecessary will occur only when management sets a moral tone that encourages open communication and provides employees with opportunities to tell their story without reprisal.

Blowing the whistle internally provides the employer with the opportunity to either demonstrate to the employee that no genuine wrongdoing has occurred, or if there is a genuine moral problem, the employer has the opportunity to resolve it (Larmer 1992). However, the problem for the whistleblower is that it sometimes places the employee in a no-win situation if management refuse to amend their behaviour. The employee will be left with little choice but to resign from the organisation or blow the whistle to an external body and risk the repercussions of losing their job and facing ostracism. Alternatively, employees can remain with the organisation with the fear of being labelled an abettor when the malpractice is eventually revealed. The relationship between external and internal whistleblowing, and the steps that should be taken before deciding to blow the whistle externally, are illustrated in Figure 12.1.

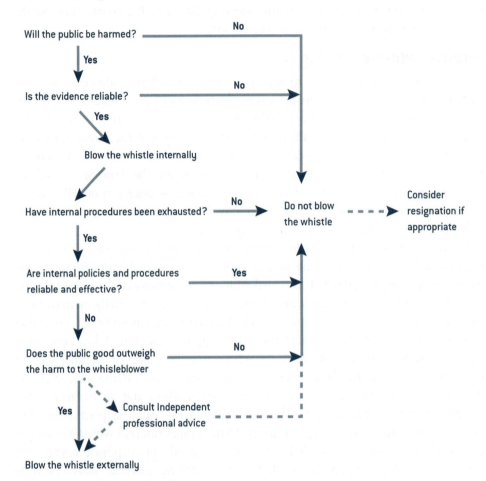

FIGURE 12.1 Blowing the whistle

Internal whistleblowing may initially appear to be a threat to the organisation, but it can potentially improve the long-term organisational effectiveness, and benefit other stakeholders such as employees, shareholders, and society. In accounting, encouraging employees to blow the whistle means that financial reporting will become more honest and businesses less corrupt. Therefore, rather than being viewed as a crisis, internal whistleblowing should be viewed as a management tool of internal control to avoid the costly effects of external whistleblowing.

## Designated officers

Designated officers are known by a number of titles; they include ethics officer, ethics auditor, ethics committee, and ombudsman. Designated officers have a responsibility to receive and act on reports received directly from employees or the firm's ethics hotline, and to provide support and guidance to employees with grievances about their employer. The effective functioning of a designated officer who encourages internal whistleblowing depends on two critical factors. First, the employee's identity remains a secret at all times to protect them from possible reprisals. Second, the system of investigation is perceived by employees to be effective, and one that will resolve the problem and instigate changes that will avoid repeat occurrences.

### Whistleblower hotline

One method that can be used to encourage internal whistleblowing is the 'whistleblower hotline'. The hotline is a mechanism for employees to disclose information when they are troubled and reluctant to discuss the issue with their supervisor. This is an effective method of internal whistleblowing when the employee feels that the supervisor is part of the problem. Hotlines are often used to augment a company's internal control reporting processes, serving as an option for employees who might feel uncomfortable coming forward. By placing a call on the hotline the employee can retain their anonymity and encourage communication, because they avoid the fear of reprisal. However, the major problem with hotlines is that they can sometimes lead to groundless accusations when employees act out of revenge or a form of sick humour. Investigating false accusations is a waste of the company's scarce resources and can damage innocent reputations.

# Gifts and hospitality //

Offers of gratitude from suppliers and clients such as gifts and hospitality are common in commercially beneficial relationships. Unfortunately for accountants, accepting offers of gratitude can give rise to self-interest and intimidation threats (IFAC 2003, paragraph C.6.2). A self-interest threat arises when offers are made to unduly influence the accountant's actions or decisions, encourage illegal or dishonest behaviour, or obtain confidential information. Intimidation threats arise when offers of gratitude received by accountants are made public.

Clearly, if the donor expects a favour in return, quid pro quo, the accountant must decline the gift. The question here is whether accountants should accept such offers when no favours are asked or expected. According to Professional Statement F.1: 'Professional Independence', an accountant, especially in cases of assurance engagements, must not accept gifts or hospitality unless the value is clearly insignificant (F.1, 'Appendix 2', paragraph 2.111). Accepting more than a token gift leaves the accountant open to allegations that they are obligated to the donor. Similar reasoning is echoed in the *Proposed Revised Code of Ethics for Professional Accountants* (IFAC 2003). Therefore, according to official pronouncements, the value of the gift or hospitality is critical in deciding whether to accept an offer of gratitude.

Unfortunately, expensive and modest values are relative to the recipients, and will vary depending on the circumstances. Therefore, a guiding rule that is based on value, unless defined, may not make the decision to accept the offer any clearer. Professional guidelines offer little direction on the meaning of the term value. However, paragraph 27 of Professional Statement F.1 states that an accountant must not accept offers of gratitude when goods or services are offered on terms more favourable than those generally available to others. Therefore, a gift is only acceptable when its value is similar to gifts or benefits offered to others. By implication, when the gift or benefit is comparatively high, it should be declined. For example, if a supplier offers its preferred customers a discount of 10 per cent on any of its products, then it is permissible for the accountant to accept any offer up to or equal to this value. However, if the discount offered to the accountant is greater than 10 per cent, say 15 per cent, then it may be seen by a third person as an attempt to influence the accountant's judgment, and must therefore be declined.

Paragraph 27 also makes reference to 'normal courtesies of social life'. It states that if the hospitality or gift is not commensurate with normal courtesies, it must not be accepted. Unfortunately, the phrase 'normal courtesies of social life' is not defined. Presumably, the term 'normal courtesies' refers to regular social events such as business lunches and gifts during important calender dates such as Christmas. In practice, accepting gifts should be interpreted sensibly and, if the gifts need to be returned, handled diplomatically. Gift givers could be offended by the sudden rejection of a gift.

In conclusion, the *Proposed Revised Code of Ethics for Professional Accountants* (IFAC 2003, paragraph C.6.3) provides the following criteria, which should be considered before a gift is accepted or rejected. It states that, when offers of gifts and hospitality are insignificant, not intended to encourage unethical behaviour, and made in an open manner, accountants may conclude that the offers are made in the normal course of business. In these circumstances, the accountant may accept the offer of gratitude or hospitality. The guidelines in deciding whether to accept or reject offers of gifts and hospitality are presented in figure 12.2.

FIGURE 12.2   When is a gift acceptable?

# A cultural perspective of ethics in business //

The increasing globalisation of business, and the internationalisation of accounting and auditing standards, combined with an accounting industry obsessed with growth, means that accountants can expect to have increasing interaction with people from a diverse spread of cultural backgrounds and moral beliefs. In this section we discuss the impact that culture has on business ethics and the problems it raises for accountants. Cultural values may collide on several issues, for instance, attitudes to women, child labour, working conditions, environmental concerns and, of course, bribery. Here, we will analyse the issue of cultural ethics through the practice of bribery. Issues such as child labour will not be discussed, because it is beyond the scope of this book; however, despite the lack of attention given in this chapter, the omission of this and other such issues should not undermine or deny their significance. For example, during an audit of its offshore manufacturers, Levi Strauss & Co discovered a contractor in Bangladesh employing underage children. Levi could not solve the problem by simply dismissing the children, because they were often the sole financial support for their families. The alternatives to work were prostitution, begging, or starvation. So, rather than force the children and their families to bear such atrocities, Levi paid the children wages while they attended school until they reached the legal working age (Rapaport 1993).

## Culture and bribery //

The issue of gifts and hospitality is always a difficult issue, but it becomes even more difficult when it is combined with international business. On an international level, the distinction between a gift and a **bribe** is not always obvious. In some cultures, there is a longstanding tradition of gift giving to cultivate long-term relationships that facilitate business dealings. In other countries, such gifts are simply bribes. Many countries such as Australia and Singapore share an aversion to pay-offs but, in other countries, certain types of bribery are an accepted element of their commercial traditions. Corruption in some countries is a major issue, and it is often the single largest component of business ethics. Refer to the section entitled, 'In Practice: Transparency International' which depicts people's perceptions of the extent of corruption in South East Asia.

In nations where gifts generate a sense of obligation, it may prove best to offer them — especially when such requests reflect the local customs. Such gifts may be gateways into the workings of the country's commercial world. However, the problem with cross-national business is that conduct that might be acceptable or legal in the host country may be offensive or may even attract penalties in the home country. For example, in some countries gifts are permissible and sometimes a necessary condition of business. Yet, in many other countries, gifts are unacceptable because they are viewed as an attempt to influence the recipient's decisions or actions. So, how should a company respond when a host country's ethical standards differ from the home country? One option is to follow whichever norm is more profitable. However, this is arguably an act of selfishness, and inconsistent with principles of good conduct. From an ethical perspective, the company has two options:

1. It can follow the norms of the host country to show proper respect for the host country's culture. This accords with the principle of 'cultural relativism'.
2. It can follow the norms of the home country. This accords with the principle of 'universalism'.

## IN PRACTICE

### Transparency International

Transparency International (TI) is a non-governmental organisation based in Berlin, with 85 national chapters worldwide. TI is devoted to monitoring and curtailing the supply and demand of corruption in the international arena. TI is best known for the Corruption Perceptions Index (CPI), which measures the degree to which corruption is perceived to exist among public officials and politicians by business people, academics, and risk analysts. The CPI builds awareness of the corruption issue and draws attention to the negative images of countries with low CPI scores. The CPI ranges between 10 (highly clean) and 0 (highly corrupt). According to TI (2003), seven out of ten countries score less than five, and five out of ten developing countries score less than three, indicating a high level of corruption. Corruption is not restricted to poor countries — it also thrives in some European countries such as Greece and Italy, and in potential wealthy oil-rich countries such as Nigeria, Indonesia, Libya and Iraq.

In 2003, TI ranked 133 countries using the CPI. The full listing of all 133 rankings can be found in TI's official report. In figure 12.3, we present the official ranking of the top twenty countries, plus countries from Indo-China and the Asia Pacific regions.

| RANK 2003 | COUNTRY | CPI 2003 |
|:---------:|---------|:--------:|
| 1 | Finland | 9.7 |
| 2 | Iceland | 9.6 |
| 3 | New Zealand/Denmark | 9.5 |
| 5 | Singapore | 9.4 |
| 6 | Sweden | 9.3 |
| 7 | Netherlands | 8.9 |

| RANK 2003 | COUNTRY | CPI 2003 |
|:---:|:---|:---:|
| 8 | Australia/Norway/Switzerland | 8.8 |
| 11 | Canada, Luxemberg, United Kingdom | 8.7 |
| 14 | Austria, Hong Kong | 8.0 |
| 16 | Germany | 7.7 |
| 17 | Belgium | 7.6 |
| 18 | Ireland, USA | 7.5 |
| 20 | Chile | 7.4 |
| 21 | Japan | 7.0 |
| 30 | Taiwan | 5.7 |
| 37 | Malaysia | 5.2 |
| 50 | South Korea | 4.3 |
| 66 | China | 3.4 |
| 66 | Sri Lanka | 3.4 |
| 70 | Thailand | 3.3 |
| 83 | India | 2.8 |
| 92 | Pakistan | 2.5 |
| 92 | Philippines | 2.5 |
| 100 | Vietnam | 2.4 |
| 118 | Papua New Guinea | 2.1 |
| 122 | Indonesia | 1.9 |
| 133 | Bangladesh | 1.3 |

FIGURE 12.3    TI's Corruption Perceptions Index 2003

The CPI 2003 complements the TI's Bribe Payers Index (BPI), which addresses the propensity of companies from top exporting countries to offer bribes in emerging markets. The BPI 2002 listed below in figure 12.4, indicates the extent to which companies from the list of 21 countries provid likely to pay or offer bribes to win or retain business (TI, 2002). A perfect score of 10 indicates a zero perceived propensity to pay bribes.

| 2002 RANK | COUNTRY | BPI 2002 | BPI 1999 |
|:---:|:---|:---:|:---:|
| 1 | Australia | 8.5 | 8.1 |
| 2 | Sweden | 8.4 | 8.3 |
| 3 | Switzerland | 8.4 | 7.7 |
| 4 | Austria | 8.2 | 7.8 |
| 5 | Canada | 8.1 | 8.1 |
| 6 | Netherlands | 7.8 | 7.4 |
| 7 | Belgium | 7.8 | 6.8 |
| 8 | UK | 6.9 | 7.2 |
| 9 | Singapore | 6.3 | 5.7 |
| 10 | Germany | 6.3 | 6.2 |
| 11 | Spain | 5.8 | 5.3 |
| 12 | France | 5.5 | 5.2 |
| 13 | USA | 5.3 | 6.2 |
| 14 | Japan | 5.3 | 5.1 |
| 15 | Malaysia | 4.3 | 3.9 |
| 16 | Hong Kong | 4.3 | n.a. |
| 17 | Italy | 4.1 | 3.7 |
| 18 | South Korea | 3.9 | 3.4 |
| 19 | Taiwan | 3.8 | 3.5 |
| 20 | China | 3.5 | 3.1 |
| 21 | Russia | 3.2 | n.a. |

FIGURE 12.4    TI's Bribe Payers Index 2002

## Cultural relativism //

The principle of **cultural relativism** holds that the standards that guide ethical behaviour are those that have been established by the host country. Cultural relativism is premised on the moral norms of the society in which the behaviour takes place. Whether an action is right or wrong depends on the moral norms of the society in which it is practised. Any act inconsistent with the host country's norms is morally wrong. The cultural relativist creed, 'when in Rome do as the Romans do', is predicated on the belief that there is no single moral standard, only local moral practices that indicate acceptable behaviour.

Relying on the principle of cultural relativism, companies claim that the only standards they are responsible for meeting are those established by the host country. The problem with this reasoning is that morally questionable activities such as bribery become morally permissible when they are acceptable to the society in which the behaviours are commonly practised. The cultural relativist creed is tempting, especially when rejecting local norms means forfeiting business opportunities (Donaldson 1996, p. 48). By adopting a 'when in Rome' attitude, companies implicitly allow the local managers to give bribes. As individuals, managers may be averse to paying bribes, but when corruption is so ingrained in the culture, refusing to pay bribes will simply lose out to the competition. In the end, corruption, which is unacceptable in most countries, becomes acceptable for companies when the alternative is to risk losing business. In this sense, cultural relativism is morally blind.

Caution should be exercised when relying on the notion of cultural relativism. Companies justify bribery on the basis that everyone is doing it, yet some practices, such as bribery, are clearly wrong, no matter how ingrained, or where they take place. Just because bribery is commonly practised, it does not necessarily follow that members of that same society accept bribery — they simply tolerate it. One should be careful in thinking that common practice makes a wrong act right.

## Universalism //

**Universalism**, also known as absolutism, maintains that there are absolute moral truths, not relative to culture, which all entities obey at all times without exception. According to this view, ethical judgments are universal — which means that if an action is wrong in one country, it is also wrong in other countries. For international business, this means the norms of the local culture are irrelevant, and companies are bound only by the standards of conduct established in their home country. For example, if bribery is unacceptable in Australia, then it is unacceptable abroad. Therefore, the same standards should be universally applied in all cultures, particularly where the host country's standards are different to those of the home country. Proponents of this view argue that businesses have a responsibility to be ethical, irrespective of culture.

The problem with applying standards universally is that this approach ignores the ethical and cultural differences between countries and may be seen by some as a form of moral authoritarianism. According to this view, the universalist sees their own culture as superior to others and, by adhering to their own standards, could be regarded as impertinent and even offensive to the local community. For example, Servcorp, an Australian company providing serviced offices in Japan, informed its Japanese staff that they were to ignore local Japanese tradition and preserve the company's Australian identity by not bowing to prospective customers. However, by prescribing Australian protocol, Servcorp failed to do business with local Japanese companies, only foreign companies. By revising its policy to respect and behave consistently with local traditions, Servcorp attracts Japanese clients and is now Australia's largest employer in Japan (Robinson 2003).

## The moral minimum //

If companies can neither adopt a host country's ethics, nor extend their home country's standard, what are they to do? The two alternative courses of action based on the notions of relativism and universalism both have shortcomings. Commentators, such as Donaldson, (1996) and De George (1999, p. 521), have subsequently argued for a middle ground, referred to in this chapter as the **moral minimum**. In brief, the moral minimum sits midway between relativism and universalism, and provides the threshold for all business activities. As a general rule, companies should respect and adapt to the norms of the local culture, while adhering to a minimum standard of conduct that transcends any particular nation or culture. In this sense, the moral minimum defines the minimum set of obligations that all companies are morally bound to observe, no matter what activity takes place. If local norms contravene the moral minimum, companies should ignore local customs and adhere to their self-imposed minimum standards. The relationship between universalism, cultural relativism, and the moral minimum is illustrated in figure 12.5.

If the moral minimum sets the floor for ethical conduct, how is the minimum standard of conduct defined? This is a complex issue, and any attempt to answer this question will always be subject to debate. In essence, however, the moral minimum binds companies to respect the basic human rights of employees, customers and surrounding communities by avoiding relationships and activities that violate people's right to health, education, safety and adequate living standards (Donaldson 1996, p. 53). This notion of the moral minimum prevents questionable activities such as slavery, the manufacture of unsafe products, racial segregation, paying less than subsistence wages, and failing to provide adequate and safe working conditions.

Despite claims that bribery in foreign cultures is a necessary element for successful business, it clearly remains a breach of the moral minimum. Companies justify their corrupt behaviour by claiming that they help local employment and

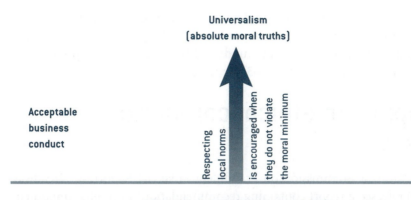

Universalism
(absolute moral truths)

Acceptable
business
conduct

Respecting local norms is encouraged when they do not violate the moral minimum

The moral minimum (basic human rights)

Unacceptable
business
conduct

When local norms violate the moral minimum they should be rejected

Cultural relativism
(standards established by the host culture)

FIGURE 12.5   The moral minimum

even promote economic efficiency. Yet, in reality, bribery stifles economic growth, because it makes industries that practise it uncompetitive. Decisions are not made on the basis of quality and cost competitiveness, but on the basis of who gives the bribes. According to Powpaka (2002), the World Bank estimates that 5 per cent of exports to developing countries (US$50–$80 billion annually) go to corrupt officials. Consequently, bribery distorts the allocation of resources, undermines competition in the marketplace, inhibits growth and development, erodes public confidence in political institutions, and leads to contempt for the rule of the law. In short, bribery denies people's right to fair and equal treatment, and a standard of living they have a right to expect.

If bribe giving is to cease, companies must articulate a culture that clearly renounces bribery and gives managers in host countries options to deal with local officials. Guidelines against giving bribes, such as a policy or a code of conduct, would significantly reduce perceived support from top management, which in turn will reduce employee fervour to give bribes. The issue of developing and managing an ethical culture is discussed in the following section. With regard to accountants, IFAC (2003, paragraph C.6.5 – 6.7) recognises that accountants in business may find themselves in situations where they are expected to offer inducements. This influence may come from within the employing organisation or from a third party. Irrespective of the circumstances, an accountant is forbidden from offering payments, knowing that any portion of the funds will have an improper influence on the judgment of the recipient (IFAC 2003, paragraph C6.8).

# Developing an ethical corporate culture //

In 1987, the National Commission on Fraudulent Financial Reporting (Treadway Commission) released a report containing recommendations to combat fraudulent financial reporting. Two aspects of the report received particular attention: first, the values of senior management and the benefits of setting an ethical tone. Second, there was the recommendation to develop and enforce a written code of corporate conduct to foster an ethical climate and open channels of communication. The incidence of financial fraud is important to the accounting profession because, in addition to the executives who misrepresent their company's financial statements, accountants who fail to detect fraud are being held accountable as well. Based on the recommendations of the Treadway Commission, creating an ethical corporate culture may be the answer to deterring fraudulent financial reporting.

The ethical climate of an organisation, known as the **corporate culture**, represents a shared set of norms, values, and practices about appropriate behaviour in the workplace. In other words, the culture of an organisation delineates acceptable and unacceptable conduct. In turn, acceptable behaviour is defined by the employees' perceptions of what is important to an organisation. Organisations can vary in terms of what they deem to be important; for example, some organisations have a culture of quality, some develop a culture for service, and others focus on profit. The problem with a profit-orientated culture is that it can subordinate issues like quality, service, and safety. Profit is a necessary condition of any business, but how profit is achieved will be influenced by its ethical climate.

Ethical decision making, particularly in times of crisis, is often a reflection of the corporate culture. In essence, a good culture will evoke good behaviour; a bad culture will evoke bad behaviour. For example, in 1982, the pharmaceutical company Johnson & Johnson recalled 31 million bottles of the pain-killer Tylenol after capsules were contaminated with cyanide by an extortionist. This action led to a one-time write-off of US$140 million. Management has been cited as saying 'they had no choice but to pull the product'. If not for the ethical culture of the company and values set by management, the decision to pull the product may never have been made. The company's actions earned the admiration of the buying public, and the company subsequently recovered from this crisis. So celebrated were management's actions, the Tylenol case is now the benchmark by which all other companies are compared.

The primary reason for developing an ethical culture is based on the notion that good ethics is good for business and good business is based on public trust and loyalty. Trust and loyalty are acquired when the public believes that they are purchasing a high quality, reliable, and safe product, made with manufacturing processes that respect the environment and its workers. In this sense, public trust and confidence are clearly valuable commodities. If trust and confidence are absent, consumers will simply turn their backs on the products and services that have a poor ethical reputation. As stated above, the cornerstone of developing an ethical climate resides with the corporate code of conduct and the commitment to the code by senior management. These issues are explored in the following sections.

## Corporate codes of conduct //

The first step towards cultivating an ethical culture is to develop a formal system of written documents outlining the firm's policy and expectations concerning the organisation's values and employee behaviour. Examples of formal controls include the corporate code of conduct, performance appraisals, and reward and punishment criteria. In this section, we focus our discussion on corporate codes of conduct.

A **corporate code of conduct** is defined as an authoritative statement of values and principles designed to set a minimum standard of acceptable behaviour and guide organisational members in resolving ethical conflicts. Corporate codes of conduct address issues such as compliance with law, conflicts of interest, stakeholder relationships, confidential information, misuse of funds, company records, gift giving and receiving, and political contributions. Corporate codes attempt to deter unethical behaviour by specifying acceptable and unacceptable behaviour. The method by which corporate codes operate is quite simple: when an employee is faced with a dilemma, they must compare the dilemma with the guidelines contained in the code and make a decision to avoid possible violation of the code.

Corporate codes are particularly useful for companies that are decentralised or fragmented into smaller divisions, such as geographic locations. When adequate supervision or guidance is lacking, divisional managers operate autonomously and not necessarily in the best interests of the company. In this situation, corporate codes are useful in providing a common value system for all divisions to adopt. A corporate code will bring companies with different cultures under one corporate umbrella and provide divisional managers with guidance in dealing with anomalies in local customs such as bribery.

## Senior management 'setting the tone' //

Employees learn acceptable behaviour through the subtle reading of signals demonstrated by the actions and reactions of senior management, which serve as a model for accepted behaviour. The rewards and penalties doled out by management in response to the actions of employees set the example for all to follow. Learning acceptable behaviours in this way does not always relate to written rules or policies; there is simply an implicit knowledge of how the organisation works and what it expects from its employees. This implicit knowledge stems from the firm's values, which are communicated by the decisions and actions of key personnel within the organisation. From this implicit knowledge, an employee can deduce appropriate behaviour to govern any specific situation. In time, employee behaviour will become increasingly congruent with the values and attitudes of senior management. Therefore, the ethics of an organisation is ultimately dependent on senior management setting the appropriate tone. Like managers, accountants in business often occupy senior positions within employing organisations, so they too are in a position to influence events, practices, and attitudes.

In the previous section, we established that corporate codes are an important influence on employee behaviour. However, codes alone are insufficient to ensure employees behave ethically. One of the most important factors in determining the power of the code's influence on employee behaviour is management's commitment to the code. Corporate codes are most effective when the values and decisions of senior management support the formally identified goals in the corporate code of conduct. Senior management has a responsibility to model its behaviour on the role expectations of the code, so that all employees are aware of acceptable and expected behaviours. In 'setting the tone', employees learn appropriate behaviour from senior management leading by example. Corporate codes supported by senior management will always be a stronger assurance of ethical culture than codes that are perceived by employees as window dressing.

In spite of the existence of a corporate code, unethical behaviour is likely to flourish when senior managers exhibit inconsistent or inappropriate behaviour, or fail to discourage employee behaviour that is in conflict with the corporate code. Incongruence between formally stated values and employee behaviour develops when senior management encourages behaviour that is not aligned with company values. As role models, senior management are most influential on employee behaviour. When senior management exhibit inconsistent or inappropriate behaviour, employees see this questionable behaviour as acceptable conduct. The influence of senior management on employee behaviour can be so pervasive that the absence of management actions against unethical behaviour is a stronger approval of questionable acts than stated policies of acceptable behaviour. When this occurs, corporate codes are perceived by employees as public relations documents, without any real intent to change behaviour. Codes eventually appear as wall hangings, collecting dust or filed in someone's office never to be seen again. The relationship between senior management and codes of conduct, and their influence on corporate culture and subsequent employee behaviour is illustrated in figure 12.6.

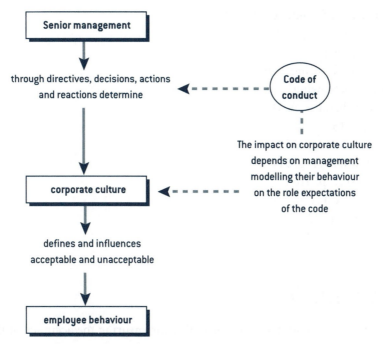

FIGURE 12.6    Managing corporate culture and codes of conduct

# Summary //

There is no shortage of ethical issues in business. Business leaders, as well as accountants, face a demanding and complex world of competing interests that question the ethical implications of their decisions. The issues discussed in this chapter include financial fraud, whistleblowing, gifts and hospitality, and culture. How accountants and managers deal with these confrontations is a likely measure of their future success. The response by business is a complex issue, but the answer to many ethical questions raised in this chapter can be addressed by developing an ethical corporate culture. Two key elements are necessary for establishing an ethical climate: the corporate code of conduct, and management setting the appropriate ethical tone. The corporate code is normally the starting point for developing an ethical culture; however, without support from senior management, its influence may be trivialised.

# Key terms //

Accountant in business ... p. 311
Bribery ... p. 323
Confidentiality ... p. 316

## Questions //

**12.1** What is the accountant's responsibility for ensuring the accuracy of the financial reports?

**12.2** Is it acceptable for an accountant in business to hold a financial interest in their employing organisation? Explain.

**12.3** Compare and contrast external whistleblowing and internal whistleblowing.

**12.4** Under what conditions is whistleblowing morally justified?

**12.5** Distinguish cultural relativism from universalism.

**12.6** What are the benefits of a corporate code of conduct?

**12.7** How does a company develop and manage an ethical corporate culture?

**12.8** Discuss the ethical issues facing accountants when:

    **a** they are pressured by management to collude in window dressing the accounts

    **b** blowing the whistle

    **c** accepting gifts and hospitality from a client or supplier

    **d** operating in a culture with ethical standards different to their own.

**12.9** Should internal audit procedures institutionalise internal whistleblowing? Why?

**12.10** What should an Australian company do when it conducts business in a foreign country that relies on bribery? What will it probably do?

**12.11** Consider the following leadership styles and discuss the potential effect they may have on the corporate culture and subsequent employee behaviour.

    **a** Paternal leader: One who is a mentor, cares for others and is always available for consultation.

    **b** Aggressive leader: One who ensures objectives are met by whatever means possible, because they feel responsible for the success or failure of the organisation.

## The Enron whistleblower

Sherron Watkins, an accounting graduate of the University of Texas, is a former Arthur Andersen accountant who joined Enron in 1993. During the 1990s Enron grew by acquisition from its origins as a natural-gas pipeline company to become America's seventh largest company. Sherron's career escalated with the company's growth and she eventually became Enron's Vice-President for Corporate Development. The 1990s were fat times for Enron, and the corporate culture wallowed in excess. The company rented ski condos in Beaver Creek, Colorado, and stocked each condo with a personal chef. Christmas parties were multimillion-dollar, black-tie affairs with ice sculptures (Morse and Bower 2002).

Jeffrey Skilling, the CEO, and Andrew Fastow, the CFO, were key players in the fraud that hid billions of dollars in debt through dubious partnership transactions. Skilling and Fastow were intimidating men who convinced others to accept the partnership transactions. Skilling also had a reputation for disciplining staff who challenged his authority. Interestingly, the board of directors, who were not directly involved in the fraud, approved most of the partnership transactions in question.

In June 2001, Sherron worked for Fastow, and she was charged with selling assets during the post technology bubble bust. In her work, she detected accounting improprieties that included allegations of conflicts of interest, related party transactions, and hidden losses that could not be supported with sound reason or documentation. At this point, Sherron began scouting for a new job. Her plan was to find new employment and confront Skilling on her last day at Enron. However, Skilling resigned before this happened.

In August 2001, at the time of Skilling's resignation, Enron Chairman, Kenneth Lay, invited employees to put any concerns in a comment box. Answering this call, Sherron lodged a one-page memo bringing to Lay's attention Enron's elaborate accounting hoax. Included in this memo, Sherron wrote:

> Enron has been aggressive in its accounting . . . I am incredibly nervous that we [Enron] will implode in a wave of accounting scandals.

The memo further stated that Enron should stop 'robbing the bank' and Sherron offered suggestions that might help the company to avoid getting caught.

The next day, Lay held a company-wide meeting but did not allude to Sherron's concerns. Sherron subsequently sought a face-to-face appointment with Lay. He appeared concerned and assured Sherron that the matter would be investigated. Lay appointed Enron's law firm, Vinson & Elkins (V&E), to conduct an inquiry. The V&E investigation concluded that the partnership transactions were proper; though, on the surface, they appeared questionable. According to Sherron's testimony, V&E provided opinions on some of the transactions in question, and therefore had a conflict of interest in conducting the investigation.

One month later, in September 2001, Lay announced to employees that Enron's 'financial liquidity has never been stronger'. This announcement came after he netted US$1.5 million by exercising personal share options. By mid-October, the company announced a US$618 million third-quarter loss and a US$1.2 billion write-off, tied to the partnership transactions that had worried Sherron.

On 2 December 2001, Enron filed for bankruptcy, which at the time was the largest bankruptcy in United States history. Enron went from being the seventh largest company in America, with a share price that once reached $75 to 72 cents on the day bankruptcy was filed. A domino-like effect eventually led to the demise of Enron's esteemed accountants, Arthur Andersen, who went down in their own scandal.

Following her memo to Lay in August 2001, Sherron continued going to work. However, in the ensuing months, she had her computer confiscated and she was demoted from her executive suite to a smaller less swish office 33 floors below her suite. At one point, the atmosphere became so ominous she sought advice from office security on self-defence. She later learned that Enron had considered firing her. Former employees have questioned why Sherron did not take her concerns to the Securities and Exchange Commission, and others were upset that she offloaded US$47 000 in Enron shares soon after her memo to Lay (Morse and Bower 2002).

From the time of the meeting with Lay in August 2001, Sherron did little until her memo was made public by congressional investigators six weeks after Enron filed for bankruptcy in January 2002. Since testifying at the congressional subcommittee investigating Enron's demise, she is known to the world as the Enron whistleblower. Since then, Sherron has co-written a book, *Power failure*, about her experiences, sharing up to US$500 000 advance payments with her co-author. On the lecture circuit, she earns up to US$35 000 per speaking engagement, telling audiences her story. As profitable as this appears, Sherron's husband claims that the money does not compare to the bonuses she earned during Enron's heyday (Reingold 2003).

In 2002, *Time Magazine* named her Person of the Year, along with two other women (Cynthia Cooper at WorldCom and Coleen Rowley at the FBI), for disclosing dubious business (Lacayo and Ripley 2002). Previous recipients of this award include Queen Elizabeth II, Pope John Paul II, Mohandas

Ghandi, Winston Churchill, and Martin Luther King. A movie deal has also been rumoured that compares Sherron's heroine status to Erin Brockovich. When the demand for public speaking dries up, Sherron plans to start a global consulting firm to advise company boards on governance and ethics.

**Required**

1 Are Sherron's actions consistent with the definition of a whistleblower? Explain.
2 What were the consequences of Sherron's behaviour?
3 Describe the corporate culture that existed at Enron, and discuss the potential effects that the culture may have had on the events that transpired at Enron.
4 In your opinion, does Sherron deserve her heroine status as 'person of the year'? Discuss.
5 At the time these events took place, the law did not protect corporate whistleblowers. Should whistleblowers be protected? Discuss.

## FURTHER RESOURCES AND WEBSITES //

Dellaportas, S and Leung, P, 2002, 'International business ethics: a cross cultural perspective', *Mt Eliza Business Review*, vol. 1, pp. 71–6.

Duska, R 1983, 'Whistleblowing and employee loyalty', in JR Desjardins and JJ McCall eds, *Contemporary issues in business ethics*, Wadsworth, Belmont California, pp. 295–300.

### Websites

Association of Chartered Certified Accountants, viewed 17 December 2003, www.accaglobal.com

Organisation for Economic Co-operation and Development, viewed 17 December 2003, www.oecd.org

Transparency International, viewed 17 December 2003, www.transparency.org

## REFERENCES //

Australian Prudential Regulation Authority, Whistleblowers or Public Interest Informants, viewed 17 December 2003. www.apra.gov.au/whistleblower.cfm

CPA Australia and the Institute of Chartered Accountants in Australia, *Joint code of professional conduct, Members' Handbook*, December 2002.

CPA Australia, *Submission on Corporate Law Economic Reform Program 9 Corporate Disclosure, November 2000*, Melbourne, viewed 8 May 2004, www.cpaaustralia.com.au

Corvino, J 2002, 'Loyalty in business', *Journal of Business Ethics*, vol. 41, pp. 179–85.

De George, RT 1999, *Business ethics*, 5th edn, Prentice Hall, Upper Saddle River, New Jersey.

Donaldson, T 1996, 'Values in tension: ethics away from home', *Harvard Business Review*, September – October, pp. 48–62.

Institute of Chartered Accountants in Australia, (2003), HIH Task Force Champions Change for the ICAA', viewed 8 May 2004, www.icaa.com.au.

International Federation of Accountants, 2003, *Proposed revised code of ethics for professional accountants*, IFAC, New York.

Jones, J B 1996, 'Whistleblowing no longer out of tune', *Australian Accountant*, August, pp. 56–7.

Lacayo, R and Ripley, A 2002, 'Persons of the year', *Time Magazine*, December 22, p. 30.

Larmer, R A 1992, 'Whistleblowing and employee loyalty', *Journal of Business Ethics* vol. 11, pp. 125–8.

Martin, M W 1992, 'Whistleblowing: professionalism and personal life', *Business and Processional Ethics Journal*, vol. 11, no. 2, pp. 21–40.

Morse, J and Bower, A 2002, 'The party crasher', *Time Magazine*, December 30, p. 52.

National Commission on Fraudulent Financial Reporting (The Treadway Commission), 1987, *Report of the national commission on fraudulent financial reporting*.

Powpaka, S 2002, 'Factors affecting managers' decision to bribe: an empirical investigation', *Journal of Business Ethics*, vol. 40, pp. 227–46.

Rapaport, R 1993, 'Import jeans export values', *Fastcompany*, November, p. 19.

Reingold, J 2003, 'The women of Enron: the best revenge', *Fastcompany*, September, p. 77.

Robinson, P, 2003, 'A room with a view puts Servcorp back on the top of town', *The Age Business*, 20 October, p. 1.

Transparency International, 2003, *Transparency International Corruption Perceptions Index 2003*, Berlin.

Transparency International, 2002, *The supply-side and the demand-side of corruption: background to the BPI and the CPI*, Berlin.

Venkatramani, S G, 2002, 'Whistleblowing failures', *Australian CPA*, May, p. 18.

# Glossary //

**AAA model:** a seven-step ethical decision-making model developed by Langenderfer and Rockness (1989) **p. 88**

**Accountability:** the responsibility ensuring the management duty is performed in the best interests of the organisation **p. 5**

**Accountability:** responsibility for the effects of actions taken **p. 206**

**Accountant in business:** is one who earns a salary rather than a fee, and is employed in commerce and industry or the public sector **p. 288**

**Accounting methods:** methods used within accounting. For example, the straight line method and the reducing balance method **p. 177**

**Accrual accounting:** accounting based on transactions whereby revenues and expenses are identified with specific periods of time, which are recorded as incurred, without regard to the date of receipt or payment of cash **p. 178**

**Adverse selection:** when the principal makes an inappropriate selection among alternatives **p. 127**

**Advocacy threats:** may occur when a professional accountant promotes a position or opinion to the point that subsequent objectivity may be compromised **p. 76**

**Affirmative action:** a program adopted by firms to reduce the effects of past discrimination on women and minorities in employment **p. 36**

**Agency theory:** a system in which owners entrust their resources to managers who then manage the assets for the benefit of the owners, giving rise to a monitoring function in the form of an audit **p. 256**

**Altruism:** the principle of living and acting for the interest or benefit of others, without the incentive of a financial or other reward **p. 238**

**Anthropocentric:** a philosophy that places the human species at the centre of importance **p. 231**

***Anton Pillar* order:** a civil court order providing rights to search property without prior warning. The main aim of such an order is to prevent the destruction of evidence **p. 154**

**Arbitration:** an alternative dispute resolution method by which an independent, neutral, third person ('arbitrator') is appointed to hear and consider the merits of the dispute, and render a final and binding decision, called an award. The process is similar to the litigation process, as it involves adjudication, except that the parties choose their arbitrator and the manner in which the arbitration will proceed **p. 151**

**Assets:** economic benefits or items of value of a long-term nature that are controlled by a particular individual or organisation, from which other parties can be excluded **p. 230**

**Audit:** the application of procedures for the purpose of expressing an opinion on the reliability of management's representation in the financial statements **p. 257**

**Audit committee:** a committee of the governing body of the company or other organisation whose function is to choose an external auditor (and agree on a fee basis) for each periodic examination of the organisation's affairs **p. 279**

**Board monitoring:** an internal corporate governance control where the role of the board of directors is to monitor the performance and management of the organisation **p. 130**

**Bribery:** involves offering, giving, receiving, or soliciting anything of value in order to influence the decisions or actions of a government or business employee **p. 323**

**Capitalise:** to record and carry forward onto one or more future periods any expenditure the benefits or proceeds from which will then be realised **p. 184**

**Capitalism:** an economic model based upon a system of private property rights that are traded within a market relatively free from constraint **p. 201**

**Carbon tax:** taxation that is imposed on the owners or users of equipment, such as motor vehicles, based on the amount of carbon that is emitted during use **p. 241**

**Cash accounting:** accounting based on cash transactions alone for a particular period **p. 178**

**Chinese Walls:** a term used to describe procedures enforced to separate a firm's departments, to restrict access to non-public and material information **p. 157**

**Client-centred conflicts of interest:** conflicts between the client and the accountant or firm of accountants **p. 287**

**Code of professional conduct:** is a set of rules designed to induce ethical behaviour and encourage public confidence in accountants and accounting practice **p. 64**

**Cognitive moral reasoning and development:** is concerned with the processes or logic that individuals use in making a decision of an ethical nature **p. 41**

**Commissions:** compensation from a third party for recommending or referring a product or service **p. 297**

**Compensatory justice:** is a type of justice that is concerned with restoring what has been lost from a wrongful act **p. 35**

**Competence:** is the attainment and maintenance of a level of knowledge from formal education, training and continued professional development that enables an accountant to render services with expertise **p. 72**

**Competence and due care:** the attainment and maintenance of an expert level of knowledge applied with diligence and for the best interests of those who rely on it **p. 296**

**Compliance:** is performing duties in conformance with accounting and auditing standards and other regulatory requirements promulgated by private and government standard setting authorities **p. 71**

**Confidentiality:** ensures that information acquired in the course of the accountant's work is not disclosed to a third party without specific authority unless there is a legal or professional duty to disclose it **p. 71**

**Confidentiality:** imposes an obligation to refrain from disclosing any confidential information on one's employment without the specific consent of the employer **p. 316**

**Conflicts of interest:** situations that undermine the judgment of a professional accountant at the expense of those the accountant has an obligation to serve **p. 285**

**Conformance:** the act of adhering to expectations **p. 5**

**Consequential:** a class of ethical theories that define right from wrong solely by the results of an act or decision **p. 108**

**Consequential theories:** define right from wrong solely by the results of an act or decision **p. 29**

**Consolidated financial statements:** financial statements of an economic entity prepared by combining the financial statements of the parent entity and each of its subsidiaries **p. 182**

**Contingent fee:** a fee calculated on a predetermined basis relating to the outcome or result of a transaction or the work performed **p. 293**

**Continuously contemporary accounting:** measurement of the effects of events and transactions on financial position made by reference to market prices **p. 179**

**Conventional level:** represents a level of moral reasoning that conforms to and upholds the rules, expectations or conventions of society **p. 43**

**Convex payoff:** benefits increase and decrease along a curved line **p. 135**

**Corporate code of conduct:** an authoritative statement of values and principles designed to set a minimum standard of acceptable behaviour and guide organisational members in resolving ethical conflicts **p. 331**

**Corporate culture:** comprise values, beliefs, and traditions that influence the behaviour of organisational members **p. 330**

**Corporate governance:** encompasses the direction, control mechanisms and all procedures and relationships involved in the economic, legal and operational performance of a corporation **pp. 5, 118**

**Corporate Governance Council (CGC):** a council consisting of 21 parties interested in improving the corporate governance practices and reporting of Australian businesses **p. 123**

**Corporate governance practice:** the process an organisation employs to ensure it is efficiently managed **p. 119**

**Corporate governance principles:** guidelines for the efficient governance of Australian businesses p. 124

**Corporate intelligence:** the collection and analysis of public information with strategic value p. 168

**Corporate social reporting:** information provided by companies in relation to their social and environmental performance. Provision is often by way of a specific social report, or as part of the organisation's annual report p. 205

**Creative accounting:** creative accounting necessarily involves an element of contrivance, applying accounting principles perversely, so as to secure a deliberately misleading result. It has also been variously described as fiddling the accounting, as manipulation, as deceit and of misrepresentation, and as abusing the accounting system. It can be described as the use of ambiguities in accounting rules to convey a different picture of the business's financial performance p. 176

**Credibility:** the trustworthiness of an entity p. 19

**Cultural relativism:** holds that whether an action is right or wrong depends on the moral norms of the society in which it takes place p. 327

**Current cost:** cost at present-day price levels of some or all of the items making up a statement of financial performance or a statement of financial position p. 179

**Current cost accounting:** conversion of financial statements based on present-day price levels, obtained by substituting historical cost prices with prevailing prices of goods and services p. 179

**Data mining:** a method of interrogating electronic data which may be downloaded from various computers or a network in an organisation, and running queries on the data to identify anomalies p. 165

**Decision making:** the process of making a choice to achieve a desired result from among two or more alternatives p. 94

**Decision rules:** rules of thumb that reduce the complexity of decision making p. 94

**Decision-making models:** provide a systematic framework to arrive at the best course of action p. 88

**Depreciation:** allocation of the cost of an asset over its useful life p. 233

**Distributive justice:** focuses on how fairly decisions and actions distribute benefits and burdens among members of the group. An unfair distribution of benefits and burdens is an unjust act and an unjust act is a morally wrong act p. 35

**Due care:** is the quest for excellence in the provision of professional services and acting in the best interests of those who rely on it p. 73

**Egoism:** is a type of reasoning that is driven by maximising self-interest p. 41

**Employer-centred conflicts of interest:** conflicts arising between the accountant in business and the employing entity **p. 288**

**Equality:** claims that every person is entitled to equal treatment under the law, be given equal opportunity, has equal worth, and should receive equal rewards **p. 35**

**Equity:** ownership interest. The equity of an organisation is the difference between the value of the assets and the value of the liabilities. If the assets exceed the liabilities, there is equity that represents wealth to the shareholders **p. 230**

**Ethical behaviour:** is behaviour that is consistent with the good reputation of the profession **p. 73**

**Ethical courage:** the strength of character to uphold ethical principles **p. 8**

**Ethical decision:** a decision on what should be done supported by more or better ethical reasons (principles of good conduct) than those against it **p. 95**

**Ethical decision making:** the process of identifying a problem, generating alternatives, and choosing among them so that the alternatives selected maximise the most important ethical values while achieving the intended goal **p. 94**

**Ethical decision-making model:** a structured systematic procedure for problem resolution that takes account of the norms and rules pertaining to the situation and gives a moral perspective to the problem and the various alternatives and their implications **p. 96**

**Ethical dispositions:** the way in which an individual behaviour demonstrates integrity and morality **p. 4**

**Ethical expectations:** the assumption that individuals will behave ethically **p. 9**

**Ethical issue:** two or more equally compelling and competing alternatives give rise to positive and negative consequences **p. 100**

**Ethical judgment:** the ability to analyse and make decisions in a responsible and ethical way **p. 8**

**Ethical priorities:** the ability to regard ethics as an interest ahead of others **p. 8**

**Ethical sensitivity:** being aware of the ethical dimensions of situations **p. 8**

**Ethical threats:** the risk or likelihood that an individual will not behave ethically **p. 16**

**Ethics:** an examination and analysis of situations and events based on generally acceptable moral principles in order to arrive at different options for action **p. 5**

**Ethics framework:** a structure of relationships which shows the influence between parties regarding their ethical expectations and behaviour **p. 4**

**Executive directors:** member of the board of directors who are also employees of the organisation or closely affiliated with the management of the organisation **p. 124**

**Expert witness:** a person who is a specialist in a subject, often technical, who may present his or her expert opinion without having been a witness to any occurrence relating to the lawsuit or criminal case **p. 152**

**External corporate governance controls:** mechanisms that external stakeholders exercise over the organisation that monitor and control the activities of employees **p. 127**

**External whistleblowing:** *see* whistleblowing **p. 314**

**Fairness:** refers to the just distribution of benefits as an equitable reward for contributions or efforts **p. 35**

**Familiarity threats:** may occur when, because of a close relationship, a professional accountant becomes too sympathetic to the interests of others **p. 76**

**Fiduciary relationship:** a relationship in which an indvidual is trusted for his or her expertise, objectivity and independence **pp. 12, 285**

**Free goods:** publicly available benefits that may be used without any direct financial cost **p. 229**

**General price-level adjusted accounting:** conversion of financial statements based on historical costs to current values using an index such as the CPI index **p. 179**

**Governance:** the authority of directing and controlling of an entity **p. 5**

**Governing body:** the section of the organisation that includes all personnel who are charged with the overall direction, control and responsibility of the organisation (usually refers to the board of directors) **p. 6**

**Greenhouse gas:** gases which, when emitted, contribute to the greenhouse effect and result in global warming. They include the carbon dioxide and sulphur dioxide gases that are common waste products from industrial and commercial activities and transportation **p. 241**

**Historical cost:** cost to the present owner at the time of acquisition **p. 179**

**Hypothecation:** the assignment of an income stream (such as a tax) for the benefit of the providers of that income. For example, the income from a hypothecated carbon tax could be used to design vehicle engines that do not emit carbon dioxide **p. 241**

**Incompatible activities:** when accountants provide professional services while engaging in any business or occupation that may create a conflict of interests in rendering such services **p. 303**

**Independence:** is achieved when accountants are free from any interests or relationships, whether in fact or appearance, that impair objective judgment **p. 70**

**Independence in appearance:** is the avoidance of facts and circumstances that are so significant that a reasonable and informed third party, having knowledge of all relevant information, including any safeguards applied, would reasonably conclude a firm's, or a member of the assurance team's, integrity, objectivity or professional scepticism had been compromised **p. 260**

**Independence in fact:** is a state of mind that permits the provision of an opinion without being affected by influences that compromise professional judgment, allowing an individual to act with integrity, and exercise objectivity and professional scepticism **p. 259**

**Independence of mind** *see* independence in fact **p. 259**

**Information asymmetry:** when the manager has private information about the firm, of which the owner is not aware **p. 119**

**Integrity:** is being straightforward, honest, sincere, and using one's convictions to withstand pressure from significant others to impair integrity **p. 69**

**Intergenerational equity:** a distribution of resources that provides a fair outcome not only for all current members of society, but also for future generations **p. 229**

**Internal corporate governance controls:** in-house mechanisms that monitor and control the activities of employees **p. 127**

**Internal whistleblowing:** occurs when the employee discloses sensitive information on company matters within the organisation rather than outside the organisation **p. 314**

**Inter-species equity:** a distribution of resources that does not benefit one

species to the detriment of other species **p. 229**

**Intimidation threat:** arises when an accountant or firm is threatened with replacement for inappropriate behaviour or a disagreement about the application of accounting principles or the way in which financial information is reported **pp. 77, 302, 313**

**Justice:** fairness; integrity; impartiality. At one level, justice is a legal concept in which laws are developed and enforced impartially and even-handedly for the benefit of all members of society. At another level, justice is the concept of fairness, and is concerned with the distribution of social and environmental benefits among members of a society, between societies, and even between species, so that no group gains advantages unfairly at the expense of other groups **pp. 35, 212**

**Lease:** a conveyance of an asset from one person (lessor) to another (lessee) for a specified period of time, in return for rent or other compensation **p. 181**

**Legitimacy:** accordance with societal norms. An action may be seen as legitimate if it is aimed at meeting the needs of society or at satisfying the wants expressed by society **p. 208**

**Liability:** amount owed to other individuals or organisations; for example, bank loan or payments owed for goods purchased on credit **p. 234**

**Linear payoff:** benefits increase and decrease along a straight line **p. 134**

**Low-balling:** the practice of bidding for audit engagements at an unreasonably low price that threatens the principle of competence and due care **p. 296**

**Loyalty:** is a devotion to protect and advance the interests of one to whom an obligation is owed **p. 315**

**Management share ownership:** an internal control designed to ensure the shares owned by management motivate managers to act in the best interests of shareholders **p. 133**

**Man-made assets:** manufactured items of a medium or long-term nature, such as buildings, equipment and motor vehicles **p. 231**

***Mareva* injunction:** an order to freeze the defendant's assets to prevent them disposing of the specified assets during the period of the injunction **p. 155**

**Mechanical decisions:** *see* routine decisions **p. 88**

**Money laundering:** the process whereby criminals conceal illicitly acquired funds by converting them into seemingly legitimate income **p. 155**

**Monitoring cost:** is the cost of monitoring the performance of managers **p. 257**

**Moral hazard:** the manager does not comply with the contractual terms **p. 127**

**Moral minimum:** defines the minimum set of obligations that all companies

are morally bound to observe, irrespective of nation or culture **p. 328**

**Natural assets:** resources that are naturally occurring and that cannot be manufactured, such as forests, mineral ores, oil and gas **p. 231**

**Non-consequential:** a class of ethical theories that define right from wrong by adherence to morally good principles regardless of whether obedience to them produces undesirable consequences **p. 108**

**Non-consequential theories:** define good by its intrinsic value regardless of whether its obedience produces undesirable consequences **p. 29**

**Non-executive directors:** independent members (non-employees) of the board of directors **p. 124**

**Non-routine decisions:** decisions that are unique and non-recurring with no clear-cut solutions **p. 88**

**Normative ethical theories:** provide the basis upon which judgment is used to solve moral dilemmas by establishing principles that are used to determine right from wrong **p. 29**

**Norms:** *see* values **p. 100**

**Objectivity:** is an impartial attitude that has regard for considerations relevant only to the facts at hand **p. 70**

**Opinion shopping:** the practice of seeking further opinions on disputed accounting or auditing issues from professional accountants until the desired opinion is obtained **p. 301**

**Partner:** a member of a firm of accountants that has overall responsibility for managing the affairs of their clients **p. 294**

**Performance:** the achievement of economic and business objectives **p. 5**

**Performance-based remuneration:** remuneration that is designed to relate some proportion of salary to individual performance within the context of overall company performance **p. 133**

**Personal ethics:** a measure of an individual's moral reasoning abilities as measured by Kohlberg's theory of moral reasoning and development **p. 109**

**Polluter pays principle:** a concept in which individuals or organisations that cause pollution are required to pay for its cleanup, or make restitution to other individuals or organisations that suffer from the detrimental effects of that pollution **p. 241**

**Pollution permits:** a system of permits that allow individuals or organisations to discharge pollutants to land, air or water up to certain permitted levels **p. 243**

**Post-conventional level:** represents the ethics of conviction to self-determined moral principles **p. 43**

**Practitioner independence:** *see* independence in fact **p. 259**

**Pre-conventional level:** reflects a level of moral reasoning that is exclusively self-centred **p. 42**

**Principles:** *see* values **p. 100**

**Private property rights:** an owner of private property rights has a legal right to sell the subject property, or rights in that property, to other individuals or organisations **p. 231**

**Procedural justice:** deals with rules or procedures that result in fair and just outcomes **p. 35**

**Profession:** is a community of people bounded by the activities they perform based on a common theoretical background acquired through formal education and professional socialisation **p. 58**

**Professional ethics:** is acting in ways that are consistent with the professional duties and responsibilities entrusted to the individual in a professional role **p. 63**

**Professional fees:** amounts charged by accountants for services rendered to clients **p. 296**

**Professional independence:** a public accountant having no financial stake or other interest in the person on whose statements they have expressed their professional opinion, that, if present, might cause the loss of their objectivity or impartiality or otherwise interfere with the free exercise of their professional judgment **p. 258**

**Professional judgment:** the process of reaching a decision that is carried out with integrity and recognition of responsibilities to those affected by its consequences **p. 94**

**Professionalisation:** is a form of licensing that includes the acquisition of formal education combined with professional development and practical work experience **p. 59**

**Professionalism:** the discharge of professional care towards an individual's responsibility **p. 13**

**Public accountant:** one who renders professional services to clients for a fee, for example, auditing and taxation services **pp. 287, 311**

**Public interest:** imposes a duty on accountants to safeguard and advance the interests of the public before others **pp. 13, 68, 316**

**Red flag:** a warning signal or anomaly that creates suspicion and demands further attention **p. 168**

**Referrals:** the process of obtaining advice or services from experts for the special needs of the client **p. 300**

**Regulatory regime:** the system of legislation, regulations and administrative requirements through which the government authority controls the market and its entities **p. 6**

**Remuneration committee:** an organisational committee with the principal role of setting executive compensation packages **p. 127**

**Rights:** is an ethical theory that imposes an obligation on people to respect the rights of others **p. 32**

**Routine decisions:** decisions based on predetermined policy or procedure **p. 88**

**Selection-socialisation:** is the process of advancement within the firm hierarchy that results from management promoting only those employees that share common values **p. 49**

**Self-interest:** a personal benefit such as career advancement, or financial or reputational advantage **pp. 13, 42, 286**

**Self-interest threat:** when a firm, or a member of a firm can benefit from a financial interest or other self-interest conflicts with a client **pp. 75, 295, 314**

**Self-regulation:** denotes control by a governing body over the activities of its members **p. 63**

**Self-review threats:** may occur when a previous judgment needs to be re-evaluated by the professional accountant responsible for that judgment **p. 75**

**Share options:** the right to buy a share in the future at the price of the option at grant date **p. 128**

**Social indicators accounting:** attempts to measure social events on a large scale (macro-social events), which involves setting objectives and assessing how these objectives are met over the longer term **p. 216**

**Socially constructed:** accounting and its methods are the result of social, economic and political events, reflected in economic transactions **p. 202**

**Socially constructing:** the use of accounting information plays a role in decision making that affects relationship within society, and societal development itself **p. 203**

**Socio-economic accounting:** a process that uses both financial and non-financial measures to evaluate publicly funded activities. For example, in relation to social welfare programs funded by government, an assessment could be made of the financial costs of providing the program, and the social benefits of a healthier population **p. 216**

**Stage of moral development:** represents a structure of thought that is concerned with how judgments are made and why judgments are made **p. 41**

**Stakeholder:** any party that can be influenced by, or that can itself influence, the activities of an organisation **pp. 110, 119, 206**

**Sustainability:** a system of development that meets the needs of the present generation without compromising the ability of future generations to meet their own needs **pp. 212, 237**

**Tax avoidance:** actions or arrangements that lawfully reduce a taxpayer's tax liability **p. 289**

**Tax avoidance schemes:** arrangements that comply with the letter of the law, but are not within the spirit of the law, allowing some taxpayers to avoid their taxation responsibilities **p. 289**

**Tax evasion:** actions or arrangements that allow a taxpayer to unlawfully escape their true tax liability **p. 288**

**Threats:** situations where ethical and professional principles may be compromised **p. 15**

**Total impact accounting:** consideration and reporting of the aggregate effect of an organisation on the environment **p. 215**

**Tradeable emission permits:** pollution permits that can be bought or sold, either in local or international markets **p. 243**

**Triple bottom line:** organisational performance in terms of financial, social and environmental issues **pp. 214, 248**

**Universalism:** maintains that there are absolute moral truths that must be respected by people and companies, irrespective of circumstances, nation, or culture **p. 327**

**Utilitarianism:** is an ethical theory that is concerned with maximising the greatest balance of pleasure over pain for the greatest number of people **p. 30**

**Values:** standards and rules that guide acceptable and morally good conduct **p. 100**

**Wealth:** prosperity, well-being, or richness. Having an abundance of valuable possessions **p. 230**

**Whistleblower:** one who has obtained knowledge of an act or decision that has caused unnecessary harm to others and has informed an external party of this fact **p. 314**

**Whistleblowing:** the activity of disclosing information externally that is normally regarded as confidential within the firm, but the disclosure of which is deemed to be in the public's best interest **p. 314**

# Index //